The Politics of International Debt

Essays prepared under the auspices of the Lehrman Institute, New York City, with funding from the Ford Foundation

Cornell Studies in Political Economy
Edited by Peter J. Katzenstein

Power, Purpose, and Collective Choice: Economic Strategy in Socialist States, edited by Ellen Comisso and Laura D'Andrea Tyson

The Political Economy of East Asian Industrialism, edited by Frederic C. Deyo

Politics in Hard Times: Comparative Responses to International Economic Crises, by Peter Gourevitch

Closing the Gold Window: Domestic Politics and the End of Bretton Woods, by Joanne Gowa

The Philippine State and the Marcos Regime: The Politics of Export, by Gary Hawes

Pipeline Politics: The Complex Political Economy of East-West Energy Trade, by Bruce W. Jentleson

The Politics of International Debt, edited by Miles Kahler

Corporatism and Change: Austria, Switzerland, and the Politics of Industry, by Peter J. Katzenstein

Small States in World Markets: Industrial Policy in Europe, by Peter J. Katzenstein

The Sovereign Entrepreneur: Oil Policies in Advanced and Less Developed Capitalist Countries, by Merrie Gilbert Klapp

International Regimes, edited by Stephen D. Krasner

Europe and the New Technologies, edited by Margaret Sharp

Europe's Industries: Public and Private Strategies for Change, edited by Geoffrey Shepherd, François Duchêne, and Christopher Saunders

National Styles of Regulation: Environmental Policy in Great Britain and the United States, by David Vogel

Governments, Markets, and Growth: Financial Systems and the Politics of Industrial Change, by John Zysman

American Industry in International Competition: Government Policies and Corporate Strategies, edited by John Zysman and Laura Tyson

The Politics of International Debt

EDITED BY

MILES KAHLER

Cornell University Press

ITHACA AND LONDON

Preface, Article 7, and Conclusion copyright © 1986 by Cornell University.
Articles 1 through 6 copyright © 1985 by the World Peace Foundation and the Massachusetts Institute of Technology.

All rights reserved. Except for brief quotations in a review, this book, or parts thereof, must not be reproduced in any form without permission in writing from the copyright holders. For information address Cornell University Press, 124 Roberts Place, Ithaca, New York 14850; and The MIT Press, 28 Carleton Street, Cambridge, Massachusetts 02142.

Most of the contents of this book first appeared in volume 39, number 3, and volume 39, number 4, of the journal *International Organization*.

This book first published 1986 by Cornell University Press.
Second printing, 1987.
First printing, Cornell Paperbacks, 1986.
Second printing, 1987.

Library of Congress Cataloging-in-Publication Data

The Politics of international debt.

(Cornell studies in policial economy)
1. Debts, External—Political aspects—Addresses, essays, lectures. 2. Loans, Foreign—Political aspects—Addresses, essays, lectures. I. Kahler, Miles, 1949–   . II. Series.
HJ8083.P65   1986   327.1'11   85-48243
ISBN 0-8014-1911-5 (alk. paper)
ISBN 0-8014-9385-4 (pbk. : alk. paper)

Printed in the United States of America

The paper in this book is acid-free and meets the guidelines for permanence and durability of the Committee on Production Guidelines for Book Longevity of the Council on Library Resources.

Contents

Contributors — 6

Preface — *Miles Kahler* — 7

Politics and international debt: explaining the crisis — *Miles Kahler* — 11

1. The debt crisis in historical perspective
Lessons from the past: capital markets during the 19th century and the interwar period — *Albert Fishlow* — 37

2. Governments and banks in the crisis
International debt: the behavior of banks in a politicized environment — *Philip A. Wellons* — 95

International debt and linkage strategies: some foreign-policy implications for the United States — *Benjamin J. Cohen* — 127

3. The political economy of stabilization
The politics of adjustment: lessons from the IMF's Extended Fund Facility — *Stephan Haggard* — 157

Democratic and authoritarian responses to the debt issue: Argentina, Brazil, Mexico — *Robert R. Kaufman* — 187

4. Crisis management and reform at the international level
International debt and international institutions — *Charles Lipson* — 219

Conclusion: politics and proposals for reform — *Miles Kahler* — 245

Contributors

Benjamin J. Cohen is William L. Clayton Professor of International Economic Affairs at the Fletcher School of Law and Diplomacy of Tufts University, Medford, Massachusetts.

Albert Fishlow is Professor of Economics at the University of California, Berkeley.

Stephan Haggard is Assistant Professor of Government at Harvard University, Cambridge, Massachusetts.

Miles Kahler is Associate Professor of Political Science at Yale University, New Haven, Connecticut.

Robert R. Kaufman is Professor of Political Science at Rutgers, the State University of New Jersey, in New Brunswick.

Charles Lipson is Associate Professor of Political Science and Codirector of the Program on Interdependent Political Economy at the University of Chicago.

Philip A. Wellons is Associate Professor of Business Administration at the Graduate School of Business Administration of Harvard University, Boston, Massachusetts.

Preface Miles Kahler

Financial crisis occupies a place in international political economy analogous to that of nuclear war in international politics, implicit as a backdrop to much of the concern about maintaining habits of cooperation but eventually unthinkable. After decades of relative tranquility in the international capital markets, however, Mexico announced a moratorium on its debt-service payments in the summer of 1982. That action appeared to some observers as the first tumbling boulder in a prospective financial landslide. The debt crisis was born. Yet in the strict sense of "crisis"—a turning point—the term was a misnomer. Global collapse did not occur; nor did default. Instead, a structure of cooperation was pieced together and maintained in the context of a deep international recession.

Popular and scholarly analyses of the causes for the debt crisis abounded; many questioned the equity of the solutions devised, but politics remained at best an ill-defined element in the various explanations that were advanced. For this aversion there was an explanation itself political: one set of actors, the creditor governments, worked assiduously to keep "politics" out of the debt crisis. Creditor governments strictly limited their interventions (and their commitment of public resources). Their attitude recapitulated one view of the buildup of developing country debt—that it was a game played in a market setting between the commercial banks and the developing countries. At the same time, however, developing country governments were working just as hard to bring politics back to center stage, arguing for multilateral solutions in which public authorities would take an active role.

However one assesses the years before 1982, there can be no question that political intervention increased after the Mexican rescue. This heightened political dimension demanded explanation. Indeed, explanation now required not only the reintroduction of politics but a historical perspective as well, for the current international financial system was not the first to suffer shocks or experience crises of confidence. Yet many "lessons" drawn as the debt crisis unfolded were based on the most superficial reading of those earlier periods.

Bringing politics into discussion of the debt crisis and its management required closer scrutiny of three ways in which politics impinged on international finance. First, the pattern of crisis management had to be explained, and particularly the renewed activism on the part of creditor governments and the International Monetary Fund (which assumed renewed importance during the crisis). Among creditor governments the United States showed a willingness to intervene that contrasted sharply with a previous pattern of benign neglect. Second, the complicated relations between commercial banks and their home governments, through the regulatory process and other, more informal channels, shaped the actions of the principal private actors in the financial system. Finally, all observers agreed that politics would play a critical role in the calculations of debtor governments required to undertake drastic adjustment programs in exchange for limited amounts of additional finance and the rescheduling of existing debt. Incentives for debtors were shaped by the political consequences of those adjustment measures—whether worsening economic conditions, overt political resistance, or declining legitimacy.

In examining the different political facets of the debt crisis, this book attempts to go beyond the confines of any one academic discipline. Assembling a group of scholars to undertake an interdisciplinary project is never easy. I was fortunate to have economists who accepted the premise that politics were important and political scientists who made an effort to understand the economic background to their work. Benjamin Cohen, Albert Fishlow, Stephan Haggard, Robert Kaufman, Charles Lipson, and Philip Wellons were as industrious and enthusiastic a band as any editor could hope for.

Equally important is a stimulating setting. The enterprise was originally suggested by Nicholas X. Rizopoulos, executive director of the Lehrman Institute; his unflagging support and the financial support of the Institute were essential to the success of the project. Linda Wrigley, associate director of studies, and members of the Institute staff gave each seminar the meticulous attention that produced a successful series. Thanks is also due to the Ford Foundation and its representative, Thomas Bayard, for their early interest and for the Foundation's generous financial support. I also thank the Council on Foreign Relations for an international affairs fellowship that permitted me the time to organize the project, and Richard D. Erb, then U.S. executive director at the International Monetary Fund, who was willing to grant me a flexible schedule during my fellowship year at the Fund. Neither the Lehrman Institute nor the Ford Foundation bears any responsibility for the results of the project.

Any author or set of authors can, of course, benefit from intelligent commentary, and we were fortunate that the Lehrman Institute seminars, where early versions of these papers were delivered, attracted an active and informed group of discussants. Most of the essays in this volume were first published in the journal *International Organization*. I thank that journal; its editor, Peter J. Katzenstein; its associate editor, Roger Haydon; and several anonymous reviewers for their invaluable suggestions in transforming promising essays into polished articles.

MILES KAHLER

New Haven, Connecticut
November 1985

Politics and international debt: explaining the crisis Miles Kahler

Since mid-1982 the existence of a "debt crisis" has been almost universally acknowledged; many would argue that the crisis had existed unrecognized for much longer, despite alarms sounded regularly over the preceding decade. The definition of the crisis in the Northern industrial countries was remarkably uniform: the onset of widespread difficulties in servicing the mountain of developing country debt threatened the stability of the international financial system. The nightmare in the North was an episode of onrushing financial collapse in the mold of those described so vividly by Charles Kindleberger— a default by a major debtor country (or domino defaults by debtors large and small), followed by the failure of a major bank or banks, a collapse of confidence in the financial system, and ultimately a sharp contraction of economic activity and international trade.[1] The model was that of a panic; the fear, that the financial system, which had appeared so robust in dealing with successive shocks in the 1970s, might prove less so in the harsher circumstances of the 1980s.

From the South—and the Southern view was heard in this crisis as it had not been heard in the past—the debt crisis was a crisis of development, one element of the deepest economic downturn since the Great Depression, which had begun for some developing countries after the first oil shock. The link between debt and economic distress varied among the regions of the Third World, however. In Latin America, which held the lion's share of private debt (and posed the greatest threat to system stability), and in Eastern Europe the sudden collapse in international lending led to sharp curbs on imports and severe economic retrenchment, complicated in the case of Eastern Europe

---

An earlier version was presented at the Lehrman Institute, New York City, in the spring of 1984 as part of its seminar series on Politics and International Debt, which was supported in part by a grant from the Ford Foundation. I particularly wish to thank Nicholas X. Rizopoulos, executive director of the Institute, and Linda Wrigley, associate director of studies.

1. Charles Kindleberger, *Manias, Panics, and Crashes* (London: Macmillan, 1978), especially pp. 201–9.

by worsening East-West relations. Africa's disastrous economic decline had begun in the early 1970s, but the roots of its economic malaise seemed to lie in a sharp worsening of its terms of trade, a decline in official development assistance, and damaging national policies; the bulk of its debt was owed to governments, not commercial banks. Asia, with the exception of the Philippines, stood outside the crisis: growth rates held up remarkably well, and the region had never entered the private financial markets with the gusto shown by the Latin Americans. Although some developing countries made clear their own interest in avoiding further weakening of the international financial system, the costs to national development objectives were paramount in Southern eyes.

Each of these competing views of the debt crisis implies a need for political intervention to resolve the crisis, even though the level and kind of political intervention espoused, North and South, differ sharply. The competing views also imply differing explanations for the crisis itself. Most analyses, however, while mentioning a political dimension to the debt crisis *sotto voce*, emphasize economic explanations for the crisis and economic paths out of it. At the risk of simplification one can discern three principal economic arguments, which, though often combined, point to quite different sources of and solutions to the crisis. These models can be labeled "macroeconomic shock," "failure to adjust," and "market imperfections."

The first is a conjunctural argument: the debt crisis was caused by surprising shifts in macroeconomic policy on the part of the major industrial countries, particularly the United States, after the second oil shock. The United States embarked in late 1979 on a turn in policy that took both the developing countries and the commercial banks by surprise. Rather than a brief recession, continuing high levels of inflation, and low or negative real interest rates, this policy shift produced the unprecedented combination of disinflation in the industrial countries, high real interest rates, and a collapse both in the terms of trade and in the volume of exports of developing countries as the industrialized economies entered a deep recession. The debtors and the banks had gambled on an economic environment that resembled the 1976–79 period; they lost. The conclusions drawn by those who take this view are that, given the present financial system, the debt crisis is manageable if the macroeconomic environment shifts toward higher growth rates in the OECD countries and lower real interest rates.[2]

Needless to say, this explanation of the debt crisis is favored by the commercial banks and the debtor countries, principal actors in the system that developed in the 1970s and early 1980s. It awards primary responsibility

2. William R. Cline, *International Debt and the Stability of the World Economy* (Washington, D.C.: Institute for International Economics, 1983), and *International Debt: Systemic Risk and Policy Response* (Washington, D.C.: Institute for International Economics, 1984); Carlos Díaz-Alejandro, "Latin American Debt: I Don't Think We Are in Kansas Anymore," *Brookings Papers on Economic Activity* 2 (1984), especially pp. 351–55.

to economic policy shifts beyond their control, not to their own actions or to imperfections in financial markets. Equally clear is the discomfort that this reading of the debt crisis causes for Northern elites. Though they (and the international organizations that tend to reflect their point of view) may accept that the change in economic conditions was swift, they also emphasize that the disinflationary change was essential to longer-term growth and that the new environment is permanent; hence adjustment, however painful, is required.

Some spokesmen for the North go further, however, shifting responsibility for the debt crisis to inadequate policies in the debtor countries. Observing the pattern of developing country experience during the 1980s—the regional divergence in economic performance noted above—they conclude that the economic environment cannot be a principal explanation for economic decline in the major Latin American debtors.[3] Even if a shift to higher growth rates in the North were desirable, the "short leash" of IMF conditionality and frequent renegotiation would have been necessary to ensure that policies in the South were set aright. The balance between financing and adjustment should shift sharply toward the latter, since one assumption of the "failure to adjust" view (an assumption held also by many of those who endorse the "macroeconomic shock" explanation) is that the limits to financing are relatively fixed (though how they are fixed remains obscure); the limits to adjustment on the part of the developing countries are far more flexible. As one International Monetary Fund (IMF) publication blandly notes,

> although a program of adjustment may involve austerity by comparison with some earlier period of policy, it cannot be considered to represent austerity by comparison with any feasible alternative.... An adjustment program involving a slower restoration of external viability, while attractive in theory, would in practice have placed in doubt the willingness of creditors to play an adequate role in the financing process, or else would have permitted a potentially threatening further increase in the external debt burden borne by the indebted countries themselves.[4]

Despite criticisms of the short-term adjustment programs urged on debtor countries, it is clear that some in the North are aiming at even more: a fundamental reorientation of the pattern of development undertaken by the major debtors during the period of easy finance. The outward orientation pushed by the IMF and the World Bank in the 1980s will now be implemented on a fast track under the pressures of adjustment.

A third set of economic explanations for the debt crisis does not exclude those given above, but awards a larger role to imperfections in financial

---

3. Of course, proponents of the first or third models can reply that *within* Latin America widely divergent policy stances seemed to fail, indicating a common external cause for failure. See Díaz-Alejandro, "Latin American Debt," p. 336.

4. *World Economic Outlook* (Washington, D.C.: IMF, April 1984), p. 25.

markets. These observers see not the efficient system of intermediation portrayed by the banks but a system prone to crisis and with no obvious lender of last resort, a system in which collective action problems within bank syndicates can threaten system stability.[5] Contagion effects and herd behavior produce "feast or famine" cycles of lending; confidence is easily undermined.[6] Some of these observers do not champion the virtues of lower regulation in international lending but prefer to point to the inadequacy of existing regulation in countering the risks of sovereign lending—risks that the banks, suffering from "disaster myopia," choose to ignore.[7] Finally, these microlevel analyses factor in the behavior of *borrowers*. Replacing the smooth allocation of lending toward economies with high growth rates and high rates of return and the easy assumption that "countries never go bankrupt" is the threat of default or repudiation, which acts as a barrier to optimal levels and distribution of lending.[8]

Such critical views of the system of commercial bank lending for balance-of-payments financing as it had developed in the 1970s were popular with none of the principal actors in the crisis. They implied that the banks acting collectively could produce perverse outcomes in the absence of external intervention. Those who viewed the threat of repudiation as a serious obstacle to the continuation of adequate lending proposed additional sanctions directed toward the developing countries or restraints on their policies, changes that borrowers hardly welcomed. Moreover, the presumption that political intervention by international organizations or national governments might be required to redress these imperfections was unlikely to win the support of Northern finance ministers and politicians increasingly inclined against regulation of or intervention in financial markets and unwilling to increase public sources of financing. These arguments at the microlevel about the existing system of international finance, however, do more than point to a possible need for political intervention in a *solution* to the debt crisis. They also raise, however obliquely, the question of a political dimension in the development of the crisis itself.

This third set of economic arguments, focused on market imperfections in the smooth-running financial system of the 1970s, calls into question the

5. Kindleberger, *Manias, Panics, and Crashes*, especially chaps. 10 and 11; Jeffrey Sachs, *Theoretical Issues in International Borrowing* (Princeton, N.J.: International Finance Section, Princeton University, July 1984), pp. 29–32.

6. Díaz-Alejandro attributes the financial shock that reinforced an external real shock to the gap between the "private and [the] collective rationality" of banks ("Latin American Debt," p. 355).

7. Jack Guttentag and Richard Herring, "The Current Crisis in International Banking," mimeo (Wharton School, University of Pennsylvania, October 1983), pp. 1–3, and their *The Lender-of-Last-Resort Function in an International Context* (Princeton, N.J.: International Finance Section, Princeton University, May 1983), pp. 2–4.

8. Jonathan Eaton and Mark Gersovitz, *Poor-Country Borrowing in Private Financial Markets and the Repudiation Issue* (Princeton, N.J.: International Finance Section, Princeton University, June 1981), chap. 2; Sachs, *Theoretical Issues*, chap. 4.

depoliticized view of international lending widely held before 1982 and helps to explain the more overt political dimension—the higher level of intervention by states and international organizations—to the debt crisis since that time. The market imperfections model also suggests a means of organizing the analysis of state intervention in international financial systems, past and present.

The means by which the world financial system has integrated economies with large capital needs, underdeveloped financial institutions, and high political risk have varied from era to era. But whenever private financial intermediaries have been central and the market imperfections described above likely to appear, governments are potentially involved in three political tasks that set boundaries for the private actors and influenced their behavior.

The first is to *ensure the stability* of the international financial system. Governments have interpreted their responsibilities for maintaining system stability in two ways. One is the classic role of lender of last resort: a willingness to lend directly to financial institutions during a threatened panic, adding liquidity at higher risk than a private actor would be willing to assume.[9] The role of state intervention here is to maintain confidence in *lenders*. Underlying the need for a lender of last resort is a belief that financial markets, and particularly international ones, are subject to instability as the result of their structure (collective action problems of large numbers of lenders), the fragility of confidence in highly leveraged institutions, and the threat of contagion.[10]

States have also undertaken a second stabilizing role, one that reinforces confidence in the system indirectly by assuring the ability and the willingness of *borrowers* to pay. At times enforcement action taken by the dominant states has underpinned stability (though the importance of such public enforcement in the past has been overstated). Kindleberger has expanded the notion of lender of last resort to imply a more general responsibility for system stability that may include additional, counter-cyclical lending to borrowing governments as well as maintaining open markets for exports.[11]

Linked to the role of lender of last resort is the second political task that governments have assumed: *regulation*. This concept should also be interpreted broadly, for regulation may mean supervision of financial intermediaries in the interest of "outsiders," particularly depositors, thereby ensuring the safety and soundness of the financial system (hence the link to the lender-of-last-resort function). Governments can also attempt to divert financial flows from their market-determined course to further other national interests, such as foreign-policy goals.

---

9. Kindleberger, *Manias, Panics, and Crashes*, p. 161; Guttentag and Herring, *Lender-of-Last-Resort Function*, p. 4.

10. Sachs, *Theoretical Issues*, chap. 5; Guttentag and Herring, *Lender-of-Last-Resort Function*, pp. 6–7.

11. Charles Kindleberger, *The World in Depression, 1929–1939* (Berkeley: University of California Press, 1975), p. 28.

16   *Miles Kahler*

Finally, governments in the borrowing economies are responsible for *adjustment* to assure scheduled repayment of debts and to guarantee continued inflows of capital necessary for development. Willingness to adjust may be influenced by the enforcement mechanisms in the system (sanctions available to private lenders) and by perceptions of the economic benefits of staying inside the system, but elites on the periphery also enter into their calculus the *political* costs that they are likely to suffer in imposing those policy changes which external financial obligations require.

Political intervention and systems of international finance

If politics, defined as state intervention, is potentially important in defining international financial outcomes, *how* important is it? Before 1945, four patterns of international lending produced different outcomes. The pre-1914 system of lending based in London and its counterpart in Paris and Berlin, as Albert Fishlow notes, seemed to provide financial system stability and an impressive flow of private capital to (richer) countries on the periphery. The New York–based system of the 1920s and its less important counterpart in London provided less capital and ended with massive defaults during the Great Depression (though the London-based system proved more resilient under strain).

These different outcomes resulted, at least in part, from different patterns of state intervention. The London-based system of international lending before 1914 was characterized by little government interference in the relations between lenders and borrowers. Fishlow's account of that era suggests that the absence of intervention to ensure system stability was not due solely to an ideological commitment to laissez-faire but to the peculiar private organization of the marketplace: merchant banks mediated between the mass of bondholders (organized in the Corporation of Foreign Bondholders) and borrowers on the periphery. Because lending in this system was based on bonds, debt-servicing difficulties did not have immediate implications for the domestic financial system, and hence the stabilizing role of the British Treasury and the Bank of England was limited. (The principal exception was the Baring Crisis of 1890, and then, through organizing a system of guarantees though not through direct lending, the Bank of England did serve as system stabilizer to preserve confidence in the City of London and stave off a panic.)[12]

The absence of a direct link between international lending and the domestic financial system also reinforced the lack of governmental supervision or regulation, though the Paris and Berlin patterns displayed stronger government efforts to manipulate financial flows to serve foreign-policy ends (perhaps

12. Albert Fishlow, "Lessons from the Past," *International Organization* 39 (Summer 1985); Kindleberger, *Manias, Panics, and Crashes*, pp. 153–56.

best considered a form of protomilitary assistance).[13] Adjustment on the periphery was seldom hindered by governments, many of them within the British formal and informal empires, committed to integrating their countries into the international economy, a stance that also assured that the burden of adjustment to financial crisis would fall squarely on them.[14] Not only did elites on the periphery fail to perceive any alternative to financial dependence on London, they also faced populations not yet mobilized to resist the harshness of adjustment.

If the pre-1914, London-based system suggests the stability of a market (organized in a particular fashion) within a set of nearly invisible political parameters, the interwar financial system offers a portrait of destabilizing political intervention in certain spheres and inadequate political intervention in others. The financial system, as Kindleberger and others have emphasized, was in transition between its old London focus and its new center in New York. Although New York became the source of new capital ouflows, as Fishlow notes, the United States as a creditor had "neither [the] trade policy nor [the] foreign perspective . . . compatible with the role."[15] When financial crisis broke in 1929-31, the American authorities were unwilling to play even the passive stabilizing role that their counterparts in London had undertaken earlier. In the absence of a governmental stabilizer the private markets proved incapable of meeting the crisis, which overwhelmed them. The shift to New York had placed the financial system in inexperienced hands: replacing merchant banks linked to their country clients through a web of financial and trade relations were New York banks that floated foreign bonds as a simple variation on the placement of domestic bonds.[16] Not only did private stabilization fail to substitute for a passive government in the New York market, self-regulation on the London model did not fill the gap left by an absence of government supervision. When the boom came to an end, the pattern of defaults divided countries in the British orbit (particularly those with an export surplus with Britain) and those in the U.S. orbit.[17] As

13. Fishlow's contrast of London with the far more politically direct Paris and Berlin financial centers holds, though on occasion the British government could make its foreign-policy wishes known to the City; see Herbert Feis, *Europe, the World's Banker, 1870–1914* (New York: Norton, 1965), p. 89.
14. David Felix, "The Baring Crisis of the 1890s and the International Bond Defaults of the 1930s: Delphic Prophecies on the Outcome of the Current Latin American Debt Crises," mimeo (Dept. of Economics, Washington University, St. Louis, Mo., November 1984), pp. 20–25; also L. S. Pressnell, "The Sterling System and Financial Crises before 1914," in Charles Kindleberger and Jean-Pierre Laffargue, eds., *Financial Crises: Theory, History and Policy* (New York: Cambridge University Press, 1982), pp. 148–64.
15. "Lessons from the Past."
16. Marcello de Cecco, "The International Debt Problem in the Interwar Period" (paper presented at the Lehrman Institute series on Politics and International Debt, New York, May 1984), pp. 15–18.
17. Carlos Díaz-Alejandro, "Stories of the 1930s for the 1980s," in Pedro Aspe Armella et al., eds., *Financial Policies and the World Capital Markets: The Place of Latin American Countries* (Chicago: University of Chicago Press, 1983), pp. 5–35; Felix, "Baring Crisis of the 1890s," pp. 46–50.

David Felix describes, the British carved out a sterling area in which London still exercised the stabilizing function that it used to offer to the world economy as a whole: its export market and promise of future capital induced some governments, such as Argentina, to undergo the risks of adjustment in order to honor their sterling debts. The United States, maintaining its nationalist stance, declined even such a "ministabilizing" role in its financial sphere.

The cascade of defaults in the early 1930s signaled more than the failure of any hope for reestablishing an open system for trade and capital exports; elites on the periphery also faced a different calculus of adjustment at home. Two critical features set the breakdown of the 1930s apart from the earlier period, and both spurred default. First, the political resistance to stabilization, particularly from a partially mobilized working class, was greater, and the political risks to any elite undertaking stabilization correspondingly elevated. Second, and equally important, economic alternatives to those imposed by the plummeting international economy were haltingly discovered. Policy experiments with import substitution and delinking from international capital markets soon expanded into acceptance of more unorthodox and state-led strategies of structural change.[18]

The financial crisis and widespread defaults of the 1930s could be explained in the purely economic terms of the macroeconomic shock model: deteriorating economic conditions for the exporters of primary products (beginning before the Great Depression) followed by a drying up of capital flows. But such a model neglects the political failure that accompanied financial failure: no clear stabilizer at the international level, an absence of regulation or self-regulation in the financial markets, and increasing political resistance to adjustment on the periphery.

Politics and international finance after 1945: to the Mexican rescue

The financial and monetary disorder of the 1930s produced a political legacy that would persist into the financial crisis management of the 1980s. After the Great Depression the principal candidate for a system stabilizer would be the United States, a continental economy whose stabilizing role would be shaped by the strong pull of domestic policy goals. The level of government regulatory involvement in the financial system took a quantum jump upward during the Great Depression; motivations, particularly in the United States, were principally domestic, but they would later prove to have international implications. And finally, as noted above, governments on the periphery took on much greater responsibility for economic development, beginning

18. Carlos Díaz-Alejandro, "Latin America in the 1930s," in Rosemary Thorpe, ed., *Latin America in the 1930s: The Role of the Periphery in World Crises* (London: Macmillan, 1984), pp. 17–50.

with the delinking of the 1930s that persisted into the postwar period. In the balance between domestic and international, incentives were skewed toward domestic economic objectives.

These shifts meant that future state intervention in international finance would be embedded in *domestic* politics, but they were easily overshadowed by the fact that private financial flows were far less significant in the years immediately after 1945. For the first time, public international institutions—the International Monetary Fund and the multilateral development banks—played a role in the international financial system; the attitude of the founders of the postwar order toward private capital flows, which were viewed as inadequate for the capital needs of reconstruction and potentially destabilizing, was at best ambiguous. It was not capital flows on the prewar model but development assistance and foreign direct investment that assumed a more prominent role. Such supply-side limitations on private finance coincided with the adoption of inward-looking, import-substitution development strategies in many of the developing countries, which reduced their demand for foreign capital.

What might have happened had New York continued its development, interrupted in 1929, as an international financial center, and developing countries had "graduated" to it, is an interesting question. What actually happened was that in the 1960s private financial intermediation between North and South found a new "technology," one born in part of regulatory changes in the United States: the Euromarkets. Refinements in the technology of bank lending through the Euromarkets—waivers of sovereign immunity in loans, syndication, and the institution of floating-rate credits—lowered risks for any individual bank participating and opened the way for a new era of sovereign lending.[19]

With the new intermediaries in place, a shift toward more outward-oriented policies by some of the larger, newly industrializing economies—Brazil, South Korea, Yugoslavia—made these new, relatively unregulated financial markets attractive. The political and economic strings of the IMF and bilateral aid donors could be avoided; Euromarket loans fitted better than did foreign direct investment with state-led industrialization and the growth of a parastatal sector.

The pattern and the intermediaries for North-South capital flows were thus established before the first oil shock, though demand for financing from this source shot up to meet the current-account deficits that oil-price increases produced. For seven years private financial markets reassumed a major role

---

19. Charles Lipson, "The International Organization of Third World Debt," *International Organization* 35 (Autumn 1981), pp. 609–10. The concept of a financial technology is from Marcello de Cecco. Among the many studies of the Euromarkets and sovereign lending by commercial banks, see Ronald I. McKinnon, *The Eurocurrency Market* (Princeton, N.J.: International Finance Section, Princeton University, December 1977), and Stefan Mendelsohn, *Money on the Move: The Modern International Capital Market* (New York: McGraw-Hill, 1980).

in financing the deficits of developing countries and their economic growth, which continued, for many middle-income countries, during a time of recession among the OECD countries. Developing country debt—highly concentrated in a relatively small number of newly industrializing countries—increased at an annual rate of 10 percent in real terms during these years; the share of that debt owed to private financial institutions grew from 25 to 41 percent during the same period.[20]

At first glance, and in many of the early analyses of this system of North-South financial intermediation, the absence of political intervention by governments or by international organizations seemed its most striking feature.[21] But the new system of bank lending to developing countries, despite its appearance of being managed by banks and dominated by market criteria, was (like previous systems) influenced by state actions and state choices in system stabilization, regulation, and adjustment. Kindleberger's questions— "Is there a lender of last resort in case of trouble? Who is it? Does he or it know it?"—suggest the anxiety that surrounded the role of system stabilizer. Apart from a vague statement issued by Group of 10 central bank governors in 1974, concrete governmental assurances to the banks were lacking.[22] International organizations also seemed to decline in importance as guarantors of system stability in the broader sense. Just before the onset of widespread debt-servicing difficulties, the *Economist* characterized the International Monetary Fund's role in the 1970s as "helpful, steadying—and very marginal," financing only 4 percent of all current-account deficits in 1978.[23] Although some observers argue that the IMF continued to play a central role in awarding its "seal of approval" to national economic policies, the Fund was only sporadically involved. The number of rescheduling cases before 1982 was relatively small (though rising), and the countries in question were not of system-threatening size: they were most often smaller, nonoil developing countries that were barely eligible for commercial bank lending in any case.

Although no obvious stabilizer was waiting in the wings, it is clear from bank behavior that many lenders assumed that such a lender of last resort existed. In Eastern Europe a belief in the "Soviet umbrella" persisted— perhaps the first Communist lender of last resort! At least part of the regional bias in bank lending—with American banks taking the preponderant role in Latin America and West German banks in Eastern Europe—must be attributed to beliefs that strategic interests would force government intervention on behalf of troubled borrowers. In sum, Eurobanks could feel reasonably

20. E. Brau and R. C. Williams, *Recent Multilateral Debt Restructurings with Official and Bank Creditors* (Washington, D.C.: IMF, December 1983), p. 25.

21. For example, Lipson, "International Organization of Third World Debt."

22. G. G. Johnson, *Aspects of the International Banking Safety Net* (Washington, D.C.: IMF, March 1983), p. 23.

23. "Survey: IMF—Ministry without Portfolio," *Economist*, 26 September 1981, p. 16.

secure—perhaps too secure—in their lending, at least to large borrowers in the regional spheres of interest of their home governments.

The stabilizing function is linked to the regulatory: a lender of last resort must know whether the financial institution or country to which it is lending is solvent or not. Obstacles to extending regulation of Eurobanks were greater than in earlier systems since the banks and their lending had moved offshore precisely to avoid regulation, and some national governments resisted a collective tightening of regulatory oversight. Commercial bank lending to the developing countries did pose risks to domestic banking systems (in contrast to the pre-1930s reliance on bond markets), making all the more striking the apparent lack of regulatory concern during the 1970s.

Part of the apparent lack of effect of national regulation is simply an illusion, however. Banks, as Philip Wellons argues forcefully, though they tried to take refuge from home country regulation in the Euromarkets, were tugged back into dependence on their home governments and home economies by cost advantages and by the direct support their governments offered through market protection and lender-of-last-resort assistance. Not only did the regulatory climate of home countries affect the behavior of banks despite the development of transnational syndicates, as Wellons suggests, the relations between governments and banks also varied *across* the industrialized countries, with implications for bank behavior.[24] Although governments were hardly as blatant in using bank lending to further their strategic interests as the French government had been before 1914, regulation, broadly defined, could go beyond government intervention to further strategic goals.[25]

Most accounts of the heyday of the Euromarkets during the 1970s also omit the third political boundary imposed by states: the politics of adjustment was only a minor theme of the period because so little adjustment seemed to take place. Stephan Haggard notes the effect that "temptation" had in undermining the willingness of elites to undertake adjustment programs; financing for current account deficits was available with few strings attached, whether in the form of economic and military assistance (Egypt, the Philippines) or in the form of commercial bank lending. The inability of banks alone to impose adjustment was demonstrated definitively in the case of Peru in 1976–77.[26]

Warning signals were apparent for those willing to see, however. Jamaica,

24. Philip Wellons, "International Debt: The Behavior of Banks in a Politicized Environment," *International Organization* 39 (Summer 1985); also Andrew Spindler, *The Politics of International Credit* (Washington, D.C.: Brookings, 1984).
25. See the examples given by Benjamin J. Cohen, "International Debt and Linkage Strategies: Some Foreign-Policy Implications for the United States," *International Organization* 39 (Autumn 1985).
26. Stephan Haggard, "The Politics of Adjustment: Lessons from the IMF's Extended Fund Facility," *International Organization* 39 (Summer 1985); William Cline and Sidney Weintraub, eds., *Economic Stabilization in Developing Countries* (Washington, D.C.; Brookings, 1981), p. 300.

22   *Miles Kahler*

a case of what Haggard terms democratic stalemate, clearly illustrated the continuing political hazards of adjustment. The government of Michael Manley, whose populist program rode the bauxite boom of the early 1970s, confronted vigorous political opposition and finally defeat when lending from the commercial banks declined. In Mexico the burst of oil revenues reinforced a pattern of state-led industrialization but did not quell political opposition to the course that had been chosen. That stalemate in the context of financial plenty produced the drift in Mexican policy that led directly to the crisis of 1982. Most of the major debtor states, however, were not pluralist: in the rest of Latin America the pattern of public-sector-led industrialization continued under "soft" authoritarian regimes, which used easy external finance to temper social divisions and lower the level of repression. Unlike Mexico, they did not face the question of stalemate in a pluralist context, but Robert Kaufman suggests that "authoritarian stalemate" had nonetheless set in by the late 1970s. Easy finance had enabled elites to postpone both political and economic choices; the development trajectory would demonstrate the shortcomings of the policy in the adverse external circumstances that were soon to arrive.[27]

In the pre-1914 London model governmental functions of system stabilization were undertaken by private actors and adjustment was viewed not as a political choice but as an inevitable element of economic life. The system of commercial bank lending to the developing countries during the 1970s, it could be argued, resembled as closely in its political outlines the unstable interwar system based on New York. In the New York system private actors could not stabilize the system and governments would not, underregulation was more characteristic than self-regulation, and the national choices of adjustment strategy were perilous for political elites. Only the threat of financial crisis would produce novel forms of political intervention that did not parallel any of the historical models. They have to date managed to stave off financial breakdown.

Patterns of cooperation in the crisis

Each of the economic models described earlier can find some evidence for its interpretation of the debt crisis in events following the second oil shock. The harsh new environment after 1979, of a different order from the recession of 1974–75, lends weight to the notion of macroeconomic shock: an even steeper recession was coupled this time with high real interest rates and a strong dollar. Terms of trade shifted dramatically against first the nonoil developing countries and then, with the emergence of an oil glut, the oil

27. Robert Kaufman, "Democratic and Authoritarian Responses to the Debt Issue: Argentina, Brazil, Mexico," *International Organization* 39 (Summer 1985).

producers. Yet a new burst of bank lending was soon under way, and developing countries received mixed signals on the need for adjustment with an apparent easing of IMF conditionality in 1979, increases in Fund resources through quota increases and borrowing, and adoption of enlarged access. The new wave of lending was characterized by several disturbing features that suggested growing weaknesses in the financial markets. Short-term debt expanded twice as rapidly as medium- and long-term debt from 1979, although this shift in composition was hardly clear at the time.[28] In addition, European and Japanese banks entered the competition more aggressively, reducing spreads and encouraging overlending. Their entrance hinted at a herd logic that the first sign of crisis could quickly reverse.

Strains in a system in which political intervention remained sporadic and even destabilizing also became clear in two reschedulings that surpassed in scale those of earlier years: first Turkey, then Poland. Poland in particular provided a critical link to the 1982 crisis in the scale of debt and its demonstration of the weakness of a wholly bank-managed rescheduling (though government urging and intervention were added). The Polish plight also laid to rest any hope of a Soviet "umbrella," and rising East-West tensions after the imposition of martial law produced the first clear signs of regional contagion in the lending patterns of the banks, affecting Romania (already in arrears), Hungary, and Yugoslavia. By early 1982 syndicated bank lending to Eastern Europe had virtually ended. The Falklands/Malvinas War and the freeze instituted by Britain on Argentinian assets directed attention to yet another heavily indebted region and increased perceptions of risk; an international red-lining of Latin America threatened. At the same time several financial institutions failed with wide publicity, notably Drysdale Securities, Penn Square Bank, and Banco Ambrosiano, heightening fears of a generalized weakening of the international financial system. Adverse economic conditions led to an accumulation of arrears by many developing country borrowers, and the shift toward short-term (and thus more unstable) debt structures continued.

The precipitant of the crisis came in August 1982 when Mexico, the largest single borrower from the international financial markets, requested a 120-day moratorium (later extended 90 days) on its debt payments. That request spurred the rapid construction of an innovative "template" for providing immediate liquidity to debtor countries while a refinancing of their debt was negotiated, a template used (with variations) in other cases in the following months. The most striking change, however, was the activist role assumed by both governments and international organizations, which now recognized the potential for dangerous instability in the international financial system. The stabilizing task, which protected the financial system by preventing an even sharper contraction of bank lending, was performed in a surprising

---

28. Brau and Williams, *Recent Multilateral Debt Restructurings*, p. 3.

24   *Miles Kahler*

display of cooperative behavior by industrial country governments led by
the United States, commercial banks, international financial organizations,
and Mexico itself.

Central banks, led by the U.S. Federal Reserve, were key players in short-
term crisis management, providing their first extra-European bridge loan to
Mexico (to be followed by similar loans to Argentina and Brazil). Central
bank cooperation, in contrast to the financial crises of the 1930s, was effective,
and the bankers' transnational network, centered on the Bank for International
Settlements, proved resilient. Central banks were effective stabilizers in the
early stages of the crisis for two reasons: as their governments' eyes and ears
in the financial markets they often had some warning of developing difficulties
on the part of borrowers (quite apart from their ties to the central banks of
the borrowers); their resources, though inadequate for more than bridging
purposes, and sometimes not even for that, could be mobilized quickly and
without political complications. Later in the crisis, as described below, their
regulatory role in national banking systems became crucial.

The *national governments of the Group of 5* (G-5) were effective in supplying
the remainder of the emergency finance—cobbled together in the American
case from accelerated oil purchases, credits from the Commodity Credit
Corporation, and, eventually, export credits. In other instances bilateral assistance was increased or accelerated. Official debt was rescheduled under
the auspices of the Paris Club.

The *International Monetary Fund*, as Kindleberger noted well before the
debt crisis, moved too slowly to serve as a crisis manager, but its stabilizer
role was perhaps the central and most expanded one in the period after the
Mexican operation. Fund conditionality became the linchpin of the system:
a Fund program or negotiations for one became a condition for rescheduling
or refinancing official and private debt; even other forms of bilateral assistance
were linked to adjustment programs. As a result, borrowing countries faced
a much tighter system of cross-conditionality. The Fund had long been an
active observer in Paris Club reschedulings; it now became much more
intimately involved in the rescheduling of commercial bank debt.[29] A more
radical innovation was introduced when the Fund used its new position to
leverage the banks into new, involuntary lending. For the first time, in effect,
a public entity was playing a direct role in credit allocation, even if only in
certain cases. A less drastic change, though one derived from precrisis lessons,
was greater Fund activity in information gathering, particularly on the debt
structure of member countries.

The *World Bank*, with development lending responsibilities, was not an
important player in the initial crisis management, but its actions ran parallel
with these actors. Its structural adjustment loans added another element of

29. Paul Mentré, *The Fund, Commercial Banks, and Member Countries* (Washington, D.C.:
IMF, April 1984), p. 31.

conditionality directed to longer-term economic policy changes, and, through accelerated disbursements and cofinancing arrangements, it could contribute modestly to the financing needs of the imperiled borrowers.

The *commercial banks* undertook debt refinancing at a new order of complexity after Mexico; the organization of large numbers of lending institutions by an advisory committee became the normal procedure, and the hierarchical and multinational organization of the lenders tightened. As Joseph Kraft said of the Mexican case, "A communications network has been created through a series of regional subcommittees. Each American member of the advisory committee took responsibility for ten different regional banks. Each regional bank took responsibility for ten smaller banks in its area and so on down the line."[30] Information sharing also became a prominent concern for the banks, and in 1983 they established the Institute of International Finance as a clearinghouse for information among lenders. The Japanese had in the meantime established their own, similar institute.

Finally, the *debtor countries* themselves undertook severe adjustment programs, under IMF standby agreements or extended arrangements, and renegotiated a means by which to continue servicing of their debts. Mexico was the first of the large, system-threatening borrowers to seek a rescheduling; others soon followed. From a relatively rare occurrence, usually requested by smaller and poorer developing countries, rescheduling became the norm: from six debt restructurings in 1981 (only one, Turkey, a significant borrower) to over twenty in 1983, including the largest borrowing countries—Argentina, Brazil, Nigeria, and Yugoslavia. Though bargaining was tough, the system established in the Mexican case held until renewed pressures in early 1984 threatened to derail it and forced modifications, managed by the same key actors.

Explaining cooperation without reform

This outcome was hardly predictable: state intervention may have been necessary to correct shortcomings in the financial markets, but overt political intervention might not have produced system stability. Two features of the debt crisis in this new, politicized phase are both striking and puzzling. First, despite the large number of state and private actors that participated in the case-by-case management of the debt crisis and their potentially conflicting interests, the level of cooperative behavior in managing the crisis—among industrialized countries, between banks and their home governments, and between industrialized and developing countries—has remained high.

The North-South division provides the second puzzle. The apparent threat to the financial systems of the North gave leverage to the borrowers. The

---

30. Joseph Kraft, *The Mexican Rescue* (New York: Group of Thirty, 1984), pp. 26–27.

Northern definition of the debt crisis and creditor solutions to the crisis nonetheless prevailed, and in the Mexican case and after the "case-by-case, on a short leash" approach remained in place. Southern complaints had not shaped Northern economic management (particularly the policy mix of the United States or the anti-Keynesian bent of the European governments), the terms of debt restructuring in the first rounds were not generous, conditionality remained orthodox in its prescriptions. The scale of the reschedulings had not shaken a template that fitted the interests of the commercial banks and Northern finance ministries far more than those of the debtors. Southern efforts to redefine the crisis and change the existing system had, it seemed, utterly failed.

"Cooperation without reform" best describes the outcome to date in the management of the debt crisis. One can attempt to explain that outcome exclusively at the international level, but I shall argue here, tracing again the political tasks of stabilization, regulation, and adjustment, that even an explanation at the level of the international financial system depends at crucial points on domestic political processes. Those processes—in particular, regulation in the industrialized countries and adjustment in the South—are essential to any effort at piecing together solutions to the two puzzles.

One superficially appealing explanation of the first puzzle is that existing sets of conventions or rules were readily transferred to the new situation, and those structures shaped national incentives and behavior in a cooperative direction.[31] Such a "regime autonomy" explanation is inadequate, not least because the existence of a coherent regime, rather than fragments of a regime, is doubtful earlier than 1982. Certainly a "case law" had been established by that time, but to posit an existing regime is to understate the level of innovation in 1982–83. Participants in the events after mid-1982 emphasize dramatic changes in ordinary procedures: as Mexico's finance minister Silva Herzog remarked, "The world was different after that. . . . The blueprints for dealing with this situation quite simply did not exist; we had to draw them up."[32] What had previously been regime fragments were linked; what had previously been a relatively leisurely means of dealing with small debtors became a crisis management mechanism for dealing with threats to the entire financial system. And perhaps most important, governments emerged as critical actors in instituting these changes.

Inclusion of the largest debtors also weakens a regime explanation. As Robert Keohane has noted, explanations of this sort are strongest in situations of shared interests, which may exclude this and other aspects of North-South relations.[33] Certainly the legitimacy of the existing regime fragments had not been tested against the interests of the larger debtors—both Turkey and

31. Stephen Krasner, "Regimes and the Limits of Realism: Regimes as Autonomous Variables," *International Organization* 36 (Spring 1982), pp. 497–510.

32. Kraft, *The Mexican Rescue*, p. 3.

33. Robert O. Keohane, *After Hegemony* (Princeton: Princeton University Press, 1984), p. 7.

Explaining the debt crisis 27

Poland had been special cases. Nor was it only Southern actors that resisted the rules of the game as they emerged in 1982–83. Bankers were also, oddly enough, resistant to the formation of a regime, in the sense of a clear-cut body of rules applied across cases: in Paul Mentré's words, "many bankers fear that precise guidelines could confer respectability and normality to a process which, in their view, should be regarded as exceptional and penalizing."[34] Thus an effort at regime consolidation faced potential resistance from lenders who preferred to maximize their bargaining power in a case-by-case approach and from borrowers who might resist the extension of existing conventions and benefit from individual treatment.

An alternative or a supplement to an explanation of cooperative and stable patterns of behavior based on regimes focuses on the renewed energy displayed by the United States in managing the crisis. Hegemonic stability arguments have been challenged both for their inability to demonstrate a close association between international power distribution and particular outcomes and for their inability to predict when and how the hegemon-designate will act.[35] Certainly, any variant of the theory would have had difficulty predicting the activism of the United States in managing this crisis "after hegemony." Yet closer examination offers reasons from *domestic* politics not only for the definition of American interests in the crisis but also for both American equivocation in the months preceding the crisis and the abrupt turnaround in the American position once the crisis had broken.

A parsimonious explanation of American actions in 1982 would revolve around the threat to a domestic financial system already under strain and the fact that it was the Mexican case that came first and provided a model for others that followed. The first set of concerns activated the Federal Reserve, and dense connections in trade and energy, as well as the strategic importance of Mexico, provided a potent glue in the often fragmented American executive. Nevertheless, as Benjamin Cohen's account of Reagan administration attitudes toward the International Monetary Fund suggests, what is most marked until the outbreak of crisis is how *little* concerned the United States appeared to be with system stability.[36] Resistance to a more active role came from two sources: the profoundly domestic orientation of American economic management and an ideological distrust of government intervention in what were regarded as efficient financial markets.

The first obstacle to American leadership has been well documented in Joanne Gowa's account of the American decision to close the gold window in August 1971: when regime maintenance or system stabilization conflicted with the autonomy of domestic economic policy making or strategic interests, regime maintenance was consistently regarded as the subordinate interest.[37]

34. Mentré, *The Fund, Commercial Banks, and Member Countries*, p. 30.
35. Keohane, *After Hegemony*, chap. 3.
36. Cohen, "International Debt and Linkage Strategies," sec. 5.
37. Joanne Gowa, *Closing the Gold Window: Domestic Politics and the End of Bretton Woods* (Ithaca: Cornell University Press, 1983), pp. 24–27.

28   *Miles Kahler*

The same pattern was apparent in 1981 and 1982: the behavior of the U.S. government (and particularly its visible internal debate) on the question of declaring Polish official debt "in default" in 1982 made clear to the worried Europeans that threats to the international financial system were not an unquestioned priority in Reagan administration policy on East-West relations. At the time of the Mexican rescue the Treasury, still dominant in international financial policy making, was run by men with little experience in international monetary affairs. They remained blinded to the onrushing crisis. Even the Federal Reserve, one of the more internationally oriented actors in the U.S. government, did not determine its monetary targets with international financial consequences as a primary concern. (One informant offered 20 percent as an estimate of its weighting.)[38]

A second obstacle to intervention by the American government was the Reagan administration's deep-seated faith in the stability and flexibility of markets and its hostility to government tampering with private transactions. Stephen Marris has captured the sea change in international attitudes toward institutions of international economic cooperation, no longer regarded as "the brightest of man's creations" but, "at best, as clearinghouses for the exchange of information or, at worst, as having a negative influence on world economic welfare."[39] The early Reagan administration shared that same revolution of declining expectations.

It is because the American government resisted acting as a stabilizer of the system for these essentially domestic reasons that the peculiarities of the situation that triggered U.S. action should be emphasized. Intervention would probably not have been so swift had Mexico not been the first of the large debtors to encounter servicing difficulties. The costs of crisis management in terms of resources and domestic political risks, despite congressional and public resistance to the IMF quota increase in 1983, were relatively small. Moreover, the United States defined the limits of intervention very narrowly. Its actions help to explain not only the stability but the conservatism of the crisis outcome: only the IMF's crisis management role was expanded; there was virtually no concession to complaints that the American economic policy mix was producing interest rates burdensome to debtors; and all of the innovations were regarded as ad hoc and temporary, unfortunate way stations on the return to the market.

The domestic dilemmas of bargaining strategies

The special, and largely domestic, circumstances of American action in the debt crisis go some distance toward explaining innovations in procedures of

38. Kraft, *The Mexican Rescue*, p. 8.
39. Stephen Marris, *Managing the World Economy: Will We Ever Learn?* (Princeton, N.J.: International Finance Section, Princeton University, 1984), p. 8.

crisis management, as well as the limits to those innovations. Nevertheless, the United States was intervening in a setting that on its own it could neither control nor even predictably influence. It required the cooperation of a host of actors, governmental and private, and it could expect resistance to its preferred solutions from at least some of the actors, particularly the debtors.

The complexities of the debt crisis after mid-1982 are difficult to simplify into a bargaining framework, but the dynamics can be viewed as bargaining between and within two coalitions, one more loosely organized than the other. The Northern coalition of the banks, the G-5 governments, and the International Monetary Fund shared an interest not only in avoiding disruption of the international financial system but also in the rough outlines of a rescheduling and adjustment regime for debtors. The coalition displayed potential fissures in the ordering of interests among its members — G-5 governments and the Fund ranked international financial stability higher than autonomy of decision making for the banks or adherence to particular payments schedules — and in the collective action problem of organizing such a large army of actors, particularly the commercial banks. Other incipient divisions among the industrialized countries depended upon regional biases in their national interests and bank lending patterns, as well as their differing attitudes toward reform — the French, for example, were relatively conciliatory toward the debtors. The Southern coalition was barely a coalition. There was little apparent coordination among the debtors until new strains in 1984 raised the possibility of a debtors' club. Much of Northern policy was directed to deepening the divergent interests among large debtors and between large debtors and those countries that could not on their own threaten the system.

Bargaining between the two coalitions most closely resembled a game of chicken: both shared an interest in avoiding financial collapse, but the Southern side was tempted to exploit the vulnerability of the North to obtain concessions in the rules of the rescheduling game or even wider reforms. The North pursued a complex strategy, offering incentives and also threatening sanctions to prevent cooperative action by Latin American debtors that could be transformed into a system-threatening moratorium on debt servicing. One incentive that the North could offer — given involuntary lending by the banks — was immediate financing on a scale unavailable outside the existing rules of the game. The sanctions were those which had always served as the principal means of enforcement in private bank lending: exclusion from private financial markets for an indefinite period and disruption of trade finance. In the longer term the promised rewards were markets for exports in the industrialized countries, renewed growth, and eventual eligibility for renewed voluntary financing from financial markets.

In pursuing this strategy the North faced several dilemmas, each of them rooted in domestic political constraints. First, it had to ease strains on the financial system that gave the debtors their principal bargaining threat. One tool for doing so — easing monetary policy and lowering interest rates — would

30   *Miles Kahler*

also provide additional incentives for the debtors to accept the preferred
G-5/IMF solution. It could, however, also conflict with other domestic economic policy goals, particularly the restraining of inflation. This conflict was
not serious as the United States recovered from deep recession in 1983, but
as the economy raced ahead in 1984 the Federal Reserve opted to tighten
monetary policy. Interest rates drifted upward in early 1984 with predictable
effects: a renewed burst of activity to organize the Latin American debtor
countries and signs of strain on the financial system (particularly the failure
of Continental Illinois). As a former vice-chairman of the Federal Reserve
Board commented, "There are times when your lender-of-last-resort responsibilities and your monetary-policy responsibilities are somewhat in conflict, and this is one of those periods."[40]

Regulation and system stability: domestic politics intrudes

The maintenance of coalition unity, and particularly maintaining the cooperation of the banks, was yet another obstacle-ridden path that governments, central banks, and the IMF had to negotiate. The strategy of the
G-5 governments and the IMF depended on bank cooperation in two respects.
In the first and purely crisis management phase the banks had to be kept
in the game: the rational response of each individual bank to reduce its
exposure as quickly as possible had to be curbed in order to prevent general
collapse. The innovation of involuntary lending added to this burden: the
banks had to be convinced not only to maintain but to increase their exposure.
Without such an increase the harsh conditions asked of the debtors would
probably have been unacceptable: as the IMF knows too well from experience,
adjustment programs are likely to fail if the amount of financing offered to
sustain them is inadequate.

The intrabank hierarchy described above was crucial to maintaining bank
cooperation, but it seems unlikely that it would have held without the intervention of public authorities, wielding both pressure and regulatory dis-
pensations. As Wellons notes, the level of "administrative guidance" varied
from case to case and depended in part on the wishes of the bargaining
parties—the banks and the debtor country—but pressure from regulators
was important in establishing the innovation of involuntary lending. As one
banker said, "It's peer-group type pressure. . . . And if that peer-group pressure
does not work, they'll get a call from some public-sector person."[41] Regulators
could also offer the incentive of relief from regulatory scrutiny. The most
prominent example was Paul Volcker's speech to the New England Council

40. Quoted in *Wall Street Journal*, 7 June 1984, p. 1.
41. Quoted in *New York Times*, 12 December 1982, p. D3; also Kraft, *The Mexican Rescue*,
p. 53.

on 16 November 1982, in which he suggested that because of unprecedented conditions, no one would question new lending to countries that had agreed an adjustment program with the IMF.[42]

The regulatory carrot offered by the Federal Reserve ran headlong into the peculiarities of the American political system. Banking supervision in most industrialized countries is, as Wellons indicates, a fairly cozy process involving the central bank and a banking sector far more concentrated than that in America. The United States, however, is host to a "crazy quilt of banking regulation," including state regulatory authorities as well as three regulatory authorities at the federal level—the Federal Reserve, the comptroller of the currency, and the Federal Deposit Insurance Corporation.[43] As the most internationally minded of the regulatory agencies, the Federal Reserve was willing to relax scrutiny in the interests of further lending as the debt crisis deepened, whatever the shortcomings of previous bank practice. Other regulators, with fewer international concerns, had different priorities. As Volcker waved his regulatory concession in November 1982 in an effort to make involuntary lending easier, the Securities and Exchange Commission was requiring banks to publish the extent of their exposure in individual "problem countries" if loans grew to more than 1 percent of the total outstanding.

Using regulation to ensure bank cooperation and system stability became even more difficult in 1983 because of the deepening politicization of regulatory questions during the debate over an increased U.S. quota in the International Monetary Fund. The quota increase was held hostage to any number of congressional concerns—efforts to target particular countries, new housing legislation—but perhaps most serious in their implications for the debt crisis were congressional demands for regulatory tightening. The American political system had once again set elements of an international strategy for stabilizing the system one against another, a necessary increase in IMF resources versus the need for U.S. banks to continue lending.

Bargaining and the politics of adjustment

In mixing sanctions and rewards to keep the debtor states in the game, the G-5 governments and the IMF had to contend with one final domestic constraint, one far more difficult than the use of regulatory instruments to influence bank behavior. They had even less control over the politics of adjustment inside the debtor countries, yet that politics was critical in de-

---

42. Mentré, *The Fund, Commercial Banks, and Member Countries*, p. 10; Kraft, *The Mexican Rescue*, p. 49.
43. Martin Mayer, *The Money Bazaars* (New York: Dutton, 1984), p. 335; Richard Dale, *Bank Supervision around the World* (New York: Group of Thirty, 1982), p. 62; David Lascelles, "US Bank Regulation after the Debt 'Crisis,'" *Banker*, January 1983, p. 21.

termining the bargaining behavior of debtor states. For not only did elites in debtor countries have to weigh the carrots and sticks waved by international actors and the economic costs of severe adjustment programs, they also had to look over their shoulder at the consequences for their domestic political position. The gains and losses implied in internal competition with their rivals formed an element essential to their calculus.

That domestic political calculus also supplies an element needed to explain the puzzles of continuing cooperation between creditor and debtor and failure of debtors to coordinate their bargaining with the banks and the industrialized countries. It is clear that, while each of the major debtors in Latin America—Mexico, Brazil, and Argentina—might threaten system stability on its own, the smaller debtors were unlikely to be able to act collectively without leadership from one or more of those three. That possibility—a coalition of the great and the small debtors in a debtors' club—was what the North regarded as most threatening of all, a prospect that their strategy of rewarding those who remained within orthodox adjustment programs was designed to thwart.

The pattern of debtor collaboration that emerged did not, in fact, involve large countries leading a program of defiance. Rather, it was the smaller economies, hardest hit by collapsing commodity prices and unlikely to regain their creditworthiness in the near term, that first began efforts at debtor organization. At meetings in Panama in March 1983 and in Caracas (under OAS auspices) in September 1983 the big debtors indicated their lack of interest. The first sign of change came at the Latin American Economic Conference at Quito in January 1984: the new Argentinian government under Raúl Alfonsín took a more prominent and activist role.

The next debtors' meeting, at Cartagena in June 1984, was the high-water mark of debtor collaboration, founded on deteriorating economic circumstances and in particular on rising interest rates. The meeting had been designed to send a signal to the London summit of industrialized countries, and the new line subsequently taken by the Federal Reserve and the IMF on better terms for rescheduling signified that they, if not industrial country leaders, may have received the signal. The Cartagena group had reached a modest consensus, but it had also been carefully managed to avoid any militant proposals despite agreement on a consultative mechanism. The chief managers of the meeting had been Mexico, Brazil, Venezuela, and the host, Colombia, arrayed against Argentina and several smaller countries. These same four countries had participated in the March 1984 "rescue" of Argentina as it approached its deadline for payment of interest to American banks. In the deal devised by Mexico the four Latin American countries and a consortium of banks contributed enough to make the necessary payments; the United States guaranteed the Latin American contributions if Argentina reached an agreement with the IMF. (Apparently, the bank contributions were also guaranteed by the Argentinian government.) Many had argued at the same time that the March action demonstrated an unwillingness by debtors to break with the system. Mexico's active role at Cartagena a few months later, however, suggested that it was playing a different strategy: keeping the other Latin Americans from actions that would, through contagion, affect its own standing with the banks, at the same time demonstrating that its leadership could be used for other purposes if a better bargain were not struck.

The reasons that Mexico and the other largest debtors did not organize a debtors' club are fairly clear: given their own bargaining power, the smaller debtors were pure free riders, unnecessary except perhaps for purposes of legitimation. Yet the contrasting courses that Mexico and Argentina followed are still puzzling: why did one become the model debtor of the IMF and the banks while the other engaged in repeated displays of brinksmanship (tied to U.S. regulatory deadlines) and foot-dragging in an effort to force a change in the rules of the game? Part of the explanation surely lies in their differing economic situations. Mexico was deeply embedded in a web of economic ties with the international economy and particularly the United States: trade disruption, particularly the disruption of food imports, would have been costly. (Brazil faced the same constraint with energy imports.) Argentina, in contrast, was not linked closely to any single industrialized country, and its economic self-sufficiency was greater.

Beneath the economic divergence, however, lay an equally important political divergence. As both Kaufman and Haggard indicate, Mexico was far better situated to undertake adjustment: the domestic political costs for its elite were lower. With the transition to the de la Madrid presidency, technocrats who were essentially in agreement with Fund prescriptions held the levers of economic policy. Alternative economic programs were advanced, but no organized group pushed hard for a coherent economic alternative; orthodox prescriptions, though hardly popular, had not been discredited by recent national experience. Most important, the corporatist or authoritarian structure of Mexico, based on a powerful presidency and a well-institutionalized political party (the PRI), provided a basis for containing resistance to stabilization, particularly from labor.

In Argentina, following the election of Alfonsín, the political landscape contrasted starkly with that of Mexico. Technocrats were hardly in control; rather, the new political leadership saw orthodox economic policies as thoroughly discredited by their association with the old regime and particularly with the government of Martínez de Hoz. Alfonsín and his cabinet repeatedly pledged themselves to no reduction in real wages and no recession. The Argentinian president, who was also institutionally powerful, acted not with the solid and centralized base of a PRI but in a setting of political flux in which the old verities had been erased by his victory. In their scramble to consolidate that surprising triumph, the Radicals had to confront a labor movement under the control of their adversaries, the Peronists. In such circumstances, given the risks of an effort to stabilize and the potential gains to be made in working-class support by resisting the IMF, the new Argentinian leaders challenged the existing rules again and again, externalizing their weakness in an effort to reduce the political burdens of adjustment.

The pattern of bargaining by Latin American states and the weakness of their collaboration reflected divergence in their domestic capabilities for adjustment. The divisions were less between democratic and authoritarian regimes than, adapting the arguments of Kaufman and Haggard, between "hard" and "soft" ones. "Hard" regimes—democratic or authoritarian—had two characteristics: they were able to curb the state sector itself in the interests of stabilization, and they were able to pursue Kaufman's containment option toward resistance to stabilization programs by labor and other groups. Although the military authoritarian regimes that took power in Latin America in the 1960s and 1970s may have begun as hard regimes—hostile in many cases to expansion of the state sector and willing to repress opposition to conservative economic policies—by the end of the 1970s (with the exception of Chile) they had softened, presiding over burgeoning public sectors and lower levels of resistance to demands from labor and other groups in civil society. The onset of economic crisis in the 1980s brought a hardening in the cases of Chile and the nonmilitary PRI government of Mexico, but it also brought great difficulties for the other, soft authoritarian regimes in pursing an adjustment program, difficulties that spurred the transition to civilian rule. In either case there was little incentive to take a tough bargaining line with the creditors. In the case of soft authoritarian regimes, such brinkmanship would risk loss of already waning middle-class support with few prospective gains in legitimation; in those regimes that could pursue adjustment programs with fewer political risks, tougher external bargaining was unnecessary. As the Argentinian case suggests, it was the "soft democratic" regime that seemed most tempted to toughen its bargaining stance and seek debtor collaboration. Such regimes were at the apogee of risk taking— not solidly grounded enough to pursue orthodox adjustment yet perceiving gains rather than losses to their domestic political base from a more resistant position toward creditors.

An end to the debt crisis?

By early 1985 each of the three biggest Latin American debtors had elected governments that enjoyed a longer time horizon than any since the beginnings of the debt crisis in 1982. Each had reached agreement with the IMF (though disbursements were soon suspended for Argentina and Brazil); each had negotiated or was nearing agreement on a multiyear rescheduling arrangement with the commercial banks. The financial system no longer looked so shaky;

year-end reports of the major banks suggested no overall weakness because of international lending. Was the debt crisis "all but over"?[44]

The answer from the South was clearly "no." The latest report of the Economic Commission for Latin America painted a picture that seemed promising only because of the bleakness of recent years. The favored, larger debtors had made some gains in economic growth, but even they were hardly successful by past standards: Mexico's per capita gross domestic product (GDP) declined in 1984; Brazil's overall increase of 3.5 percent only offset the decline in 1983. Among the smaller countries the record was catastrophic: declines in per capita GDP from 1981–84 of 25 percent in Bolivia, 16 percent in Uruguay, 11 percent in Chile.[45]

Northern countries saw a much brighter picture. The evolving bargain, which remained highly favorable to the creditors, looked as though it would hold. Certainly the evolution of economic parameters—interest rates, commodity prices, OECD growth rates—provides a major element in any prediction. My argument suggests, however, that the structure of international finance is now far more politicized and that political unknowns, *domestic* political unknowns, are equally important in predicting the outcome of the debt crisis. System stabilization continues to rest on cooperation among the industrialized countries and on continuing engagement by the United States. Despite its activism in crisis management since 1982, the United States is an unstable stabilizer, constantly tugged toward domestic policy goals that may conflict with its systemic role and seduced by a faith in the virtues of the unleashed market.

The domestic regulatory environment in all of the industrialized countries and particularly in the United States is likely to continue to influence the management of the debt crisis. On the one hand, the crisis itself induced a tightening of the regulatory environment for international lending. Some observers contend this new strictness could have a chilling effect on any new lending to Third World borrowers, but it could also, paradoxically, strengthen the hand of the debtors in their bargaining with the banks.[46] On the other hand, an opposite trend—hardly interrupted by the debt crisis—is also likely to have contradictory effects on bank behavior, and that is the continuing *deregulation* of financial institutions in the United States and elsewhere. Deregulation offers incentives for money center banks in the United States to turn away from their riskier international business, but it could also, as a by-product of the financial supermarkets of tomorrow, produce new financial

44. *New York Times*, 4 February 1985, p. D1.
45. Economic Commission for Latin America and the Caribbean, "Preliminary Overview of the Latin American Economy during 1984," LC/G. 1336 (Santiago, 17 January 1985).
46. Robert A. Bennett, "Bankers Fear Effects of Regulators' Moves," *New York Times*, 17 November 1984, pp. 31, 33; Karin Lissakers, "Bank Regulation and International Debt," in Richard E. Feinberg and Valeriana Kallab, eds., *Uncertain Future: Commercial Banks and the Third World* (New Brunswick, N.J.: Transaction, 1984), pp. 66–67.

technologies to sustain capital flows to the developing countries. Commercial banks, in this last view, may be the dinosaurs of international finance; the needs of developing country borrowers, like those of domestic consumers, may be better served by new, diversified institutions.[47]

Perhaps most unpredictable, however, is the course of politics and economic policy in the debtor countries. As soft authoritarian regimes give way to democratic regimes, whether hard or soft, the historical record is not encouraging: both authoritarian and democratic regimes in Latin America have been weighed in the stabilization balance and found wanting. Conservative, dependency, and neodependency models of Latin American development also seem wanting as the region (and other indebted countries) grope toward a new model that will fit the changed international economic circumstances. As in the 1930s, so it is in the 1980s: the gambles that political elites on the periphery take or decline to take—weighing both their economic and their domestic political prospects as well as their hunches about the international economy—will set the final political boundary to the future of the debt crisis.

47. The future of the commercial banks is considered by Mayer, *The Money Bazaars*, especially chap. 2.

Lessons from the past: capital markets during the 19th century and the interwar period
Albert Fishlow

On Friday, 13 August 1982, Finance Minster Jesus Silva Herzog of Mexico made a series of visits to the International Monetary Fund, the Federal Reserve, and the U.S. Treasury. His message to each was the same: Mexico could no longer continue to service its debt. Thus began a dramatic weekend of negotiations that marked the end of the preceding decade's buoyant expansion of developing country debt and the start of a still continuing response to the sudden collapse.

Joseph Kraft describes the Mexican action as "a bombshell that shook an entire universe. It was like Columbus setting out on an uncharted sea, and taking with him on the leap into the dark some of the stuffiest people in some of the world's most hidebound institutions."[1] Kraft, like many others, is too much struck by the novelty of the event. More than a century earlier, in a paper read to the Statistical Society in London, Hyde Clarke had lamented the "unparalleled disaster... which has inflicted not only pecuniary, but moral and even physical distress, on every family of Western Europe which had the industry to secure and the thrift to save."[2] One could go back even farther than the crisis of the 1870s to find similar reactions attending the defaults of the 1820s, in which Latin America, and Mexico, played a principal part.

International capital markets functioned, and failed, long before this latest episode. And they played even more central roles than in recent years. From 1870 to 1914, for example, a truly global economy was forged for the first time, extending from the core of Western European industrializers to latecomers in Eastern Europe to raw material suppliers on the periphery. At the

---

An earlier version was presented at the Lehrman Institute, New York City, in the spring of 1984 as part of its seminar series on Politics and International Debt, which was supported in part by a grant from the Ford Foundation.

1. Joseph Kraft, *The Mexican Rescue* (New York: Group of Thirty, 1984), p. 3.
2. Hyde Clarke, *Sovereign and Quasi-Sovereign States: Their Debts to Foreign Countries* (London, 1879), p. 9.

International Organization 39, 3, Summer 1985 0020-8183/85/030383-57 $1.50
© 1985 by the Massachusetts Institute of Technology and the World Peace Foundation

heart of this extension of trade was a system of expanding finance that girded the globe with railways and opened new areas for primary production. Large infusions of capital provided the savings, and the foreign exchange to import track and equipment, that were beyond the capacities of recipient countries. The amounts were enormous: in the four decades before the First World War something like $30 billion, the equivalent in 1984 dollars of $270 billion or one-third of contemporary developing country debt, in a world economy perhaps one-tenth as large.

For the suppliers of capital, such flows meant large allocations from their own savings. Britain, the largest source of foreign capital, invested abroad an annual average of 5 percent of gross product during the period 1873–1913, reaching a peak of 10 percent just before the outbreak of war. For France, the commitment was about half as large, both on average and also for the final surge in 1910–13. Germany was a latecomer. Its more rapid growth and absorption of saving in domestic capital formation left a small 2 percent of income for overseas assets, and a lesser tendency for acceleration. The contrast to the recent expansion of lending to developing countries is marked: even during the peak transfers of the 1970s only about 1 percent of industrialized countries' incomes was being channeled in that direction.[3]

Foreign investment was central to the trade and growth performance of most of the recipients in the late 19th century. Australia, Canada, Argentina, and Brazil all experienced surges of capital imports that accounted for a third to a half of all domestic investment undertaken. The United States, despite its position as the largest capital importer in the 19th-century world economy, was an exception. Foreign lending accounted for no more than 10 to 15 percent of investment, and that only for selected peak years. That lower level is much more the standard of recent years. During the most buoyant phase of increasing debt in the last decade foreign saving financed about 20 percent of developing country investment, higher only for the low-income and poorly performing African countries.[4]

The First World War marked a decisive break. For one, it marked the emergence of the United States for the first time as a net creditor nation. For another, the position of the principal European lenders was much changed. Germany became a leading importer of capital; French assets abroad were dramatically reduced by the repudiation of extensive Russian holdings, diminishing the appetite for overseas holdings as domestic reconstruction re-

3. Information on the creditor countries comes from R. C. O. Matthews et al., *British Economic Growth* (Stanford: Stanford University Press, 1982); Rondo Cameron, *France and the Economic Development of Europe, 1800–1914* (Princeton: Princeton University Press, 1961); and B. Mitchell, *European Historical Statistics* (New York: New York University Press, 1980), containing national income and balance-of-payments series of Walther Hoffmann. Contemporary data are from the World Bank and the International Monetary Fund.

4. For data on the importance of investment to a variety of recipients see Arthur I. Bloomfield, *Patterns of Fluctuation in International Finance before 1914*, Princeton Studies in International Finance no. 21 (Princeton, N.J., 1968), Appendix 3, and the country-specific sources later cited.

quirements increased; Britain experienced a marked decline in savings rates. A larger U.S. presence did not compensate for European withdrawal, and global foreign investment declined.

In addition, developmental finance for the periphery took second place during the 1920s to capital flows among the industrialized countries and lending for war reconstruction. Reparations and the interally loans were a constant source of irritation. Then came the Great Depression, the demise of the gold standard, and widespread default. The level of world trade rapidly declined after 1929, and interdependence produced perverse consequences for peripheral participants. This post-1914 failure of the international capital market was in stark contrast to pre-1914 success. No wonder, then, the nostalgia for 19th-century conditions that W. A. Lewis reflected in the introduction to his survey of the interwar period: "The sixty years before 1914 witnessed an astonishing expansion of the world economy, in area, in production, in interdependence, and in complexity. Why did progress reduce, not indeed to a halt, but to a much slower pace after 1918?"[5]

The subject of international capital flows over more than three-quarters of a century is a vast one. Several works, some classics, have been dedicated to the topic.[6] My objective here is not to retell the vivid and fascinating story nor even to rehearse earlier debates of the causes and the consequences of foreign investment. I seek rather to distill some of its important features for comparison with the present. For the pre-1914 period, the central issues are why the market worked so well and how it managed the periodic fluctuations in economic activity that afflicted borrowers and lenders alike. For the interwar period, parallel questions relate to the breakdown of the earlier model.

I shall stress four determinants of capital market performance. The first is the principal use that borrowing countries made of international finance. Recipients could use the resources to supplement their own domestic savings and increase investment or to enhance consumption. In practice, before 1914 and to some extent even before 1929, this was a decision to invest in infrastructure or to finance current governmental expenditures. The former almost always translated into greater capital formation, the latter into consumption outlays. Note that the distinction is *not* between private and public borrowing.

5. W. A. Lewis, *Economic Survey, 1919–1939* (London: Allen & Unwin, 1949), p. 12.
6. Among such classics, still highly useful, must be counted L. H. Jenks, *The Migration of British Capital to 1875* (New York: Knopf, 1927); H. Feis, *Europe the World's Banker: 1870–1914* (New Haven: Yale University Press, 1930); A. K. Cairncross, *Home and Foreign Investment, 1870–1913* (London: Cambridge University Press, 1953); and B. Thomas, *Migration and Economic Growth* (London: Cambridge University Press, 1954). For a summary of some of the discussion and selected readings see A. R. Hall, ed., *The Export of Capital from Britain, 1870–1914* (London: Methuen, 1968). A recent and highly useful reexamination of some of the basic hypotheses surrounding British capital export is M. Edelstein, *Overseas Investment in the Age of British Imperialism: The United Kingdom, 1850–1914* (New York: Columbia University Press, 1982).

Governments could and did apply resources to state-owned projects; but then they would have to find the means to service their debts. Not all had and have the political capacity to do so.

A second important factor is the ease with which debtor countries increase exports. Foreign capital inflows imposed the requirement of subsequent outflows to service interest and profits, as well as amortization. There was a question not only of whether borrowed resources would earn an adequate rate of return but also of how to transfer those earnings. The answer depends, in the last analysis, upon export capacity and the structure of world trade.

The third characteristic I single out is the institutional form of financial intermediation. Results are not independent of the way that funds are channeled, whether through the large investment banks centered in London before 1914, banks in the United States in the interwar period, or the Euromarket in the 1970s and 1980s. Very obviously, the International Monetary Fund is a central and new actor on the scene, but private agents and national governments performed at least some of its functions earlier.

Finally, the source of finance shaped the quantities and consequences of capital flows. The degree of politicization and the consequent direction of foreign investment differed with its national origin. London, Paris, Berlin, and New York were not perfect substitutes, and capital markets were not and are not fully blind to the identity of transactors. There is also a second indirect route of influence via international trade. The ability of borrowers to apply their proceeds freely, and to find markets for their exports to service their foreign obligations, varies with the policies and practices of creditor countries.

Together, these four characteristics add up to distinctive equilibrating mechanisms of trade, capital movements, service payments, and income of the global economy, both historically and at the present time. Such relationships embody an important political component, as noted above, but also a dominant economic content. The appeal of the profit motive, and the private returns that could be earned, mobilized capital. The search for profit did not mean a perfect capital market, but it did mean a market and an international economy within which it functioned.

This emphasis consciously contrasts with Herbert Feis's valuable, monumental, and still influential study of the 1870–1914 period. His concerns were shaped by the times in which he wrote: in the troubled interwar period it was virtually inevitable that political considerations would loom large and, ultimately, largest:

In short, the financial transactions between western Europe and the other areas were an important element in political affairs. They became all the more important because the official circles of lending countries gradually came to envisage the foreign investments of their citizens, not as private financial transactions, but as one of the instruments through which national destiny was achieved. Financial force was often used to

Lessons from the past

buy or build political friendship or alliance, was often lent or withheld in accordance with political considerations.[7]

The vision, without denying the validity of the conclusion, is only partial. Moreover, it impedes rather than facilitates our understanding of capital flows not only then but especially in comparison with the 1920s and 1930s and with the 1970s and 1980s.

I begin with a quantitative overview of lending that spans both the pre- and the interwar periods. Section 2 then examines the workings of the capital market before 1914 in more detail, and section 3 similarly focuses on the interwar market. I conclude with some observations about the debt crisis of the 1980s, drawing on the lessons from the past.

1. Trends in international lending

Table 1 sets out estimates of net overseas assets of the capital-exporting countries at regular intervals from 1855 to 1938. Changes in the stock of assets before 1914 approximate flows of foreign investment. Neither widespread default nor significant changes in valuation occurred. In 1876 the Corporation of Foreign Bondholders reported a total of $1.5 billion in default, the prewar peak; much of it was restored to paying status by 1885, albeit partially written down.[8] After 1914 the problem is more serious. Corrections have been applied to offset write-downs and write-offs, and a series on direct capital flow data for the United States used.

In consideration of the different character of the subperiods 1870–1913 and 1913–38, I present two aggregate foreign investment series. One considers only the major European creditors, treating the United States solely as a recipient of funds rather than a source. The other, more relevant after 1914, consolidates the U.S. net position and thus better reflects investment in areas outside the core countries. These estimated flows have been deflated to 1913 dollars using a British export price index before the war and an American export price index for finished manufactured products thereafter. From such constant dollar investment data, it becomes possible to aggregate a constant dollar stock series over the entire period.

Finally, Table 1 presents an estimate of real resources transferred to recipients of capital inflows. The calculation of the transfer subtracts from investment the return flow of interest and dividend payments required to service outstanding debt and equity holdings. Real resource transfers thus reflect the net addition to domestic savings provided by foreign capital. Income receipts are estimated reasonably accurately for Britain and the United

---

7. Feis, *Europe the World's Banker*, p. xxvi.
8. Corporation of Foreign Bondholders, *Thirty-third Annual Report, 1906* (London), p. 11.

TABLE 1. *Growth of net overseas private long-term assets, 1855–1938 (end of year, in U.S. $ billions)*

Country	1855	1870	1885	1900	1913	1930	1938
United Kingdom	1.0	3.5	7.6	12.3	20.4	27.2	20.8
France	.5	2.4	3.5	5.0	8.7	3.8	3.3
Germany			1.8	3.6	5.5	−.9	−2.1
Netherlands[a]		.5	1.0	1.1	1.2	3.0	4.8
United States	−.4	−1.3	−1.8	−2.5	−3.7[b]	9.5	4.8
Total European Assets	1.8	6.4	13.9	22.0	35.8	33.1	26.0
Total European and American assets	1.4	5.1	12.1	19.5	32.1	42.6	30.8
European Foreign Investment	4.6	7.5	8.1	13.8	4.7[c]	−3.7[d]	
European and American Foreign Investment	3.7	7.0	7.4	12.6	16.4[e]	−6.2[f]	
Net European Resource Transfer	1.5	−.2	−4.2	−2.3	−18.0	−12.2	
Net European and American Resource Transfer	1.2	.6	−3.1	−2.6	−13.3[g]	−17.4	
Constant 1913 Dollars:							
Total European Assets	1.7	5.3	11.9	21.4	36.1	39.6	35.5
Total European and American Assets	1.3	4.2	10.3	18.9	32.3	44.4	37.5
European Foreign Investment	3.6	6.6	9.5	14.7	3.5	−4.1	
European and American Foreign Investment	2.9	6.1	8.6	13.4	12.1	−6.9	
Current Foreign Assets[h]/Primary Trade	1.1	2.0	3.4	3.3	2.9	2.1[i]	2.2
Constant Foreign Assets[h]/Primary Trade			2.4	2.9	3.0	2.8[i]	2.5

a. Gross. b. 1914.
c. Change in assets less losses in value owing to war estimated in U.N., *International Capital Movements during the Inter-War Period*, pp. 4–5.
d. Change in assets less estimated defaults of British assets implicit in Mathews's estimates of net investment and asset values.
e. Excludes intergovernmental debts.
f. European investment plus direct estimates of U.S. net long-term foreign investment.
g. Excludes income from interallied debts.
h. Foreign assets are European until 1914, European and American thereafter.
i. 1929 trade level.

Sources. For *net assets* of **United Kingdom**: R. C. O. Matthews et al. *British Economic Growth*, p. 128, for net assets at specified dates, interpolated by annual net foreign investment reported in B. Mitchell, *European Historical Statistics*, and 1930 extrapolated from 1924. For **France**: 1855–1914, R. Cameron, *France and the Economic Development of Europe, 1800–1914*, p. 79, interpolated by estimated net flows; 1938, Cleona Lewis, *Debtor and Creditor Countries: 1938*, 1944, pp. 60–62; 1930, extrapolated from 1938 by foreign investment series in Mitchell, *Historical Statistics*. For **Germany**: 1914, W. Woodruff, *Impact of Western Man*, p. 154 (less Cameron's estimate of French investments in Germany); 1885–1900, extrapolated from 1914 using annual investment flows in Mitchell, *Historical Statistics*; 1930, Woodruff, *Impact* (less estimated U.S. investments in Germany in C. Lewis, *America's Stake in International Investment*, p. 486); 1938, Lewis, *Debtor and Creditor Countries*, pp. 62–63. For the **Netherlands**: 1855–1914, Woodruff, *Impact*, p. 150; 1938, Lewis, *Debtor and Creditor Countries*, pp. 67–68; 1930, extrapolated from 1938 using annual investment flows in Mitchell, *Historical Statistics*. For the **United States**: 1855–1930, *Historical Statistics*, Series U-40; 1938, Lewis, *Debtor and Creditor Countries*, pp. 78–80.

For *investment*: Change in assets, adjusted as described in the notes.

For *resource transfer*: foreign investment less income. For U.K. income I use Imlah, *Economic Elements in the Pax Britannica*, for 1855–1914 and thereafter estimate from Mathews, *British Economic Growth*. Same implicit rate of return applied to other European investment. For the United States, income estimates from *Historical Statistics*.

For *foreign investment deflators*: 1855–1914, U.K. export index, weighted by annual investment, both from Imlah. 1855 fixed asset deflator is equal to unweighted 1850–55 average. 1914–38, U.S. export index of finished manufactures, weighted by annual net investment, excluding government, 1914–38. Investment taken from *Historical Statistics*, and the price index from R. Lipsey, *Price and Quantity Trends in the Foreign Trade of the United States*, p. 143.

For *primary trade*: 1913–38, P. Lamartine Yates, *Forty Years of Foreign Trade*, p. 39; 1885–1900, 1913 value from Yates extrapolated by value and volume indexes in W. A. Lewis, *Growth and Fluctuations, 1870–1913*, pp. 282–83; 1855–70, 1889 value from Lewis extrapolated by world trade estimates of W. Rostow, *The World Economy*, pp. 666–67. (1855 is average of 1860 and 1850.) The procedure assumes constancy in relative value of primary trade, confirmed in the data for 1876–1900.

States, the largest sources of pre- and post-1914 investment respectively, and the entries for resource transfer are therefore equally valid.

Table 1 registers the sharp break in international finance at the time of the First World War. Even taking into account the American conversion from net debtor to net creditor, annual real investment abroad is two-thirds as great in the period 1914–30 as it was between 1900 and 1913. A decline in the 1930s leaves even the cumulated real assets about where they had been more than two decades earlier. The previous record of continuous increase over 75 years came to an end.

Reported interwar investment flows exclude almost $10 billion of Allied War Loans granted by the U.S. government as well as another $9 billion in loans advanced by Britain and France. A large portion of these loans net out in aggregating the three countries: eighty percent of U.S. loans went to Britain and France, 20 percent of the British loans to France. In the end about $8.5 billion was transferred to third parties, principally Russia and Italy.[9] Since these loans financed current outlays and were later adjusted (and defaulted on), they are best excluded from the calculation of overseas assets. Their exclusion does not, however, mean they are of no interest. On the contrary, in conjunction with reparations payments these governmental obligations created important distortions in interwar financial markets. (I discuss their effects in section 3.)

The First World War also marks the shift in financial preeminence from London to New York. Although Britain would resume its lending in the 1920s, U.S. investment was quantitatively more important in that decade and thereafter. Shortly after the war began, European holdings of American securities were liquidated to meet the new expenses and the United States, a prominent investor in Latin America since the 1890s, became a net creditor for the first time. France and Germany never recovered their earlier positions. The former's large portfolio of Russian bonds suffered repudiation after the Revolution, canceling about one-fourth of reported 1913 assets. Overall French losses were estimated at more than $4 billion. A similar fate befell Germany, which actually became a net debtor after 1924. It was not only forced to sell off assets and to accept repudiation on many of its European holdings, it was also forced to borrow extensively in order to meet reparation payments. The Netherlands increased its creditor role by larger commitments in its colonies as well as continuing portfolio investment in Europe and the United States.

Despite the rapid prewar growth in the stock of foreign capital, at an annual average rate of 4.6 percent between 1870 and 1913, foreign investment did not fully keep up with the reflow of income from interest and dividends. Return income flowed at a rate close to 5 percent a year on outstanding

9. Harold G. Moulton and Leo Pasvolsky, *War Debts and World Prosperity* (Washington, D.C.: Brookings, 1932), Appendix A.

balances, meaning that on average creditors transferred no resources to debtor nations over the period. During shorter intervals of peak investment outflows could exceed income, but such episodes did not outweigh the opposing tendency. Likewise, individual recipients could enjoy import surpluses for years when external flows were heavy, but the need to generate export surpluses soon compensated for them.

Such an aggregate result casts doubt on the conventional description of the regular debt cycle that capital recipients were supposed to experience. That cycle has four parts. The first phase is characterized by an import surplus and an increasing debt. In the second stage the mature debtor generates an export surplus, but it is inadequate fully to meet service obligations and the debt continues to increase. In the third or "immature creditor" phase the export surplus more than covers interest costs and allows for a reduction in outstanding foreign debt. Finally, the country achieves net creditor status. In reality, however, most countries experienced only brief periods of import surplus. For most of the time they were compelled to export more than they imported in order to meet their debt payments. Such negative resource transfer was not continuous; it depended upon long swings in capital availability that would set up another period of intense foreign investment. Thus Table 1 shows a smaller negative resource transfer in 1900–1913 than in 1885–1900. Still, European investors were not even reinvesting the income they had earned in the former period.

If the evidence suggests a modest negative balance before 1914, after the war the reverse transfer is massive and unambiguous. Debtors were returning far more to their creditors than was being reinvested. It was only because the inflation accompanying the war sent export values to a much higher plateau that the debt could be serviced. Despite the 1920–21 recession and accompanying deflation, unit values for world trade in the 1926–29 period stood perhaps 40 percent higher than their 1913 level.[10] Then, as real trade growth slowed and primary prices weakened in the late 1920s, foreign-exchange limitations loomed. Even without the further complicating burden of the war debts and reparations, the negative resource transfers of the post-1914 period would have posed new difficulties for global equilibrium.

Trouble had been averted earlier by the successful expansion of primary exports at rapid speed and by rising commodity prices after 1896. The latter was critical; it shows up in the decline recorded in Table 1 in the stock of foreign capital relative to trade in primary exports between 1885 and 1913 when both are expressed in current values. Trade growth in constant terms is slower, causing the ratio of capital to trade to go up by one-fourth. Since the measure is crudely comparable to present debt-export ratios as an indicator of the payment capacity of borrowers, the decline in current dollars indicates a smaller debt burden. We can similarly explain the large disparity between

10. P. Lamartine Yates, *Forty Years of Foreign Trade* (London: Macmillan, 1959), p. 204.

46   *Albert Fishlow*

the constant and current dollar values in 1929 and 1938. As pointed out above, rising prices were of considerable assistance to debtors in the first instance, whereas the deflation of the Great Depression resulted in a constant ratio rather than the reduced level implicit in recovery of the volume of primary trade.

This brief quantitative overview highlights important features of the evolution of international debt. It conveys the discontinuity between the pre- and post-1914 periods with regard to the volume of investment and resource transfers, the size of the capital stock relative to primary exports, and the roles of the leading creditor countries. With this record as backdrop, I now examine both periods in more detail.

2. Capital markets before 1914

Table 2 indicates the distribution of foreign assets held by the major creditors on the eve of the First World War. It tells us much about the pattern of investment over the preceding decades, and in particular the data trace two overlapping processes. One is market-oriented foreign investment, largely undertaken by Britain and directed to the resource-rich, European-settled countries of the periphery: North America, Latin America, and Oceania. These three regions together account for more than half of all gross foreign assets in 1914, but more than 70 percent of British investment. The other type of investment was Europe-oriented and accounted for more than a quarter of all assets. Russia was the largest debtor, with other eastern European and Scandinavian countries also recipients. France and Germany were the principal sources. In this kind of investment, as well as in holdings in China, Turkey, Egypt, and some of the African colonies, political considerations clearly played a part.

Developmental finance

Developmental investment of the first, market-oriented kind was largely directed to railroads and other infrastructure. Railroads alone represented more than 40 percent of British asset holdings in 1913. (With full allowance for the direct governmental loans also applied for this purpose, one contemporary placed the total at 60 percent). Matthew Simon's breakdown of all borrowing between 1865 and 1914 by economic sector allocates 69 percent to social overhead capital, with extractive industry in second place, far behind at 12 percent. By contrast, holdings of foreign governments outside the Empire made up less than 10 percent of the portfolio in 1913. Not only had foreign holdings fallen from almost one-half of British investment in 1870, there was even a decline in absolute terms.[11]

11. Matthew Simon, "The Pattern of New British Portfolio Foreign Investment, 1865–1914,"

These data derive from securities that were publicly issued. Of them, about four-fifths in 1913 were debentures and one-fifth was in the form of equity participation. Direct investment in enterprises and activities not represented by issues traded on the Stock Exchange might have accounted for something like 10 percent of total British investment at the time of the war.[12]

The intent underlying all this investment was well understood. Sir George Paish could take satisfaction in 1909 at the role capital exports had played in contributing to British trade and prosperity: "By building railways for the world, and especially the young countries, we have enabled the world to increase its production of wealth at a rate never previously witnessed and to produce those things which this country is especially desirous of purchasing—foodstuffs and raw materials. Moreover, by assisting other countries to increase their output of the commodities they were specially fitted to produce, our investors have helped those countries to secure the means of purchasing the goods that Great Britain manufactures."[13] Credit advanced in the first stage would lead to the purchase of British capital goods. In the second stage a return flow of peripheral primary exports would cover the requisite payments of interest and dividends, lowering the cost of living at the center as well.

Flows of capital from Britain thus went where real returns were likely to be greatest, that is, where new lands to be exploited were receiving labor through immigration. Large waves of emigration from overcrowded Europe moved in conjunction with financial credits. Foreign investment went not to the poorest countries but to the richest, those where incomes even exceeded those of the capital-supplying countries. The tropical countries, already burdened with high population densities, even an India favored in British capital markets, received very little investment. Simple two-factor models suggesting income equalization through capital and trade flows are inappropriate to the 19th-century reality.

Nor can we stress secular trends to the exclusion of long swings of approximately twenty years in British foreign and home investment. Not only did such long cycles characterize the flows of people and capital abroad during the 19th century, they did so in a fashion inverse to British domestic investment. When foreign investment was buoyant, as in the late 1860s and early 1870s, again in the mid- and latter 1880s, and once more in the first decade of the 20th century, domestic investment tended to remain at low

---

in Hall, *Export of Capital*, p. 23. The contemporary estimate is that of George Paish, "Great Britain's Capital Investments in Other Lands," in *Journal of the Royal Statistical Society*, rpt. in Mira Wilkins, ed., *British Overseas Investments, 1907–1948* (New York: Arno, 1977), p. 479 (original).

12. Calculated from Michael Edelstein, "Realized Rates of Return on U.K. Home and Overseas Portfolio Investment in the Age of High Imperialism," *Explorations in Economic History* 13 (1976), p. 295 n. 16 and p. 305, Table 5.

13. Paish, "Great Britain's Investment," p. 480.

TABLE 2. *Geographical distribution of foreign investment of the United Kingdom, France, Germany, and the United States in 1914 ($ U.S. millions to the nearest $50 million)*

To\From		U.K.	France	Germany	U.S.A.	World
Europe	Total	1,050	4,700	2,550	700	12,000
North America						
U.S.A.		4,250	400	950		7,100
Canada		2,800	(100)	200	900	3,850
	Total	7,050	500	1,150	900	11,100
		(63.5%)	(4.5%)	(10.4%)	(8.1%)	(100%)
Latin America						
Mexico		500	400	n.a.	850	2,200
Cuba		150			350	(500)
Argentina		1,550	400	(200)		2,950
Brazil		700	700	(500)		2,200
Chile		300	50	n.a.	450	
Peru		150		(100)		1,000
Uruguay		200	50	n.		
Rest		100	n.	n.		100
	Total	3,700	1,600	900	1,650	8,900
		(41.8%)	(18.1%)	(10.2%)	(18.5%)	(100%)
Oceania						
Australia		1,700	(100)			1,800
New Zealand		300				300
Rest		(200)				(200)
	Total	2,200	(100)			2,300
		(95.7%)	(4.3%)			(100%)
Asia						
Turkey		100	650	450		1,200
India and Ceylon		1,850				1,850
Indo-China			(200)			(200)
Straits Settlements		150	n.	n.	n.	200
Dutch East Indies		200	n.	n.	n.	750
China		600	150	250	50	1,600
Japan		500	(200)	n.	50	1,000
Rest		(150)	n.	n.	150	300
	Total	3,550	1,250	700	250	7,100
		(50.0%)	(17.6%)	(9.9%)	(3.5%)	(100%)
Africa						
Egypt		(200)	(500)			(700)
British West Africa		1,550	(100)			1,650
South Africa		250				250
Rhodesia		150				150
Anglo-Egyptian Sudan						
Rest of British Africa						
French North Africa			(200)			(200)
French Africa (South of Sahara)			100			100
German Colonies				400		400
Belgian Congo				(100)		300
Rest		100				100
	Total	2,450	900	500		4,050
		(60.5%)	(22.2%)	(12.3%)		(100%)
World	Grand Total	20,000	9,050	5,800	3,500	45,450
		(44.0%)	(19.9%)	(12.8%)	(7.8%)	(100%)

Notes. n.a. = not available. n. = negligible.
Source. William Woodruff, *Impact of Man* (New York, 1967), p. 154.

levels. On the lending side, therefore, approximately constant saving behavior could be applied now to foreign, now to domestic, uses without provoking large changes in interest rates. At the same time the balance of payments did not suffer special strain despite large outflows of investment, because the positive effect these outflows had upon export activity was not directly transmitted to domestic income. Instead, the positive stimulus was damped by the decline in home investment, precluding a rise in imports and thus achieving the current-account surplus required for capital export to occur.

An important source of such swings was the longer period required to absorb infrastructure investment in the capital-receiving countries. Railroads took time to build, and the new areas that they opened took time to exploit. There were also longer lags in the construction activity required to meet the increasing demand for housing.

Considerable controversy has arisen about the precise interrelationship between the pull of these peripheral investment booms and the push of diminishing British construction. What is at question is not the relative weight of these factors but the role to be assigned to the forces that tied the cyclical patterns together: the balance of payments versus the indirect influences of migration and wage rates. A. R. Hall's judicious conclusion, echoed in the bulk of M. Edelstein's statistical findings, that a combination of domestic and international factors was at work in both Britain and the new settlements suffices for our purposes here.[14] One should add that neither France nor Germany, whose foreign investment was largely of a different kind, apparently experienced such pronounced, or inverse, movements.

Central to the successful capital transfer of the magnitude of the pre-1914 period is a less noted characteristic of the long-swing, inverse pattern. It took a *sequential* form in incorporating new regions into the world economy: first the United States, in the boom of the early 1870s (and even earlier in the 1830s and the 1850s), then Australia and Argentina in the mid- and latter 1880s, and then Canada and Brazil with renewed Argentine investment in 1900–1913.

Investment was thus concentrated, rather than spread evenly over time. Two consequences followed. Bunching together investments on a large scale was more likely to realize the high returns latent in infrastructure investment. Projects in these new countries were largely indivisible, unlike in Europe or even in the United States before the Civil War, and large increments of railroad track were needed to make the undertakings profitable and to make local production available for export.

Economies of scale also helped in raising funds on the London market. The exaggerations of many prospectuses, all singing the praises of expansion

14. Hall's introduction to *Export of Capital* is a useful summary of the debate surrounding the causal mechanism underlying the transmission of long swings internationally. See also Edelstein, *Overseas Investment*.

50   *Albert Fishlow*

at the same time, could be mutually reinforcing rather than arousing doubts. Positive expectations were, in turn, self-fulfilling. Large capital inflows financed large increases in investment while keeping the balance of payments strong amid a local prosperity that was welcome to foreign investors. A net transfer of resources was achieved in the upswing of the cycle even if service payments, averaged over the whole cycle, ate up most of the proceeds.

The moving frontier, responsive to new supply opportunities, facilitated real transfers of resources in another way. Earlier beneficiaries of capital inflow, with more of their investment now in place, could finance later ones. In the case of the United States, for example, outflows on income account in the boom of the 1880s offset about 60 percent of recorded foreign investment. For Argentina and Australia the proportions were respectively 38 and 53 percent during the same interval, 1884–90.[15] By the 1900s the United States was barely a net recipient.

The inverse pattern itself, independent of the geographic sequence just described, made its own contribution to the transfer problem. A recovery in British home investment as foreign investment faltered brought with it a rise in demand for imports. This rising demand was not adequate to avert declines in the terms of trade of primary producers, whose output was greater thanks to expanded infrastructure, but at least some endogenous, equilibrating mechanism helped to ease the burden of required service payments. If a cyclical mechanism tended to carry investment to excess, a compensating mechanism absorbed some of its increased product.

The net result was a set of favorable, realized financial returns from developmental investment. British income from overseas assets, as we have seen in Table 1, accumulated at rates of between 4.3 and 5.0 percent annually throughout the period 1870–1913. Edelstein's calculations of realized earnings, taking account of capital gains and adjusted for risk, show a clear margin favoring foreign holdings. Compared to Consols, with an adjusted real yield of −1.7 percent, U.S. railway shares stood at 2.2 percent and debentures at 1.9; Latin American railway bonds yielded 1.2 percent and shares, much less important, −0.1. Australian and Canadian governments, a principal vehicle for railroad investment, each earned −0.1 percent. Thus the margin of superiority of foreign returns, taking into account their potentially greater fluctuation in value in response to cyclical variation as well as to political news, ranged from 3.9 to 1.6 percent. Only shares in Indian and East European railways fared worse than the return on Consols. Even if we extended the

15. For data on inflows of net investment for the United States see U.S. Department of Commerce, *Historical Statistics of the United States* (Washington, D.C., 1975), pp. 865ff; for Argentina, A. G. Ford, *The Gold Standard, 1880–1914: Britain and Argentina* (Oxford: Oxford University Press, 1962), p. 142; for Australia, N. G. Butlin, *Australian Domestic Product, Investment and Foreign Borrowing, 1861–1938/39* (London: Cambridge University Press, 1962), pp. 405ff.

comparison to include other domestic applications, the advantage lies with foreign investment.[16]

Not surprisingly, the advantage is not uniform over time. During the long waves of intense foreign investment, when the market evaluated overseas ventures most optimistically, such assets enjoyed a larger margin. In periods of rising home investment, domestic securities actually outperformed their foreign counterparts, but to a smaller extent. Even in such intervals realized real private financial gain from foreign securites exceeded 5 percent (except 1910–13). In no period, morever, did foreign debentures fail to outperform domestic bonds; the margin over Consols sometimes extended to more than two to one. Overseas assets yielded especially handsome returns during the last prewar surge of investment abroad, between 1897 and 1909, when domestic assets yielded but 1.35 percent while foreign assets produced 5.2 percent.[17]

The British capital market mediated between the real social benefits of peripheral infrastructure investment and financial gains to individual investors. It did so quite successfully, as these very large differences attest, to the point that later observers questioned whether the market was not biased against domestic capital formation and in favor of foreign portfolio investment.[18] No such bias appears to have existed, but the more telling point is that there was no discrimination against foreign investment. Neither lack of information nor lack of direct control was a powerful inhibiting influence.

One of the reasons for the positive reception accorded foreign securities was the favorable return earned on holdings of U.S. railroad bonds and shares. Even in 1870–76, when average domestic investment yielded more than average foreign holdings, these bonds earned 7.8 percent compared to the 4.4 percent of domestic debentures; shares returned 8.1 percent.[19] Contrary to the over-cited American defaults arising from initial state borrowing in the 1830s, almost all of which was shortly thereafter made good, the United States was a positive influence, a "demonstration effect" eliciting British investment in other parts of the periphery. American railroads had patently increased the productive capacity and trade of that country and were the implicit model elsewhere. Few noted the exceptional qualities of the American experience: the very small supplement to domestic saving entailed and the consequently limited share that interest and dividend payments took of export earnings.

Another reason why foreign investment successfully rose was the frequency with which loan proceeds were applied to the purchase of British exports. Britain's semimonopoly position in the supply of capital goods linked financial

16. Edelstein, *Overseas Investment*, pp. 133–34.
17. Ibid., p. 148.
18. Edelstein, *Overseas Investment*, finds no evidence of such a bias, dubbed a "Macmillan gap" because it arose in the report of that parliamentary inquiry in 1931.
19. Edelstein, *Overseas Investment*, pp. 153–54.

52   *Albert Fishlow*

and real transactions. That had two effects. One was a much greater international familiarity, characteristic of a trading nation, and therefore a greatly
reduced cost of information. The other was a private internalization of the
social externalities inherent in infrastructure investment. Provincial manufacturers understood that their prosperity was related to successful flotations
of securities on the London Exchange, and they helped to make a market
in them.[20]

The capital market performed its task with virtually no official intervention
or restriction. To be sure, official dissatisfaction was registered as defaults
followed the virtual halt in the mid-1870s of the first wave of investment.
The Foreign Loan Investigation of 1875 found much to criticize in the activities of merchant bankers, including market rigging, exorbitant commissions, and interest payments withheld from principal to service the loan
initially.[21] Yet no regulation of the increasing overseas activities of the City
ensued. Nor was there a government presence to encourage or discourage
commitments, especially notable as increased lending progressively assumed
the cloak of developmental investment. Loans flowed with a high degree of
responsiveness to market forces.

In such circumstances the Foreign Office did not need to provide official
guarantees in the event of default. British policy was forged in an earlier era
when foreign securities were virtually all governments' and when default
was commonplace. Canning's reluctance to intervene in the 1820s when
confronted with the defaults of the new Latin American governments was
reiterated by Palmerston in the 1840s, when some £50 million of governmental securities lay in default. The government offered friendly offices but
no intervention, diplomatic or more forceful, on behalf of bondholders. L.
H. Jenks's assessment of the policy rings true: "For it need not be supposed
for a moment that disregard of the bondholders arose from any fine sen-
sitiveness about using the resources of the nation to forward the interest of
a few subjects. It simply had not been conceived as a national interest to
help bondholders."[22] Indeed, Palmerston had so stated publicly, in 1847.
Nonintervention was a matter left to the government's discretion rather than
a matter of principle, as some later defaulters would learn.

Investors settled instead for a voluntary association organized in 1868,
the Corporation of Foreign Bondholders. Its principal sanction was the closing
of access to further borrowing. Although initially intended to be international,
and therefore more effective, its membership was in the end only British.

20. Jenks, *Migration of Capital*, p. 306, cites the success of the Turkish loan of 1858: "The
Stock Exchange . . . was hostile to the affair. . . . But the loan was taken up in the provinces
where the market for manufactures seemed more important." We have too little knowledge of
how this externality was internalized, especially in the latter part of this period.

21. For a brief discussion of the report of 1875, the forerunner of the U.S. Senate Finance
Committee investigation of 1932, see Jenks, *Migration of Capital*, pp. 292–93.

22. Ibid., p. 123.

Nonetheless, London's increasing, and changing, international role gave force to the corporation: the City outgrew its earlier competition with Paris as a center for government finance, becoming the unchallenged source of developmental capital.

The two markets were roughly equal in 1870, but by 1885 British foreign investment was more than double the French, and the lead continued to increase. The discontinuity created by the Franco-Prussian War and the French indemnity was one factor, but so, too, were accelerating international trade flows, which contributed to London's financial preeminence.

Trade acceptances flowed to London even for unrelated exchange, and the profits earned by merchant banking houses contributed to their evolution into underwriters of international issues. The role was a broad one. Individual firms established a client relationship with borrowing governments and firms, took responsibility for remittances and advanced short-term finance in anticipation of their later incorporation in long-term bonds. The international loan business was based not upon discrete open bidding but rather upon a continuous set of services. Britain required no major institutional innovation, like the French Credit Mobilier or the German Great Banks, to compete. Merchant banks fulfilled the function, and the London market attracted new participants from Europe and the United States. The more enduring of them understood that their long-run profits depended upon their reputation for bringing worthy securities to market.

Revenue finance

As London increasingly financed peripheral extension and trade expansion, Paris and Berlin focused instead on financing government expenditures in Eastern and Central Europe and the Middle East. As Table 2 records, half of their portfolios on the eve of war were composed of European securities. Of the rest, Turkey (and for France, Egypt also) made up a sizable part. Rondo Cameron gives more detail for the French holdings: 25 percent in Russia, 4 percent in the Balkans, 12 percent in the Near East, 8 percent in Central Europe, 12 percent in Italy, Spain, and Portugal. Feis's estimates of the German distribution still remain as good as any: Russia, 8 percent; the Balkans, 7 percent; Turkey, 8 percent; Central Europe, 13 percent; and Spain and Portugal, 7 percent.[23]

But the similarity of these static proportions is deceptive on two counts. First, Germany did not participate to the same degree as France in the boom of 1900–13, for domestic financing requirements dominated. Second, German enthusiasm for financing its immediate neighbors diminished in favor of investment in Latin America and of colonial undertakings in China and

23. Cameron, *France and Economic Development*, p. 486; Feis, *Europe the World's Banker*, p. 74.

54   *Albert Fishlow*

Africa. As holdings in Austria-Hungary, Rumania, and Russia stagnated or declined, Germany made its only new large European commitments in Turkey.

Revenue, as opposed to developmental, lending characterized these portfolios. Borrowing was more often to balance government accounts than to undertake infrastructure investment. Frequently it was occasioned by the need to fund a growing floating debt that had in the interim financed deficits on current account. While national debt grew as a liability, on the asset side there was nothing. In a moment of unusual jocularity, M. G. Mulhall recorded in the national balance sheet for Egypt a large equalizing sum for "ballet dancers, etc.," an item that exceeded the outlay for public works. More soberly, the financial report filed by Stephen Cave in 1876 pointed out "that for the present large amount of indebtedness there is absolutely nothing to show but the Suez Canal, the whole proceeds of the loans and floating debt having been absorbed in payment of interest and sinking funds."[24]

Unproductive borrowing was, however, very profitable lending. The commissions to be gained were large and guaranteed, and in addition a potential for speculative capital gains existed if the debentures increased in price. Issue prices were set much below par in order to market them, and values of 60 to 70 percent of par were not uncommon. Even at such rates of interest to purchasers and despite the pledge of specific sources of state revenues (among them customs, land-holdings, and other natural resources), willing takers could not always be found. Then short-term finance would require even higher rates for the issuing bankers while efforts were undertaken to persuade the public of the soundness of another issue.

Getting the money was for borrowers frequently a Pyrrhic victory. The considerable cost of funds, which had no corresponding domestic application in productive assets, required increases in domestic revenues that were not always forthcoming, requiring loans to meet the interest on the previous debt. Borrowers were very much in a debt trap. At some point, and usually after a sustained upsurge in foreign investment had petered out, default was a likely outcome. Explicit hypothecation of public revenues and resources set the stage for outright intervention, to reform the offending state and to guarantee the repayment of interest.

This lending to governments had its institutional counterpart in a regulated capital market. Private investment decisions, in the absence of favorable real economic prospects, could not be relied upon to produce the desired outcome. High returns could work only for a short while, and thereafter the greater the private gain, the higher the probability of government default. Even bankers who initially profited at the expense of weakened nations eventually required some way to dispose of their overextended holdings.

24. M. G. Mulhall, *Dictionary of Statistics* (London, 1899), p. 272; the Cave report is quoted in *Fenn on the Funds*, 14th ed. (London, 1889), p. 447.

Default could become for them a source of gain rather than of loss, but only when some implicit guarantee of intervention promised to bring order to the financial chaos of mismanaged states and lead to refunding of prior debt. Public assurances that supported the continued lending required to avert default could work equally well. Both circumstances qualify David Landes's judgment that the "great international bankers... have always understood that prosperous, independent states make the best clients."[25]

Not surprisingly, both the Paris and the Berlin capital markets provide abundant evidence of the public intervention required for large-scale revenue lending to flourish. Intervention was of two kinds, financial and real. In the first category, listing on the Paris and Berlin exchanges was an important decision in which foreign political considerations explicitly figured. The decision provided positive signals, and it also provided the inconvenience (but not the impossibility) of transacting elsewhere. But the informal and continuing contacts between the financial community and the French and German foreign offices were perhaps even more vital in signaling official enthusiasm and displeasure. They could determine whether Italian or Russian or Turkish loans should be taken up with enthusiasm or rejected. Whichever the course, the financial press could be counted upon to rationalize the decision on the grounds of economic fundamentals and to ease the task of distributing the securities. In turn, as we shall see below, the government could be counted upon for support in dealing with the dependent and impoverished borrowers sometimes favored for political reasons.

Still, the official attitude to overseas commitments was not always eager. In the German case, especially, the foreign capital market was occasionally seen as an unwelcome competitor, and the role of regulation was not to direct investment abroad but to restrict it. In the words of Finance Minister Adolf von Scholz in 1886, "the government will have to desist from supporting any effort on the part of domestic capital that might seek a higher interest rate abroad. . . . Also it seems necessary to me to reserve domestic capital as much as possible for domestic purposes and enterprises and to keep it serviceable for our own state credit against all eventualities." Such an attitude reflects itself in the relatively diminishing share of German national income devoted to the purchase of foreign assets after the 1880s.[26]

On the real side, the French and Germans consciously attempted to tie finance to a return flow of orders for domestic industry. What Britain could take for granted as an externality contributing to foreign investment, the others could not. In the decade before the war, in particular, French loans carried provision for tied trade at the insistence of French industrialists. They claimed that they needed special provisions to equalize their competitive

25. D. S. Landes, "Some Thoughts on the Nature of Economic Imperialism," *Journal of Economic History* 21 (1961), p. 505.
26. Quoted in Fritz Stern, *Gold and Iron* (New York: Knopf, 1977), p. 424.

position with German producers aided by mandated orders. Yet it was France, it seems, that employed the practice more consciously. By about 1910 German manufacturers could compete effectively on their own and required no special treatment. In France larger objectives dominated and loans seemed attractive on their own merits, but even there no such restriction could be imposed, as the history of the large Russian loans shows.[27]

The greater politicization of German and French lending largely aimed to obtain advantage in dealing with foreign governments, and it went hand in hand with securities markets that specialized in public debentures. A more modest current of colonial preference intruded. As Table 2 reveals, the capital flow to such possessions was quite small, for they could not absorb much. While conflict could and did arise over Africa and China, these areas were economically marginal. Profits and markets might be emblazoned on the banner of late-19th-century imperialism, but they were portrayed larger than life. More accurate were Bismarck's laments about the timidity of German capitalists.

Peripheral developmental lending did not automatically exclude loans to governments; much of the borrowing by Australia, Canada, Argentina, Brazil, Mexico, and other Latin American countries obviously took this form. Nor, on the other hand, did the proceeds of loans to eastern European states and Turkey and Egypt go entirely for current consumption. In particular, it is important to understand that French investment in Russia did not merely respond to political signals; there was a surge in industrialization dating from the 1890s. Finally, Britain also defended its security interests. It created favorable conditions for foreign investment in Turkey and Egypt, not to mention the active role that the British government took in securing concessions in Persia and China.

The two processes that describe 19th-century capital flows partially overlap. But they intermingle in a way that reinforces the importance of attention to the prospects for private profit even where lending satisfied larger political objectives.

Developmental and public revenue defaults

Capital markets did not operate smoothly before 1914. Lenders and borrowers conducted their activities against the backdrop of large cyclical swings in international economic performance. Rebellion and war superimposed political shocks on economic fluctuations. Part of the task of the capital market was to cope with periodic failures to meet contractual obligations.

The failures, like the motivations for lending, took two basic forms that required and received different treatment. On the one hand were develop-

---

27. For the discussion of tied loans in France and Germany see Feis, *Europe The World's Banker*, pp. 124–33 and 176–81.

mental defaults: the counterpart debt of rapid investment in physical assets created temporary service burdens that exceeded capacity to pay. On the other were public-sector insolvencies, the result of a slowing in continuing capital flows that had hitherto financed the shortfall between government expenditures and revenues.

Countries experiencing developmental default showed rising exports and government revenues, were attractive to foreign investment in private undertakings in addition to public securities, paid moderate rates of interest, and were integrated into the world economy. Public-sector insolvency plagued stagnating economies whose governments financed current outlays with loans that they were able to get by paying exorbitantly high interest rates even while they were benefiting from temporarily favorable conditions of capital supply. Private securities were not issued.

The two modes of default shared a sensitivity to variation in foreign investment and a governmental inability to pay, but there the similarity ends. Developmental default governments could not pay because their revenues, closely tied to imports, declined sharply as slowing exports and capital inflows reduced import capacity. Investment was sensitive to performance, and the descent was self-reinforcing. Inflationary finance bid up the exchange rate and the cost of the required foreign exchange while discouraging new capital flows; even noninflationary finance could not help, since limited foreign exchange necessarily elevated the real debt burden. Such countries had a transfer problem.

The appropriate remedy was time: time for exports to rise and to increase internal prosperity, imports, and governmental revenues. Investment bankers helped provide that time in funding loans that consolidated debt and allowed for brief periods of reduced, or no, interest payments and amortization. With recovery, new loans would again flow, for the capital market bore no long-lasting grudge. In the interim there would be periods of export surplus and slowed domestic expansion. Development default was part of the long-swing pattern of peripheral expansion.

Revenue default was part of the same pattern, but more incidentally: it was linked through the conditions of access to capital markets. As flows diminished, so did capability to meet service payments. Investment had started in the first place because, with little debt, there were relatively large revenues to cover obligations. But interest costs rose more rapidly than revenues, soon eroding that initial capability. Revenue default was a case of genuine insolvency, with the interest cost on resources actually received after discounts far exceeding revenue growth. Little, if any, real resource transfer occurred. Lending might be sustained, but it was for political rather than for long-range economic reasons. And default might even be welcomed as a way of enhancing political influence.

The solution for revenue defaults was frequently drastic. By the 1870s it involved direct intervention to overhaul both public finances and public

58   *Albert Fishlow*

administration. Debt was significantly written down, either through much reduced interest payments or through lowered capital values (or both). Balancing such generosity was the assignment and sometimes even the external collection of the revenues required to service the debt. Latin America in the 1820s escaped such a fate despite a spate of public-sector insolvencies, because British policy of the time emphasized nonintervention. (Britain's position would change with time and the strategic location of the defaulter.) Instead, Latin American borrowing was precluded for almost fifty years and only resumed after settlements, sometimes costly ones.

These two types of default and their solutions flowed naturally from the distinctive lending processes inherent in the operation of the pre-1914 capital market. Table 3 applies quantitative indicators to discriminate between the two groups and between countries that defaulted and that did not.

The two categories differ obviously in the composition of their foreign capital. Developmental borrowers, even where governmental participation was important (as in Australia, Argentina, and Brazil), attracted investment in complementary activities. Revenue borrowers, with the partial exception of Russia, did not. Such additional inflows tended to increase the ratios of foreign capital to exports for developmental borrowers. Yet their service payments are not correspondingly higher, because of the lower interest rates and smaller amortization charges that derive from longer-term debt. The large values for Brazil and Mexico in 1914 are misleading: they presume equivalent returns on nongovernmental securities as governmental obligations when private payments were likely to have been partial at best.

For the revenue borrowers, the ratio of public debt to revenues tends to be higher (the Argentine value is an anomaly associated with very low revenues in 1891 that provoked default). Correspondingly, the service requirements from public receipts are even greater because of the high interest costs on even the nominal values of the debt.

Development borrowers are further distinguished by their higher growth rates of exports and revenues and by their greater variance. The last is what gets them into trouble and provokes inability to pay. After a settlement is reached, they grow out of their problem and return to the good graces of the financial community. Revenue borrowers have indifferent export performance both before and after default; their economies are not significantly integrated into the world economy. Nor do revenues pick up significantly, despite interventions in Turkey, Egypt, and Greece. Creditors must simply settle for less because of the insolvency of the borrowers, and payments are reduced to conform with the debtors' capacity to pay.

The typical developmental default story of Table 3, then, is one of export growth rates that immediately prior to the default are variable and lower than previously. At the same time foreign investment slows. The balance-of-payments problem translates into a public finance problem and eventually governmental default. After a settlement provides temporary relief, export growth and public revenues recover, investment resumes, and creditors eventually accept even higher ratios of capital to exports.

The typical revenue default of Table 3 is provoked by slowing inflows of capital that no longer obscure the underlying insolvency of interest rates, and hence inertial debt growth, higher than either export or revenue growth. Even when revenue growth had been strong, it was the consequence of exceptional resources—guano—or new taxes, neither of which could be projected to continue. With no expectation of recovery, radical solutions are necessary to reduce debt service. Since debt had initially been sold at substantial discount, a ready expedient is available: nominal debt can be scaled down in exchange for direct assignment and collection of revenues adequate to yield some low but potentially increasing return.

Nondefaulters are included in each category: Australia and Canada among the developmental borrowers, Russia among the revenue borrowers. Putative default dates, corresponding to slowing foreign investment, are used to calculate comparable values. It is clear from the comparison that nondefaulters are in a stronger position. Their service requirements are markedly smaller, abetted by interest rates relatively lower than what other countries in the category are paying. The effective rate on foreign capital invested in Canada implicit in Table 3 is less than 3 percent and only slightly higher for Australia. For Russia, it is 4.5 percent. Moreover, export growth for Australia and Canada, and revenues for Russia, were strong, and they were therefore able to maintain more satisfactory access to the capital market than defaulting countries could.

Canada, because of continuing export growth, was spared the full effects of a cyclical downturn provoked by a shortage of foreign exchange; Australia was not. Australian real product declined between 1890 and 1895 at an annual rate of 2.7 percent. Australia met its obligations by compressing imports while it stayed on the gold standard. Argentina, with its inconvertible currency, partially sought to avoid the deflationary path by maintaining domestic demand and reducing debt-service charges. Brazil, when it finally defaulted in 1898, had to accept a deflationary recipe from its bankers and so had to check income growth in addition.

Brief comments on the Russian case are also in order, for it is held to epitomize the mixture of politics and finance characteristic of the prewar capital market. As Feis expresses it, "This movement of capital was influenced and guided not only by pecuniary calculation, by economic plans, but by the stir of political arrangements. No capital movement was more important in shaping the destinies of the continent."[28] Indeed, there is no denying the political content of decisions regarding the placement of Russian securities in Berlin or Paris, nor even the use of such capital inflows to support military expenditures. Two points should, however, not be obscured. One is that this

---

28. Ibid., pp. 211–12.

TABLE 3. Default indicators before 1914

	Default Date	Total Foreign Capital (mill $)	Public Debt (mill $)	Foreign Capital/ Exports	Service Payments/ Exports	Foreign Public Debt/ Revenues	Public Debt Service/ Revenues	Annual Export Growth Rate[a]		Annual Revenue Growth Rate[a]	
								Before Default	After Agreement	Before Default	After Agreement
Developmental Borrowers											
Australia	[1893]	1303	807	7.5	.28[b]	7.0	.28[b]	5.8%	5.9%*	0	2.8%*
Canada	[1893]	1043	187	9.2	.26[b]	5.1	.21	7.2%*	8.4%*	−1.9*	7.4*
Argentina	1891	808	443	8.1	.59	15.8	1.00	4.2	3.7	−15.3*	11.8*
	1898		395	197	3.1	.21	4.2	.38	−6.3*		
Brazil	1914	1985	740	8.7	.59	3.2	.30	−6.2	8.3	3.9	6.3*
Mexico	1914	2200	328	15.2	.88	5.6	.33	3.6*		−2.8	
Revenue Borrowers											
Russia	[1913]	3869	2746	5.1	.23	1.6	.07	1.7		2.0	
Turkey	1875	930	930	12.6	.77	9.7	.63	.1[c]	3.3	7.1*	−.2[d]
Egypt	1876	412	373	6.5	.62	7.3	.65	.7	−.8	6.4*	2.0
Peru	1876	176	159	7.4	.55	6.6[e]	.55	1.0	−2.7	1.4	4.0*
Greece	1893	117	117	6.6	.35	6.2	.33	−5.7	−1.9	9.0	2.0*[g]
										5.1[f]	

a. Annual average growth rate calculated by least squares trend of five years. An asterisk indicates statistical significance at 10% level.
b. Interest payments only.
c. Percentage change between 1870 and 1875.
d. Percentage change of net revenues of the Public Debt Administration from 1882/3–1886/7 to 1887/8–1892/3.
e. Average of revenues 1873–78; includes guano receipts.
f. Percentage change of tax revenue from 1887 to 1893.
g. Growth rate of revenues assigned for debt service is 1.6% (not statistically significant).

Sources. **Australia**: total foreign capital and foreign public debt is a cumulation from 1861–93 of estimates of total British investment and of government borrowing from N. G. Butlin, *Australian Domestic Product, Investment and Foreign Borrowing, 1861–1938/39* (Cambridge, 1962), p. 424; exports and revenues from B. R. Mitchell, *International Historical Statistics: The Americas and Australasia* (New York, 1983); and total and public-debt interest payments from Butlin, *Australian Domestic Product*, p. 414. **Canada**: total foreign capital, 1900 estimate from M. C. Urquhart, ed., *Historical Statistics of Canada* (Toronto, 1965), ser. F 195 (from Viner, *Canada's Balance of International Indebtedness, 1900 to 1913*) less accumulated current-account deficit from 1894 to 1900 estimated by Urquhart, "New Estimates of Gross National Product, Canada, 1870 to 1962," mimeo (NBER, 1984), Table 4; foreign public debt for 1893 from *Historical Statistics*, ser. G 60, adjusted for foreign holding by use of 1886 ratio reported in *Fenn's Compendium of the English and Foreign Funds*, 14th ed. (London, 1889), p. 185; exports and total interest payments from M. C. Urquhart, "New Estimates," Table 4; and revenues and public-debt service from *Historical Statistics*, ser. G 21 and G 37, adjusted as above. **Argentina**: total foreign capital and foreign public debt is estimates of Finance Minister Hansen for 1891 cited by H. Peters, *The Foreign Debt of the Argentine Republic* (Baltimore, 1934), p. 34; exports and revenue from *Extracto Estatístico, 1915*, pp. 3, 225; debt service, 1890, from A. G. Ford, *The Gold Standard, 1880–1914* (Oxford, 1960), p. 139 (following J. H. Williams, *Argentina's International Trade under Inconvertible Paper Money* [Cambridge, 1920]). Public debt service is estimated by applying .07 service charge on total debt service. **Brazil**: for 1897, total foreign capital is public debt as below plus an estimate of direct investments and private-sector loans up to 1895 from Marcelo de Paiva Abreu, "A divida pública externa do Brasil, 1824–1931," Discussion Text no. 83 (Economics Department, Catholic University of Rio de Janeiro); foreign public debt from Anibal Villela and Wilson Suzigan, *Política do governo e crescimento da economia brasileira, 1889–1945* (Rio de Janeiro, 1975), p. 437; exports and federal revenues from *Anuário estatístico do Brasil, 1939–40*, Appendix; debt service from Abreu, "A dívida." Implicit interest rate is applied to private debt to estimate total service. For 1914, total foreign capital and foreign public debt is from Abreu, "A dívida"; exports, federal, state, and municipal revenues, and debt service are as for 1897. **Mexico**: total debt from W. Woodruff, *Impact of Western Man*, p. 154 (as in Table 2); foreign public debt, 1913, from Edgar Turlington, *Mexico and Her Foreign Creditors* (New York, 1930), p. 318. This estimate, from the 1920s, includes internal debts held abroad as well as loans guaranteed. It excludes the Huerta loans of 1944. Direct foreign obligations come to only half this estimate (cf. Turlington, p. 345). Export, Federal revenues, and peso exchange rate from *Anuário estatístico, 1939*, pp. 557, 665 and 700; debt service figure from average interest rate of 5.8% on direct foreign obligations (from Turlington, p. 345) applied to foreign capital and public foreign debt estimates. **Russia**: total foreign capital from L. Pasvolsky and H. G. Moulton, *Russian Debts and Russian Reformation* (New York, 1924), pp. 173ff., without adjustment for postwar reduction; foreign public debt (including guarantees) from ibid.; exports and revenues from B. R. Mitchell, *European Historical Statistics* (New York, 1980); debt service from Pasvolsky and Moulton, pp. 177, 189. Paul R. Gregory, "The Russian Balance of Payments, the Gold Standard and Monetary Policy," *Journal of Economic History*, June 1979, has slightly larger estimates for total investment income and public debt service, but these would not alter the calculated ratios very much. Pasvolsky and Moulton are used for consistency with the total debt estimates. **Turkey**: total foreign capital from W. H. Wynne, *State Insolvency and Foreign Bondholders*, vol. 2 (New Haven, 1951), pp. 452, 453, capital outstanding of loans contracted between 1854 and 1875; foreign public debt as above; revenue and exports from *Fenn's Compendium*, pp. 620, 623, 624; B. Mitchell, *International Historical Statistics, Africa and Asia* (New York, 1982) for exports after 1878; R. Owen, *The Middle East and the World Economy* (London, 1981), p. 106, for revenue 1860–1880, and p. 193 for later period; debt service is an estimate of 13.6 £T in C. Issawi, *The Economic History of the Middle East, 1800–1914* (Chicago, 1966), p. 103, corroborated by estimate in *Fenn's Compendium*, p. 620. **Egypt**: total foreign capital and foreign public debt is foreign public debt from Wynne, *State Insolvency*, p. 584, plus value of Suez Canal shares; exports, revenue from B. Mitchell, *International Historical Statistics, Africa and Asia*; debt service is estimated from Wynne, *State Insolvency*, p. 584. Ratio to exports includes Daira obligations; ratio to public revenues excludes them, since they were to be met from the khedive's estates. **Peru**: total foreign capital and foreign public debt is from J. F. Rippy, *British Investments in Latin America, 1822–1947* (Minneapolis, 1959), p. 25. 1880 estimate corresponds to 1896 level. For exports, *Fenn's Compendium*, p. 542—exports to U.K. for 1875 were used, slightly greater than total reported in B. Mitchell, *International Historical Statistics, The Americas and Australasia*, and also shown in J. V. Levin, *The Export Economic* (Cambridge, 1960), from Peruvian sources. For predefault growth the latter series was used, and for postsettlement growth R. Thorp and G. Bertram, *Peru 1890–1977: Growth Policy in an Open Economy* (New York, 1978). Revenue from C. A. McQueen, *Peruvian Public Finance*, U.S. Dept. of Commerce Trade Promotion Series no. 30 (Washington, 1926), p. 36; debt service from McQueen, *Public Finance*, p. 87. **Greece**: total foreign capital and public foreign debt from Wynne, *State Insolvency*, p. 327; Exports and revenues: Mitchell, *European Historical Statistics*, and J. A. Levandis, *The Greek Foreign Debt and the Great Powers, 1821–1898* (New York, 1944), p. 73. Debt service: Wynne, *State Insolvency*, p. 303.

62   *Albert Fishlow*

lending, unlike those cases which ended in revenue default, was carried on at favorable market terms for both borrower and lenders. Returns were large enough, in comparison with French *rentes*, to provide a positive inducement to private investors without burdening the Russian fisc with an impossible carrying capacity. Even if the securities were not listed, German bankers could and did participate in response to differential interest rates. On the other side, Russia's external debt service on the eve of war did not absorb much more than 10 percent of revenues or 20 percent of exports.

The fact that capital flows were channeled from particular countries for overt political advantage does not necessarily imply that the flows lacked economic basis, and that is the second point to remember. Capital could be elicited from France not merely because of the warmth of Franco-Russian relations but also because of the obvious improvement in Russian economic fundamentals. Russian revenues, despite Feis's view "that the revenue-collecting power of the government remained small and handicapped," were expanding at a favorable rate, as Table 3 reveals.[29] Exports, too, were growing, in part because of rising prices but also because a large rail network was starting to facilitate foreign sales.

Without arguing that Russia was an investor's paradise, and the subsequent Soviet decision to default showed that the risk had been badly underestimated, one can usefully differentiate its attractiveness from the cases of revenue default. Here I limit myself to comment on the refunding arrangements for four defaulters: Argentina, Brazil, Turkey, and Peru. The arrangements shed additional light on the institutional characteristics of the pre-1914 capital market.

Argentina, Brazil, Turkey, and Peru

The story of the Baring Crisis of 1890, precipitated by the overexposure of a merchant banking house in Argentine securities, is well known. The chancellor of the exchequer and the Bank of England rapidly intervened, preventing a major financial collapse by guaranteeing Baring's liabilities and the orderly reorganization of the firm. The Bank's willingness to act as a lender of last resort did not forestall a diminished ardor for overseas investment that rapidly spread through the capital market. Not only did Argentine issues immediately move to substantial discounts, so did those of other peripheral countries. As S. F. Van Oss noted, however, prices of European securities moved inversely, partially smoothing realized foreign investment flows.[30] Note that Greece did not default until 1893, and then only because a new government rejected the funding loan already agreed.

29. Ibid., p. 211.
30. S. F. Van Oss, *Stock Exchange Values: A Decade of Finance, 1885 to 1895* (London, 1895), p. lxxvi: "The alternating *rage* for South American and European securities and its result upon their quotations has been one of the most interesting phenomena of the Stock markets during recent years."

payment of interest claims for a period of three years in new bonds to be issued for that purpose. Amortization, which had begun to bunch in the mid-1890s and again in 1911–13 and therefore was an important source of pressure, was to be suspended for thirteen years in each case. The formula, that is to say, was designed to alleviate a liquidity crisis. In 1898 the principal problem was a decline of 64 percent in coffee prices over the preceding five years, and especially in the last two. In 1914 it was a fall in prices of 38 percent in two years, reducing export proceeds that had already been adversely affected by the end of the rubber boom.[34]

The government's accounts were directly affected because of the close association of revenue with the value of trade. In addition, with an inconvertible currency in the former period the premium on foreign exchange rose with balance-of-payments problems, even overshooting an equilibrium value and making payments of interest and amortization more expensive. In the latter period the rising premium led to the progressive loss of gold from the conversion account and forced a return to inconvertibility.

The second funding loan is a purer example than the first of managing externally provoked developmental default. It followed a period of orthodox domestic policy in which the rate of inflation was minimal and the exchange rate, stable. Thus the default escaped contamination by the expansionary internal policies of the 1890s when the founding of the Republic unleashed a stimulative surge in the monetary supply that contributed to a first decade of significant import substitution in the industrial sector. The second default also came when the burden of indebtedness relative to export earnings was considered higher than in the 1890s. Brazil was a major recipient of capital in the final surge of foreign investment before the First World War. Moreover, the second default came more suddenly. In the 1890s the government had resorted to short-term loans from branches of foreign banks to permit it to meet its external obligations. The Funding Loan in 1898 took form only when that expedient had failed and pressure was building from the banks for a more far-reaching plan.

Finally, and as a result of these differences, the second loan was characterized by less conditionality than the first. In 1898 the problem had been defined much more in terms of the failure of domestic policy. Accordingly, not only was it necessary to pledge the entire customs receipts of the country and to accept a moratorium on new debt issues, internal or external, and even governmental guarantees, but the government was committed to withdrawing from circulation paper money equal in value to the £10 million loan. While it is hyperbolic to claim that the "foreign banks practically demanded the *control of the country's economy*," it is clear that the element of intervention was greater than in the case of Argentina.[35] Funding loans were not "all finance and no adjustment."

---

34. These trade data are taken from the *Anuário Estatístico, 1939–40*, Appendix, pp. 1359ff.
35. Aníbal Villela and Wilson Suzigan, *Política do governo e crescimento da economía brasileira: 1889–1945* (Rio de Janeiro, 1975), p. 318. (My translation, authors' emphases.)

64   *Albert Fishlow*

But the contrast on this score with revenue defaults remains considerable. There direct official intervention was the rule, not merely at the moment of default but sometimes much sooner, and political considerations frequently loomed. Turkey is the classic case. The first foreign loan contracted was issued in London in the Crimean year with the encouragement of the British government, then Turkey's ally. Implicit approval had a value: the first attempt to float the securities, without such a cachet, had been withdrawn, but the second was oversubscribed at a price of 80 and an interest rate of 4 percent. In the next year Britain, in conjunction with France, explicitly guaranteed another issue that went above par with an interest rate of 4 percent. One condition of the loan was that commissioners should oversee the expenditure of the proceeds. The intention was wider still, to encompass the "introduction of a wholesome foreign agency into the financial operations of the Porte."[36]

The subsequently rapid growth of the Turkish debt was due to a continuous deficit in the public accounts, first covered by floating debt offered by the Galata bankers, then funded by an external issue, and eventually enlarged to pay interest on itself. Loans faced a skeptical public and could be sold only at deep discounts. The last of the series, in 1874, carried a price of only 43.5, an interest rate of 5 percent, and a guarantee that "at last the finances of the really great and rich empire of Turkey are to be administered by first rate English men of business. . . ."[37]

In 1874 the Porte unilaterally reduced the cash payments for interest and amortization by half and substituted new 5 percent certificates for the rest. Two years later, after insurrection and open war, it could not meet even these reduced debt charges. The default was inevitable from the very beginning. Of a total nominal issue of £217 million the Turkish Treasury realized only £107; the effective rate of interest thus exceeded 11 percent, well beyond the revenue capacities of the Turkish empire even without the extraordinary expenditures that military requirements imposed.

Eventual settlement awaited the Congress of Berlin in 1878 and was not reached until 1881. It involved a drastic decline in outstanding debt to £106 million including capitalized arrears in interest. The minimum interest rate was to be 1 percent, with any excesses that might become available to be applied four-fifths to interest and one-fifth to amortization. Bondholders had to accept the outcome as the "best that the condition of Turkey permits. Though the amount of the revenues is comparatively small, the security for

36. This discussion of Turkey follows W. H. Wynne, *State Insolvency and Foreign Bondholders*, vol. 2 (New Haven: Yale University Press, 1951), pp. 393–528. The quotation is from the dispatch of the British ambassador at Constantinople as cited in Wynne, p. 396 n. 13.

37. Wynne, *State Insolvency*, p. 411, quotes the comments of the *Money Market Review* in reaction to the extension of the responsibilities of the Imperial Ottoman Bank. It is merely one of a series of mistaken declarations about both the potential of Turkey and the role of foreign administration that filled the prospectuses.

On the Argentine side the seriousness of the situation was already apparent prior to the crisis in November 1890. Railway net profits had peaked in 1888, and the gold premium on paper pesos rose to 94 percent through 1889 despite the record capital inflows of that year. Imports rose to new highs, responding not only to real investment but also to expansive domestic monetary incomes. Service requirements on the foreign debt amounted to 50 percent of export earnings. Throughout 1889 new loans were being contracted on the London market at a rate much reduced from that of 1888. And by mid-1890 it was necessary to suspend payment of interest. Indeed, in August mounting domestic pressures led to the resignation of the president and an attempt to substitute more restrictive fiscal and monetary policies. But the Baring Crisis intervened.[31]

When it broke, it brought a new urgency to the need for a solution to Argentina's economic problems. The stratagem of guaranteeing the liquidation of Baring Brothers required the restoration of the good credit of Argentina and the marketability of Baring's portfolio of Argentine securities. An international committee of bankers headed by Lord Rothschild had been formed to seek resumption of interest payments on the governmental securities. They considered three alternatives: insistence upon immediate domestic reforms, adjustment coupled with a small loan to keep current, and a more liberal funding loan. The committee, dominated by English bankers, opted for the last, rationalizing it on the argument that the default was developmental. The *Economist*, however, speculated that the bankers' concern was to shore up market prices for the sale of overhanging Argentine securities.[32] If that was the case, they did not succeed; securities prices continued to slide after the agreement of March 1891. Nor did the Argentine economy show signs of improvement.

The first funding loan failed for two reasons. One was that Argentina's domestic policy continued unsettled and political uncertainties intruded. Landowners had favored an inflationary environment, for their debts, fixed in nominal pesos, had diminished with rising domestic prices; they also stood to gain from direct earnings in foreign exchange. In the midst of a real decline in output, it was difficult to reverse the strategy, especially with an election to be held in April 1892.

The second reason was an inadequate transfer of resources. Although the £15 million loan was considered generous, its function was exclusively to cover in full the interest payments that were to come due over the next three years. It afforded relief at the expense of further indebtedness, but it was insufficient to restore private flows and to assist in recovery. The coupons could also be used to pay for customs duties collectible in gold, and to that

---

31. This discussion of the Argentine default draws on Ford, *The Gold Standard*, and H. S. Ferns, *Britain and Argentina in the Nineteenth Century* (Oxford: Oxford University Press, 1960), especially chap. 14.

32. *Economist*, 7 March 1891, pp. 301–2.

66   *Albert Fishlow*

extent they reduced the government's revenues. Despite the moratorium on public interest transfers, therefore, the arrangement was not as liberal as it seemed. Private railway firms continued to remit payments, although sometimes reduced. Imports had to be compressed to equilibrate the balance of payments, which helps to explain the adverse reaction in Argentina to the Rothschild agreement and the anti-English sentiments that it unleashed.

Underlying both reasons was the fact that the developmental cycle had not run its course. Intervention would have had to have been much more substantial to contribute to an earlier recovery. In fact, the data on railway receipts suggest a less severe and prolonged downturn than what other peripheral economies experienced in the 1890s, in part because real wages adjusted downward and in part because domestic production and exports increased profitability.

A new settlement was reached in July 1893, in anticipation of the need to resume interest payments the following year. The Arreglo Romero, at the insistence of the Argentines, substituted a set period of reduction in service obligations for the increased indebtedness and full payments of the earlier formula. For five years interest payments were to be reduced by an average of 30 percent and amortization suspended until the beginning of 1901. Under its auspices the defaulted provincial debt was consolidated and the railway guarantees phased out. Despite an initially cool reception in both London and Buenos Aires, the agreement held.

H. S. Ferns attributes the success of the Arreglo to "the way in which it directed the growing surpluses of the Argentine Government into the channels of investment. The supreme defect of the Rothschild Loan Agreement had been the opportunity it presented to the Government to spend revenues on current needs, for the simple reason that debt service was being taken care of by the Funding Loan."[33] That is to confuse the causality. Return flows to Britain did not create the basis for an improving Argentine economy, nor was fiscal discipline the cause. Rather, it was the great subsequent acceleration in export performance that underlay both, and one that Table 3, because of its five-year calculation, does not fully reflect. In 1899, after full interest payments were resumed, service payments made up a smaller proportion of exports than they had done during the partial suspension. The Arreglo Romero would quite likely not have worked in 1891.

In corroboration of that judgment is the fact that the Brazilian Funding Loans of 1898 and 1914 were of the same genus as the initial Rothschild Committee settlement. Since the merchant bankers of Brazil were the Rothschilds themselves, that is perhaps not surprising. Yet it also suggests a deeper understanding of peripheral foreign investment than the narrow motivation (easing the liquidation of Baring) sometimes attributed to the Argentine policy. As in 1891, so in 1898 and 1914: the Brazil agreements provided for a full

33. Ferns, *Britain and Argentina*, p. 473.

its payment rests on the solid and substantial basis of an actual administration, possessing an international and independent character...."[38] As it turned out, the average annual net revenue available to the bondholders remained virtually stationary for the following twenty years, yielding no more than the minimum stipulated. Only thereafter was there a modest rise.

Britain had lost financial interest well before this time. The Paris market took up the bulk of the new loans floated after 1881, with Germany becoming more active in the first decade of the 20th century. The two governments were not merely rivals; they also cooperated as capital flows rose to finance "railways and other enterprises, and in addition assisted the Porte to continue excessive and wasteful expenditures."[39] For the initial bondholders, the latter item, at least, was familiar, one for which some, but by no means all, had paid a price.

The Peruvian case differs from the Turkish, Egyptian, and Greek model of revenue default in that there was no significant official presence. Yet it shares most of the other features of the group: borrowing on public rather than private account; limited application of loans to real infrastructure assets; stagnation of revenues, other than the diminishing windfall of guano, as an antecedent to default; protracted negotiations as a prelude to settlement; and significant write-down of external obligations. And if intervention was not to be found, the Peruvian case, with its recurrent exclusive assignment of guano exports to foreign interests, certainly saw foreign influence at a level far above what is characteristic of peripheral investment. Even a defender of British trade and investment policy in Latin America in the 19th century, W. M. Mathew, is forced to concede about the monopoly of Gibbs & Sons that "They represented metropolitan finance, and held out to a weak, insecure and inadequately financed governmental system in Lima irresistible temptations to sink ever more deeply into a costly and debilitating indebtedness. They did not thrust money on the Peruvians, but of course they rarely denied them it either."[40]

The second Peruvian default—the earlier one dating to the war for independence was settled in 1849 after the discovery of guano had made reentry to the capital market possible—came well after the exit of Gibbs & Sons in 1861. Upon their departure another concessionaire, Dreyfus Brothers, was extended comparable rights, including the servicing of the debt from guano export proceeds. The debt rapidly expanded as a result of two large issues in the early 1870s, the second of which in 1872 found no public market but was taken up at a substantial discount by Dreyfus and other firms associated with them. As a result Peru found itself in 1873 with a nominal

38. Wynne, *State Insolvency*, p. 450, citing Robert Bourke, the British delegate nominated by the Council of Foreign Bondholders to the negotiations leading to the settlement.
39. Ibid., p. 478.
40. W. M. Mathew, in chap. 9 of D. C. M. Platt, ed., *Business Imperialism, 1840–1930* (Oxford: Oxford University Press, 1977), p. 370.

68   Albert Fishlow

debt of over £35 million and annual service charges of £2.6 million, representing a rate of 10 percent against actual resources obtained. After an abortive effort by Dreyfus to cancel service remittances in that year, another contract was signed extending coverage through 1875. At that point yet another concessionaire was sought, but no contract was ratified because the Peruvian government received an inadequate advance. Suspension began with the coupons due on 1 January 1876.[41]

The subsequent history is replete with new concessions, legal actions in the English, French, and Belgian courts, the war between Peru and Chile, loss of the province of Tarapaca and its guano deposits, and futile representations by European governments. Peru rejected diplomatic intervention on the grounds that the debts had been contracted with private parties and therefore had no international character. Britain refused to accept the terms of a proferred settlement between Chile and the bondholders, leading the latter, at least, to believe that they "cannot now possibly do better than leave the whole case . . . entirely in the hands of Her Majesty's Government."[42] In fact, the denial of stock exchange listing to a prospective Chilean issue in 1888 proved to be a more effective tactic.

Out of these complications emerged a settlement with both countries. Under the Grace contract of 1889 Peru exchanged its extant debt for the creation of the Peruvian Corporation. This private company was ceded the state railways for a period of 66 years, assigned the guano deposits up to a maximum of two million tons, guaranteed a subsidy from customs revenues, and endowed with a land grant of five million acres. In the 1890s Chile eventually settled the bondholders' claims deriving from the cession of Tarapaca. Yet so complex was the array of claims, and so intense French insistence that its national creditors received equal status, that final disposition awaited arbitration at The Hague in 1921.

As a financial assessment, it is perhaps true that "from the Peruvian standpoint the settlement . . . was a good bargain. The country was enabled to wipe out its foreign debt and in time to redeem its credit at small direct cost to the Treasury."[43] Nor did stockholders of the Peruvian Corporation reap a great advantage. Returns on the preferred shares were a mere 0.25 percent, beginning only in 1900, and they averaged less than 1.2 percent until the First World War; the common paid nothing. The debenture holders fared little better as the Corporation paid less than the stipulated 6 percent from 1896 through 1903.

---

41. Wynne, *State Insolvency*, pp. 190–95, traces the complex history of Peruvian foreign debt defaults and negotiations.

42. Ibid., p. 153 n. 64, cites the reaction of Sir Henry Tyler of the Peruvian Bondholders' Committee to the communication of the Foreign Office to Chile. Britain thus rejected an official role endorsing a proposed private settlement, while at the same time offering, and requesting, reopening of negotiations that did not seem favorable to the British bondholders.

43. Ibid., p. 179.

From a Peruvian perspective, however, it was another stage in the long history of foreign domination. The Corporation was quite unpopular and disproportionately powerful. It was the exclusive link with external capital markets and thereby exercised considerable influence beyond its immediate franchises. It was not unwilling to do so: "The directors and management of the Peruvian Corporation actively intervened in the market against Peru. In 1896 the Corporation successfully prevented a French consortium from lending to the Peruvian government."[44] If there were no overt international intervention and occupation, there certainly was a powerful foreign presence not fully identified with Peruvian developmental aspirations and committed exclusively to putting affairs in order.

Intervention on behalf of the bondholders did not occur in part because Peru was not relevant to European political concerns. In the 1890s it was reported in *Fenn's Compendium* that "a scheme is under consideration by which a new Peruvian State loan of £2,000,000 will be issued, secured by a mortgage on all the revenues of the republic not already pledged, these revenues being administered by an International Commission somewhat on the lines of the Egyptian model."[45] Peru was, however, too unimportant for such an arrangement to be consummated.

Summary

The large capital flow from 1870 to 1914 occurred within a larger economic and political system. Britain stood at the center of that system. Its prosperity was seen as linked to the performance of the international economy, which gave a prominent position for foreign securities on the London exchange in competition for a large share of British saving (large enough to recycle large and increasing return flows of income). Its prosperity also meant a free market to receive imports from the rest of the world. Capital importers had to expand exports, eventually the only means to pay interest and principal on their loans. Financial and real flows went together.

On their side, the recipients of capital were obliged to apply their proceeds effectively. If they bought British capital goods in the process, as so many did, so much the better—they thus closed the circuit and reinforced the interrelationship between trade and finance. Migration provided another direct link that enhanced the productive capacity of capital importers. Ultimately the market test would be a growth of primary exports large enough to satisfy debt-service charges.

The political and economic preeminence of Britain assured enforceability of the debt contracts. Peripheral countries had powerful incentives to remain inside a rapidly expanding world economy. Repudiation made it impossible

---

44. Rory Miller, chap. 10 of Platt, *Business Imperialism*, p. 384.
45. S. F. Van Oss, ed., *Fenn on the Funds*, 18th ed. (London, 1898), p. 427.

to tap the London capital market for funds, which is why initial defaults rarely persisted. Investment and imports were essential to growth. The confidence of British investors in the power of their denial of new capital made the cost to borrowers cheaper than it otherwise would have been. Overt intervention was largely unnecessary. It was reserved for the subset of cases where political motives dominated, providing less of a cause than a pretext. Intervention was refused too frequently on exclusively economic grounds to argue otherwise.

When developmental default occurred, and the long swings in finance and economic activity that defined the rhythm of the prewar cycle assured that it would, adjustment became necessary. The capital market was an exigent but not unyielding taskmaster. Assistance could be extended, but domestic accommodation was also necessary. If Argentina escaped some of the burden, though by no means all, it was in some measure because of the importance of the Baring Crisis for the British money market and economy. Australia, on the other hand, never defaulted, but it did experience a severe retrenchment in growth.

Revenue defaults were a matter more specific to the profligate habits of recipient governments and to political priorities than generic to the international economy. They declined as a problem in the 1890s compared to the 1870s as developmental lending increased in importance. Moreover, as France and Germany became the sources of finance, and these countries were less subject to cyclical swings in investment, public-sector insolvency was less likely to be triggered by reductions in capital inflows. When they happened, they evoked stronger responses. Economic recovery could not be depended upon to provide a cure, and even when direct intervention did not occur, as in the case of Peru, much greater foreign control was exercised.

France and Germany were on the margins of this late-19th-century capital market centered on Britain. Their capital investment, smaller and oriented toward European governments, inevitably had greater political content. Without the export domination that Britain enjoyed on the global level, until the 1890s at least, they had less incentive to cast their nets widely. As Germany grew, its foreign investment declined relative to domestic investment; Germany also reached out to Latin America and wherever the potential for trade penetration provided a linkage with finance.

Even as capital flows were rising to unprecedented peaks in the first decade of the 20th century, however, the liberal system in which they flourished was under attack. British preeminence was being challenged economically, and the balance of power on the continent was unraveling. The war and its disruptions accelerated the transition to a far different international economy, one in which capital flow was of a different kind.

3. Capital markets between the two world wars

Changing patterns of lending and borrowing

The postwar period saw the United States emerge not merely as a net creditor country but as the principal source of new international capital flows. This transition followed from the neutral status of the United States early in the war and its expanded exports to the European belligerents, paid for by the sale of American securities in New York. That reduction in liabilities was great enough that private American foreign investment in Canada and Latin America showed a net positive balance for the first time.

But there was another, and larger, official component to American creditor status after the war, one that was to weigh heavily on international economic adjustment in the 1920s. War-related expenditures produced interally debts of more than $16 billion at the time of the Armistice, to which subsequent American credits of $1.5 billion should be added. Of this total, the United States was a net creditor of about $9 billion and Great Britain of about $3.3 billion; all other European countries, including France, were debtors. The British credit position, moreover, included $2.5 billion in loans to Russia that were substantially written down.[46] For all practical purposes, therefore, war debts were exclusively American credits.

Their inevitable counterpart was the reparation claims against Germany. If the Allies were to pay, and the United States steadfastly insisted that they do, then allied debtors needed credits to match their liabilities. It was no accident that the British and French proposed soon after the war not only a collective treatment of the debt issue but also a direct linkage with the reparations claims under discussion. Lloyd George wrote to Woodrow Wilson in 1920 to press the advantage of an "equitable arrangement for the reduction or cancellation of inter-Allied indebtedness, but that such an arrangement must be one that applies all around." Wilson's reply reiterated U.S. opposition to such a linkage, making it clear "that it cannot consent to connect the reparation question with that of inter-governmental indebtedness."[47]

So the matter stood. Britain eventually acceded to American pressures in 1922, negotiating a funding of the war debt at interest rates more favorable than originally proposed; other countries followed, France not until 1926. From an American perspective, the allied debtors had been more than fairly treated. With long amortization periods (62 years) and interest rates of 3.5 percent (even less for an initial period, varying with the debtor), the settlement contained a grant element. But it did not avert a continuing need for the European countries to send significant interest and principal payments to the United States, making them eager not only for compensating income from Germany but also for export surpluses in order to accomplish the transfer.

---

46. Moulton and Pasvolsky, *War Debts*, pp. 426, 428.
47. Quoted in ibid., pp. 66, 69.

TABLE 4. *Foreign capital issues, 1920–31*

| | Annual Averages ($ million) | |
	New York	London
1920–23	531	416
1924–28	1142	587
1929–31	595	399

Source. U.N., *International Capital Movements during the Inter-War Period*, p. 25.

War debt and reparations were inevitably linked; so were the reparations question and a restoration of private lending. As long as European financial arrangements remained muddled, foreign investment by the United States was limited. Not until the acceptance of the Dawes Plan in 1924 fixed what were seen to be more reasonable German obligations and contributed to German internal stability after the preceding hyperinflation did overseas securities begin to attract attention in the United States.

That connection is brought out clearly in Table 4, which presents the annual flow of new issues in New York and London between 1920 and 1931. Beginning in 1924 the U.S. capital market is much the more active and clearly outstrips Britain for flotation of new issues. But New York was also more volatile and turned away from international finance after 1928. The British pattern is more even and always constrained by attention to a weakened balance of payments, to which the decision to return to the gold standard at the prewar par contributed. Indeed, capital flows to foreign governments were embargoed before 1922 and again in 1925, 1929, and 1931. When there was no embargo, uncompetitive British interest rates required to sustain the value of the pound drove potential borrowers to New York.

Table 5 describes the functional distribution of lending in the two markets. It makes clear the parochial quality of postwar British foreign investment. Almost half of all British lending took the form of Empire government securities. Even so, London could not even compete effectively for the Canadian business, which was substantially transacted in New York, and for that reason the total U.S. purchase of Empire governmental issues was not much inferior to the British total.

What also stands out in Table 5 is the magnitude of public borrowing relative to the security issues of private companies. Almost three-fourths of total American and British portfolio investment, and there were few other lenders, was allocated to government or public-agency bonds. National governments borrowed, state and city governments were eager supplicants, and so were public corporations. Of U.S. placements registered in Table 5, 52 percent were issues of national governments, 17 percent state or provincial, 12 percent municipal, and 19 percent in government-controlled or guaranteed enterprises.

Lessons from the past

TABLE 5. *New capital issues, 1920–31*

	New York ($ bill.)	London (£ mill.)
Governments	7.5	803
Empire	2.1	591
Foreign	5.4	211
Europe	3.0	103
Germany	.9	21
Latin America	2.0	51
Corporations	1.9	496
Railways	n.a.	96
Other	n.a.	400
Total	9.4	1299

Source. John T. Madden, Marcus Nadler, and Harry C. Sauvain, *America's Experience as a Creditor Nation* (Englewood Cliffs, N.J., 1937), pp. 76–77; J. M. Atkin, *British Overseas Investment, 1918–1931* (New York, 1977), pp. 130, 154, and 336.

Postwar lending was thus much more like the pre-1870 variety than the 1870–1914 kind. Peripheral railroad investment was no longer important, and it was replaced by large American capital flows to Europe and especially to Germany. For, in the wake of the stabilization of the mark and the apparent resolution of the reparations question, Germany became the largest debtor country in the world. But there were also others. In fact, Albania, Lithuania, Latvia, Spain, Portugal, and Russia were the only European countries not to borrow long term from the United States after the war.

Latin America also received its share, as Table 5 shows. Proximity to the United States was an advantage. In the early 1920s, before lending to Europe picked up, Latin American and Canadian issues made up about two-thirds of the business transacted in New York. "At first the principal borrowers were the national governments of the stronger countries such as Argentina, Brazil, Chile, and Cuba; but as the boom in security underwriting developed in the United States, numerous obscure provinces, departments, and municipalities found it possible to sell their bonds to American investors."[48] More than a quarter of Latin American lending was for the benefit of state and local governments, but direct foreign investment, shared largely by Canada and the larger Latin American countries, also increased.

The purposes for which governments borrowed during the 1920s were diverse. For many of the smaller European countries, security issues bolstered reserves, either directly in the form of gold or in dollar holdings that worked equally well under the gold exchange standard. Indeed, currency stabilization

48. J. T. Madden, M. Nadler, and H. C. Sauvain, *America's Experience as a Creditor Nation* (Englewood Cliffs, N.J.: Prentice-Hall, 1937), p. 74.

74   *Albert Fishlow*

and return to convertibility was a requirement for the reconstruction loans authorized under the auspices of the League of Nations. Paul Einzig attributed to the policy a large share of the blame for the eventual crisis, not least because it created a false sense of security to ultimate lenders and established the basis for the large capital flows to Europe.[49] Reconstruction loans did not necessarily find their way exclusively into reserves. They were also intended to cover governmental deficits and thus avert inflationary finance. The Dawes and Young loans to Germany, and the League Loans to Austria, Hungary, Greece, Bulgaria, Estonia, and Danzig, amounted to about $1 billion, less than 10 percent of the foreign capital issues registered in Table 4.[50]

Ordinary governmental placements were also intended to finance expenditures. Unfortunately, it is impossible to provide an accurate, or even an approximate, assessment of what kind of expenditure. From the perspective of the 1930s, one survey found much to be wasteful: "Later, when these [reconstruction] needs became less urgent, in many European countries and particularly in Germany, they borrowed to construct swimming baths, public libraries, and theatres which, although they raised the standard of life of the community, did not help very directly to increase the efficiency of the borrowing countries' export industries. Finally, they borrowed in order to rearm."[51] Nor was Latin America spared: "The purpose of Argentine borrowing in the post-war period, both internal and external, was only in small part to provide for productive improvements. . . . By far the greater part of the burden has been incurred as the result of inefficient management of state enterprises and an unbalanced national budget, neither of which have resulted in any social gain."[52]

Whether these claims are extravagant, and respected observers maintained they were, it is clear that postwar lending differed from the prewar type. Critics of reparations, among them John Maynard Keynes, warned: "If European bonds are issued in America on the analogy of the American bonds issued in Europe during the nineteenth century, the analogy will be a false one; because, taken in the aggregate, there is no natural increase, no *real* sinking fund, out of which they can be repaid. The interest will be furnished out of new loans, so long as these are obtainable, and the financial structure will mount always higher, until it is not worth while to maintain any longer that it has foundations."[53]

Even in the case of foreign capital flows to Latin America, Australia, and

49. Paul Einzig, *World Finance, 1914–1935* (London: Macmillan, 1935), pp. 140ff.
50. Royal Institute of International Affairs (RIIA), *The Problem of International Investment* (Oxford: Oxford University Press, 1937), p. 21.
51. Ibid., p. 20.
52. H. E. Peters, *The Foreign Debt of the Argentine Republic* (Baltimore: Johns Hopkins University Press, 1934), pp. 144, 146.
53. RIIA, *Problem of International Investment*, p. 12, reprints a section of his *A Revision of the Treaty*. (His emphases.)

Canada, moreover, the commitments of the 1920s differed from the developmental investment of a mere two decades earlier. Foreign capital flows were not part of a systematic and integrated system of population and trade exchanges. They were not responsive to favorable opportunities to bring new exports of primary products to the world market. Commodity overproduction and weak prices were already a problem by the mid-1920s; indeed, one of the objectives of Brazilian borrowing, by the state of São Paulo, was to finance a growing stockpile of unsold coffee. Demand was more critical than supply.

Postwar institutional structure

The new pattern of lending and borrowing in the postwar period could be sustained only within an altered institutional framework. Two significant changes occurred. One was more pervasive political influence, if not intervention. The other was a new foreign orientation of U.S. banks.

Postwar lending could not help but be more political. At the outset is the sheer size of the governmental interallied debts intruding into economic relationships. For the United States the official credit balance just about matched the private creditor position reported in Table 1, which set in motion bilateral negotiations that lasted until the late 1920s. France and its war debtors did not conclude final agreements until January 1930.

In the second place are the League reconstruction loans and the Dawes and Young loans, which were consciously directed to national stabilization. Even though private resources were used to finance such issues, public interest was keen. As Secretary of the Treasury Andrew Mellon testified before the House Ways and Means Committee in 1926, "The countries of Europe must be restored to their place in civilization.... America, with its excess of capital seeking profitable investment must aid by making private loans to Europe for productive purposes."[54]

Third, the sheer volume of governmental loans implies an analysis of sovereign risk and thus political considerations. These considerations did not have to be reflected in actual exclusion from the market to be effective; they could and did manifest themselves in price. Foreign government issues varied substantially in the interest rates they returned, and the public press and official stance could influence investor perceptions.

But outright intervention also presented itself with greater frequency in the interwar period. The United States enunciated in 1922 an official (but voluntary) policy: "The flotation of foreign bonds issued in the American market is assuming an increasing importance and on account of the bearing of such operations upon the proper conduct of affairs, it is hoped that American concerns that contemplate making foreign loans will inform the De-

---

54. Reprinted in Moulton and Pasvolsky, *War Debts*, pp. 379–80.

76   *Albert Fishlow*

partment of State in due time of the essential facts and subsequent developments of importance."[55] Britain, also in a break with past noninterventionist tradition, imposed embargoes on foreign loans at various times to prevent undesired capital outflows.

In addition, the volume of capital inflows inspired recipients to examine the entry of foreign investment more closely. As early as 1924 Germany sought to bring municipal and state borrowing under the authority of the Ministry of Finance. In 1925 control of public foreign loans was given to a formal board whose advice, while not binding, was usually followed. The Beratungsstelle rejected 46 percent of applications for municipal borrowing between its creation and September 1927 while approving almost all loans for industrial or agricultural purposes. Colombia, Australia, and Poland similarly centralized their publc borrowing. Italy in 1928 brought all foreign borrowing under the auspices of the Ministry of Finance.[56]

Yet one must not exaggerate the degree of regulation or coherent political motivation. The U.S. requirement of prior State Department approval for foreign government placements did not lead to much. Its operational importance was to embargo loans to allied war debtors that had not yet settled. Rumania, France, and Russia were the overt victims, but of course other countries were inhibited from public issues in the same way, and the need for approval is credited with the Belgian and Italian settlements. Two cases, the German Potash loan and the São Paulo Coffee Institute loan, provoked disapproval because of opposition to monopoly control of trade. Both loans were successfully floated in London.

The regulation later came under attack, during investigations of lax lending practices in the 1920s. Then it was argued that prior State Department approval might have led the public to believe there had been official endorsement. Although no mention could be made in the prospectus or otherwise, there was an implied authorization, as a State Department official recognized during the Johnson Committee hearings. Indeed, officials in Commerce and State did express their disquiet on occasion, but on economic rather than political grounds, and their arguments carried insufficient weight to disallow the issue. By 1932, in the face of public dissatisfaction and limited use, it was easier to abandon than to defend the policy.[57]

Nor did British intervention greatly influence the operations of the capital market. Not only was it temporary, it had no distorting consequence. The preference to Empire issues did not deter Canada from seeking out the New York market. European issues would have preferred cheaper and possibly less exigent American issuing houses. On the other side of the market, internal

55. Reprinted in J. T. Madden and M. Nadler, *Foreign Securities* (New York: Ronald, 1929), p. 223.
56. Ibid., chap. 10.
57. Madden, Nadler, and Sauvain, *America's Experience*, pp. 241ff.

controls in borrowers did not prevent large, and sometimes wasteful, increases in indebtedness.

Rather, the formal regulations of this period were a precursor of what was to come during the Depression. Politics mattered not because of these rules but because of the different character of the interwar economy and the unsettled relations of European nation states.

Later attention to and criticism of the ease with which foreign resources were extracted from the American public gave little weight to political considerations. The focus instead was upon the corrupting quality of private profit. In the aftermath of default in 1932 an extensive Senate inquiry, reminiscent of the British parliamentary investigation of 1875, turned up numerous examples of excessive enthusiasm by American banks new to foreign investment. "Overseas agents, finders fees, direct bribes to officials of borrowing governments, and deceptive prospectuses became standard operating procedure. . . ."[58] Hotels in Germany were reputed to be especially profitable because of their high occupancy rates by representatives of American banks. Max Winkler, who had foreseen disaster throughout the boom, was especially caustic after the fall: "American bankers were endeavoring merely to transfer and apply to the rest of the world the installment selling system which had been flourishing in the United States. American bankers and manufacturers made the masses buy, regardless of whether or not they needed what was sold them, and irrespective of whether or not they would be able to repay."[59]

The conclusions of the Senate Committee on Banking and Currency were equally scathing, if less ironic:

> The record of the activities of investment bankers in the flotation of foreign securities is one of the most scandalous chapters in the history of American investment banking. The sale of these foreign issues was characterized by practices and abuses which were violative of the most elementary principles of business ethics.[60]

That the United States experienced a speculative surge in foreign investment is clear, just as domestic construction, land, and equity markets went through dramatic rises and falls during the 1920s. Too much blame, however, has been lavished on the lax morality of the newcomer American issue houses in contrast with the more responsible attitudes of the venerable British merchant banks. If anything, the problem was excessive competition among American banks eager to enter a growing market. The actual average commissions were hardly exorbitant, on average 3.7 percent and thus comparable with British practice.[61] But the weaker the issue, the larger was the spread,

---

58. David Felix, "The Baring Crisis of the 1890s and the International Bond Defaults of the 1930s," mimeo. (Washington University, St. Louis, Mo., November 1984), citing the conclusions of the Senate Finance Committee inquiry.
59. Max Winkler, *Foreign Bonds* (Philadelphia: Swain, 1933), p. 90.
60. Reprinted in Madden, Nadler, and Sauvain, *America's Experience*, p. 205.
61. For the analysis of the commissions actually earned, as calculated from the Senate Finance hearings, see ibid., pp. 226ff.

78   *Albert Fishlow*

giving new firms an incentive to search out poor credit risks and to find gullible buyers. Even when competitive bidding eroded profits, the market consequences were far from optimal. Instead of a continuous relationship, dependent upon the reputation of the country and the issuing house, there was a discrete transaction. Foreign capital markets require more than competitive conditions for effective intermediation between borrowers and lenders.

In the last analysis, foreign bonds sold in the United States, and they were successfully mass marketed by the banks, because they offered a large premium over domestic returns. During the peak period of flotations, from 1924 to 1928, an interest-rate differential of between 1.7 and 1.9 points favored new foreign issues—a stable percentage advantage of between 35 and 41 percent and an average return of 6.4 percent. While generous relative to domestic bonds, even BAA-rated issues, such a yield could not compete effectively with the greater gains to be obtained from the equity market at the end of the 1920s. The realized return, including capital gains and allowing for lapses in interest payments, was a higher but still inadequate 7.2 percent.[62] The prospect of still higher gains in the stock market in the dizzying days of 1929 was the decisive element in the reduced outflows of 1929.

The lack of a strong institutional counterweight did not help. In stark contrast to the British case (both before and after the war), in which overseas investment was a sizable share of the capital market, in the United States foreign lending always remained marginal. No more than 18 percent of all security issues during the 1920s were foreign, with an annual average of 14 percent; if mortgages are also considered, the average participation falls to 10 percent. No important financial interest was involved, therefore, in guaranteeing an adequate and smooth flow. As a result, the share went from its near-maximum of 17.7 percent in 1927 to 6.7 percent in 1929. American banks were both too much *and too little* engaged in lending abroad.[63]

The United States at the center of the system

More generally, the fundamental problem with postwar lending was not the overeagerness of specific lenders responding to market signals but its systemic deficiency. Trade and capital flows were consistent in the short term but not in the long term. European borrowers, even Germany despite its reparations payments, had import surpluses sustained by capital inflows. (Reparations payments to Allies were partially channeled back to the United States, to pay some $2 billion in interest on the war debts.) Great Britain

62. For the yield on new foreign bonds based on prices at time of issue, see RIIA, *Problem of International Investment*, p. 170, drawing on a publication of the U.S. Department of Commerce. The analysis of the actual rate of return, including capital gains and allowances for nonpayment, is found in Madden, Nadler, and Sauvain, *America's Experience*, pp. 154ff.

63. These are the Federal Reserve Board estimates presented in Madden, Nadler, and Sauvain, *America's Experience*, p. 96.

ran progressively larger import surpluses as well, financed by income from past investments and earnings on service account. These sources of foreign exchange permitted a return to lending, although at rates much below income receipts. As a result, some old borrowers, even those that were recipients of new capital, had to find export surpluses to transfer their interest and dividends. The critical last piece of the puzzle was the United States. Its long-term capital outflows were a necessary adjunct to its export-surplus position and its receipts of short-term capital. They were what equilibrated the world economy in the 1920s.

The U.S. move to the center of the system after the war was of central importance. But its capacity to perform the needed functions suffered from serious limitations. The 1922 Fordney Act served notice that the war had not changed American attitudes about protection. The legislation, enacted in response to domestic concern with falling prices in the 1920–21 recession, raised tariffs back to the higher levels that had prevailed before the 1913 liberalization. It also reverted to the principle of equalized cost, authorizing discretionary increases when the United States was at a disadvantage. If anyone had wondered whether the United States might come to see its creditor role as central to foreign economic policy, the Fordney Act laid that possibility to rest.

British free trade had served to assure debtors a certain market for their produce and thereby encouraged the rising exports essential to debt service. The U.S. refusal to provide an equivalent guarantee meant that other markets would have to be found. As we have seen, large merchandise import surpluses, abetted by an overvalued pound, found their way to Britain. If U.S. prosperitiy in the 1920s was a source and a reflection of its new role as capital exporter, Britain's slow growth under the pressure of import competition was a component of the same interwar global economic system.

The other route to global equilibrium was to attach no importance to the generation of export surpluses by debtors. Then all that was needed was continuing American capital exports to provide the foreign exchange required to service outstanding debts. The success of such a policy was manifest in the reestablishment of the gold standard and the stabilization of Germany. As Harold Moulton commented, not many years thereafter, "The loans stimulated American export trade and contributed greatly to the prosperity of the ensuing years. They also enabled European countries to return to the gold standard; to maintain stable exchanges for a period of years; and to restore, in substantial measure, industry, agriculture, and trade.... So great was the success of this policy that the fundamentals of the problem were soon obscured and nearly all sense of reality was lost."[64]

The difficulty was that the policy required an ever larger debt to accomplish short-term consistency, thereby leading to lending and borrowing that might

---

64. Moulton and Pasvolsky, *War Debts*, p. 380.

80   *Albert Fishlow*

prove excessive in the long run. Trade and debt were part of an integral whole; the latter could not perpetually substitute for the former. In addition, interwar real interest rates were substantially greater than those which had prevailed before the war. During the 1920s, on average, yields on foreign bonds at their time of issue (and thus what countries had to service) came to 6.59 percent. In conjunction with price stability such costs required expectations of both high returns on domestic applications and high rates of growth in exports.

Contemporaries were aware of the danger, but some, even in 1928, thought it was exaggerated. As George Auld said,

> The dollar exchange created by the new loans takes care of the old loans and finances new American exports. . . . This expansion, the English tell us, is dangerous to the United States. But I have yet to hear any sensible reason advanced why it is dangerous or why it cannot go on indefinitely to levels scarcely yet dreamed of. . . .
>
> It seems to me, that on the evidence, we may safely conclude that those who have feared that the debts . . . cannot be paid because the debtor countries will not have an export surplus, have been unnecessarily concerned. For so long as the debtor countries have no export surplus, they will be in the market for new foreign loans, and the debts will be paid by new loans.[65]

The inability of the United States to continue supplying capital betrayed this impeccable logic, even before the crisis struck. In the late 1920s investors turned their profit seeking to the stock market, and foreign issues were crowded out. That change created problems, not only for the new European borrowers but for peripheral countries as well.

No help came from the Federal Reserve System. Domestic considerations primarily governed policy, as seemed approriate for a country whose exports amounted only to 10 percent of product and whose saving was overwhelmingly applied internally. But there was a policy dilemma. Higher interest rates to discourage speculation served to attract short-term capital from abroad; lower interest rates, as in 1927, did not stimulate so much real investment as a stock market boom. Central bank coordination was still primitive and subordinated to continuing political differences. France and Britain disputed spheres of financial influence within Europe; the United States tended to side with the former and resisted the efforts of the latter to curb foreign lending. Instead, "Strong and J. P. Morgan & Company partner Dwight Morrow denied that it was possible or even desirable for any agency— domestic or international—to regulate loans on an economic basis."[66] France

65. George C. Auld, former accountant general of the Reparations Commission, and cited as a "leading economist" by Madden, Nadler, and Sauvain, *America's Experience*, p. 169.
66. Frank C. Costigliola, "Anglo-American Financial Rivalry in the 1920s," *Journal of Economic History* 37 (1977), p. 929.

TABLE 6. *Default and export earnings*

Percentage Decline of Export Earnings 1928/9 to 1932/3	Default Status, 31 Dec. 1935	
	Fully Serviced[a]	More than 50% U.S. Bonds in Default
40–50%	1	1
50–60	3	4
60–70	3	9
70+	0	6
	7[b]	19

a. Includes Argentina, current on sterling and delinquent on interest for about 25% of dollar bonds.
b. Original data exclude Ireland and Haiti.
Source. Adapted from David Felix, "The Baring Crisis," as computed from S. G. Triantis, *Cyclical Changes in Trade Balances of Countries Exporting Primary Products, 1927–33* (Toronto: University of Toronto Press, 1967), Table 7, and Madden, Nadler, and Sauvain, *America's Experience*, Appendix Table 2.

and Germany remained bitterly divided over reparations and could not be counted on for cooperation.

Sporadic efforts across the 1920s to liberalize trade through international agreement under the auspices of the League of Nations were equally ineffectual. The United States was not interested in bringing down the increased barriers since they seemed no hindrance to its prosperity. Continental Europe retained its high tariff tradition. Britain was tempted by Imperial Preference as a way of compensating for its poor economic performance. Freer trade, moreover, could have worked only to the degree that it simultaneously expanded the volume of exports and directed more of those exports to the United States.

With the United States at the center, therefore, the postwar international economy had a greater potential instability. Nor was it susceptible exclusively to the European repayment problem; the considerable investment in Latin America and elsewhere in the periphery was also fundamentally precarious. From the mid-1920s onward, prices of agricultural prices declined despite an increase of 75 percent in stocks (financed indirectly by capital flows). Because agricultural and mineral exports remained the main sources of income for peripheral debtors, and almost three-fifths of world trade, the real debt burden was becoming a matter of concern.

It is unnecessary to detail the eventual slide into crisis, beginning with the decline on the New York Stock Exchange and ending with the destruction of the multilateral trading and financial system. But it is useful to glance at the wreckage of defaults to confirm what went wrong.

82   *Albert Fishlow*

Defaults in the 1930s

The first country to default on its dollar obligations was Bolivia, on 1 January 1931. Within a short time it was joined by its Latin American neighbors. By the end of 1933 Argentina was the only South American country maintaining full service on its external debts, and even it could not remain fully current. Peripheral borrowers defaulted because of the collapse of commodity prices. Table 6 establishes the association more broadly. Of nineteen primary exporting countries that had more than half of their bonds in default as of the end of 1935, fifteen had experienced declines in export earnings of more than 60 percent between 1928–29 and 1932–33. Only two of the six countries fully or virtually fully servicing their debts were in a similar position. The relationship is direct. While it was not impossible to meet one's obligations, the cost in domestic adjustment could be severe, and few were inclined to accept it. However efficiently debt had been applied, the transfer problem was insuperable because of lack of world demand.

Among the nondefaulters, as in the 1890s, were Canada and Australia, but in this case their roles were reversed. Canada bore the brunt of the Great Depression, experiencing a real income decline of 30 percent between 1929 and 1933 and barely regaining the earlier level by the end of the decade. Australia grew at an annual rate of 3 percent between 1932–33 and 1938–39 after an initial drop of 8 percent in income. Australia's better performance derives from early abandonment of the gold standard and expansionary domestic policies as well as recovery of trade due to preferences within the sterling bloc.

Closer ties to British than to U.S. markets were an advantage since recovery in Britain proceeded more successfully. But preferences did not help Canada, despite some trade diversion. Canada's policy of splitting the difference between sterling and the dollar when Britain left the gold standard meant that its currency appreciated against competitor raw material producers. Nor does this explanation in terms of trade blocs, emphasized by David Felix, do justice to the importance of Argentina's suspension of convertibility at the end of 1929 and its willingness to expand internal demand. Argentina's acceptance of the Roca-Runciman Treaty in 1933, which provided limited guarantees for Argentine exports in return for substantial return concessions that included maintaining debt service payments, was not the essential factor. Argentine export quantum in 1935–39 had not regained its 1925–29 level.[67]

The decisive determinant of better performance by peripheral countries was their abandonment of integration into the international economy in favor of domestic stimulus. Default went hand in hand with a proliferating variety of quantitative controls over imports, exchange controls and multiple ex-

67. See Felix, "The Baring Crisis," pp. 46ff. For Argentina in the 1930s see Carlos Díaz-Alejandro, *Essays on the Economic History of the Argentine Republic* (New Haven: Yale University Press, 1970), chap. 2.

change rates, and increasing reliance on barter arrangements to sell exports. It also helped to concentrate export earnings upon imports regarded as necessary for the programs of import-substituting industrialization that flourished. Thus a trade solution to the crisis emerged, but it was one that destroyed rather than rescued the international capital market.

Default was made easier by its very commonness. The failure of the entire system went far beyond the capacity of individual bankers to ameliorate, and none tried. The Great Depression was not a Baring Crisis. It required an international lender of last resort when the obvious candidate, the United States, lacked even a national source of support. Capital markets were essentially closed to long-term movements and only functioned to sustain short-term flight to the United States, providing little incentive for conformity with the rules. In the absence of the lure of future capital flows (and the threat of their blockage) the power of the U.S. Bondholders Protective Council was nil.

Nor was official punishment meted out. Peripheral default was secondary in the foreign economic policies of the Roosevelt administration. Resumption of payment was not central to the New Deal strategy of economic recovery, nor was it crucial to restoring the solvency of the banks, because they were intermediaries rather than ultimate investors in the securities. Default was also inconsequential to the continuing surpluses in the U.S. balance of payments. Indeed, making reciprocal trade agreements and assuring markets for U.S. exports were the principal objectives in dealing with the Latin American countries. The potentially divisive subject of debt, to the disappointment of the bondholders, was not even discussed.

Germany's default, like the European lending, was in another category. The U.S. failure to provide continuing long-term capital is part of the story but far from the entirety. German exposure was aggravated by an accumulation of short-term liabilities that in 1930 managed to exceed even its long-term obligations. Its debt export ratio equaled about two in 1930 and was substantially offset by German holdings abroad. These figures would have yielded net service payments for debt of about 6 to 7 percent of export earnings, clearly manageable. Reparations payments were an additional 15 percent and made the situation more difficult. But the prime source of ultimate vulnerability was $2.5 billion in short-term indebtedness. In 1930 alone there were withdrawals of credits amounting to about 10 percent of the outstanding balance.[68]

It was a situation in which political circumstances played a critical role. The gains of the National Socialist party in the parliamentary elections of September 1930 contributed to uncertainty, accentuating the flight of capital as well as claims on short-term liabilities. In March 1931 came the announcement of the German-Austrian customs union, precipitating an inter-

68. Moulton and Pasvolsky, *War Debts*, pp. 285, 306.

national political crisis. It also helped to precipitate an economic crisis by speeding the collapse of the principal Austrian commercial bank, the Creditanstalt, a large holder of short-term liabilities that were under increased pressure.

The effects were soon felt in the diminishing gold and foreign-exchange reserves of the Reichsbank. The German manifesto of 5 June, warning that "the limits of the privations . . . on our people have been reached," only inspired new withdrawals, setting the stage for Hoover's 20 June call for a one-year moratorium on all intergovernmental debts.[69] A credit of $100 million was arranged to which the central banks of the United States, Britain, and France and the Bank for International Settlements contributed. When the credit did not help, a standstill agreement on withdrawals of foreign credits was reached. As a result, Germany was able to avoid a severe deterioration in its balance of payments despite declining exports.

British depreciation of sterling in September was the next shock. Within months the deutsche mark had appreciated by 40 percent, leading to rapid deterioration in German export earnings. The Bruning government sought accommodation through domestic deflation, with the apparent intent of enforcing an end to reparations not by default but by making clear the cost of compliance. The specter of inflation caused the alternative, devaluation, to be rejected. The government held firm, and reparations eventually did come to an end at Lausanne, in July 1932.

But the end came too late and at too high a price. The National Socialists came to power in January 1933. One of the early decisions of the new government was to call a conference of representatives of foreign bondholders to consider restructuring of the debt. Foreign exchange had already been refused in 1932 for repayment of principal, although transfers of interest had been permitted. A decree in June 1933 centralized access to foreign exchange for private, state, and municipal debtors. Initially a combination of cash and scrip was offered, but by the middle of 1934 cash payments ceased. Coupons due on the Dawes and Young loans were initially payable in registered marks, but they too eventually saw full default.

The unilateral German transfer moratorium provoked one contemporary to condemn the action as an "abuse of confidence, amounting to nothing less than vulgar dishonesty. . . . Germany will not be able to raise money again in Great Britain, France or the United States during our lifetime."[70] The penalty, if not the outrage, was entirely beside the point. Germany was not a typical debtor country nor was the Depression a typical setting for default. The failure was that of the system.

69. Quoted in ibid., p. 311.
70. Sir Arthur Samuel, quoted in Winkler, *Foreign Bonds*, p. 252.

4. Capital markets in recent years

The 1970s and 1980s

Another surge of private foreign lending on long term had to wait for more than a generation. When it came, developing countries, and especially the middle- and higher-income ones, were the principal recipients. The subject has drawn much attention in recent years, and so there is no need to provide a full account here. The essential features will suffice.[71]

Although developing country borrowing in the Eurodollar market had begun before the oil crisis, the sudden injection of petrodollars altered the pace and purpose of debt. Oil importers, faced with a fourfold increase in their costs, relied on external loans to sustain their purchasing. Countries did not have to borrow; they could have cut back on imports of oil or restricted other imports. But such options implied passing along the oil tax in the form not only of reduced real income but also of diminished output and employment. The other alternative, acceleration of export growth, implied reduced consumption, but such a strategy was at least not contractionary. None of these possibilities appealed to Latin American countries, basking in the legitimacy of improved economic performance and still with a tradition favoring import substitution rather than export promotion.

Not surprisingly, therefore, the Latin Americans were in the forefront of countries that borrowed to finance more gradual adjustment. Those that were eligible were the more successful developers, countries that would become known as the newly industrializing countries or NICs. Many had even borrowed previously from the Eurodollar market. Now they turned from debt-led growth to growth-led debt. These countries fared better than their poorer neighbors who were forced to adjust immediately, and more painfully, despite larger official lending mobilized in their behalf.

For some of the borrowers, again especially in Latin America, the new credits became habit-forming. Even after industrial countries began to recover in 1975, balance-of-payments deficits persisted. They did so because banks were prepared, and indeed eager, to lend to finance them and the attendant public-sector shortfalls. As a result of bank preference for official guarantees, private capital markets imparted a systematic bias in favor of government and state enterprise expansion.

Countries were eager to borrow because it was cheap to do so. Nominal interest rates deflated by the prices of the exports that paid them were highly negative. In addition, the speed and minimal requirements of the commercial banks were a welcome contrast to the rigidities of official loans and their implicit interventionism. Banks were happy to lend because it was profitable to do so. They made their Euromarket earnings from the up-front com-

---

71. I have followed the discussion in my "Revisiting the Great Crisis of 1982," to appear in a symposium published by the Notre Dame Press in 1985.

missions on syndicated loans and the spreads over the cost of money, the London Interbank Offered Rate (LIBOR). Both were higher for developing countries. In addition, the money center banks, which were the innovators of syndication, gained from their domestic operations in the largest borrowers. Citicorp's Brazilian subsidiary, for example, generated 20 percent of all corporate earnings in 1982.

The strategy of growth-led debt on which some countries embarked was nonetheless a risky one, subject to special vulnerabilities. Nations were financing medium- and long-term capital formation from credits whose maturity varied between six and ten years and whose cost was variable. One innovation in the 1970s that helped the outpouring of bank lending was to place all the risk of changing interest rates on the borrower. Inherent in any debt strategy is an ignorance of real cost since future export prices are uncertain. But the unpredictable cost of funds from one six-month period to another created a whole new vulnerability.

Yet up to the second oil price shock in 1979 the gamble was worth taking. Countries that borrowed did, on the whole, increase their investment and rates of growth. Debt translated more than proportionally into productive physical assets. Public-sector deficits were for capital expenditures rather than for the expansion of current services. Foreign capital thus was earning a real rate of return, and one obviously greater than its minimal cost. At the same time there was no transfer problem in servicing it. Despite worries about protectionism, developing country export growth was sustaining itself at favorable prices. Despite continuing import-substitution programs, the external market received attention. As a consequence, the ratio of debt to exports for nonoil developing countries was more favorable in 1979 than in 1970–72.

International capital markets had successfully intermediated between the surplus position of the oil producers and the deficit position of the developing countries. Without official intervention, and despite predictions of gloom and doom, private commercial banks had averted a potential oversavings, non–full employment global equilibrium. Without debt, incomes would have had to fall to erase the record imbalance of international payments ushered in by the rise in oil prices. With debt, there could be an early recovery to which the exports to the borrowing, middle-income developing countries contributed.

So favorable a state of affairs did not survive the changed international environment ushered in by the 1979 oil shock. Oil prices more than doubled. The economies of industrialized countries again contracted, but this time more seriously than in 1974. As a consequence, developing countries faced a more adverse impact on export demand and terms of trade. And, in addition, they confronted sharply rising interest rates that were a by-product of the anti-inflationary restraint of the industrialized countries. Where before the capital market facilitated deficit finance, it now not only made borrowing more expensive but also penalized the stock of past debt contracted on a floating basis.

Among the influences involved, the second oil shock is paramount in timing and magnitude. Second is the recession-induced reduction in export earnings, the result of a combination of slower volume growth and weaker prices. Higher interest rates are third in importance. But they were highly significant for the largest borrowers, which had contracted increasing quantities of bank debt.

The more precarious position of oil-importing debtor countries in 1980 and thereafter ushered in higher spreads and shorter maturities on bank loans that were simultaneously more difficult to obtain. Recession in the past had been accompanied by more abundant and cheaper credit to finance balance-of-payments deficits. Now expensive money was added to expensive oil just when export earnings faltered.

Yet the sharp initial rise in the current-account deficit of developing countries between 1978 and 1980 must also be explained. Even if one allows for the rise in oil prices and the recession shock, there was an increase of about 75 percent. Inadequate domestic policy and excessive readiness of the banks to lend are responsible.

For one thing, Chile and Argentina greatly increased their borrowing as an integral component of their new conversion to international monetarism and reliance upon the balance of payments to regulate domestic inflation. These two countries alone accounted for 12 percent of the increment in developing country borrowing in the four years 1978–81. For another, oil exporters, especially Mexico, relied on external finance to sustain disproportionately high rates of import growth. They borrowed not to accommodate adverse external circumstances but on the basis of their new riches, and they were therefore especially sought-after clients of banks awash in new Eurodeposits in search of application.

Increased indebtedness of these countries did not translate fully into real resource transfers, let alone productive application. Indirect estimates based on debt and balance-of-payments statistics suggest that between 1978 and 1981 Argentina experienced a capital outflow of 60 percent of the debt contracted; Mexico, 40 percent; and Venezuela, more than 100 percent. Public obligations were converted into private assets overseas. For Chile, this pattern does not seem to have been a problem. But critics of its liberal policies could point to the deficiencies of an investment boom in construction that failed to support expansion of the industrial sector.

In addition, some oil-importing countries, habituated by this time to debt-financed adjustment, prominently Brazil, underestimated what would prove a more persistent recession and a less elastic and higher-cost capital market. Prudence would have required greater attention to the danger posed by the already large outstanding debt.

The industrial country recession transmitted itself to most of the developing countries by 1981. Instead of buffering the oil price shock, as previously, developing country debt now transmitted it. Growth-led debt required for its success growing exports and growing debt at low interest rates. It made little difference that it had seemed to be working before 1979. What counted was that the strategy chosen was no longer viable and also not easily reversible.

Once in debt, countries found it more difficult to maneuver. Growth-led debt, especially for Latin American borrowers, had been converted by high interest rates into debt-led debt. And as the supply of debt could not be sustained, debtor (and global) equilibrium was achieved at lower levels of real income compatible with finding the means to service outstanding liabilities. What was for the world a sharp recession was for the Latin American debtors a great depression. Even then that dramatic meeting on 13 August 1982 could not be averted.

Policy makers improvised an imaginative solution to the Mexican crisis. It has become generalized and is the basis of the optimism reigning in many circles that the debt problem has been resolved without default and ensuing financial chaos, and without resort to the more radical solutions that were being put forth. There are three components to the present strategy.

One is a larger official role, especially for the International Monetary Fund. The Fund has imposed a new conditionality on commercial bank lenders, requiring them to make continuing loans to sustain the liquidity of borrowers. This involuntary lending counteracts the profit-maximizing instinct of each bank in isolation to reduce its commitments and substitutes instead a systemic perspective. In addition, the IMF has made contributions from its own resources, replenished in 1983 under the impulse of the crisis. Finally, the Fund has devised and monitored adjustment programs for countries, assuring that the debtors are acting in good faith and that good money will not be thrown after bad.

In the second place, the commercial banks have played a more active part. They have renegotiated the terms of their loans, initially each year but in the fall of 1984, for the first time, on a multiyear basis. In so doing, the new bank groups have also made concessions on spreads and commission rates that were conspicuously absent earlier when they were exacting higher risk premiums, and profits, on rescheduled lending. Such private activities have been coordinated with and thus far have been dependent on the official stabilization programs countries have agreed to fulfill.

The third component of the strategy has been industrial country recovery and renewed growth of international trade. The importance of the recession shock in the downturn has its counterpart in the beneficent impact of cyclical recovery upon the exports of the debtor countries. Tentatively in 1983 but more firmly in 1984, export growth of the major problem-debtors has underwritten large trade surpluses that have permitted the continuing service of debt obligations.

A new global equilibrium of sorts has emerged. The United States has

Lessons from the past

become the buyer of last resort, absorbing imports and capital at a record rate. Foreign capital inflows from Europe and Japan finance the internal public-sector deficit in the United States, permitting fiscal stimulus and high growth rates. These are accompanied by high interest rates, low inflation, and a strong dollar consistent with the continuous attraction of external finance. Debtor countries, laboring under the handicap of large debt-service requirements without new lending—the growth rate of new commercial bank credits, including involuntary credits, has plummeted from 25 percent to about 5 percent—sell their exports primarily to the United States.

The strategy devised for dealing with the debt problem has thus far worked. What we have learned is that within such a global framework large debtors, for example Brazil and Mexico, have managed to turn around their balances of trade in unprecedented fashion. At the same time domestic targets such as growth, employment, price stability, and income distribution have proved not only to be more recalcitrant but to have been sacrificed for the improvement of the balance of payments.

There has been no financial panic and collapse. Banks, even if buffeted by a skeptical stock market, have remained solvent. Debtors, even if weary of austerity, have continued to accept by far the largest burden of an adjustment accompanied by skimpy external finance. Industrialized countries, especially the United States, even if coping with mounting protectionist pressures, have not closed their markets.

Some believe it cannot last. Past experience can be instructive.

Lessons for the future from the past

The story of the last decade is a unique episode, but there are historical parallels. In common with the pre-1914 experience, lending was for the most part directed to the peripheral developing countries. Unlike in the 19th century the periphery is now defined not by abundance of land but by potential industrial capacity. The modern NICs, also capital-scarce, offer the possibility of high returns on foreign investment, as indicated by their growth records over the past three decades and sometimes longer. And like that earlier period, the NICs' growing ability to export manufactured products as part of a changing international division of labor augurs positively for the long term.

Yet as in the interwar period the surge of sudden borrowing in the 1970s was an unnatural event, one whose magnitude was occasioned by disequilibrium in the global balance of payments rather than by accelerated developing country growth. And the apparent excess supply of commodity production and the weak prices for raw materials that have afflicted many of the smaller debtors bear a strong resemblance to the 1920s.

It is in dealing with the failures of the market that the present arrangements are most distinctive. In contrast to the 19th century there is an official, multilateral presence. Then it was less needed. The rhythms of an expanding global economy, with free-trade Britain at its center, in conjunction with attentive investment banks, smoothed over the problems of developmental borrowers afflicted by growing pains.

These experienced merchant banks vetted potential borrowers and distributed their securities to a larger investing public. First-class houses stood by their domestic clients and their foreign borrowers both, hoping for continuing business on the basis of their reputations. They dealt in long-term securities that were publicly marketed. Valuation on the exchange provided a market test. But the banks were quite aware that their decisions were of influence. The salvage of the Argentine situation in the 1890s may not have led to an immediate recovery in bond prices, but it stabilized the fall even while easing the Argentine plight. The more favorable results from the Brazilian rescue stemmed primarily from the reversal in coffee prices rather than the harsher domestic policies imposed.

But the banks, through their influence in the Corporation of Foreign Bondholders, were also alert to the fact that not all problems were mere liquidity crises. Capital market booms also opened the gates to creditors of another stripe, borrowers whose longer-term prospects were far inferior. Insolvency was not beyond their capacity to recognize and resolve. Then the remedy was large and immediate write-offs and ceilings on interest payments in accordance with the capacity to pay. The other side of the coin was overt intervention. It was no accident that such treatment went hand in hand with governmental political objectives.

In the 1920s the emergence of the United States as the principal source of international lending diluted this institutional framework. Long-term securities were still the currency of portfolio investment, and they were listed on the stock exchange and traded. But the competitive structure of a multiplicity of issue houses failed to provide checks on quality as satisfactory as might have been hoped, nor did it encourage a close relationship with foreign borrowers. There was no hope of a continued flow of finance even before the crash, let alone after.

But the nature of the debt problem at that time also called for more than an easing of the difficulties of a few borrowers. Official intervention was required and eventually came in the Hoover moratorium. By that time peripheral default had begun, and resolution of the reparations and war debt issues that had plagued international economic relationships in the 1920s could not reverse the downward slide of trade and finance. The United States was unprepared to play the role of international lender of last resort and Britain could not.

That experience helped to dispose the financial community to firm and innovative response in 1982 and thereafter. The reaction rests upon a diagnosis of the debt problem as exclusively a temporary lack of liquidity. Modest finance is regarded as adequate, assuming continuing industrial country growth and an eventual, spontaneous restoration of former conditions of capital supply. I have dealt with this question at length elsewhere.[72] Here I wish only to point out the variance of present practice from historical precedent.

If we have a developmental debt problem comparable to those of the pre-1914 period, two important ingredients of the historical solution are missing. One is a willingness to finance a large proportion of continuing debt-service obligations in the short term and even temporarily to reduce their magnitude. This was the treatment meted out to Argentina and Brazil in return for their willingness to avert default. The other is the prospect of renewed capital flow to permit resumption of investment and economic growth. Short-term assistance was provided in the context of a continuing capital market relationship, and investment banks expected to remain engaged.

What we now see, on the contrary, is an insistence on payment in full and little willingness to consider such expedients as capitalization of interest to compensate for variation in Eurodollar interest rates. Finance is being provided, but at a level that has forced most of the adjustment upon developing country production and income. Nor is there a promise of capital inflow. Instead, banks ask for more foreign direct investment, repatriation of capital flight, and evidence of domestic austerity.

The present institutional structure has much to do with the difference. Unlike in the past commercial banks are not merely intermediaries but also the final holders of loans. Investment banks were immune from financial loss from a declining value of foreign securities. That market verdict affected the wealth of others; the banks' task was to make the best of it, which depended upon some sharing of the burden between debtor and creditor in order to facilitate recovery. The dispersion of bondholders concentrated decision authority in the hands of the merchant banks. One of the objectives of present policy is to preserve bank solvency and to prevent systemic distress. The means of doing so is forcing more of the real burden upon the debtor countries. When Baring Brothers was caught with Argentine securities in 1890, moreover, the bank was bailed out (at some expense to the partners) rather than letting it fail; Argentina was not held responsible.

While it is true that holding the debt predisposes the banks to accept involuntary lending, and hence partial finance, the sums provided fall far short of the return flow of interest payments received. And banks are eager to retrench as soon as possible. Development lending has proved a less interesting business than it first seemed, making it impossible to hold out realistic prospects of resumed capital flow even to diligent debtors. Long-term renegotiation is an incentive that does not recur. The debt problem is being treated not by prospects of renewed development but rather by penalties for failing to meet IMF stabilization targets.

72. See my "The Debt Crisis: A Longer Perspective," *Journal of Development Planning*, April 1985.

Investment banks were also prepared to recognize their more serious mistakes of revenue default. Capacity to pay, not adherence to principles of property rights, determined their assessments. While we retain the same case-by-case approach, we seem less able to differentiate among borrowers. There are some countries whose prospects for transferring their debt service are, at best, limited. Instead of the slate being wiped clear, they are the ones laboring under the most severe terms. In the case of Chile the government has even been required to guarantee a private debt that was patently a private risk. Favorable treatment is offered to the countries that have made most progress in improving their external accounts. Sometimes the lack of improvement is the fault not of the country but of commodity prices.

Insolvency was a verdict rendered easier, historically, because it was accompanied by a large say in managing revenues and even governments. Countries did not choose such a path willingly. We lack an analogue. The IMF is unable to force a readjustment of private debts and seems reluctant to try. The deficiency is serious in dealing with the debt problems of many smaller countries whose circumstances are less favorable than those of the NICs. In some respects these countries are the equivalent of the historical revenue defaulters.

Intervention was not the only recourse of lenders to such defaults. It occurred where there was a direct political interest. There was also refusal to lend. There was a long interval between loans to Latin American countries in the 1820s and their resumed borrowing in the 1860s and even later. It was the 1970s before bankers and the public forgot the debacle of the 1920s. Access to the capital market is a powerful policy instrument. But it requires a continuing capital market—precisely what is absent now.

Despite the similarities of the balance-of-payments borrowing of the 1970s and that of the 1920s, we have so far managed better, in part because of greater understanding of economic interdependence and advance in coordination. But the different political climate is also fundamental. Developing countries have accepted the sacrifices of adjustment and large transfer of resources abroad, just as they did periodically in the 19th century. They have not resorted to default as many did in the 1930s, when they were ignored in the midst of the continuing deterioration in Europe. Nor have developing countries demonstrated the defiance of a Germany, increasingly committed to break with the system.

In the last analysis, the issue is not whether countries can service their debt but whether they choose to do so. By exacting sometimes severe domestic sacrifices, many developing countries can continue to pay provided that world trade growth does not collapse as it did in the 1930s. The relevant question is whether we want them to try. There are economic costs of reduced growth as domestic savings and potential imports are paid abroad as interest. There are also political consequences. By setting too hard a task, we may wind up with a new surge of nationalism and a very different set of international economic relationships. The current debt overhang, no less than reparations and the interallied debt, is not merely a technical and financial matter. It has already become politicized and is likely to become more so. We are more the heirs of the interwar problem than the simple developmental defaults of the 19th century.

International debt: the behavior of banks in a politicized environment Philip A. Wellons

"All politics is local politics."

Thomas P. "Tip" O'Neill

The debt crisis riveted attention on political issues at the international level. Groups of states clash, and the North-South divisions are very noticeable. As conflict and cooperation among governments, banks, and multilateral agencies make headlines, three blocs appear to contend: the banks, the debtor governments, and the creditor governments. These are the obvious players in the workouts, and it is important to understand the conventions that bind them.

Attention on the crisis period, however, misses one very important element. The debt drama reached a climax in late 1982, as first Mexico and then other developing countries failed to service their debt. Governments and multilateral agencies then stepped in, but this official activity after August 1982 should not beguile one into thinking that the major governments were absent from the game earlier. At no time did international banking occupy a market free of such exogenous factors as governments.

In this article I examine an extremely important but neglected form of political activity: relations between the big banks, which account for most lending across borders, and their home governments in the United States, the United Kingdom, Japan, France, and West Germany (the Group of Five or G-5).[1] The crisis period has largely been discussed from the perspective

---

An earlier version was presented at the Lehrman Institute, New York City, in the spring of 1984 as part of its seminar series on Politics and International Debt, which was supported in part by a grant from the Ford Foundation. For their help, I thank Joseph Badaracco, Joseph Bower, Dennis Encarnation, Richard Vietor, Louis Wells, Jr., David Yoffie, members of the Lehrman Institute's colloquium, and three reviewers.

1. Cross-border lending by banks occurs when the bank is located in one country and the borrower resides in another. International credit markets are highly concentrated. According to one study, "about 25 large banks based in OECD countries" make up the inner circle, accounting for some 60 percent of lead managements and over 50 percent of all bank lending. See Paul Mentre, *The Fund, Commercial Banks, and Member Countries*, IMF Occasional Paper 26 (Washington, D.C., April 1984), pp. 5–6.

of governments, but my focus here is on the big banks. How does the political process affect the big banks in their cross-border lending?

My broader argument is simply put. The crucial actors in the system of international debt have been the individual governments of the Group of Five. In Robert Gilpin's terms, national economic and political objectives take precedence over global economic efficiency. Gilpin provides a useful statement of contrary views, one of them being the notion that

> increasing economic interdependence and technological advances in communications and transportation are making the nation state an anachronism. In the interest of world efficiency and domestic economic welfare, the nation-state's control over economic affairs will continuously give way to the multinational corporation, the Eurodollar market, and international institutions better suited to the economic needs of mankind.[2]

This view, while recognizing a political dimension to the international system, emphasizes the primacy of economic forces, particularly in the literature about international banking.[3]

Indeed, much of the extensive literature prompted by the debt crisis is implicitly built around the concept of global economic efficiency. One central question for analysts, therefore, is why the banks loaned as much as they did to developing countries, and the treatment of this specific issue captures the more general approach. For most observers, the 1973 oil shock was key, but as a starting point rather than as a full explanation.[4] Analysts usually emphasize one of five different economic variables to explain the banks' lending: macroeconomic forces, market disequilibria, structural changes in the international economy, the dynamics of intermediation, and structural disequilibria.

For those who focus on macroeconomic forces, the banks loaned to developing countries because of the response by the industrial countries to the first oil shock. Expansionary policies by the OECD governments permitted

2. Robert Gilpin, *U.S. Power and the Multinational Corporation* (New York: Basic, 1976), p. 232.

3. On the political dimension see Robert O. Keohane and Joseph S. Nye, *Power and Interdependence* (Boston: Little, Brown, 1977).

4. See Benjamin J. Cohen, *Banks and the Balance of Payments* (Montclair, N.J.: Allanheld, Osmun, 1981), p. 22; Richard S. Dale and Richard P. Mattione, *Managing Global Debt* (Washington, D.C.: Brookings, 1983); William R. Cline, *International Debt* (Cambridge: MIT Press, 1984); Darrell Delamaide, *Debt Shock* (Garden City, N.Y.: Doubleday, 1984), p. 27; Irving S. Friedman, *The World Debt Dilemma: Managing Country Risk* (Philadelphia: Robert Morris Associates, 1983), p. 53; and the "Church Committee Report"—Staff Report, "International Debt, the Banks, and U.S. Foreign Policy," Subcommittee on Foreign Economic Policy, Committee on Foreign Relations, U.S. Senate, 95th Cong. 1st sess. (Washington, D.C., 1977), p. 31. Since "deficits in developing countries require loans," whether deficits or loans come first "can be a chicken and egg question," according to David Gisselquist, *The Political Economy of International Bank Lending* (New York: Praeger, 1981), p. 155.

world inflation and led to the "breakdown in the world adjustment process."[5] The results included low real interest rates and high commodity prices. Banks, assuming this environment would continue indefinitely, loaned to developing countries.[6] Bankers tend to see this decision as an honest mistake, but others see it as "administrative miscalculation and outright bungling and ... the misjudgment of Western lending institutions...."[7] Both views capture a permissive environment but fail to explain why the banks acted as they did.

A related explanation focuses on disequilibria in the banks' major markets, looking particularly at demand, performance, and returns. In major developing countries, compared with industrial markets, the banks found higher returns and a history of strong growth based on exports of manufactured goods.[8] Opportunities for higher profitability extended beyond lending to encompass many related services: deposits, correspondent banking, local branch operations, and corporate finance.[9] In a conducive environment such conditions gave the banks strong incentives to lend. These multiple ties to developing countries did not exist for many banks as recently as 1970, however, and as a result this interpretation misses certain changes in the structure of world finance.

A third view holds that structural changes in the international economy, under way for over a decade by 1973, prompted the banks to act. One set of writers finds important changes in the environment. "Multinationalization" prompted some banks to follow multinational corporations abroad and then prompted others to follow the first wave of banks.[10] These new entrants

---

5. On inflation see Alexander Fleming, "Private Captial Flows to Developing Countries and Their Determination: Historical Perspectives, Recent Experience, and Future Prospects," *World Bank Staff Working Paper* no. 484 (Washington, D.C., August 1981), p. 13. The quotation is from William A. Noellert, "The International Debt of Developing Countries and Global Economic Adjustment," in Lawrence G. Franko and Marilyn J. Seiber, eds., *Developing Country Debt* (New York: Pergamon, 1979), p. 270.
6. Robert Z. Aliber, "International Banking: A Survey," *Journal of Money, Credit, and Banking* 16 (November 1984, pt 2), p. 661. See also Carlos F. Diaz-Alejandro, "Latin American Debt: I Don't Think We Are in Kansas Anymore," *Brookings Papers on Economic Activity* 2 (1984), p. 337.
7. Dan Dimancescu, *Deferred Future* (Cambridge, Mass.: Ballinger, 1983), pp. 58–59.
8. On returns see George E. Phelan, "Discussion," in *Key Issues in International Banking* (Boston: Federal Reserve Bank of Boston, 1977), p. 42. A survey by the Group of 30 later confirmed that bankers found stronger growth and better returns in developing countries: Group of 30, "How Bankers See the World Financial Market" (New York, 1982), p. 8. On growth see Jeff Frieden, "Third World Indebted Industrialization: International Finance and State Capitalism in Mexico, Brazil, Algeria, and South Korea," *International Organization* 35 (Summer 1981), pp. 407, 409. On exports, Noellert, "International Debt," p. 273.
9. Richard O'Brien, "Private Bank Lending to Developing Countries," *World Bank Staff Working Paper* no. 482 (Washington, D.C., August 1981), p. 15.
10. R. M. Pecchioli, *The Internationalization of Banking: The Policy Issues* (Paris: OECD, 1983), p. 52; see Herbert Grubel, "A Theory of Multinational Banking," *Banca Nazionale del Lavoro Quarterly Review*, December 1977, p. 349. Norman S. Fieleke, "The Growth of U.S. Banking Abroad," in *Key Issues in International Banking* (Boston: Federal Reserve Bank of Boston, 1977), pp. 9, 30, found, for example, that U.S. foreign direct investment was associated with the level of U.S. branch assets in various countries.

pushed the search for new customers, which led banks to developing countries that were newly industrializing as part of a long-term transformation of the world economy.[11] World financial markets opened as many countries relaxed such regulations as exchange controls and barriers to access by foreign banks.[12] The greater role of the International Monetary Fund (IMF) reduced the risk associated with lending to developing countries.[13] These four changes are all outside banking itself. A second set of writers focuses on changes in lending procedures that permitted banks to make the kind of loans that fit developing countries' needs. New techniques included syndication and cross-default clauses; new technologies included the computer and improved telecommunications.[14] New conventions permitted banks to go directly to the prospective customer rather than through correspondent banks, creating "a less tidy market."[15]

The story of the preceding discussion is that changes in the international economy prompted banks "to bravely go where few banks had gone before." Another interpretation, also built on the idea of global economic efficiency, is that the dynamics of international lending — seen in banks' strategies, long since at work — explain the response of the banks. Writers assert that the global money markets were "in place" by the time of the oil shock.[16] They then trace different causal lines. One approach assumes competitive strategies: lead banks made their money from fees and so had to find and arrange ever more loans; as lending grew, banks continued to lend even more in order to retain market share.[17] Another approach notes the cooperative strategies of the players, especially compared to prewar antagonisms: by working together, banks and borrowers reduce the risk of default.[18] A third approach, that the banks were simply diversifying their assets, is difficult to demonstrate, either by showing that the banks' rate of return was higher abroad than at home or by showing that the variance of returns declined as banks loaned to more countries.[19] The best-known explanation is Charles Kindleberger's. He argues that euphoric lending as in the mid-1970s is inherent in international banking. The many players match one another's lending, overestimating the upswing in the economic cycle. In the absence of an international lender of last resort, a crash follows the euphoria. The boom-bust pattern has extended over centuries of international banking, in his view, the episode in the mid-

11. Michael Moffitt, *The World's Money* (New York: Simon & Schuster, 1983), p. 93; Frieden, "Third World Indebted Industrialization," pp. 407, 430.

12. Pecchioli, *Internationalization*, p. 53.

13. Charles Lipson, "The International Organization of Third World Debt," *International Organization* 35 (Autumn 1981).

14. Dale and Mattione, *Managing Global Debt*.

15. M. S. Mendelsohn, *Money on the Move* (New York: McGraw-Hill, 1980), p. 88.

16. Moffitt, *World's Money*, p. 94.

17. Mendelsohn, *Money on the Move*, p. 83; Aliber, "International Banking," p. 678.

18. Jeffery Sachs, "LDC Debt in the 1980s: Risk and Reform," in Paul Wachtel, ed., *Crisis in the Economic and Financial Structure* (Lexington, Mass.: Lexington, 1982), p. 200.

19. Pecchioli, *Internationalization*; Fieleke, "Growth of U.S. Banking Abroad."

1970s being merely one of many.[20] This interpretation comes close to a structural argument.

Finally, advocates of global efficiency explain the lending of international banks by looking for the competitive advantage that some banks have over others. At least two approaches—one based on theories of industrial organization and the other on theories of international trade[21]—find that that advantage comes from structural imbalances. In the first, banks from countries in which margins are narrow are presumed to be more efficient than others and hence have opportunities to grow abroad at the expense of the less efficient. In the second, countries whose banks have greater scale, technology, or access to information, or a lower cost of capital, have an advantage in foreign competition.[22] Unfortunately, these approaches are too general to explain why banks loaned so much to developing countries in the 1970s.

These five approaches hold in common the view that global market forces, independent of the politics of nations except to the extent that states create market imperfections, explain the behavior of banks. Even Robert Aliber, after admitting that "there are few uniquely international" banks, proceeds to concentrate on market phenomena.[23]

A different approach focuses on economic and political objectives at the national level. To quote Gilpin, "the mercantilist model . . . views the nation-state and the interplay of national interests (as distinct from corporate interests) as the primary determinants of the future world economy."[24] It follows that "the management and the analysis of interdependence must start at home."[25] However, little in the literature about banks' international lending examines this perspective. One common view does hold that banks go abroad in response to low demand at home, but it is outside a mercantilist interpretation, which presupposes an active state.[26]

It is in the work of two writers who draw upon the notion of competition among nations that the literature about international banking comes closest to the mercantilist paradigm. To explain the banks' lending, David Gisselquist notes that the "major nations compete for current account surpluses."[27] He

20. Charles P. Kindleberger, *Manias, Panics, and Crises* (New York: Basic, 1978).
21. Aliber, "International Banking," and Yoon S. Park and Jack Zwick, *International Banking in Theory and Practice* (Reading, Mass.: Addison-Wesley, 1985).
22. See Ian H. Giddy, "The Theory and Industrial Organization of International Banking," in Robert G. Hawkins et al., eds., *The Internationalization of Financial Markets and National Economic Policy*, Research in International Business and Finance vol. 3 (Greenwich, Conn.: JAI, 1983), p. 195, cited in Park and Zwick, *International Banking*, p. 25. See Grubel, "A Theory," on multinational wholesale banking.
23. Aliber, "International Banking," p. 661.
24. Gilpin, *U.S. Power*, p. 232.
25. Peter J. Katzenstein, ed., *Between Power and Plenty* (Madison: University of Wisconsin Press, 1978), p. 22.
26. On low demand see the *Annual Reports* of the Bank for International Settlements in the early 1970s; Richard Russell, "Three Windows on LDC Debt," in Franko and Seiber, *Developing Country Debt*.
27. Gisselquist, *Political Economy of Lending*, p. 156.

does not, however, explicitly connect government action to win these surpluses and the lending of banks. In a study of foreign policy and international banking Andrew Spindler finds that Japanese banks act abroad to "support . . . broader Japanese strategic objectives."[28] Other writers recognize the role of apparently disparate home government policies but fail to connect them. Many have noted that banks establish foreign offices because of legal restrictions in home markets, for example, tax laws and foreign-exchange controls among them.[29] In 1977, by contrast, a study by the Church Committee of the U.S. Senate suggested an incentive to lend if banks expected that their home government would bail them out should their developing country borrowers defaulted.[30]

These two approaches—global efficiency and mercantilism—actually describe very different relations between governments and international banks. In the model of global economic efficiency the big banks are transnational agents, independent of any nation including their own home. In this article I use the phrase "transnational bank" as a shorthand reference to banks as understood in the global economic efficiency model. I agree, however, with Aliber that the world has few if any transnational banks. We can best understand the expansion of international debt and the ensuing debt crisis, I argue, in terms of the interests and policies of the major home countries and the process by which those policies are shaped.

I first examine the pervasive impact that their home has on the international lending of banks. The source of these effects is important. The evidence does not confirm the argument that powerful transnational banks force weak home governments to create a favorable banking climate. Instead, that climate reflects complicated bargaining among many players at the national level. Not surprisingly, the five nations differ, and these differences among the G-5 countries affect the international system. They help to explain economic behavior by the banks—entry, exit, allocation, pricing, rescheduling—that in turn affects the stability of the system. How they affect that stability is the subject of part 3.

The general implications of this view are clear. If the home really plays such an important role in international debt, we should expect structural and policy changes at home to affect the flow of international debt. Perhaps the most important way to increase the flow of private credit across borders is through change in the home countries of the intermediaries.

Several refinements to this interpretation should be noted. First, players other than the G-5 governments and the major banks have a role. Big debtors have leverage and borrowing countries can manage their economies to attract

28. J. Andrew Spindler, *The Politics of International Credit* (Washington, D.C.: Brookings, 1984), p. 175.
29. Pecchioli, *Internationalization*, pp. 53 and 56.
30. Church Committee Report, pp. 67–68.

Debt and the banks 101

or repel credit. Home government policy must, however, be conducive to the flow of new credit. Second, politics and economics are linked in banking. Banking is so highly regulated within national markets that a pure market model does not adequately explain lending behavior, even though banks in the G-5 countries maximize profits. Third, politics at home is more than a matter of Walter Wriston talking to George Schultz. The bureaucratic politics of contending ministries, the interest-group politics of banks and other blocs, the so-called high politics of secretaries of state and defense—all frame home government policy.[31]

1. Home is an integral part of big banks' international strategy

If banks were truly transnational, they would be affected no more by their home government than by the governments of other countries. The true transnational is, after all, independent of nation states and so independent of any particular state, including the home. A close look reveals, however, that the home's impact is much more pervasive and important than the impact of other governments.

The home government policies that directly and indirectly affect the international lending of their banks raise important political issues for the banks. The major issues are control (who decides how to allocate credit) and cost (who pays for divergence from the market). Home governments affect the banks' relations with competitors (other banks or financial institutions), other governments, and other borrowers.

Banks, as profit maximizers, manage the components of profitability, expressed simply as [(unit revenue less unit costs) times (volume)]. Bankers thus relate their net income after tax to their asset volume and report it as return on assets. But to restate the equation as [(revenue times volume) less (costs times volume)] reveals the special importance of the home country to international banking. For, more than any other country, the home affects both the type and the volume of revenues and costs.

Of ultimate concern to the bank is overall profitability, not just domestic or foreign profitability. This truism is grounded in the business itself, for it is very difficult to compartmentalize banking operations in geographic terms. Banks have a hard time in their own analyses allocating revenue, costs, and volume among countries or between domestic and international operations. How should a bank allocate revenue from serving multinational clients worldwide or from such fee-earning services as syndication? How should it allocate costs of capital or headquarter costs that benefit the entire organi-

---

31. For a typology of relevant political issues see John T. Wooley, "Political Factors in Monetary Policy," in Donald R. Hodgman, ed., *The Political Economy of Monetary Policy: National and International Aspects*, Conference Series no. 26 (Boston: Federal Reserve Bank of Boston, 1983), p. 177.

102   *Philip A. Wellons*

zation? Should it account for money deposited in its London branch by the
headquarters of a U.S. corporation as a U.S. or as a foreign deposit? To deal
with these and other problems, banks have evolved rules of thumb that are
often arbitrary and vary among banks. In this article I consider the effect
of the home on overall revenues and overall costs. The alternative, allocating
costs and revenues between home and abroad to estimate domestic and
foreign net income, yields no useful insights.

The pervasive impact of home policies is apparent in the activities of the
big banks. For years banks have used the political process at home to affect
cross-border loans in several ways: to change their own cost structure, to
maintain or change barriers to entry or mobility, to maintain or expand their
freedom from regulation, and to protect against imminent loss. In reviewing
these aims I begin with cost, which is important for lending.

a. The cost structure at home

The home has more influence than other countries on [(cost times volume)]
because the banks' volume at home is so large. At home, moreover, the
bank has substantially greater opportunities to reduce costs.

For all the big banks, the home market is by several orders of magnitude
the dominant geographic market. For most, the home accounts for the majority of assets, liabilities, and profits; for big U.S. banks, the United States
is by far the largest market. From 1979 to 1983, for example, the domestic
earnings of the ten largest U.S. banks ranged from 44 to 56 percent of all
earnings. Domestic deposits ranged from 44 to 49 percent of all deposits,
and loans by domestic branches averaged 53 to 54 percent of all loans.[32]
Thus costs in the home country are crucial for the banks.

Even the extreme case—one of the world's most international banks, Citicorp—shows the importance of the home market as a volume base. Citicorp's
income statement for 1983 (Table 1) suggests in very rough terms how the
bank's net revenue and gross expenses fall between domestic and foreign
offices.[33] Even a bank as international as Citicorp has at least 40 percent of
its costs in its home country, and no other political jurisdiction comes remotely
close to a 40 percent share. Almost every other big U.S. bank would report
a much higher share of costs as domestic in origin.

The cost of money swamps other banking costs, and any action that reduced
it even a little would have a big impact on expenses. For Citicorp, borrowed
money (largely deposits) is 71 percent of gross expenses, overhead is 25

---

32. Salomon Brothers, Inc., *A Review of Bank Performance* (New York, 1984). Given the
vagaries of booking, the quoted ranges are rough approximations.

33. This allocation by Citicorp shows, at best, orders of magnitude. It is extremely difficult
to allocate income and costs geographically. Since it reports bookings in U.S. and other offices,
it probably underestimates the U.S. component. It discloses, however, more than do non-U.S.
banks.

TABLE 1. *Citicorp's expenses and revenue (in $ billions), 1983*

	U.S.	90 Other Countries	Total
a. Gross expenses	$6.2 (40%)	$9.1 (59%)	$15.5 (100%)
Borrowed money	(26%)	(45%)	(71%)
Provisions[a]	(1%)	(2%)	(3%)
Overhead[b]	(13%)	(12%)	(25%)
b. Net revenue	$2.9 (49%)	$3.0 (51%)	$5.9 (100%)
c. Net expenses and profit			(100%)
Overhead			(64%)
Loan losses and provisions			(8%)
Taxes			(14%)
Dividends			(3%)
Retained earnings			(10%)

a. Includes losses. Author's allocation based on distribution of actual loan losses.
b. Author's allocation based on distribution of employees in 1983.
Note. Percentages may not sum to 100 due to rounding.
Source. Citicorp, *Annual Report*, 1983.

percent, and "provisions"—as close as the bank comes to allocating for possible as well as actual losses—are only 3 percent. But all banks have similar costs for funds in international lending because they fund so much of their cross-border lending in Euromarkets. This common source puts them on an almost level playing field—one that they try to leave. Squeezed between the common cost of funds and price-sensitive customers, banks compete in wholesale lending on fine price differentials, and thus a large part of the game is to keep one's own costs lower than those of competitors. Consider the following example. On a Eurocurrency loan the bank typically earns the London interbank offer rate (LIBOR) plus a margin (assume no other fees). The bank typically has several costs—the cost of funds (LIBOR), overhead, risk, and capital (dividends and, to increase the capital base as assets rise, retained earnings).[34] In this simple equation LIBOR cancels out on both sides, and the margin must meet all other costs. Margins are typically small, just 1 to 3 percent, and in syndicated loans they are the same for all banks. A bank can achieve above-average profitability only by reducing costs, and that is where the home comes in.

The home can change some of these costs. Home government action, for

34. I have classified capital expenses as costs for convenience in this example. One could legitimately treat dividends and retained earnings separately as profits.

104   *Philip A. Wellons*

example, affects costs of funding, translation or exchange, and transactions, costs that can be shared with others, and even costs that are reduced by an implicit guarantee from the government. These costs represent overhead, risk, and capital costs. If Citicorp were to net out the cost of funds and account simply for net income, its distribution of costs (broadly defined) would look different (see "Net expenses and profit" in Table 1). Few if any costs are insignificant.

In short, any home action that changes costs from what we might call the free-market level has a much more powerful effect on the banks' profitability than a similar cost change elsewhere. In this formulation costs at home need not fall below those abroad (although in some cases they may do so). The following sections explore where the opportunities for changing costs at home exceed those abroad. Many involve government action, raising overtly political issues.

i. Cost advantages in the home financial system. The financial system at home, even without direct action by big banks, changes some costs of banking. For example, big banks from Japan and France have pursued low-price strategies in international markets, with the aid of systemic cost advantages.[35] In France government ownership reduces risk for depositors and private shareholders, and therefore cost to the bank. In Japan systemic effects accrue in several ways. Savings are encouraged by government policy and by institutional practice. Risk is reduced, in part by an implicit guarantee from the government (no bank has been allowed to fail in Japan since World War II) and in part by the structure of the financial system, in which a small number of banks lend to industry, the government is a direct intermediary, and ties with business are close.[36] Compared to what costs would otherwise be, the overall cost of funds is lower; leverage is higher, reducing capital costs; reserves to provide against loss may be lower; and the cost of complying with prudential regulations, such as reporting requirements, may be lower. Higher leverage is particularly important since it allows the bank to lend at lower prices, both at home and abroad, even if exchange controls impede the export of domestic capital.

But there is no evidence that these systemic effects arise from government attempts to improve its banks' position in loan markets. Typically, however, big banks do support their home country's system: the Japanese banks, for example, are the single largest contributors to the governing party, while the nationalized French banks engage more in bureaucratic than in party politics.[37]

35. See, for example, Cary Reich, "Spreads: The Search for Solutions," *Institutional Investor,* June 1978, p. 33.

36. I make this argument in detail in "Competitiveness in the World Economy: The Role of the U.S. Financial System" (paper for the Harvard Business School 75th Anniversary Colloquium on United States Competitiveness in the World Economy, 1984).

37. Stephen Bronte, *Japanese Finance: Markets and Institutions* (London: Euromoney, 1982), p. 13. In France, prior to nationalization, the private banks appear to have helped the private sector evade restrictions that were essential for the system to remain self-contained.

Debt and the banks

Rather, governments are motivated by interests beyond the competitiveness of the financial system. In Japan the government uses the system to promote industrial development. In France the government uses the system to redistribute income, its implicit guarantee holding down the costs of the investment in the banks it owns. These lower costs help compensate banks for government involvement in their lending activities. Such compensation is necessary: in Japan, for example, the banks take large portions of governmental debt at below market prices. Nationally owned banks in France are expected to lend to the public sector and to distressed areas of political importance.

ii. Overhead and transaction costs: privileged relations. Access to privileged information about borrowers reduces risk and overhead. Banks rarely have an insider relationship with borrowers from other countries, especially with governments of developing countries. Some banks own equity in or have exclusive relationships with corporate customers in their home country. As a *haus bank* or as part of a *keiretsu*, for example, a bank has access to information not available to ordinary lenders. In this sense the bank-as-owner shares costs with the bank-as-lender, and the cost of individual transactions is thus lowered. As home firms go overseas and the banks follow their customers, they take these competitive advantages with them.[38]

The banks' acquisition of these privileged relations is a complex story. To the extent that privileged relations give banks an independence from their home government greater than they otherwise would have had, autonomy results from national forces exerted over decades rather than from some transnational aspect of the banks' operations. Such privilege is limited to banks from the firm's home country.[39]

iii. Home government resource allocation to lower costs. Government subsidies and implicit guarantees reduce risk and such overhead costs as country and credit analysis. The prospect of such aid lures banks into the political process. They actively mobilize allies inside and outside the government to win official aid when they believe a customer may win its deal. Two obvious examples are export credits and the guarantees implicit in international lending.

Export promotion agencies such as the U.S. or Japanese export-import banks and some foreign aid agencies change the cost structure of transactions,

---

38. The extent to which relations between banks and their home customers remain tight abroad varies among the G-5 countries, as I discuss below.
39. Privileged relations with home customers also benefit the banks on the pricing side. If they choose, they can accept lower prices than in an arm's-length loan to foreign borrowers yet keep the same margins. A bank that holds equity in the borrowing firm may take a longer view, accepting lower interest rates in return for eventual appreciation in the value of the firm's stock. The alternative is to use their power as equity holders to force higher margins on these customers. In either case the base allows more competitive pricing elsewhere.

particularly in financing large projects that generate many visible jobs at home. By taking the long-term end of the financing, they reduce the risk a bank might otherwise have borne. Such a subsidy may make a project viable, allowing the borrower to pay market rates (at least) to private banks.

These export programs draw more on home than on foreign banks. Programs in the G-5 are now open, at least in part, to banks headquartered in other countries. In practice, however, home banks take the lion's share of such programs, if only because of their close ties with home customers that export.[40]

In the export credit war among industrial countries the banks are more like foot soldiers than generals. They do little to help formulate the basic policies of their home government. A country's aggressive export credit program represents a broader government commitment to promote trade. Support comes from a combination of domestic groups whose interests are vitally affected: the exporting firms, their employees, and their suppliers. Banks do, however, help promising customers move reluctant agencies, such as a finance ministry, with all available means of persuasion commensurate to the likely return. Lobbying for support from an existing program is, however, far removed from the idea that transnational banks manipulate their governments' policy.

The second example is the guarantee implicit in international lending. An official guarantee to a bank reduces its cost of funds, in the abstract, to the risk-free level paid by government itself. All G-5 governments support the overall international exposure of their biggest banks. The financial system defines these biggest banks; each bank's job is to make sure it is in the inner circle and hence able to make riskier loans without commensurate increase in costs. Both banks and governments recognize that the home financial system is hostage to the performance of its biggest banks. But this status is due not to the transnational status of the big banks but to their position in the *home* financial system.

The more explicit the guarantee, in theory, the more beneficial will be the cost effect for the bank. Yet big banks have generally not been able to wrest explicit guarantees from their governments. The implicit assurances that do exist tend to be based on broader systemic rationales rather than on the international action of the banks. For example, Japanese banks see the participation of the Industrial Bank of Japan in a project as a guarantee. The government's rationale is, of course, to promote the development needs of the nation, but the broader the implicit guarantee, the greater the benefit to home banks when competing with other banks at home and abroad.

In sum, a cost effect at home is, by virtue of the home's size as a market, qualitatively larger than what other countries can provide. The cost effect at home comes at several levels: in the financial system as a whole, in

40. Interviews, Europe and Japan.

Debt and the banks

individual transactions, and for individual big banks. Privileged relations between banks and customers also reduce costs at home. Most of these effects came about not because banks gained independence from their home by becoming transnational but precisely because of the banks' intricate role in the home economy. Some occurred for purely domestic reasons. Here is an economic rationale, based on costs, for the view that even the biggest banks are creatures of their home country.

b. Protection at home

As it is in the case of costs, so it is for [(revenue) times (volume)] for the big banks: the home has by far the greatest impact. Compared to other countries, it provides the largest volume of business and offers the greatest opportunity to affect revenue. Whatever increases revenue at home has, due to high volume, a much more powerful effect on the banks' profitability than would a similar shift elsewhere. Given narrow margins, even fractional improvement is important.

The government's ability to protect home markets offers an important opportunity to affect bank revenue. A protected home base gives banks a competitive advantage in international lending and, if domestic competitors do not compete the advantage away, ties them more closely to their home. In countries that protect their banks, credit allocation restricts competition in France and interest ceilings carefully balance the needs of the banks and other intermediaries in Japan. The important point in such cases is that these controls are carefully negotiated among various interest groups over a long period of time—the essence of politics.

In their own markets all governments protect banks—even banks from other countries—against some forms of competition, if only by regulating standards for banking. One would expect the home, if of special importance, to provide substantially more protection for its own banks than they can receive elsewhere. As with costs, the effect hinges on the mix between volume (the size of the protected base relative to the bank's total business) and scope (the extent of the protection). As we saw above, the sheer volume of a bank's business at home overshadows its business in other countries that might provide protection. The real question concerns the extent of protection at home in the G-5 countries. Markets are protected in many ways. Banks may be protected against foreign banks, and their special relations with domestic borrowers may also be protected.

i. Protection from foreign competitors. At first blush, it would appear that the G-5 markets are not protected. In all five countries many foreign banks do business locally. Their markets shares are low, averaging 13 percent of the assets of deposit-taking banks in the G-5 countries, but that alone does not suggest protection because national markets do not integrate at once.

108   *Philip A. Wellons*

One must look for a growing supply of foreign banks without a commensurate growth in market share. We find this pattern in Japan. Although the number of foreign-bank offices has increased considerably in the last ten years, their share of the domestic market has remained at about 3 percent.[41] Access to Japan's financial services market has become a matter of diplomatic contention in recent years, also suggesting protection.

Among the G-5 countries the degree of foreign penetration varies widely, as do the supporting government policies. The source of protection is another matter. Banks from the G-5 countries typically find it difficult to break into one another's home markets.[42] The difficulty does not always stem from home government policy. Chase Manhattan Bank attributes its failed efforts to enter the German retail banking market in the 1970s to the market power of the big German banks.[43] Elsewhere, official policy seems to be the main factor. In France, as I argue below, the method of monetary management discriminates against new entrants. There is no simple explanation for the flat market share of foreign banks in Japan, but Japanese banking is a highly managed system.

ii. Protection of privileged relations. One major source of a big bank's competitive strength is its close ties with major firms in its home country. Often extending over decades, sometimes broadened to include equity interests in the firm as well as loans to it, these ties make it hard for competing banks to take business simply by underpricing. In several of the G-5 countries, however, these ties are challenged by groups outside the financial community.

The growth and volume of international lending by the big banks periodically inflame domestic political debate about the allocation of credit at home. The banks are denounced, particularly in times of tight money and economic hardship, for lending abroad rather than to those in need at home. The attack quickly expands to include the banks' ties with their large corporate clients at home. Critics often assert that the big banks lend in a way that cripples the country's industrial growth and competitiveness. By financing established firms and foreigners, the banks are said to be ignoring the dynamic and innovative small business sector. In the United Kingdom, for example, Lord Lever of the Labour party made this argument in 1980, and the same view has been heard in Germany, France, and Japan.[44] One part of the proposed solution in West Germany and Japan has been an attempt to reduce

41. Interviews with foreign bankers in Tokyo. Data for the 1970s have not been published, although they have been shown to individual foreign bankers there.

42. Interviews in all G-5 countries.

43. Interviews, West Germany, 1980 and 1983.

44. Lord Lever and George Edwards, "Banking on Britain," *Sunday Times* pamphlet (London, 1980). The Labour party argued thus during the 1970s. See also D. Vittas and R. Brown, "Bank Lending and Industrial Investment: A Response to Recent Criticisms" (London: Banking Information Service, March 1982).

the banks' equity stake in companies to which they lend.[45] Banks typically try to avoid meeting these political challenges head-on. They stall, make small changes, and try to influence opinion. Because the controversy extends beyond the financial system, however, the banks' power is relatively limited. The outcome varies by country.

In both areas of protection—from foreign banks and from challenges to privileged relations with firms—the political process usually draws players from a narrow band on the political spectrum: the banks, others in the financial system, and the home government. The very act of international lending threatens to reduce protection, however, and so the banks, if international markets are important to them, must try to balance protection at home with reciprocity abroad. Others in the financial system are concerned with preserving their own power and prerogatives with the banks. For the home government, the interests of the banks are merely one part of the political equation; other issues include management of the monetary system, control over cross-border flows, the structure of the financial system, and control over economic policy in a broader sense. As long as the political debate stays within the financial system, bargaining among the players is relatively manageable. Thus when the threat to protection comes from foreign players, as is the case for protected home markets, the big banks are better able to maintain the barriers. When the threat comes from other domestic groups, however, as is the case for the protected customer base, the big banks are in a weaker position and must rely on broader political affiliations.

Certain home governments protect the markets and customer relationships of their big banks. Does official action reflect the strength of banks as transnationals? Do banks win protection from their home government because their international operations give them independence and power? In France the government owns its banks, so independence does not describe the relation. In Japan the banks' international operations are too small a share of total assets (15% at most) to grant them independence. In Germany protected ties with firms existed for over a century, surviving the destruction of the German banks' international networks during both world wars. We must look to factors other than the banks' independence from their home countries to explain this protection.

c. The vanishing frontier: freedom from regulation

Much of the argument that banks are transnationals independent of government authority centers on the multiplicity of legal jurisdictions in which banks do business. Given fungible money, inventive financiers, and financial

---

45. Other responses are joint ventures by government and the banks that are supposed to finance the credit-poor sectors. The Deutsche Wagnis Finanzierungs Gesellschaft in Germany, Sofinnova in France, and the Industrial and Commercial Finance Corporation in the United Kingdom are examples.

havens, the argument holds, the banks operate as free agents outside the jurisdiction of any one nation's laws. The implication is clear: a government cannot restrict the international operations of banks against their will. Such a view may reflect the limited power of many host countries, but it vastly underrates the power of the home countries.

The home is the one jurisdiction that can regulate the international operations of banks. When the Basle Concordat placed ultimate lender-of-last-resort responsibility with the home country, it was merely acknowledging the existing lines of authority. No government other than the home is in a position to get a complete view of the banks' worldwide operations. Moreover, this authority is more than a legal nicety: the big banks' interests in their home country are, as we have seen, so strong and so interrelated that the banks cannot extricate themselves. As Federal Reserve Board chairman Arthur Burns has said, the U.S. regulatory system prompts competition in laxity, in part because banks can switch regulators. Ties at home are so constraining, however, that the big banks do not switch citizenship.

The idea that banks move abroad to escape home regulation is a commonplace, but no bank escapes completely.[46] Japanese banks, for example, report all credits to the Finance Ministry, checking many in advance. The regulation of banks' international lending, done for prudential and systemic reasons, raises broad political issues.[47] Governments have various policy reasons to regulate banks; they are concerned with safety and soundness, the structure of finance and industry at home, demand management, the balance of payments, and even issues of national security. The result for most G-5 banks is a complicated set of rules that shapes international lending in terms of safety and soundness, structure, tax, credit allocation, lending in the home currency, antitrust laws, and restrictions on types of services that banks can provide.

We have here more than Glendower's empty command.[48] The Bank of England is attentive to the prudential aspects of cross-border loans by British banks. U.S. and Japanese authorities regulate the number of new foreign branches that their banks may open. French authorities effectively prohibit their banks from lending francs across borders for most purposes. It is certainly true that the G-5 governments have not enforced all laws, but the circumstances of each asserted lapse must be carefully reviewed. One of the most blatant cases involves a U.S. rule limiting loans to a single borrower to 10 percent (later 15%) of capital. Even when loans were made to agencies of

46. To the extent that the banks do succeed in escaping regulation, their response to a politicized environment could be called avoidance through alternate markets.

47. See, for example, James W. Dean and Ian H. Giddy, *Averting International Banking Crises*, New York University, Graduate School of Business Administration Monograph Series in Finance and Economics no. 1981-1.

48. "I can call spirits from the vasty deep," says Owen Glendower in *Henry IV Part I* (2.1). "Why, so can I. . . . But will they come when you do call for them?" is Hotspur's reply.

the Mexican government as part of a coordinated borrowing scheme by the central government in 1981, U.S. authorities chose to treat them as outside the 10 percent rule. Close examination suggests that other government policies took precedence, including Mexico's needs as a troubled neighbor. The lapse does not appear to have occurred because U.S. banks were able to ignore government policy; rather, the U.S. government needed the lapse for its own reasons.

The extent to which and arenas in which big banks are able to minimize home regulation varies widely among the G-5 countries, as I argue below. Most countries do, however, have the authority and the power to regulate the international lending of their big banks. In one way or another all G-5 governments exercise this authority over the entire international operations of their own banks more effectively than can any other jurisdiction.

d. The threat of imminent loss: getting help at home

The most effective anchor to the home country is the allocation of international lender-of-last-resort responsibility among the G-5 governments. Each country looks after its own banks. Each also has de facto responsibility for debtor countries that are important to it: West Germany for Poland, for example, or the United States for Mexico. Bankers can "read" the system in advance: they know that in a crisis they can turn to the home government, and they know not to burn their bridges in advance of crisis. Indeed, they cannot turn elsewhere. To put it crudely, only their home government will bail them out directly. This is hardly the stance of an independent, transnational firm.

Faced with the threat of a large and imminent loss on loans to a foreign country, the big banks turn for help with rescheduling to other interested parties at home, the other lending banks and the government. The big banks have two goals in such circumstances. They need to deal with the immediate prospect of loss, and they need to preserve or augment their competitive position in the long run. In seeking government action, the banks must ensure that policy makers see a danger to the home country. Often the danger is obvious even to the most myopic, and so the banks need take no direct action to convince officials that a crisis exists. Their earlier lending has already affected the system in which policy makers operate and reflects their own reading of the government's strategy.

From the perspective of the big banks, political action is necessary in three political arenas at home: interbank politics, "bailout" politics, and the politics of competitive positioning. In each arena they require the help of their home government.

i. Interbank politics. Part of rescheduling is the effort to keep the small banks in the game—a matter of no small concern to big banks. Interbank

112   *Philip A. Wellons*

politics draws the home government in when, from its perspective, important state interests must be represented. The task of the big banks is to demonstrate that these interests are affected by the crisis. The home government, despite its great concern about the stability of the financial system, will be even more active in interbank politics when the debtor country is strategically important.

The special involvement of the U.S. government in Mexico's rescheduling and of the West German government in those of Poland and Yugoslavia exemplifies the home's role in interbank politics. Precise measurements of involvement are difficult to make. The Federal Reserve Board was clearly active in the case of Mexico, but in that of Brazil it was not active in the first phase, from September 1982 to May 1983.[49] Paul Volcker in late May 1983 urged the big U.S. banks to change their policy, participated in high-level discussions of the new Brazil package at the IMF meeting in September 1983, and addressed the Honolulu conference of the American Bankers' Association on the topic of Brazil in October 1983. Nevertheless, the Fed was less active in contacting small banks that were holdouts in the case of Brazil than it was in the case of Mexico.[50] Indeed, many small banks were still holding out from the new loan to Brazil as late as February 1984.

ii. "Bailout" politics. Any hint of a "bailout"—the government providing public funds that allow the banks to withdraw from ill-judged loans—stirs the political cauldron at home, particularly in the United States. When the danger is geographically close, government expenditure is easier to justify. Even a threat to the international financial system is important less for the stability of the system as a whole than for its consequences at home. Foreign-policy interests seem to mobilize the G-5 governments. Mexico received more funds than Brazil and got them faster: in one weekend $3 billion was raised within the U.S. government for Mexico. Brazil, on the other hand, got a Treasury swap of $1.23 billion very early (September 1982), but no Commodity Credit Corporation money until June 1983 (and then only $250 million, compared to Mexico's $1 billion) and practically no U.S. Eximbank guarantee materialized even though $1.5 billion had been promised in mid-1983.

The big banks' strategy for bringing in government funds has been twofold: keep the policy debate within the financial system and shift the costs or tradeoffs out. Banks want debate about the fact and scope of assistance to take place among them, their regulators, and the treasury; the common interests of the participants discourage awkward questions about responsibility

49. Some people interviewed in 1982–83 in New York assert that the big banks and the government of Brazil wanted the U.S. government to remain aloof from the rescheduling process to keep it in the market. Even if this were true, the U.S. government acquiesced in this approach. Would the United States have allowed the Mexican government to founder for nine months?

50. Interviews, New York, 1984.

Debt and the banks   113

for the crisis. In Japan and Europe debate has in fact stayed within these groups. Banks shift costs outside the financial system both at the level of the debtor country and at the systemic level. Each of the G-5 governments, for example, provides aid to the country in distress or to multilateral institutions rather than to the banks. The banks gain an advantage from this practice, which focuses political attention away from the lenders. Banks from different countries have had varying success with this strategy.

iii. The politics of competitive positioning. So much of rescheduling requires banks to cooperate that it may seem grotesque to identify a politics of competitive positioning designed to secure the bank's place when the dust settles. Yet a crisis offers opportunities to the agile bank. The government, after all, plays a part that depends on its own strategy and on the financial system. The more highly structured the home financial market, the greater is the role of the government in legitimizing potential leaders and the less the government simply reacts, accepting the market's identification of leaders. In Japan the Bank of Tokyo has played the main leadership role because of its close relation to the Finance Ministry. One might suppose that the home government plays a neutral role among banks, but in practice the stronger banks can use the regulatory system to erode the position of weaker banks. Tighter prudential rules are, for example, a competitive weapon. When U.S. regulators in effect require on-site inspection for country analysis, they exclude many smaller U.S. banks from the international loan market.

Home government help for the international lending of big banks is an intricate story. There are at least two phases, and current interest in the crisis phase should not obscure the importance of the lending phase. Home policy can provide a low-cost base and protection for banks, increasing profitability. The home market is such a large part of the business of big banks that even slightly lower costs and protection can have a strong effect. The home is the market that is willing to protect its banks. Banque Nationale de Paris cannot expect the Japanese Ministry of Finance to protect it, for example, but even if the Finance Minstry did so in Japan, the effect on the bank's overall earnings would be insignificant. The home helps to direct the flow of credit abroad through incentives to lend in certain ways, such as export credit and implicit guarantees, and through the selective application of prudential rules.

The home plays a special role during and in anticipation of crises. Only the home government will bail out a bank directly; Japan's Finance Ministry will not come to the aid of Banque Nationale de Paris. This, the home government's ultimate weapon in dealing with its banks, can also bestow potent benefits in the lending phase. Such weapons are important, for the home is the one central jurisdiction that can regulate the international operations of banks.

Banks are one of many competing groups; they sometimes win and sometimes lose. Their success hinges on their ability to identify their own needs with some broader purpose that motivates their home government. The relation between home government and its big banks is not easy, but the government is far from subordinate to the big banks as pictured in the transnational model.

That the home government has a qualitatively greater influence than others over its big banks' international lending makes sense. The home has the greatest opportunity to influence costs and to control credit allocation, and it also plays an important role in the banks' international business strategy. Banks, after all, are in a commodity business. One of the hardest tasks for a firm selling a commodity is to differentiate itself from its competitors. In international credit markets a bank's home affiliation permits it to differentiate itself from banks from other countries. The market holds the fact that a bank is from Japan or from the United States as important. This attitude reinforces the banks' ties with their home country and weakens their transnational status.

2. The G-5 nations differ

Much of this discussion has treated bank-government relations in the G-5 countries as essentially similar. In fact, important differences exist among the G-5 countries. They affect the international lending of the banks and the stability of the world financial system as a whole.

If we were dealing with transnational banks, we would expect them to win and use government resources in ways not linked to their home country. If big banks were truly transnational, we would not expect to see big differences among them, when grouped by home country, in the extent to which they enjoy a low-cost base or protection at home. Nor would we expect to see big differences in the extent of their freedom from regulation or of the help they get when threatened with imminent loss. In practice, however, the differences are large.

a. Cost structures

Cost structures differ among G-5 countries, as exemplified by leveraging (a systemic cost) and export credits (a form of resource allocation). In both cases Japanese and French banks make one group, German and U.S. banks a second. British banks are closer to the former group on export credit, closer to the latter on leveraging.

These groups reflect basic differences in government policy in the five countries. Banks from some countries can leverage their equity a great deal, others much less, and the differences have a dramatic effect on asset growth.

TABLE 2. *Extraordinary export support programs, 1981*

	France	U.K.	Japan	Germany	U.S.
Inflation insurance	3	2	0	0	0
Exchange risk insurance	3	2	2	2	0
Mixed credits/tied aid	3	2	2	2	1
Local cost support	2	2	3	3	1
Foreign currency loan	2	3	0[a]	0	0
Frequency of use:	\multicolumn{5}{l}{0 = not available}
	\multicolumn{5}{l}{1 = used only to match competing offers}
	\multicolumn{5}{l}{2 = available, moderately used program}
	\multicolumn{5}{l}{3 = extensively used program}

a. An exporter may on-lend in foreign currency, however.
Source. Export-Import Bank of the United States, *Report to the United States Congress on Export Credit Competition and the Export-Import Bank of the United States for the Period January 1, 1982, through December 31, 1982* (Washington, D.C., 1983).

In 1982, for example, one dollar of equity would support $80 of assets for French banks and $44 for Japanese banks, compared with $22 for U.K. and U.S. banks and $34 for German banks.[51] As a result, a bank from Japan or France could lend more than other banks in world markets on a smaller equity base or could lend the same amount at narrower margins. Increased lending contributed to the rapid growth of bank credit in the 1970s; narrower margins contributed to intense price competition.

The export credit policies of home governments also vary widely. In the 1980s the U.S. and German governments pushed for market rates while other countries were much more willing to subsidize exports and to mix aid with export credit to win important export bids. France and the United Kingdom helped their exporters most, as Table 2 shows, and Japan did so somewhat less. Long central to the French and Japanese strategies, aggressive export promotion using the financial system became important in the United Kingdom under the Thatcher government.

These differences affect the international lending of banks in several ways. In particular they determine, to the extent that they help the banks' home customers win bids, which country's banks will supply collateral finance. In

51. *Euromoney*, June 1983, pp. S6–S12. Due to accounting differences, the comparison of debt/equity ratios is very rough. Other comparisons find the same ranking. See "The Top 500," *Banker*, June 1982, p. 177. A more systematic approach that is not sufficiently disaggregated for this analysis is R. Revell, *Costs and Margins in Banking: An International Survey* (Paris: OECD, 1980). In Japan, where no bank has failed since World War II, a complex web of official policy and industry structure reduces risk and permits higher leverage. In France, where the state as dominant shareholder does not require market returns on its equity investment and the government offers subsidized rediscounting for favored credit, structure has an even more direct impact on the cost of capital for the banks.

116   Philip A. Wellons

TABLE 3. *Market share of foreign banks in G-5 host countries, 1982–83*

	U.K.	France	U.S.	Germany	Japan
Assets: foreign banks as a share of					
All deposit banks	21%	17%	14%	10%	3%
Largest banks	52	33	30	27	7
Loans: foreign banks as a share of					
All deposit banks	23	18	16	11	3
Largest banks	52	34	30	29	8
Largest banks are	Clearers (5 banks)	Big 3	10 large NYC banks	Big 3	12 city banks

These comparisons are rough. For example, the United Kingdom shows only sterling loans
and assets; the United States shows 1,738 commercial banks with assets over $100 million;
Japan shows ordinary banks (city banks, long-term credit banks, and regional banks), but
adding other deposit-taking banks would reduce the foreign banks' share by only 1%; France
excludes *banques d'affaires* even though they can take deposits.
Sources. Central bank bulletin of each country, except for controller of banks in France.
Data are as of the end of December 1982 for the United Kingdom, February 1983 for
Japan, June 1983 for the United States, July 1983 for West Germany, and as of 5 January
1983 for France.

this way they change the flow of credit. Subsidies have mainly gone to developing countries and Eastern Europe, thus encouraging banks to lend to
these groups of countries.

b. Home protection

Foreign banks hold considerably different shares of the domestic markets
in the G-5 countries (see Table 3). Japan is an extreme case: the market
share of foreign banks there is less than one-third of the share of foreign
banks in West Germany, the closest country. Such differences reflect official
policies, shaped in part by the needs and pressures of the home banks and
in part by other governmental concerns.

Barriers to market entry are most pervasive in Japan. One major reason
seems to be that Japan's Finance Ministry has closely controlled its borders
to maintain a domestic financial system that promotes industrial competitiveness. The interests of the Japanese city banks have been consistent with
the Finance Ministry's goal of closed markets: over 85 percent of the city
banks' earnings at home come from highly segmented domestic markets to
which they want to retain privileged access.[52] As a result Japan, alone among

52. Bronte, *Japanese Finance*, pp. 67ff.

the G-5 countries, still has "a substantial lack of national treatment and equality of competitive opportunity in practice for U.S. and foreign banks" operating in the country, according to the U.S. government.[53]

More subtle forms of protection are found in France and West Germany. France controls the money supply through the *encadrement* system of ceilings on the growth of credit. The effect is to limit every bank to the market share it had when the system went into effect in the mid-1970s.[54] From their pivotal position in the financial system, the big German banks can discipline newcomers greedy for market share.[55]

London's long-standing role as the world's premier financial center encouraged both the government and the big banks to protect domestic markets less. The largest British banks are international, and they depend on substantial foreign earnings. They are inclined to encourage reciprocity at home, even though to do so could increase competition in the lucrative, inefficient domestic market. Barriers remain strong, however, in matters critical to the informal management of banking and monetary policy in the United Kingdom, among them control of the London and Scottish clearing banks.[56] Despite the efforts of the British Foreign Office and Board of Trade, for example, the Bank of England thwarted an attempt by the Hong Kong and Shanghai Banking Corporation to take control of one clearer, the Royal Bank of Scotland, in 1981.

In the United States government has long followed a policy of limiting the power of the big banks. Among other constraints, banks have been prohibited from crossing state lines in their operations. In the 1970s, however, the big banks began aggressive political action to challenge these barriers. In their quest to open their own national market the banks have allied themselves with some regulators (notably the comptroller of the currency) and with foreign banks against the smaller and regional U.S. banks.

53. Department of the Treasury, "Report to Congress on Foreign Government Treatment of U.S. Commercial Banking Organizations" (Washington, D.C., 17 September 1979), p. 77. Only in the last few years have restrictions on foreign banks in Japan been reduced. Many survive. Many foreign branches "were required to submit pledges . . . not to solicit local deposits," making them subject to Bank of Japan quotas on currency swaps (p. 75). They have had to obtain advance approval for yen loans to non-Japanese, unlike the big banks with foreign-exchange licenses. They have been limited in their ability to expand their branch network. Foreign banks are not part of the syndicate that can trade in government securities. They can issue certificates of deposit for up to 30% of their yen assets while domestic banks' CD issues may reach 75% of capital.
54. Because of the long-term decline in the exchange rate of the French franc, foreign banks are reluctant to increase their capital, the only way to raise one's market share within this corset. Some negotiation with the authorities is possible, but a dramatic increase in share is not.
55. See, for example, John Zysman, *Governments, Markets, and Growth: Financial Systems and the Politics of Industrial Change* (Ithaca: Cornell University Press, 1983). Chase Manhattan Bank's failed effort to establish a retail base in Germany is an example.
56. See, for example, William Hall, "Bank of England Seeks Stronger Financial Sector Merger Controls," *Financial Times*, 23 September 1981, p. 1. More recently the Bank of England has instructed foreign banks not to break into the sterling market by underpricing in the acceptance credit market, which is where the Bank "conducts its daily money market operations" ("The Bank Squeezes the Bankers," *Banker*, June 1983, p. 13).

c. Independence from home regulation of overseas lending

In their attempts to escape regulation by moving overseas, big banks from the G-5 countries have had very different experiences. The European banks have much more independence abroad than banks from either Japan or the United States. Consider, for instance, the ceilings on foreign loans by home banks in the aggregate or by individual banks to individual foreign borrowers. French regulators essentially leave the question to their big banks. The Bank of England works through individual consultation with each bank. Over the past decade the German banks avoided the imposition of ceilings, while the U.S. banks were at least nominally subject to ceilings and the Japanese banks were regulated in form and in practice. In West Germany the banks fought the regulators, going outside the financial system for allies, while in the United States the banks joined forces with the regulators against Congress, and in Japan the banks ended up cooperating with their regulators in return for systemic tradeoffs elsewhere.

In West Germany clear regulatory principles applied to banks and their foreign branches but not to their foreign subsidiaries, which consistently made substantial loans.[57] Since the mid-1970s technocrats in the German Finance Ministry and regulators in other industrial countries have urged consolidation of the operations of foreign subsidiaries, even though such a move would force the banks to increase their equity or greatly reduce their foreign lending. By early 1984, however, the big private German banks had still managed to elude consolidation, and they were supported by big German firms, which could borrow deutsche marks from the unregulated Luxembourg subsidiaries of German banks at lower cost.

The political strategy of the banks was to delay legislative action and to prove that they could manage what problems might arise as a result of nonconsolidation.

They informally reported figures that consolidated 100 percent or nearly 100 percent owned subsidiaries in order to avoid formal change.

They gained time from the disintegration of the Schmidt government after 1979 and the slow start of the succeeding Christian Democrat government.

They had the support of the economics minister, a leader of the. Free Democratic party and a proponent of free markets.

To make government assistance unnecessary, they aided small banks that went bankrupt partly because the absence of rules allowed them to behave imprudently.

---

57. Principle I limits a bank's total credit to eighteen times equity. Section 19 of the banking law limits credits to a single borrower or related group to 75 percent of equity. Schneider, Hellwig, & Kingsman, *The German Banking System* (Frankfurt/Main: Knapp, 1978), pp. 141–43. That this limit is much higher than what one sees in the United States reflects the importance of the ties between the big German banks and the major corporate customers, both to the banks and to the state.

They did not adjust their own balance sheets to comply with the intent of the law setting credit-equity ratios.

As late as February 1984, when the finance minister submitted his draft law on consolidation, the economics minister still opposed him.[58] Even though the act passed in early 1985, the five-year transition period means that the Big Three banks will have delayed consolidation for over ten years.

In the United States a similar debate about loan limits led to a formal decision against the banks. Implementation of the 10 percent rule, however, favored them.

In Japan, under the authority of the Banking Law of 1981, the government has limited to 20 percent of capital and reserves the loans that a city bank can make to any one customer, including medium- and long-term loans to any one country.[59] The move was preceded by years of informal discussions, during which time many banks moved toward the new government standard. By the time the limit was imposed, only Mitsui Bank lacked adequate capital to cover its outstanding loans to *keiretsu* customers.

The long period of discussion, compromise, and adjustment is characteristic of the regulatory system in Japan. So is the government's extensive reach. Since the mid-1970s the Finance Ministry had:

> Twice pulled Japanese banks out of syndicated loan markets, once between 1974 and 1976, the second time in 1979–80.
>
> Limited the share Japanese banks as a group could take in any dollar syndicated loan (the limit was 20% in late 1983).
>
> Fixed six-month ceilings on offshore loans to be allocated among the banks.[60]
>
> Set rules for matching the maturities of foreign liabilities to foreign assets.
>
> Required the banks to report all offshore lending, though foreign subsidiaries could report loans after they were made.
>
> Reviewed in advance the lending program of each bank, through the ministry every six months and through the central bank monthly.

---

58. See John Davies, "Bonn Wrangles over Bank Laws," *Financial Times*, 23 December 1983, p. 2, and Peter Norman, "Germany Drafts Tougher Rules for Its Bankers," *Wall Street Journal*, 3 February 1984, p. 27.

59. The city banks did oppose rigorous application of the 20 percent limit to overseas lending. In an interview published one month before the Finance Ministry's action, the president of Fuji Bank said "Suggestions are being made by the Ministry of Finance for guidance but I believe decisions should be to the individual banks' management. Of course, whether 20% of capital or 25% is a good limit is open to discussion, but the decision should be made by the individual bank. There are some banks that are going into international lending, and others that are not. So a universal application of the 20 percent limit is unrealistic." Quoted in "Bank's Leader Pushes for Reform," *Euromoney*, March 1983, pp. 125, 128.

60. For the six months starting in April 1983, for example, the banks received ¥700 billion ($2.9 billion) for yen loans and $8 billion for dollar loans. Yoko Shibata, "Limits Raised on Offshore Loans by Japanese Banks," *Financial Times*, 19 April 1983, p. 18.

120   *Philip A. Wellons*

Once agreement was reached on lending ratios, Japanese banks were expected to comply with both the spirit and the letter of the law.[61]

These outcomes illustrate relations between the banks and their regulators in the international field. In West Germany and the United States no constituencies outside the financial system coalesced around the goal of limiting the international lending of the banks. Thus German regulators were unable to change the status quo and U.S. regulators did not feel compelled to do so, despite congressional interest. In Japan, on the other hand, the Finance Ministry did not need to look outside the financial system for support to regulate international lending. Maintaining control was the status quo.

The results also reflect the broader political strategies of various home governments. The Japanese, taking an activist role in international economic affairs as a whole, could not let their banks escape unregulated. The American regulators, concerned about the international financial system and the needs of such neighbors as Mexico, responded to global systemic issues. The German regulators fell afoul of the governing coalition's strategy of nonintervention in foreign economic affairs and its reliance on the big banks to help coordinate those affairs.

A final factor was the banks' position in each country's financial system. The Big Three German banks occupy a pivotal position in the financial system, responsible for functions ranging from shareholding to trade finance. They have had the greatest success in evading regulation. The U.S. banks are important in absolute terms but occupy a very small part of the financial market. Their partial success in evading a stringent application of the rules seems to be due primarily to the broader concerns of the regulators rather than to their own power. The Japanese banks, though large, are roughly comparable in size and numerous enough to be competitive with one another. They were least successful in evading regulation.

d. G-5 government support for big banks threatened by imminent loss

Truly transnational banks when threatened by imminent loss should receive no special treatment from any government, not even from that of their home country. We know, however, that no G-5 government has agreed to provide lender-of-last-resort support to a bank from another country. We also know that each G-5 government has agreed to support its own banks.[62] Differences among governments are differences of nuance. The German government presents the appearance of arm's-length relations; so does the U.S. govern-

---

61. It might be argued that the Japanese banks violated the spirit of the limits on medium- and long-term lending when they dramatically increased their short-term loans in 1981 and 1982. I believe they acted within the spirit of the rule, which was intended to leave them free on the assumption that short-term lending finances trade.

62. The effort by the Italian authorities to escape the terms of the Basle Concordat at least suggests that governments outside the G-5 may not subscribe to it wholeheartedly.

ment, but that did not prevent U.S. authorities from assisting large depositors in the case of Continental Illinois.

Substantial differences emerge in the extent to which banks from various countries get and use home government resources. If one assumes that the banks themselves seek or acquiesce in the treatment they receive, then on matters of substantive policy banks from different home countries vary widely. They appear to hold different priorities among the four goals set out in section 1.

The big German banks rate freedom from regulation above the other goals; self-help is a principle that dominates all goals, underlying the banks' role in the whole West German economy.

The big British banks couple freedom from regulation with protection of home markets and are less preoccupied with reducing costs or the threat of imminent loss. The City of London benefits the British economy, so protection cannot be excessive, yet some protection is necessary to meet the needs of the clearing banks as domestic financial institutions.

The Japanese city banks repeatedly place least emphasis on freedom from regulation in their international lending, by choice or by necessity. They look instead to their government for protection, lower costs, and safety from imminent loss.

The big French banks seem to focus on government help in reducing costs and guarding against loss, but they receive freedom from regulation by default.

The big U.S. banks subordinate independence to a larger goal: reduction of barriers within their own country. They use international credit markets as one of several means to this end.

These various priorities represent major political tradeoffs. Japanese banks, for example, are the most regulated in their international lending but also the most protected and most assisted by various cost advantages. Government assistance may represent, at least in part, compensation for tighter controls.

3. Differences among homes affect international debt

Banks from various G-5 nations should act differently in markets for international debt if these national differences are important determinants of banking behavior. In practice they do. Bank behavior varies for entry and exit from international markets, regional allocation of credit, and rescheduling. These differences are not adequately explained by such international economic criteria as size, experience, market share, or market imperfections. The home is critical. As we have seen, much more than home regulatory policy is at work, but all the various critical forces affecting bank behavior (some political, others economic) share one characteristic: they stem from the specific home countries of the banks.

When banks from the same country enter and leave international markets, they often seem to be marching to the beat of the same drummer. Japanese banks appeared on the international scene as a group in 1970. They cut back their syndicated lending dramatically in 1974, reentered in 1977, exited en masse in 1979, and entered once again by 1981. Their stop-go pattern may be extreme, but it is not unique. French banks have also reduced their international activities in 1978 and in the early 1980s. The big German banks withdrew from lending to developing countries in 1980. When an executive vice president of Dresdner Bank told President Marcos of the Philippines in November 1980 that the bank would not be able to help the country float a bond in West Germany, he was expressing a position toward such countries that officials of Deutsche Bank had initiated earlier that year.

Banks from the same country move together in response to more than economic stimuli, including some form of oligopolistic reaction. In Japan, for example, home regulation was critical. The Finance Ministry and Bank of Japan held the banks on a short leash, pulling them out of and allowing them to enter international markets as conditions in Japan warranted. The French banks pulled out of the interbank market in 1978 when other banks demanded higher spreads on deposits. The others feared that a new Socialist government would harm the economy and the banks; political uncertainty in France prompted the market to treat all *French* banks as being at greater risk. The second pullback occurred as French banks began to respond to domestic financing needs that grew as the country's current account grew progressively worse. In the first instance the market treated all French banks alike, while in the second the banks gave precedence to customers from their home country. The Germans pulled back as they recognized their exposure in Poland, the dangers in Latin America, and the need to retrench. Bank regulators were certainly concerned about the banks' exposure, but the banks themselves appear to have prompted the retreat. Their behavior is consistent with the German banks' view that freedom from control is the main goal. To maintain this independence, they must appear to be able to manage their own debt problems.

That banks from the same country are dominant or weak in particular regions of the world is a commonplace. British banks dominate markets in certain countries in Asia and Africa, as do French banks in parts of Africa. In Mexico, U.S. banks made 36 percent of all loans outstanding in mid-1982, German banks made less than 4 percent, but in Poland these positions were reversed. In Latin America and in Pacific Asia, U.S. banks have a much larger market share than they have in other regions (see Table 4).

The home plays an important role even as market shares shift. In 1981, for example, Mexico raised some $20 billion in new debt, much of it short-term and much from Japanese banks. The fast, indeed excessive rise in

TABLE 4. *U.S. interests and U.S. banks' market shares*

	U.S. Banks' Market Share of All Cross-border Loans		
Regions	over 40%	30–39%	below 30%
a. Distribution of U.S. banks' loans as of 30 June 1979			
Latin America	31.1%	20.3%	0.1%
Pacific Asia	13.6	4.8	—
South Asia	—	0.2	0.8
Mideast	0.2	0.8	3.8
Africa: anglophone	0.1	—	3.3
Africa: francophone	—	0.1	4.2
Western Europe[a]	—	4.1	6.5
Eastern Europe	—	—	6.4
TOTAL	45.0%[b]	30.0%	25.1%
b. Distribution of U.S. banks' loans as of 31 December 1982			
Latin America	19.7%	37.5%	0.2%
Pacific Asia	13.3	2.9	—
South Asia	—	0.6	0.7
Mideast	—	1.6	1.5
Africa: anglophone	0.1	0.2	3.8
Africa: francophone	—	—	1.9
Western Europe[a]	—	1.1	9.4
Eastern Europe	—	—	3.2
TOTAL	33.1%	43.9%	20.6%

a. Developing countries in Europe are Greece, Spain, Portugal, Yugoslavia.
b. That is, 45.0% of all U.S. banks' claims are in countries where the U.S. market share (i.e., the U.S. share of all cross-border loans) exceeds 40%.
Sources. For U.S. banks, Federal Financial Institutions Examinations Council, Statistical Release E.16, semiannual. For all banks, Bank for International Settlements, "The Maturity Distribution of International Bank Lending," semiannual.

lending did not occur merely because Japanese banks with surplus funds overloaned in ignorance of one anothers' activities, as an explanation built on market inefficiencies would suggest. Rather, the Japanese government began to strengthen ties with Mexico after the second oil shock in 1979 to secure another source of oil, and as part of that move Japanese banks were encouraged to lend to Mexico. The Japanese government thus lowered risk by sponsoring big projects in Mexico—but, as noted above, home regulations placed a ceiling on the banks' medium- and long-term credit. So Japanese banks switched to short-term debt. As this case illustrates, one must understand the dynamic at home to understand why the banks loaned as they did.

Home affiliation is important in debt crises. Banks from particular countries group together and act in concert during the workouts: U.S. banks led the Mexican rescheduling (indeed, the Latin American reschedulings), German banks led the Polish rescheduling. Existing exposure does not adequately account for this pattern. If it did, one would expect the banks' role in re-structurings to reflect the degree of their exposure. In Mexico, however, the Japanese banks as a group had the second-largest exposure but did not take an active leadership role in the restructuring. In contrast, French as well as German banks were active in the Polish restructuring.

As home governments were caught up in the debt crises, transnational conventions—which had seemed to create a community of international banks during the 1970s—broke down. Sometimes the breakdown occurred because of contradictions in those very conventions, sometimes because of problems in banks' home countries. In either case coalitions formed around the home. One example is the Brazil rescheduling.

In the case of Brazil a major conflict arose over the treatment of interbank deposits placed with Brazilian banks outside Brazil. The conflict split creditors along home-country lines. For the banks and governments of some countries, the interbank market, particularly for developing countries, was more important than the medium-term or sovereign-risk markets. To protect not merely their interbank loans to Brazil but their worldwide interbank operations, Swiss banks and the Swiss government actively opposed efforts that would have kept them in the long-term rescheduling. The French government, having just nationalized many banks, felt too weak at home to oppose smaller French banks that wanted to pull out their interbank loans to Brazil. The Swiss and the French banks were in a sense opposing conventions built around the syndicate model. Banks from the same homes successfully distinguished the treatment of short-term interbank lenders from that of medium-term lenders.

National differences affect the stability of the international system. The enforcement of credit ceilings, coupled with a well-articulated Japanese interest in Mexico, led Japanese banks to lend too much in the short term, as described above. In general, different systemic costs and resource allocation (such as high leverage, implicit guarantees, export credits) encouraged excessive lending. Protection of the banks impeded market forces that would have led to equilibrium.

In sum, political issues at home have logical implications for international lending. If their home government is most concerned about the threat to the home financial system, then the logic for big banks is to lend big. Their instability will threaten the home, and their home government will step in. If, on the other hand, the government is most concerned about the importance of the debtor country to the home's economy and security, then the big banks should choose to lend to countries that are strategically important to their home.

International lending patterns suggest that the banks do indeed anticipate the economic and security interests of their home country in debtor nations. From 1979 to 1982, for example, U.S. banks retained a relatively higher market share in Latin America and Pacific Asia, which are zones of U.S. interest for trade, investment, and security reasons (see Table 4). This pattern, in turn, suggests that the banks responded to home interests rather than leading them. Recall that the U.S. government helped Mexico faster than Brazil, though both owed equally large amounts to the banks. It appears that the banks can help cement their home's interest in a borrowing country, but that other home interests are also important. Trade and investment ties, proximity, and the country's importance to the security interests of the home country have a crucial bearing on whether the home government will take extraordinary action when a borrowing country gets into trouble.

This rationale for lending destabilizes the world economy. There is no clear consensus about who has responsibility for particular regions. For instance, other governments, as much as or more than their banks, have pushed the United States to assume greater responsibility for working out the Latin American debt. The position of the European and Japanese governments reflects their perception of the regional dominance of the United States. The United States, however, wants the others to provide more support.

That home governments play different roles in workouts underlines the importance of the home in international credit. As I have argued, the enduring economic and political ties of banks to their home country go to the heart of the factors that affect business decisions most profoundly: cost and control. As lending grew, the banks influenced, and were influenced by, these ties. Cost reduction, protection, regulation, and help in debt crises shape the banks' competitive position in world credit markets. All of these factors involve the home government, raising political issues for banks at home in which their international status is often irrelevant. To understand the flow of credit across borders, one must understand the dynamic relationship between the banks and their homes.

International debt and linkage strategies: some foreign-policy implications for the United States   Benjamin J. Cohen

Recent debt crises in Eastern Europe and the Third World have vividly highlighted the close connections between high finance and high politics. "Money brings honor, friends, conquest, and realms," said John Milton; or, as the old French proverb puts it, "l'argent fait le jeu"—money talks. The connections, however, are anything but simple. Money may talk but it does so, as it were, out of both sides of its mouth. The game that money makes is a highly complex one in which it is not at all clear who conquers, who is conquered, or even what conquest means.

My purpose in this article is to explore some of the foreign-policy implications of international debt from the point of view of a major creditor country. Specifically, my focus is on the United States, whose banks have been among the heaviest lenders to sovereign borrowers in recent years. Foreign policy, in this analysis, is understood to encompass the full range of strategies and actions developed by the U.S. government's decision makers in America's relations with other nations. Foreign policy aims to achieve specific goals defined in terms of national interests as decision makers themselves perceive them. National interests may include economic objectives no less than political or security concerns. The central issue for analysis is the extent to which, if at all, the global debt problem has influenced the power of the U.S. government in foreign affairs, power being understood to imply leverage or control not only over resources and actors but also over the outcome of events. Has the global debt problem altered the ability of public officials in Washington to realize their foreign-policy preferences?

What makes this question analytically interesting is the fact that most international debt is owed to private creditors rather than to governments or multilateral agencies. Following the first oil shock in 1973 the private

---

An earlier version was presented at the Lehrman Institute, New York City, in the spring of 1984 as part of its seminar series on Politics and International Debt, which was supported in part by a grant from the Ford Foundation and directed by Miles Kahler of Yale University.

financial markets, and in particular the major commercial banks, became the principal source of external finance for much of Eastern Europe and the Third World, and banks have been intimately involved in all of the major debt crises of recent years. In short, banks have become full participants in the realm of foreign policy: they are now important independent actors on the world stage. Yet there is no assurance at all that the banks' interpretation of their private interests in the marketplace will necessarily converge with the public interest as interpreted by policy makers in Washington. As one astute observer has commented, "U.S. foreign policy actions and the overseas activities of the private banks have come increasingly to overlap. The interests of the two sides do not always coincide and indeed may at times be contradictory."[1] Or to quote Ronald Reagan's first under secretary of state for economic affairs,

> There are areas of shared interests . . . as well as areas of potential friction. . . . The bankers must be guided by the interests of their stockholders. . . . Governments, on the other hand, are guided by a mix of political, humanitarian, strategic and economic objectives. . . . Banks may differ with government in their assessment of political factors. . . .[2]

In formal terms the situation described here corresponds to Robert Keohane and Joseph Nye's "complex interdependence," in which direct interstate relations are affected by the presence of important transnational actors, including banks. As Keohane and Nye write, "These actors are important not only because of their activities in pursuit of their own interests, but also because they act as transmission belts, making government policies in various countries more sensitive to one another."[3] Certainly the lending practices of banks, insofar as they have contributed to the origin or exacerbation of the debt problem, have increased the mutual sensitivities of the United States and major sovereign debtors and complicated considerably the U.S. government's pursuit of policy objectives in relation to those countries. Complex interdependence, Keohane and Nye remind us, means that power in foreign policy must be exercised through a political bargaining process. The participation of banks in the process, with their own interests to pursue, can significantly affect outcomes. Through their ongoing commercial decisions vis-à-vis sovereign debtors, the banks affect the general foreign-policy environment—and their effects may substantially alter the issues of salience for policy or the nature and scope of policy options available to government officials.

In short, high finance intersects with high politics. Strategic interactions

1. Karin Lissakers, "Money and Manipulation," *Foreign Policy* no. 44 (Autumn 1981), p. 123.
2. Meyer Rashish, "Bank Lending Overseas Has Become Intertwined with Politics," *American Banker*, 15 January 1982, pp. 4–5.
3. Robert O. Keohane and Joseph S. Nye, *Power and Interdependence: World Politics in Transition* (Boston: Little, Brown, 1977), p. 26.

between governments—the traditional focus of foreign-policy analysis—are increasingly linked with strategic interactions between public and private institutions in both debtor and creditor countries. The roster of players in the "money game" is rich and varied.

From the point of view of a major creditor country, such as the United States, the principal impact of these interactions is on the number and substance of potential "linkages" in foreign policy (that is, the joining for bargaining purposes of otherwise unrelated policy instruments or issues). Policy makers may be forced to make connections between different policy instruments or issues that might not otherwise have been felt necessary; opportunities for connections may be created that might not otherwise have been thought possible. In a world of complex interdependence power in foreign affairs is very much a function of a government's "linkage strategies"—that is, how well the government can make use of instruments or issues where its bargaining position is relatively strong in order to promote or defend interests where it is weaker.[4] These considerations shape the analysis to follow. My discussion will center on the implications that the global debt problem holds for the linkage strategies of the United States as a major creditor country.

I start by introducing some general considerations that bear on the relationship between international debt and the foreign-policy capabilities of the United States. The discussion is deliberately abstract, in effect creating a set of empty analytic "boxes." In the following three sections I attempt to put some empirical content into those boxes by looking at a limited selection of recent experiences—the Polish debt crisis of 1981–82, the Latin American debt crisis (or crises) of 1982–83, and the International Monetary Fund quota increase of 1983. In all three cases the cutoff point for discussion is mid-1984. The treatment in the three sections is necessarily cursory but nonetheless suggestive. I conclude the article with a brief summary of conclusions and implications for the politics of stabilization of the international financial system.

1. Debt and foreign policy

The intersection of high finance and high politics in the context of the global debt problem highlights the potential for reciprocal influences between governments and banks.[5] Changes that banks induce in a government's decision-

---

4. Ibid., pp. 30–32.
5. Surprisingly, there have been few formal attempts by scholars to explore systematically, in a foreign-policy context, the question of reciprocal influences between governments and banks. But see Jonathan David Aronson, *Money and Power: Banks and the World Monetary System* (Beverly Hills: Sage, 1977); Janet Kelly, "International Capital Markets: Power and Security in the International System," *Orbis* 21 (Winter 1978), pp. 843–74; and J. Andrew Spindler, *The Politics of International Credit* (Washington, D.C.: Brookings, 1984).

making environment may alter foreign-policy capabilities; in turn, a government may be able to supplement its power resources by relating bank decisions, directly or indirectly, to foreign-policy considerations. Either form of influence could affect the power of a government in foreign affairs, but neither can be predicted a priori with any confidence.

Some observers do not doubt that the banks' lending practices in Eastern Europe and the Third World have weakened the ability of the U.S. government to realize its foreign-policy preferences. By their decisions affecting sovereign borrowers—to lend or reschedule debt? to which countries? how much? when? at what cost? under what conditions (if any)?—banks establish priorities among capital-importing nations that amount, in effect, to decisions about foreign aid. And since these decisions may depart quite substantially from the goals and priorities of official policy, they can significantly hamper the effectiveness of existing policy instruments. The government may find it more difficult to support or reward its friends or to thwart or punish its enemies. Generous debt assistance to countries with poor records on human rights, for instance, or to regimes that support international terrorism may easily undermine efforts by Washington to exercise influence through the withholding of public moneys; states deemed vital to U.S. security interests may be seriously destabilized if they are suddenly "red-lined" by the financial community. Contends Congressman Jim Leach of Iowa, "The large money center banks are the true foreign aid policy makers of the United States."[6]

Clearly, there is some truth in this charge. As the *Banker* has commented, "bankers assume a political role . . . through the mere act of lending on any large scale. The provision of finance to sovereign borrowers . . . immediately involves financial intermediaries in passively helping to determine priorities."[7] But equally clearly, it is an exaggeration to argue, as Jack Zwick and Richard Goeltz do, that therefore "private banks are effectively making United States foreign economic policy."[8] Public officials still make policy. What has changed is the nature of the constraints and opportunities that now confront those public officials in the international arena. It is not at all clear that these changes are, on balance, necessarily disadvantageous for foreign policy.

In the first place is an empirical question: How serious is the problem? The fact that banks *may* establish priorities at variance with the goals of official policy does not mean that they inevitably *will* do so. Banks naturally pay attention to foreign relations in the ordinary course of business and, to some extent at least, tailor their commercial decisions accordingly. It is obvious that insofar as movements of finance correlate positively with movements of the diplomatic barometer, bank decisions may actually enhance rather than diminish the effectiveness of existing foreign-policy instruments. The

6. As quoted in *New York Times*, 11 November 1982, p. D3.
7. "The Politics of Banking," *Banker*, September 1977, p. 21.
8. Jack Zwick and Richard K. Goeltz, "U.S. Banks Are Making Foreign Policy," *New York Times*, 18 March 1979.

drying up of private credits in Chile, for example, undoubtedly strengthened the Nixon administration's campaign against Salvador Allende after his election in 1971. Current U.S. government support of such strategic allies as South Korea and the Philippines is undoubtedly reinforced by a continued high level of bank lending there. Sometimes private and public interests converge and sometimes, as we shall see in the discussions of Poland and Latin America, they do not.

Furthermore, even where bank operations appear to diverge from official priorities, the resulting impacts on policy effectiveness could turn out to be little more than trivial. To say that policy *could* be affected is not to say that any such influences are necessarily *significant*. That remains to be seen.

Finally, and most importantly, any impacts on foreign-policy capabilities will depend a great deal on the policy linkages that bank decisions generate. Debt-service difficulties are a natural breeding ground for policy linkages. When key sovereign borrowers get into trouble, Washington may feel forced to respond, however reluctantly, with some sort of support—in effect, to underwrite the debts in some way. Some borrowers are considered crucial for U.S. interests and cannot be ignored. As the Senate Foreign Relations Committee staff has written, America "has important security interests in other debtor countries.... It can hardly afford to stand by and watch the economies of these countries collapse, or to have their governments undermined politically by financial difficulties."[9] In other cases borrowers may stimulate concerns about possible repercussions on the health and stability of American banks or the wider financial or economic system. Either way, debtors gain a new kind of political leverage to extract from the U.S. government concessions that might not otherwise be obtainable. These concessions may be financial, trade, or even political.

Financial concessions are the most familiar variety. Back in 1979, for example, at a time of near-bankruptcy, Turkey was able to exploit its strategic position within NATO to persuade the United States and other Western allies to come to its rescue with pledges of special assistance totaling nearly one billion dollars. Subsequent aid packages for similar amounts were pledged for 1980 and 1981 as well.[10] Likewise, more recently, financial assistance has been arranged for several Latin American debtors when they had trouble meeting their obligations to foreign creditors.

There may also be trade concessions, which have been increasingly mooted lately despite strongly protectionist domestic pressures. U.S. policy makers have been forced to acknowledge the obvious linkage between trade and finance—that import liberalization by industrialized countries may be the only way to enable major borrowers to earn their way out of their debt morass. In the words of Meyer Rashish,

9. U.S. Senate, Committee on Foreign Relations, *International Debt, the Banks, and U.S. Foreign Policy*, A Staff Report (Washington, D.C., 1977), p. 7.
10. *IMF Survey*, 18 May 1981, p. 162.

We must face the interdependence of the financial and trading systems. External debt only makes sense if the borrower has a reasonable prospect for servicing the debt by exporting goods and services to the lenders. . . . Ultimately, we, the lenders, will be confronted with a decision —either to open our markets in order to provide outlets to the borrowers for their exports, thus generating revenues in the borrowing countries for debt repayment, or to yield to protectionist pressures and be forced to deal with resultant financial failures. . . .[11]

Finally, even political concessions may be felt necessary. In 1977 the Senate Foreign Relations Committee staff worried that "there appears to be a direct correlation between economic hardship and political repression in many countries. The Carter Administration may therefore have to choose between pressing its international human rights effort, and supporting creditor demands for drastic austerity programs that can only be achieved at the expense of civil liberties in the countries that undertake them."[12] In the first half of the 1980s this dilemma confronted the Reagan administration as well, in Latin America and elsewhere. In the case of the Philippines, for example, Asia's second-largest debtor to the banks, the United States clearly chose to maintain support for the martial law "New Society" of Ferdinand Marcos on broad foreign-policy grounds. U.S. policy makers justified strict Filipino controls, including the continued stifling of political opposition, by the need to preserve the financial viability of an important strategic ally.

Can we generalize about the implications of these policy linkages for the foreign-policy capabilities of the United States? I shall stress three considerations that bear on this question. First is the nature of the concessions themselves. Concessions are not necessarily disadvantageous. In fact, the constraints and opportunities created for the U.S. government's linkage strategies in individual instances may actually enhance rather than diminish U.S. power in foreign affairs. The constraints imposed by the debt problem are evident—the risks of possible financial disruption, loss of export markets, souring of political relations, or instability or disorder in areas of vital strategic importance. But opportunities to promote U.S. policy preferences may be generated as well. The key is whether debt-related concessions may be regarded as advantageous *outside the immediate area of financial relations.* Do the concessions, while effectively underwriting debt, also serve to reinforce other U.S. policy interests? Or do they work at cross-purposes, demanding trade-offs among interests? Concessions will be disadvantageous only when inconsistent with other foreign-policy objectives.

Of crucial importance in this connection is whether U.S. relations with troubled debtors are adversarial or not. Where relations are adversarial, as they were in the case of Poland, efforts to cope with debt-service difficulties

11. Rashish, "Bank Lending Overseas," p. 6.
12. Committee on Foreign Relations, *International Debt,* p. 7.

Debt and U.S. policy 133

may actually undermine the effectiveness or credibility of other policy measures, weakening U.S. power in foreign affairs. Concessions in such instances may be regarded as disadvantageous. But where relations are nonconflictual, as in Latin America, helping others can, under appropriate circumstances, also help ourselves. Concessions may be of mutual benefit and may even lead to matching political or economic concessions from debtor governments. In such instances a potential certainly exists for promoting foreign-policy preferences.

A second consideration bearing on policy linkages is whether, or to what extent, the government may be able to supplement its own power resources by relating bank decisions, directly or indirectly, to foreign-policy considerations. Insofar as bank behavior has a significant influence on the general foreign-policy environment, public officials could, hypothetically at least, try to alter that behavior to conform more closely to policy objectives—in effect, to deploy the banks as part of the government's broader linkage strategies. How effective are such attempts likely to be in reality?

In principle the international activities of American banks are supposed to be independent of politics. But in practice political considerations are rarely absent, even if in most instances they remain fairly subtle. At times they become overt. The U.S. government has long had an arsenal of policy instruments available in order, when deemed appropriate, to relate the commercial activities of U.S. banks to foreign-policy questions; among those instruments are loan guaranty programs, restrictions, and outright prohibitions as well as prudential supervision, general monetary policy, and "moral suasion." During the years of the Cold War, for instance, loans to communist governments were strictly prohibited on political grounds (as they still are to Cambodia, Cuba, North Korea, and Vietnam). The prohibitions were reversed with the coming of detente. At their summit conference in 1972 Leonid Brezhnev and Richard Nixon declared that "the USA and the USSR regard commercial and economic ties as an important and necessary element in the strengthening of their bilateral relations and thus will actively promote the growth of such ties." Quite clearly the activity was to include promotion of credits from American and other Western banks. By mid-1982 U.S. banks alone had built up an exposure in Soviet-bloc countries in excess of $7 billion. The exposure of all Western (including Japanese) banks was in excess of $60 billion.

Other examples can also be cited. Prohibitions on lending were employed in support of UN sanctions against Rhodesia, for instance, in the years following that colony's unilateral declaration of independence as well as in support of Washington's economic sanctions against the revolutionary government of Iran during the months of the hostage crisis. Conversely, in early 1982 the State Department went out of its way to make plain its hope that banks would keep open their credit lines to Yugoslavia, lest that nation be driven closer to the Soviet Union.[13]

But the fact that such efforts are not unprecedented does not mean that they are uncontroversial. On the contrary, any attempts by Washington to influence bank behavior on foreign-policy grounds—either to encourage or discourage lending, to individual debtor countries or in general—have tended to generate lively public debate. Some observers, indeed, feel that the only problem is that the U.S. government has not gone far enough to link foreign policy and the commercial decisions of American banks. As Zwick and Goeltz argue, "This step must be taken to preserve not only the financial integrity of the banking system but also the discretion of the Government in the formulation of foreign policy."[14] For others, Robert Russell among them, the problem is precisely the opposite: "It would seem better to keep public policy and private investment at arm's length to the extent possible. . . . Injecting foreign policy considerations into private bank decision making . . . seems likely to exacerbate both the problems of foreign policy and bank soundness."[15]

The key issue here is effectiveness. *Can* public officials effectively influence the commercial decisions of banks? In an era when much of the international activity of American banks takes place beyond Washington's direct jurisdictional reach in an almost totally unregulated environment (the Eurocurrency market), the answer is no simple matter. Today most foreign lending takes the form of bank credits booked through financial centers where official supervision is by definition minimal. Moreover, with the evolution of the Eurocurrency market has come a blurring of the strictly national identity of banking institutions. The largest part of bank credits is now the product of syndicates of mixed nationality. The ease and intimacy with which financiers from different countries work together today would have seemed unthinkable, if not treasonous, three-quarters of a century ago. As a result it is difficult indeed for Washington effectively to control or manipulate bank behavior on foreign-policy grounds.

But it is not impossible; government officials are not entirely without leverage. In the first place, while national identity may have become blurred, it has certainly not been forgotten. As Herbert Feis wrote half a century ago, "Bankers are subject to the forces of national feeling as are their fellow men."[16] The men and women who run America's largest banks can still be moved by "moral suasion" when the national interest appears to be at stake.

13. "State Department Calls in U.S. Bankers to Warn against Cutting off Yugoslavia," *Wall Street Journal*, 22 April 1982, p. 33.

14. Zwick and Goeltz, "U.S. Banks Are Making."

15. Robert W. Russell, "Three Windows on LDC Debt: LDCs, the Banks, and the United States National Interest," in Lawrence G. Franko and Marilyn G. Seiber, eds., *Developing Country Debt* (Elmsford, N.Y.: Pergamon, 1979), pp. 263–264.

16. Herbert Feis, *Europe, the World's Banker, 1870–1914* (1930; rpt. New York: Norton, 1965), p. 468.

Debt and U.S. policy 135

Furthermore, despite the extent of their overseas operations, the banks are still ultimately dependent on a domestic financial base and subject to the influence of domestic monetary policy and prudential supervision. What is implied, however, is that any government attempts at leverage are likely to be effective only within rather broad limits—that is, control is likely to be "loose" rather than "tight." As we shall see, control is especially likely to be loose when the government aims in individual instances to encourage rather than to discourage lending.

The third and final consideration bearing on the question of policy linkages is whether, or to what extent, Washington might be able to supplement its power resources by pursuing policy objectives through the intermediation of a multilateral agency such as the International Monetary Fund—in effect, to deploy the Fund as part of the government's broader linkage strategies. Because of the global debt problem, the IMF has gained considerable leverage over the behavior of both debtor governments and banks. But the Fund itself is subject to substantial leverage from the U.S. government, which still retains unparalleled influence over IMF decision making. In effect, therefore, an opportunity seems to have been created for U.S. policy makers to accomplish indirectly, via the IMF, what they cannot accomplish (or can accomplish only at a higher economic or political cost) on a direct, bilateral basis.

2. Solidarity suppressed

The Polish debt crisis of 1981–82 provides a particularly apt case for empirical investigation. Rarely in recent American experience have the complex connections between high finance and high politics been quite so manifest. After the rise of the Solidarity trade union movement in 1980, Poland became the touchstone for U.S. foreign policy in Eastern Europe. Yet Washington's ability to exercise leverage over the course of events in that troubled country was plainly compromised by the high level of Western bank exposure in Poland. Polish debt added to the difficulties experienced by the United States in trying to prevent suppression of Solidarity after martial law was declared in December 1981.

Even before December 1981 Polish debt was becoming a problem. As early as 1979 Poland's economy had stopped growing, in good part because of a deterioration of export revenues; and in 1980 and 1981 national income actually dropped at a rate of 5 percent a year. To maintain imports, Warsaw resorted to accelerated borrowing from the West. As a result, between 1978 and 1981 Polish foreign debt increased by nearly half, from under $18 billion to an estimated $26 billion; and its debt-service ratio (the ratio of interest and amortization to export revenues) more than doubled, from an already

136   *Benjamin J. Cohen*

high 79 percent to an incredible 173 percent.[17] By the start of 1981 it was
an open secret that Poland could not meet its scheduled obligations. Warsaw
formally notified its creditors in March that it would no longer be able to
guarantee debt service.

At the time the attitude of the U.S. government was clear: do everything
possible to avoid destabilizing the situation inside Poland, and do nothing
to jeopardize the achievements of Solidarity. Throughout 1981, therefore,
Washington maintained an essentially benevolent posture toward the Polish
debt problem. While it contemplated no massive new credits, it did undertake
several actions to ease Warsaw's financial difficulties. As early as the previous
summer, in an obvious attempt at a linkage strategy, Washington had openly
pressured American banks to keep a substantial refinancing loan from failing.
(Washington was not alone in this instance: in Bonn the West German chancellor, Helmut Schmidt, personally telephoned the presidents of the three
largest German banks to back a similar Polish loan.) And in April 1981 the
United States joined with fourteen other industrial nations (later fifteen) in
agreeing to postpone for four years $2.3 billion of Polish debt payments due
in 1981 to official creditors. In the first week of December, after some difficult
negotiations, there followed an agreement among Western banks to reschedule
$2.4 billion of commercial debt due in 1981 as well. The concurrence of
Western banks was crucial inasmuch as almost two-thirds of Poland's debt—
some $16 billion—was owed to private lenders, reflecting a decade's growth
in Western bank lending to the East. West German banks held the largest
amount—about $6 billion. American banks accounted for about $3 billion.[18]
The December 1981 rescheduling was made contingent on Poland's payment
of $500 million in interest obligations for the last three months of 1981.

In addition, in the spring of 1981 the Commodity Credit Corporation
(CCC) of the U.S. Department of Agriculture raised the interest-rate guarantee
for private agricultural export credits to Poland (used to finance grain sales)
from 8 percent to 12 percent; this exceptional provision for the Poles was
not generalized to any other country. And even as late as early December
plans were going forward for $100 million of new CCC credits that would
have fully guaranteed, for the first time and for any country, all interest
payments as well as principal.[19]

But then came General Jaruzelski's declaration of martial law on 13 December 1981, followed by suppression of Solidarity. Washington's attitude
quickly hardened. Western governments immediately suspended talks with
the Jaruzelski regime about a possible rescheduling of Poland's 1982 debt
to official creditors, at Washington's behest, and numerous other economic

17. U.S. Treasury and State Department Fact Sheet on Polish Debt, in U.S. Senate, Committee
on Foreign Relations, Subcommittee on European Affairs, *The Polish Economy*, Hearings, 17
January 1982 (hereafter *Polish Economy Hearings*), p. 12.
18. *New York Times*, 5 December 1981.
19. Interview, U.S. State Department, August 1984.

sanctions were levied against both Poland and the Soviet Union, including termination of all subsidized food shipments and most U.S. government-guaranteed bank credits to Poland (including the planned new CCC credits), restrictions on Polish fishing rights in American waters, suspension of talks (due to have begun in February 1982) with the Soviet Union on a new long-term grain agreement, and an embargo on materials for Russia's natural-gas pipeline from Siberia to Western Europe. The aims of the sanctions were clear—to persuade Poland and its patron the Soviet Union to end martial law, free all political prisoners, and restore Solidarity to its previous domestic status. Pressure would be maintained, the Reagan administration insisted, until these goals were achieved. In the words of the assistant secretary of state at the time, Robert Hormats,

> In these circumstances, our continuing objective is to apply sustained pressure on both Poland and the Soviet Union to have martial law lifted, the prisoners released, and the dialog between the government, the church and Solidarity begun in earnest in a free atmosphere. In short, our goal is the restoration of the process of reform and renewal in Poland.[20]

The impact of the sanctions, however, was diluted by the continuing problem of Poland's debt. For 1982 alone the country was estimated to owe Western creditors a total of $10.4 billion in principal and interest—yet Warsaw had still not even gotten current on the interest due for its rescheduled 1981 debt.[21] Clearly, some additional relief would be required if default were to be avoided, and Washington had no desire to precipitate a Western banking crisis. It was recognized, of course, that the direct exposure of Western banks was not large (certainly not as compared with their exposure in Latin America or the Far East). Of the $16 billion of outstanding bank claims on Poland, almost half (about $7 billion) was guaranteed by creditor governments. Of the $3 billion owed to American banks, the CCC guaranteed $1.6 billion, and the remainder was spread so thinly among some sixty institutions that for most American banks guarantee-adjusted exposure amounted to less than 5 percent of capital.[22] The fear of financial disruption was nevertheless genuine. Who knew what might happen if a major debtor like Poland were compelled to default?

The biggest question was whether a default could be contained. Many U.S. officials were concerned about the possibility of a "domino effect"—a scramble by banks to reduce their exposure elsewhere in Eastern Europe, which might lead to a chain reaction of defaults throughout the region, and perhaps in

---

20. Robert Hormats, "Statement," *Polish Economy Hearings*, p. 4.
21. Treasury and State Department Fact Sheet, *Polish Economy Hearings*, p. 12.
22. Ibid., pp. 11–12. Bank capital is defined to include shareholders' equity, undistributed profits, and reserves for contingencies and other capital reserves—in essence, what a bank would have after paying off depositors and creditors.

other areas of the world as well, endangering the entire Western banking structure. The flow of new bank credits to other Soviet bloc countries, as well as to Yugoslavia, had already started drying up as a result of Poland's debt-service difficulties.[23] American policy makers were convinced by their conversations with bankers that their fears of a regional "contagion" were not unfounded.[24] Banks, after all, had their own interests to protect.

Indeed, Washington's concern was such that despite its tough rhetoric, it even started servicing some of Poland's debt itself when Warsaw failed to meet payments due on part of its $1.6 billion of CCC-guaranteed credits beginning in January 1982.[25] In such an instance creditor banks would ordinarily have been required to declare the debtor formally in default in order to qualify for CCC payments. But in this case, for the first time ever, the Reagan administration circumvented the legal requirement by quietly adopting an emergency waiver to avoid triggering cross-default clauses in other bank loans to Poland. In effect, by meeting the CCC's guarantees and then transferring the overdue credits to its own books, the U.S. government unilaterally rescheduled a portion of Poland's debt. Most importantly, it did so *unconditionally*, without extracting any price from Warsaw—no formal default, no attempt to attach Polish assets, not even a public announcement. From a foreign-policy point of view this action was undoubtedly the turning point of the whole affair.

The CCC decision did not go unopposed within the administration. Defense Department officials in particular, led by Under Secretary for Policy Fred Iklé, argued vigorously for maintaining the hardest possible line vis-à-vis Poland, up to and including a formal declaration of default. But the prevailing view among policy makers, reflecting a de facto coalition of the Treasury and State departments, ruled out default under almost any circumstance, for three principal reasons. First was the fear of financial disruption, described above. Second was a fear of political disruption in the Western alliance, reflecting Western Europe's far greater loan exposure in Poland (amounting, in fact, to about three-quarters of all Polish debt). Given that West European banks and governments had so much more of an investment to protect, there was a considerable risk that they might respond favorably to any Polish overture to negotiate a separate deal. American bankers were especially concerned about the prospect. As a confidential working document prepared by one large U.S. bank warned, "There is every reason to believe that European banks and governments would cooperate with the Poles. . . . There is [therefore] not only a significant probability that such a default action would fail, but it would also impose massive costs on the alliance."[26]

Finally, there was a fear of losing a possible instrument of leverage over

23. See, for example, *New York Times*, 26 May 1982, p. D1.
24. Interview, U.S. State Department, August 1984.
25. *New York Times*, 1 February 1982, p. 1.
26. "Polish Default: Bankers' Perspectives on the Issues," 22 March 1982, p. 4.

Debt and U.S. policy 139

the Poles. Policy makers reasoned that by taking over the debt itself, Washington could actually hope to reinforce its pressure on the Jaruzelski regime — "keep Poland's feet to the fire," to quote a leaked State Department memorandum. With new lending at a standstill, Warsaw's interest payments represented a net transfer of financial resources *to the West*. A formal declaration of default, however satisfying to the emotions, would only have relieved the Poles of that burden. The Jaruzelski regime would no longer have had to find precious foreign exchange to meet its debt-service obligations to Western banks. Instead, the martial-law regime would have been freed to consolidate its authority with even greater force and harshness. According to one administration official, "keeping the pressure on this way is the real hard line."[27] The view was summarized by Assistant Treasury Secretary Marc Leland:

> What should we do about the debt? Our feeling is that we should try to collect it. The more pressure we can thereby put on the East Europeans, particularly on the Soviet Union, to come up with the funds to help Poland, the better....
>
> To maintain maximum leverage ... they should be held to the normal commercial concept that they owe us this money, so they should come up with it....
>
> In this way we hope to maintain the maximum amount of pressure on them to try to roll back the actions of December 13th and to enter into an internal political dialog.[28]

The proof of the pudding, however, is not to be found in the chef's fine words. In practice this "real hard line" proved scarcely effective at all, and it may even have been counterproductive in Washington's attempt to exercise leverage over the Poles. For once having signaled the depth of its apprehensions about default in its decision to pay off CCC-guaranteed credits unconditionally, the U.S. administration actually made itself *more* vulnerable to the threat of financial disruption; and the Jaruzelski regime was not above making veiled hints about possible default as a form of policy leverage of its own.[29] Washington's constraint, in effect, became Warsaw's opportunity. Western bank assets could be held as a sort of hostage, and perhaps a wedge could be driven between the U.S. government and its West European allies. The CCC decision handed the Poles, despite their desperate economic straits, some additional room for maneuver.

At a minimum, the action strained the credibility of the Reagan administration's commitment to sanctions. The key question at the time was why the CCC guarantees were paid off unconditionally. Observers were entitled to ask why no quid pro quo of any kind was demanded of the Poles, for

---

27. As quoted in *New York Times*, 1 February 1982, p. 1.
28. Marc Leland, "Statement," *Polish Economy Hearings*, p. 7.
29. See, for example, *New York Times*, 8 June 1982, p. D1.

140   *Benjamin J. Cohen*

instance, by attaching some of their foreign assets as collateral for eventual repayment. Officials argued that few such assets were available: perhaps a few airplanes and ships plus some meager hard-currency reserves. But their response missed the symbolic value of the opportunity thus lost. Psychologically, the appearance of vacillation by policy makers quickly dissipated the impact of Washington's sanctions. What was left was an impression — right or wrong — that the administration, simply put, was more concerned about a Western banking crisis than it was about the future of Solidarity. Public perceptions at the time were accurately, if colorfully, summarized by columnist William Safire:

> The secret regulation giving the junta extraordinarily lenient treatment makes a mockery of pretensions of pressure.
>   In an eyeball-to-eyeball confrontation, the Reagan administration has just blinked. Poland's rulers can afford to dismiss the Reagan rhetoric because they have seen that the U.S. is ready to do regulatory nip-ups to save them from default.[30]

In the end, of course, as we know, the administration achieved few of its goals. Poland neither "came up with the money" nor "rolled back" the actions of 13 December. Martial law was formally lifted after two years, to be sure, but many of its key features still remain, now incorporated into Polish civil law. And while most political prisoners were released in 1984, Solidarity still remains an outlawed organization, replaced by tame government-sponsored trade unions. In short, the process of "reform and renewal" was not restored. Yet, one by one, most of the sanctions imposed so dramatically in 1981 were either eased or eliminated. In July 1983 a new long-term grain agreement with the Soviet Union was announced. In November 1983 the most stringent sanctions directed against the Soviet gas pipeline were lifted, and restrictions on Polish fishing rights were relaxed. And the following month Washington joined other Western governments in reopening the suspended talks with Poland on rescheduling some of its debt to official creditors.

Admittedly, apprehensions about default were by no means the only — or even the most important — reason for such seemingly conciliatory behavior. The Soviet grain agreement, for example, was best understood in terms of President Reagan's 1980 campaign promises to American farmers. Similarly, the easing of sanctions against the Soviet pipeline was most evidently motivated by a desire to improve roiled relations with Western European allies. Even the reopening of debt negotiations was a response, at least in part, to growing discontent on the part of other Western governments that viewed Washington's continued refusal to talk as essentially self-defeating. From the time discussions were first cut off, following the declaration of martial law,

30. William Safire, "Payoff for Repression," *New York Times*, 1 February 1982.

Debt and U.S. policy 141

Warsaw had suspended all payments of interest as well as principal on its official debt (although interest payments to banks were maintained, albeit with delays). As a result, U.S. allies began to argue, Poland was actually able to save precious foreign exchange, in effect at the expense of Western taxpayers. Other Western governments had initially gone along with the suspension of negotiations.[31] But as the situation dragged on, they eventually started to lobby the Reagan administration vigorously for agreement to an early resumption of talks.[32]

It must also be admitted that the easing of sanctions might have occurred even *without* apprehensions about default. The use of economic sanctions in pursuit of foreign-policy goals is a tricky business in the best of circumstances. The success rate of sanctions varies greatly, depending among other factors on the type of goals being pursued.[33] The more modest the policy changes targeted, the greater is the probability of success. Conversely, in instances where "major" policy changes have been sought, as in the Polish case, the evidence suggests that economic sanctions have rarely been effective. Washington was fighting an uphill battle. Even with *no* Western bank exposure in Poland, the Reagan administration would have experienced difficulties in trying to prevent the suppression of Solidarity.

Poland's debt, therefore, cannot be blamed per se for the evident failure of the administration's policies. Washington's leverage in the situation was at best limited. But debt can be blamed for adding to the administration's difficulties, by undermining the effectiveness and credibility of its other policy initiatives. The effort to avoid Polish default worked at cross-purposes with other policy interests. I would not go so far as to argue with John Van Meer that the default issue thus "allowed the tyranny of the debtor to replace the tyranny of police-state Communism as the key to Western calculations."[34] But I would contend that debt helped to undercut whatever power the U.S. government might otherwise have had in its confrontation with Warsaw. The negative effect of the linkage may have been only marginal, but it was not trivial. Foreign-policy capabilities were indeed diminished.

3. The debt storm in Latin America

In Latin America the situation was different. Although here too Washington feared financial disruption—indeed, such fears were rampant—the U.S. government's foreign-policy capabilities in the region were, for a time at least, enhanced rather than diminished by the sudden explosion of a debt crisis

---

31. Interview, U.S. State Department, August 1984.
32. See, for example, *New York Times*, 30 July 1983, p. 34.
33. Gary Clyde Hufbauer and Jeffrey J. Schott, *Economic Sanctions in Support of Foreign Policy Goals* (Washington: Institute for International Economics, 1983), pp. 73–75.
34. John Van Meer, "Banks, Tanks and Freedom," *Commentary*, December 1982, p. 17.

in 1982. The principal reason seems to have been that U.S. relations with the major Latin borrowers were at the time not adversarial, as they had been with Poland. Initially, this general sense of cooperation created an opportunity for Washington, through a series of financial concessions, to win considerable goodwill and influence for itself at comparatively little economic or political cost. Over time, however, these gains proved essentially transient. As the region's debt crisis wore on, and particularly as Washington's efforts to revive private lending to Latin America proved largely ineffective, relations grew gradually more strained. Two years after the crisis began, in mid-1984, the continued goodwill of our hemispheric neighbors appeared to depend on new concessions of some kind from Washington. Foreign-policy leverage, it seemed, needed nourishment to remain effective.

The roots of the Latin American crisis go back at least to the late 1960s, when a number of governments made a deliberate decision to finance accelerated domestic investment with borrowing from private and public institutions abroad—"indebted industrialization," in Jeff Frieden's phrase.[35] Then came the first oil shock, which spurred further borrowing to pay for higher-priced oil imports, and after 1976 a trend toward negative real interest rates in global financial markets, which whetted appetites even further. By the time of the second oil shock, at the end of the decade, many Latin governments had seemingly become addicted to foreign finance, and debt was piling up at a dizzying pace. By mid-1982 total debt in the region had swollen to an estimated $295 billion, including $90 billion in Mexico, $75 billion in Brazil, $30 billion each in Argentina and Venezuela, and $15 billion in Chile.[36] Two-thirds of the total was owed to private banks.

The banks, not surprisingly, were getting worried. Two years earlier they had already begun to shorten the maturities of new credits, hoping to position themselves to get their money out quickly should something go wrong. The policy would have been rational for any one creditor acting alone. With all banks doing the same thing, however, the practice merely added to the risks of lending in the region by greatly increasing the aggregate amount of debt that repeatedly had to be rolled over. By mid-1982, according to Morgan Guaranty Bank, the debt-service ratio (including amortization) of the five largest debtors had grown to 179 percent for Argentina, 129 percent for Mexico, 122 percent for Brazil, 116 percent for Chile, and 95 percent for Venezuela.[37] Interest payments alone for these five were expected to eat up from 35 to 45 percent of export revenues. Clearly, a storm was brewing.

The first threatening clouds appeared in early 1982, during the Falklands/

35. Jeff Frieden, "Third World Indebted Industrialization: International Finance and State Capitalism in Mexico, Brazil, Algeria, and South Korea," *International Organization* 35 (Summer 1981), pp. 407–31.
36. Pedro-Pablo Kuczynski, "Latin American Debt," *Foreign Affairs* 61 (Winter 1982–83), p. 349.
37. Morgan Guaranty Trust Company, *World Financial Markets*, October 1982, p. 5.

Debt and U.S. policy

Malvinas conflict, when Argentina began to fall behind on its debt service because of the British government's freeze of Argentinian assets in London. But the really rough weather did not set in until the middle of the year, when political and economic uncertainties in Mexico sparked a major capital flight. In June 1982 the Mexicans had still been able to raise $2.5 billion in the Eurocurrency market, albeit with considerable difficulty. By August, new private lending had ceased, the peso had to be devalued, and the government was forced to announce that it could no longer meet its scheduled repayments of principal on external public debt. Suddenly, one of the Third World's two largest debtors seemed on the edge of default, and the tempest had broken.

Like the cavalry of old the U.S. government rushed to the rescue (but this time *on behalf* of the Mexicans), quickly providing more than $2.5 billion of emergency assistance—$700 million via the Federal Reserve's swap arrangement with the Bank of Mexico, $1 billion from the Commodity Credit Corporation, and an advance payment of $1 billion on oil purchases by the Department of Energy for the U.S. Strategic Petroleum Reserve. In addition, the Treasury Department's Exchange Stabilization Fund (ESF) and the Federal Reserve together contributed about half of a $1.85 billion bridging facility provided through the Bank for International Settlements. And Washington also backed a proposed $3.9 billion credit from the International Monetary Fund.[38] By September the Mexican situation seemed, for the moment at least, in hand.

But the storm kept spreading. Largely because of the Mexican crisis, bank confidence sagged, new private lending dried up throughout Latin America, and soon other debtors in the region were finding themselves deep in trouble too. More rescue packages had to be organized. In the latter part of 1982 the ESF made some $1.23 billion available to Brazil. And in December and January bridging loans were arranged through the Bank for International Settlements, with substantial U.S. participation, for both Brazil and Argentina.[39] In addition banks were constantly exhorted by Treasury and Federal Reserve officials, in the name of the public interest, to resume their lending in the region despite already high exposure levels. Typical was a well-publicized speech by Federal Reserve chairman Paul Volcker in November 1982, in which he laid great stress on easing the difficulties of major Latin borrowers. "In such cases," he said, "new credits should not be subject to supervisory criticism."[40] Translated, his message was that considerations of banking prudence would not be allowed to prevail over the objective of keeping key debtors afloat. On the contrary, banks were reportedly threatened with closer

---

38. For detail, see Paul A. Volcker, "Statement," in U.S. House, Committee on Banking, Finance and Urban Affairs, *International Financial Markets and Related Problems*, Hearings, 2 February 1983, Appendix I, pp. 80–81
39. Ibid., pp. 81–83.
40. Paul A. Volcker, "Sustainable Recovery: Setting the Stage," Remarks before the New England Council, Boston, 16 November 1982 (processed), p. 17.

scrutiny of their books if they did *not* go along with fresh loans for countries like Mexico.[41] The pressures on the banks were not inconsiderable.

Nonetheless, they proved largely ineffective. Banks simply did not regard it as in their own interest to increase their exposure in the region significantly. In 1980 and 1981 total bank claims in Latin America had risen by some $30 billion a year. In the eighteen months from June 1982 to December 1983, by contrast, they increased by no more than $9 billion in all, less than the total of so-called "involuntary" lending arranged in connection with parallel IMF credits (discussed below), meaning that there was absolutely no "spontaneous" new lending at all.[42] Accordingly, no important borrower in the region was able to maintain debt service without some difficulty. All had to enter into protracted and difficult negotiations with private and public creditors, and most were forced to initiate painful—as well as politically risky—domestic austerity measures. In the words of Pedro-Pablo Kuczynski, "Undoubtedly, the interruption of significant new lending by commercial banks has been the major stimulus for such measures."[43]

Still, Washington continued to press the banks for a more accommodating attitude. One example was Argentina in late 1983 after that country's presidential election. According to the *New York Times*,

> The bankers . . . said that they were already coming under pressure from the United States . . . to aid the country's new democracy after nearly eight years of military rule. Many are resigned to making some concessions.
>
> "We don't want to look like the bad guys," one American banker said.[44]

Officials also urged the banks to consider limiting the interest rates they charged on loans to hard-pressed debtors. In another well-publicized speech in early 1984 Federal Reserve chairman Volcker suggested that "one of the things certainly worth looking at is what arrangements could be made so that one particular important threat to their financial stability, the continued rise in interest rates, could be dealt with."[45] What he had in mind was some kind of a cap on interest payments, with any excess of market rates over the cap being added to loan principal ("capitalization"). A specific proposal along these lines, for a cap tied to real interest rates, was floated by the Federal Reserve Bank of New York at a meeting of central bankers in May 1984, though nothing ever came of the idea.[46]

41. *New York Times*, 14 January 1983, p. D1.
42. Bank for International Settlements, *International Banking Developments, Fourth Quarter 1983* (Basle, April 1984).
43. Pedro-Pablo Kuczynski, "Latin American Debt: Act Two," *Foreign Affairs* 62 (Autumn 1983), p. 24.
44. *New York Times*, 5 November 1983, p. 46.
45. As quoted in ibid., 13 May 1984, p. 1.
46. Ibid., 11 May 1984, p. D2.

Debt and U.S. policy 145

Moreover, to encourage the banks Washington continued to put its own money where its mouth was, for example in the U.S. contribution to the IMF quota increase, finally approved by Congress in late 1983. Another example was the decision of the Export-Import Bank in the summer of 1983 to extend new loan guarantees of up to $1.5 billion to Brazil and $500 million to Mexico—the largest such package ever proposed by the Bank. William Draper, the Bank's president, made no secret of official intentions to prompt further private lending in these and other Latin countries. "We expect the proposed financing will strengthen the Mexican and Brazilian recovery," he said, "by acting as a catalyst for continuing support by the international financial community."[47] What was highly unusual about this initiative was that, unlike most guarantee proposals, these guarantees were not tied to specific projects. Clearly, the U.S. government wanted to send a signal.

It is not difficult to discern why the government took such an active role in the crisis. Latin America has always been regarded on broad foreign-policy grounds as a region vital to U.S. national interests. From the moment Mexico's difficulties began, there was never any doubt among policy makers that America's own security, not just Mexico's, was at stake—that the United States too would be threatened by serious economic or political instabilities south of its border. Nor was there any doubt that the contagion might spread to other Latin American nations as well. Washington simply could not ignore the potential for disorder in its own backyard that financial default might have sparked. As the *Economist* commented at the time,

> How to resolve these difficulties is one of the biggest foreign policy questions facing Washington, for behind Mexico there stretches a line of other burrodollar [sic] debtors. Brazil, Argentina and Venezuela between them owe $140 billion. The United States dare not risk the political consequences of calling default on any of them.... Those in the Reagan administration who have calmly contemplated pulling the plug on Poland's debt, which is only a third of Mexico's, have to recognize that the problem facing them in Latin America is far bigger.[48]

More narrowly, of course, policy makers were also worried about the direct risks to American banks, particularly the large money-center banks, whose loan exposure in Latin America far exceeded that in Poland. For Mexico alone, at the end of 1982, exposure in relation to capital exceeded 40 percent in nine of the twelve largest U.S. banks; taking Latin America's five biggest borrowers (Argentina, Brazil, Chile, Mexico, and Venezuela) together, the exposure of these same dozen banks ranged from a low of 82.5 percent of capital (Security Pacific) to a high of 262.8 percent (Manufacturers Hanover); most banks fell in a range of 140 to 180 percent.[49] The banking system was

47. As quoted in ibid., 18 August 1983, p. 1.
48. *Economist*, 21 August 1982, p. 11.
49. William R. Cline, *International Debt and the Stability of the World Economy*, Policy Analyses in International Economics no. 4 (Washington, D.C.: Institute for International Economics, September 1983), p. 34.

146   *Benjamin J. Cohen*

clearly vulnerable. If Poland had provoked fears of financial disruption, Latin America triggered nightmares.

Finally, there was also concern about U.S. trade interests in Latin America. By 1982 the region had surpassed all but Western Europe as a market for U.S. goods; Mexico alone was America's third-largest customer. Once the Mexican crisis broke, commerce and real-estate markets throughout the American Southwest were seriously damaged.[50] U.S. government officials never tired of stressing how many exports, and hence jobs, would be lost if something were not done for troubled debtors. Washington's motives were neatly summarized by Paul Volcker: "The effort to manage the international debt problem goes beyond vague and generalized concerns about political and economic stability of borrowing countries. . . . The effort encompasses also the protection of our own financial stability and the markets for what we produce best."[51]

It is hardly surprising, then, that the government would take so active a role. Nor is it surprising, given the reluctance of private banks to resume lending in the region, that Washington's concerns might give debtors the leverage to extract official concessions of some sort. What is striking is how much goodwill and influence were initially generated for the United States, and therefore how much easier it became to realize U.S. foreign-policy preferences. Officials in Washington reported a marked shift on the part of Latin governments toward a more accommodating spirit on various international issues.[52] The United States was now in a position to say, when looking for cooperation, that "we were there when you needed us, now we need you." In Brazil, Washington's efforts to help out financially were reported to have given the United States "more leverage . . . than it has enjoyed in more than a decade."[53] Suddenly the Brazilians were willing to talk about problems that had been roiling relations with the United States for years, most important among them nuclear policy and military cooperation. Likewise diplomats noted that Mexico toned down criticisms of U.S. policy in Central America; and also the Department of Energy was given permission to buy even more oil than originally agreed, at attractive prices, for the U.S. Strategic Petroleum Reserve.[54] In the short run Washington's investment in these countries' financial stability seemed to yield significant foreign-policy dividends.

But it did so only in the short run. As the debt crisis wore on, and domestic resistance to prolonged austerity measures grew, Latin governments were bound to grow more impatient. Riots and street demonstrations, as well as election results, suggested a decreasing tolerance for belt tightening in the region. Latin governments increasingly asked why the burden of adjustment

50. *New York Times*, 6 December 1982, p. D9.
51. As quoted in ibid., 4 June 1983, p. 29.
52. Interviews, U.S. Treasury, November 1983 and January 1984.
53. *New York Times*, 15 November 1982, p. D1.
54. *Miami Herald*, 30 August 1982.

Debt and U.S. policy 147

should fall entirely on the shoulders of the debtors. What was first perceived as generosity on Washington's part came to be viewed more as miserliness and insensitivity. U.S. concessions, it was noted, had been strictly financial and, for the most part, strictly short-term. (All of the loans included in the emergency packages for Argentina, Brazil, and Mexico, for example, had to be repaid within one year.) No trade concessions had been forthcoming at all—indeed barriers to key imports from Latin America, such as copper and steel, were on the rise—while at the same time rising U.S. interest rates, universally blamed on the Reagan administration's huge budget deficits, were adding to current debt-service burdens. Washington's emphasis on domestic "stabilization" translated, to Latin observers, into nothing more than retarded development, increased unemployment, and declining living standards. The risk was that this changing mood might eventually push Latin American governments toward alienation and confrontation with the United States. It could even lead to their replacement by regimes far less friendly to U.S. economic or security interests.

By 1984 the straws were in the wind. In May the presidents of four of the region's largest debtors—Argentina, Brazil, Colombia, and Mexico—meeting in Buenos Aires issued a joint statement warning that they "cannot indefinitely" accept the "hazards" of current approaches to the debt crisis. Expressing concern over the effects of "successive interest rate increases, prospects of new hikes and the proliferation and intensity of protectionist measures," they cautioned that "their peoples' yearning for development, the progress of democracy in their region and the economic security of their continent are seriously jeopardized."[55] Such sentiments were emphasized when eleven Latin debtors met in Cartagena, Colombia, in June and concluded with a plea to the United States and other creditor countries, as well as to the banks, to accept a greater share of the burden of adjustment. The dramas of Argentina and Venezuela, both of which had deliberately chosen to go into arrears on their debt rather than submit to harsh austerity programs, attested to the decline of patience in the region. And other regional governments were also considering a reordering of their domestic and foreign priorities. As a report of the Americas Society pointed out, "In virtually every Latin American and Caribbean country, there are major pressures to turn inward, . . . to turn their backs on existing obligations, and to look to solutions which stress a higher degree of protection and greater state control."[56] Washington's initial foreign-policy dividends in the region seemed after two years of crisis in danger of evaporating without a new investment of financial or trade concessions.

55. *New York Times*, 21 May 1984, p. D1.
56. Western Hemisphere Commission on Public Policy Implications of Foreign Debt, *Report* (New York: Americas Society, February 1984), pp. 19–20.

4. The role of the IMF

One issue raised by the gradual erosion of Washington's early gains in Latin America was whether the government's power resources, in the context of the global debt problem, could be supplemented through the intermediation of the International Monetary Fund—in effect, by using the IMF as an instrument of U.S. linkage strategy. The U.S. government's attitude toward the IMF changed dramatically over the first years of Ronald Reagan's presidency. Initially cool to any significant or rapid enlargement of Fund resources, the Reagan administration eventually became one of its strongest advocates. This policy shift appears to have reflected, at least in part, an altered perception of how a strong IMF might serve U.S. interests. Yet here too, as the crisis wore on, Washington's short-run gains in foreign policy came to be significantly eroded.

During its first year and a half the administration actively sought to discourage any early increase of Fund quotas (which determine a member-country's borrowing privileges). The Seventh General Review of Quotas, which raised quotas by half, from approximately SDR 40 billion to SDR 59.6 billion (the value of the SDR in recent years has ranged from $0.95 to $1.05), had just been completed in November 1980, and another review was not formally required before 1983. Yet it was clear that the IMF's usable resources would soon be running low. Mostly as a result of the second oil shock and the subsequent recession in the industrial world, deficits of non-oil-developing countries grew enormously, from $41 billion in 1978 to $89 billion in 1980 and $108 billion in 1981. Net borrowing from the Fund rose quickly, from under SDR 1 billion in 1978 (new loan commitments less repayments) to SDR 6.5 billion in 1980 and SDR 12 billion in 1981.[57] As early as the spring of 1981 the Fund's managing director, Jacques de Larosière, was warning of an impending threat to the Fund's own liquidity position. Without a new quota increase, he insisted, the Fund itself would need to borrow as much as SDR 6-7 billion annually to meet all of its prospective commitments.[58]

Nonetheless, the Reagan administration remained adamant. Its opposition was to a large extent rooted in a critical view of IMF lending practices as they had developed during the presidency of Reagan's predecessor, Jimmy Carter, particularly after the second oil shock. In early 1979 the Fund's Executive Board had issued a revised set of guidelines on conditionality that put new emphasis on the presumed "structural" nature of many members' balance-of-payments difficulties. The traditional period for a Fund standby arrangement had been one year. But the revised guidelines extended standbys for up to three years if considered "necessary," confirming the trend toward

---

57. *IMF Survey*, 6 February 1984, p. 40.
58. See, for example, ibid., 18 May 1981, p. 152.

longer adjustment periods already evident in programs financed through the Extended Fund Facility, first introduced in 1974, and the Supplementary Financing Facility (Witteveen Facility) established in 1977.[59] To the Reagan administration these changes smacked of development lending in disguise — totally inconsistent with the Fund's intended role as a limited revolving fund for strictly short-term assistance for balance-of-payments problems. The administration was especially critical of large, low-conditionality loans, such as the SDR 5 billion credit arranged for India in late 1981, and was not at all eager to facilitate more such loans in the future.[60] At most, the administration stated, it might be prepared to contemplate a quota increase of perhaps 25 percent, and even for that there was no particular hurry.

But then came the Mexican crisis — and with it the dramatic shift in U.S. policy. Suddenly the administration *was* in a hurry. Not only did it now pronounce itself in favor of an accelerated increase of quotas (and a more sizable one at that), it wanted to go even further. At the Fund's annual meeting in Toronto, in September 1982, Treasury Secretary Donald Regan suggested "establishment of an additional permanent borrowing arrangement, which would be available to the IMF on a contingency basis for use in extraordinary circumstances."[61] And in the following months the secretary pushed hard for formal consideration of such a proposal, surprising observers who had become accustomed to administration recalcitrance on the size and timing of any new IMF funding. Said one private banker, "Maybe there's a problem out there that we don't know about."[62]

With Washington no longer dragging its heels, the details did not take long to work out. In February 1983 the IMF announced agreement on an increase of quotas from approximately SDR 61 billion to SDR 90 billion — a rise of 47.5 percent. Furthermore, the Fund's General Arrangements to Borrow (GAB) were to be tripled, from approximately SDR 6.4 billion to SDR 17 billion, and for the first time made available to finance loans to countries outside the Group of Ten — thus converting the GAB into precisely the sort of emergency fund that Secretary Regan had earlier suggested.[63] The U.S. share of these increases, which at prevailing exchange rates came to a total of some $8.5 billion ($5.8 billion for a quota increase, $2.7 billion for the GAB expansion), was finally approved by Congress, after protracted lobbying by the administration, in November 1983. In the following month the enlargement of Fund resources formally came into effect.

A policy shift of this magnitude demands some explanation. At one level

59. Ibid., 19 March 1979, pp. 82–83.
60. Ibid., 23 November 1981, p. 365, for the India loan.
61. As quoted in ibid., 4 October 1982, p. 327.
62. As quoted in *New York Times*, 12 December 1982, sec. 3, p. 1.
63. The United States for a time held out for a slightly smaller quota increase, to only SDR 85 billion, but was unsuccessful. It *was* successful in preventing expansion of the General Arrangements to Borrow to the figure of SDR 20 billion favored by European governments. See *Economist*, 22 January 1983, pp. 62–63.

150   *Benjamin J. Cohen*

the explanation was simple: there really *was* a problem "out there"—the threat of a chain reaction of defaults in Latin America and elsewhere that could have plunged the whole world into the abyss of another Great Depression. The Reagan administration did not want to go down in history alongside the Hoover administration; in any event, there was a presidential election coming up in 1984. It had to do *something*, and the IMF was there. It seemed only natural to use what was already available.

At a deeper level, however, the explanation was more complex. Use of the IMF, some administration officials began to believe, might actually serve U.S. policy interests more effectively than attempts to deal with debt problems on a direct, bilateral basis. "A convenient conduit for U.S. influence," one high-level policy maker called it.[64] Any effort by Washington itself to impose unpopular policy conditions on troubled debtors would undoubtedly have fanned the flames of nationalism, if not revolution, in many countries. But what would be intolerable when demanded by a major foreign power might, it seemed, be rather more acceptable if administered by an impartial international agency with no ostensible interests other than the maintenance of international monetary stability. Likewise, the Fund could apply pressures to banks, to maintain or increase lending exposure in debtor countries, that the banks might have resisted had they come from national officials. As the country with the largest share of votes in the Fund (just under 20%), and as the source of the world's preeminent international currency, the United States still enjoys unparalleled influence over IMF decision making—in effect, an implicit veto on all matters of substantive importance. Through its ability to shape attitudes at the Fund, therefore, Washington could hope to exercise more leverage over debtors and banks indirectly than seemed feasible directly, and at a lower political cost.

On the issue of policy conditions the Fund had begun to tighten its standards even before the Mexican crisis, owing in good part to the Reagan administration's active disapproval of earlier lending practices. By the summer of 1982 its institutional attitude had already shifted back toward more rigorous enforcement of domestic austerity measures. Thus once the storm hit, Fund officials needed no persuasion to take on the role, in effect, of the "cop on the beat"—setting policy conditions for new or renewed credits and ensuring strict compliance with their terms. Following the Mexican crisis nearly three dozen countries fell into arrears on their foreign loans; and over the next year nearly two dozen of them found it necessary to negotiate debt relief of some sort with private or official creditors, or both. In all of these negotiations the Fund became a central arbiter of access to, as well as of the terms of, new external financing. Creditors began to insist formally that a debtor country, as a precondition to their own financial assistance, first conclude a standby arrangement with the IMF subject to upper-credit-tranche conditionality.

64. Interview, U.S. Treasury, January 1984.

Debt and U.S. policy

Many restructurings were also made conditional upon continued compliance with Fund performance criteria; and on occasion disbursements of new loans were even timed to coincide with drawings scheduled under Fund stabilization programs.[65] The IMF spelled financial relief and, as such, exercised considerable leverage over the policies of troubled debtors.

That leverage, however, was clearly resented. Throughout the Third World the IMF became a dirty word. And the hand of the United States behind the IMF was increasingly evident to many. In this respect, too, Washington's gains proved essentially transient. Initially, U.S. interests were served by letting the Fund get out in front. But as the crisis persisted the veil tended to wear thin, and criticism came to be focused more and more on the perceived power behind the throne—the United States. This criticism helped stimulate the widespread and growing dissatisfaction with what was viewed as Washington's miserliness and insensitivity toward the problems of debtor countries.

The story is similar in the IMF's relationship with the banks. Initially, it seemed, U.S. interests might also be served by the Fund's ability to apply effective pressure on banks. Washington's own exhortations to banks to resume lending in Latin America or elsewhere fell, as already indicated, largely on deaf ears. Not so, however, with the Fund, which in several key instances successfully demanded specific commercial commitments as a precondition for its own financial assistance. In connection with its $3.9 billion arrangement for Mexico, for instance, which took some four months to negotiate, the Fund refused to go ahead until each of the country's fourteen hundred creditor banks first agreed to extend additional credit amounting to 7 percent of their existing loan exposure (amounting overall to some $5 billion in new bank money for Mexico).[66] Likewise before approving a loan of $5.5 billion for Brazil, in February 1983, the IMF laid down a number of requirements for the banks: restoration of interbank credit lines to $7.5 billion; new loans of $4.4 billion; rollover for eight years of $4 billion in principal due in 1983; and maintenance of short-term trade credits at $8.8 billion.[67] Similar conditions were attached to agreements with other countries as well, most notably Argentina and Yugoslavia.[68] The IMF's message to the banks was clear. In the words of de Larosière, "Banks will have to continue to increase their exposures . . . if widespread debt financing problems are to be avoided."[69]

Not that all the banks were eager to cooperate—not at first, at least. Many, pursuing their private interests, simply wanted to get their money out as quickly as possible. Managing Director de Larosière had to "knock heads

---

65. *Recent Multilateral Debt Restructurings with Official and Bank Creditors*, IMF Occasional Paper no. 25 (Washington, D.C., December 1983), pp. 10, 26.
66. *Economist*, 19 February 1983, p. 89.
67. *New York Times*, 1 March 1983, p. D1.
68. Ibid., 22 January 1983.
69. As quoted in *New York Times*, 9 January 1983, sec. 3, p. 10.

152   *Benjamin J. Cohen*

together," as one official phrased it.[70] But eventually the banks themselves came to recognize the crucial public interest in such "involuntary" lending in critical cases. Said one prominent U.S. banker: "It was clear that somebody had to step in and play a leadership role."[71] Said another: "The IMF sensed a vacuum and properly stepped into it."[72] Could anyone imagine the U.S. government taking such interventionist initiatives? In the first place, Washington had no jurisdiction over the banks of other countries (which accounted for well over half of total loan exposure). And second, even American banks would have been highly reluctant to take such direction straight from government officials. U.S. banks have traditionally placed great store in their arm's-length relationship with authorities, insisting vehemently on their right as competitors in the marketplace to make their own commercial decisions. In this respect, too, U.S. interests seemed to be served by letting the Fund get out in front.

But this gain also proved to be essentially transient. What the banks were willing to tolerate in certain critical cases, they would not accept as a general rule. Certainly they might again be prepared, should similar emergencies arise in the future, to surrender temporarily some of their traditional operating autonomy. But they would not accept a permanent role for the IMF in the management of private international credit flows, and increasingly they reasserted their right to go their own way. Washington could not long rely on Fund intermediation with the banks either.

5. Conclusion

The limited selection of experiences that I have briefly examined suggest some interesting insights into the foreign-policy implications of international debt for the United States as a major creditor country.

In the first place, it is evident that America's foreign-policy capabilities are indeed affected, and that the influence is in fact significant. In Poland and Latin America alike, bank priorities turned out to be substantially at variance with the goals of public officials in Washington; and as a result the effectiveness of existing policy instruments in each region was to some extent compromised. For banks, the main goal was simply to avoid default while limiting the extent of any new loan exposure. In Poland this attitude made it more difficult for the Reagan administration to make its economic sanctions stick. In Latin America it undercut efforts to keep friendly governments financially secure without new concessions from Washington. In neither case could the negative impacts on policy effectiveness be described as trivial. In both cases money did indeed "talk"—but not to U.S. advantage.

70. Ibid.
71. Ibid.
72. Ibid.

Moreover, it is evident that in the complex intersection of high finance and high politics the government had at best only limited influence over the behavior of banks, given the traditional arm's-length relationship of the public and private sectors in the United States. The limitation was most obvious in Latin America, where despite both carrots (e.g., new Export-Import Bank loan guarantees) and sticks (e.g., threatened closer scrutiny of books), banks could not be induced to resume significant new amounts of voluntary lending. Bank behavior in this instance was not difficult to understand: Why should bankers accept the risk of increasing exposure more than they themselves consider prudent? In fact, much more could have been expected only if bankers could have been persuaded that vital national interests were at stake.

Third, it is evident that policy linkages were indeed created, though their consequences for U.S. power differed in the two instances. In Poland debt acted marginally as a constraint limiting Washington's ability to influence the ultimate outcome of events. Despite its proclaimed opposition to martial law the Reagan administration felt compelled by its concern over default, when push came to shove, to make a key financial concession to Warsaw— namely, the unconditional decision to pay off CCC-guaranteed credits as they came due. As a result Washington's leverage over Poland was reduced. The United States may not have been "conquered," but it did not "win" either.

In Latin America, by contrast, foreign-policy capabilities were initially enhanced after the Reagan administration acted to help out some of the region's major debtors. The crises of Mexico and others offered Washington, at least for a time, an opportunity to gain considerable goodwill and influence for itself in return for only limited financial concessions. The difference between the two cases was that in one U.S. relations were nonconflictual while in the other they were adversarial. In both cases avoidance of default was treated as an important policy goal. When dealing with an enemy like the Jaruzelski regime, this goal tended the handicap the realization of U.S. foreign-policy preferences, since it undermined the credibility of other policy measures; when dealing with our friends in Latin America, on the other hand, it meant that we were able to help ourselves even as we helped others. The lesson seems clear. Linkage strategies bred by the debt issue are more apt to work when the interest we share with others in avoiding default is reinforced by other shared economic or political interests.

Even in Latin America, however, the initial foreign-policy gains proved essentially transient. As the region's debt crisis wore on, Washington's ability to determine the course of events there declined. Additional concessions, it appeared, would be necessary if the U.S. government wished to retain its newly won leverage. Power in such situations seems to be a wasting asset. Repeated investment is needed to avoid the depletion of goodwill and influence.

Finally, it is evident that any tendency toward power depletion in such situations can only for a time be countered by reliance on the intermediation of a multilateral agency. In the immediate aftermath of the Mexican and other Latin rescues, the IMF gained considerable leverage over the behavior of both debtor governments and banks; and insofar as Washington still retained paramount influence over IMF decision making, U.S. interests, it seemed, could be served more effectively via the Fund than on a direct, bilateral basis. This realization helps to explain the sudden policy shift by the Reagan administration in mid-1982 in favor of a strong, well-endowed IMF. Money seemed to talk best indirectly. But this too, in time, proved to be an essentially transient opportunity.

All of these considerations have very serious implications for the politics of stabilization of the international financial system. The global debt problem appears to suggest an urgent need for some actor, or set of actors, to provide the "collective good" of stability. According to the popular "theory of hegemonic stability," that stabilizing role can be played only by a hegemonic power—meaning, in the contemporary era, the United States. But if my analysis is correct, America does not seem to have the capacity to play that role. Only at the outset of the series of crises in Latin America was the United States able to exercise significant influence over the course of events. The financial collapse of Mexico and others in effect threw those nations willy-nilly into the arms of the only country capable of organizing rescue packages on short notice (just as Poland's financial difficulties pushed it more under the influence of its patron, the Soviet Union). Emergency conditions gave Washington leverage. But once the emergency was past, even this gain was eroded. American power has been insufficient to stabilize the system.

In part, this insufficiency explains why Washington was prepared to try relying to the extent it did on the intermediation of the IMF. Why accept the constraints of operating indirectly through a multilateral agency unless power resources to act directly are inadequate? Unfortunately, even this tactic proved effective only in emergency conditions.

The key to the dilemma lies in the U.S. government's limited influence over the banks, which can best be understood in terms of the continuing dialectic between the "market" and the "state." At Bretton Woods, in 1944, an international monetary regime was designed that in principle excluded private markets from decisions affecting the creation of international liquidity. But the gradual emergence of the Eurocurrency market as a major source of balance-of-payments financing to a significant extent "privatized" the creation of liquidity.[73] In effect, the market moved beyond the influence of any one state, even that of the former hegemonic power. The pendulum can swing

73. Benjamin J. Cohen, "Balance-of-Payments Financing: Evolution of a Regime," in Stephen D. Krasner, ed., *International Regimes* (Ithaca: Cornell University Press, 1983), pp. 315–36.

Debt and U.S. policy

back only if the jurisdiction of states catches up once more with the domain of the market—which means *collective* action by governments in lieu of reliance on a single stabilizer. The United States, it would appear, can no longer win the game on its own.

The politics of adjustment: lessons from the IMF's Extended Fund Facility Stephan Haggard

The international debt crisis has forced painful economic adjustments on the developing world. In the short run it has forced governments to seek to correct payments imbalances through stabilization programs, usually undertaken with conditional assistance from the International Monetary Fund (IMF). The crisis has also revealed deeper weaknesses in many Third World economies, weaknesses demanding more basic reforms in the structure of incentives, prices, and investment.

Yet efforts at stabilization and structural adjustment are routinely stymied by domestic political forces.[1] Taking as a sample the thirty adjustment programs launched under the auspices of the Extended Fund Facility (see Table 1), twenty-four were renegotiated, or had payments interrupted, or were

---

An earlier version was presented at the Lehrman Institute, New York City, in the spring of 1984 as part of its seminar series on Politics and International Debt, which was supported in part by a grant from the Ford Foundation. I thank, in addition to participants at that meeting, Don Babai, Derrick Boston, David Menzie Chinn, John Cohen, Jorge Dominguez, Laurel Fitzpatrick, Merilee Grindle, Mary Hildebrand, Vera Joffe, Peter Katzenstein, Robert Keohane, David Mednicoff, Craig Murphy, Michael Shafer, Scott Sidel, Evelyne Huber Stephens, John Stephens, and participants at seminars sponsored by the Harvard Institute for International Development and the Brown Center for the Comparative Study of Development. I have profited in particular from extended discussions with Robert Kaufman, Miles Kahler, and Joan Nelson.

1. On the politics of stabilization see Joan Nelson, "The Politics of Stabilization," in Richard E. Feinberg and Valeriana Kallab, eds., *Adjustment Crisis in the Third World* (New Brunswick: Transaction, 1984); Alejandro Foxley, *Latin American Experiments in Neoconservative Economics* (Berkeley: University of California Press, 1983); John Sheahan, "Market-Oriented Economic Policies and Political Repression in Latin America," *Economic Development and Cultural Change* 28 (January 1980); Carlos Diaz-Alejandro, "Southern Cone Stabilization Plans," in William Cline and Sidney Weintraub, eds., *Economic Stabilization in Developing Countries* (Washington, D.C.: Brookings, 1981); David Pion-Berlin, "Political Repression and Economic Doctrines: The Case of Argentina," *Comparative Political Studies* 16 (April 1983); Thomas Skidmore, "The Politics of Stabilization in Postwar Latin America," in James Malloy, ed., *Authoritarianism and Corporatism in Latin America* (Pittsburgh: University of Pittsburgh Press, 1977); and Roberto Frenkel and Guillermo O'Donnell, "The 'Stabilization Programs' of the IMF and Their Internal Impacts," in Richard Fagen, ed., *Capitalism and the State in U.S.–Latin American Relations* (Stanford: Stanford University Press, 1979).

158   *Stephan Haggard*

quietly allowed to lapse. Of these twenty-four, sixteen were formally canceled by the IMF, virtually all for noncompliance.

The IMF itself has recognized that cancelations are linked with the political inability to meet program requirements. The IMF review of 1980 standbys and 1978–80 Extended Fund Facility agreements found that, in the view of the staff, "political constraints" or "weak administrative systems," or both, accounted for 60 percent of the breaches of credit ceilings. Exogenous shocks, by contrast, were the most important factor in only 26 percent of the cases.[2] What determines the political capacity to stabilize an economy and to make medium-term structural adjustments? Are some political systems better suited than others to sustain the reforms associated with IMF programs?

The problem of structural adjustment

Established in the wake of the first oil shock in 1974, the Extended Fund Facility was the first of a wave of Fund reforms that vastly enlarged members' access to credit.[3] Targeted at developing countries, the EFF was designed to meet conditions that were virtually synonymous with underdevelopment itself. EFFs would be appropriate for:

a. an economy suffering serious payments imbalances relating to structural maladjustments in production and trade where prices and cost distortions have been widespread;
b. an economy characterized by slow growth and an inherently weak balance of payments position which prevents pursuit of an active development policy.[4]

Programs under the EFF did not represent a sharp departure from the Fund's traditional strategies for adjustment. Adjustment still rested on traditional instruments—the exchange rate and monetary and fiscal restraint—and the goal of short-term stabilization often took precedence over more difficult structural changes. Many countries had already become prolonged users of Fund resources by running one year standbys back to back.

Nonetheless, the EFF reflects a subtle change in ideas on stabilization, adjustment, and conditionality. Standby agreements already seek "understandings" that go beyond fiscal, monetary, and exchange-rate policies to policies on prices, taxes and subsidies, interest rates, and even wages.[5] EFFs

2. Cited in Tony Killick et al., *The Quest for Economic Stabilization: The IMF and the Third World* (New York: St. Martin's, 1984), p. 261.
3. EFFs were designed to run for three years. When coupled with the liberalizing policy of "floating" a facility, i.e., excluding currency holdings under a specific facility in determining potential drawings under the reserve and credit tranche policies, the EFF, enlarged access policy, and supplementary financing facility permitted cumulative access to up to 600% of quota by the early 1980s.
4. Dec. no. 4377 (74/114), 13 September 1974, in IMF, *Annual Report 1975*, pp. 88–90.
5. M. Guitián, *Fund Conditionality: Evolution of Principles and Practices* (Washington: IMF, 1981), p. 26.

TABLE 1. *Programs under the IMF's Extended Fund Facility*

Country and period	Status
Bangladesh, 8 December 80–7 December 83	Disbursements interrupted for noncompliance, June 81. Canceled for noncompliance, 12 June 82.
Brazil, 1 March 83–28 February 86	Disbursements interrupted for noncompliance and program renegotiated, June 83–March 84.
Costa Rica, 17 June 81–16 June 84	Disbursements interrupted for noncompliance, November 81. EFF canceled, 20 December 82.
Dominican Republic, 21 January 83–20 January 86	Negotiations on compliance break down, March 84; interim agreement reached August 84.
Egypt, 28 July 78–27 July 81	Disbursements interrupted mid-1979 for noncompliance; negotiations for a new EFF fail, 1980.
Gabon, 27 June 80–31 December 82	Program completed.
Guyana, 25 June 79–24 June 82	Guyana seeks renegotiation of conditions, October 79; EFF canceled for noncompliance, replaced by new EFF.
25 July 79–24 July 83	Increase in resources negotiated, June 81; canceled for noncompliance, 22 July 82.
Haiti, 25 October 78–24 October 81	Disbursements interrupted for noncompliance, February 81.
Honduras, 28 June 79–27 June 82	Disbursements interrupted for noncompliance, September 81; program revised, December 81.
India, 9 November 81–8 November 84	India announces intention not to draw further funds, 15 January 84.
Ivory Coast, 27 February 81–22 February 84	Program completed.
Jamaica, 9 February 78–8 June 81	Targets revised but initial program canceled, 10 June 79.
11 June 79–10 June 81	Program effectively ended with breakdown of waiver negotiations, March 80; formally canceled, 12 April 81.
13 April 81–12 April 84	Program augmented, June 81. Disbursements interrupted for noncompliance, waiver granted June 83; program canceled for noncompliance, September 83.
Kenya, 7 July 75–6 July 78	Kenya forfeits access to EFF in 1976 for noncompliance; not formally canceled.
Mexico, 1 January 77–31 December 79	Oil boom allows early repayment.
1 January 83–31 December 85	In progress.
Morocco, 8 October 80–7 October 83	Canceled for noncompliance, 8 March 81.
9 March 81–7 October 83	Canceled for noncompliance, 25 April 82.
Pakistan, 24 November 80–23 November 83	Canceled, 1 December 81.
9 March 81–23 November 83	Program completed.
Peru, 7 June 83–6 June 85	Disbursements interrupted, November 83; canceled for noncompliance, 25 April 84.
Philippines, 2 April 76–1 April 79	Program completed.
Senegal, 8 August 80–7 August 83	Canceled, 10 September 81.
Sierra Leone, 30 March 81–22 February 84	Canceled for noncompliance, 6 April 82.
Sri Lanka, 1 January 79–31 December 81	Payments suspended 3d quarter of 1980 for noncompliance; resumed 6 June 81 and program completed.
Sudan, 4 May 79–3 May 82	Program renegotiated and augmented, November 80; canceled for noncompliance, 17 February 82.
Zaire, 22 June 81–21 June 84	Canceled for noncompliance, 22 June 82.
Zambia, 8 May 81–7 May 84	Canceled for noncompliance, 3 July 82.

Note. Status of programs in progress is through 1 January 85.
Sources. International Monetary Fund, *Annual Report 1984*, and various other sources.

are representative of a growing emphasis among development economists on the importance of microeconomic instruments and on the role of resource utilization and production as the basis for longer-term structural adjustment. EFFs often call for fundamental shifts in policy, such as liberalization of trade, decontrol of prices, and restructuring of public-sector corporations.[6] Though the problems facing the countries that signed EFF agreements are obviously varied, the adjustments entailed are politically ambitious.

How to judge the success or failure of Fund programs is not self-evident, however.[7] Should success be judged against what went before, what would have happened in the absence of policy change, or some normative standard such as plan targets? On the other hand, failure, argue critics of the IMF, indicates only the inappropriate design and unrealistic goals of Fund programs.[8] Exogenous economic factors also affect the capacity of governments to pursue certain policies, of course, among them unexpected trends in interest rates or export markets.

Indeed, it could be argued that economic policy is best explained by economic circumstance. Political forces may have room to operate in the short run, delaying "necessary" decisions, but the starting point of a stabilization program is by definition a position that is unsustainable. In the end economic constraints swamp political ones. Yet such economic determinism says nothing about alternative routes to a new equilibrium (or disequilibrium). Economic factors may force changes in policy, but politics drives elite perceptions of acceptable economic advice and thus shapes the path to adjustment. Economists explain success and failure in meeting plan targets by calling on such institutional and political factors as "capacity" and "will."[9] These are, of course, things to be explained, not an explanation.

6. For longitudinal studies noting the difficulties of compliance with fiscal targets see Thomas M. Reichmann and Richard Stillson, "Experience with Programs of Balance of Payments Adjustment: Stand-by Arrangements in the Higher Tranches, 1963–1972," *IMF Staff Papers* 25 (June 1978), and W. A. Beveridge and Margaret R. Kelly, "Fiscal Content of Financial Programs Supported by Stand-By Arrangements in the Upper Credit Tranches, 1969–1978," ibid. 27 (June 1980).

7. For a discussion of this problem see John Williamson, "On Judging the Success of IMF Policy Advice," in Williamson, ed., *IMF Conditionality* (Cambridge: MIT Press for the Institute for International Economics, 1983), and Guitián, *Fund Conditionality*.

8. For the debate on alternatives to the "IMF model" of stabilization and adjustment see William Cline, "Economic Stabilization in Developing Countries: Theory and Stylized Facts," in Williamson, *IMF Conditionality*; Foxley, *Latin American Experiments*; Rudiger Dornbusch, "Stabilization Policies in Developing Countries: What Have We Learned?" *World Development* 10, 4 (1982); Lance Taylor, *Structuralist Macroeconomics* (New York: Basic Books, 1983), chap. 11; Killick et al., *Quest*, and the companion volume of case studies, *The IMF and Stabilization: Developing Countries' Experiences* (New York: St. Martin's, 1984); and Tony Killick, ed., *Adjustment and Financing in the Developing World: The Role of the International Monetary Fund* (Washington, D.C.: IMF in association with the Overseas Development Institute, 1982).

9. See for example Christine A. Bogdanowicz-Bindert, "Portugal, Turkey and Peru: Three Successful Programmes under the Auspices of the IMF," *World Development* 11, 1 (1983), and the case studies in Cline and Weintraub, *Economic Stabilization*; Williamson, *IMF Conditionality*; Feinberg and Kallab, *Adjustment Crisis*; Killick et al., *The IMF and Stabilization*; and William Cline et al., *World Inflation and Developing Countries* (Washington, D.C.: Brookings, 1981).

Distributional coalitions, regime types, and stabilization

The most controversial political issue in recent debates about the IMF concerns the relationship between stabilization, repression, and authoritarianism.[10] Are authoritarian regimes better suited to undertake IMF stabilization policies? Conversely, are IMF programs politically destabilizing in ways that elicit repressive and authoritarian responses?

Mancur Olson has posed the dilemma over adjustment in terms of the power of "distributional coalitions."[11] According to Olson, organizations for collective action have little incentive to make social sacrifices; they will emerge only in attempting to seize the largest share of national income for themselves. Groups lobby for, and come to have an interest in, market-distorting policies: an administered price, an "artificially" high wage, a subsidy, a tax break, or inflation itself. Where such groups flourish, Olson argues, they slow economic adjustment by entrenching economic rigidities and resisting the efficient allocation of resources.

The identity and the power of the "distributional coalitions" important to any particular adjustment effort vary with the structure of the economy. Stabilization generally entails a decline in real wages, but many policy reforms have cross-cutting distributional effects.[12] Allowing food prices to rise, for example, may benefit the rural sector while hurting urban marginals and the working class. In general terms, however, "adjustment" demands the reduction or elimination of rents accruing to favored groups.[13]

Interestingly, Olson's analysis fits well with the conventional wisdom in political science on the relationship between regime type and stabilization, most of it drawn from the semi-industrialized Latin American countries. Thomas Skidmore, writing in 1977, argued:

(1) governments in competitive political systems find it *extremely* diffi-

---

10. The most general critique of the IMF along political lines is still Cheryl Payer, *The Debt Trap: The IMF and the Third World* (New York: Monthly Review Press, 1974). See also Sheahan, "Market-Oriented Economic Policies"; Frenkel and O'Donnell, "Stabilization Programs."

11. Mancur Olson, *The Rise and Decline of Nations* (New Haven: Yale University Press, 1983); Robert Bates, *Markets and States in Tropical Africa* (Berkeley: University of California Press, 1981); Anne Krueger, "The Political Economy of the Rent-Seeking Society," *American Economic Review* 64, 3 (1974). For a review of recent literature on rent-seeking with reference to protectionism see Robert Baldwin, "The Political Economy of Protectionism," in Jagdish Bhagwati, ed., *Import Competition and Response* (Chicago: University of Chicago Press, 1982), and the trenchant "Comment" by Stephen P. Magee.

12. See Nelson, "Politics of Stabilization"; Richard Cooper, *Currency Devaluation in Developing Countries*, Princeton Essays in International Finance no. 86 (Princeton, N.J., 1971), pp. 28–29; and Omotunde Johnson and Joanne Salop, "Distributional Aspects of Stabilization Programs in Developing Countries," *IMF Staff Papers* 27 (March 1980).

13. While Olson's pluralist analysis assumes that "distributional coalitions" will be made up of societally based interest groups, his analysis can be extended to include state actors, including civil servants, parastatal managers, and the military. In fact, these groups may be the most difficult to control or circumvent.

cult to reduce inflation once it has exceeded 20 percent and they have paid a very high political price for their efforts; (2) no such government has proved able to pursue a successful . . . anti-inflation effort; (3) all the cases of successful stabilization have been carried out by authoritarian (or one-party) governments; and (4) even authoritarian governments must have a high degree of internal consensus to carry through a successful stabilization.[14]

The gloomy prognosis regarding the ability of democratic regimes to sustain adjustment is matched by equally dire generalizations about the political consequences of stabilization. Devaluation, Richard Cooper found in 1971, doubled the likelihood that a ruling group would be removed from power and tripled the chances that finance ministers would lose their jobs. "Market-oriented" policies, according to John Sheahan, are associated with increases in repression in Latin America. Most dramatically, efforts at stabilization have been associated with the installation of authoritarian governments. As Skidmore argues, democratic regimes permit the formation of alliances "in which each [element] thinks it can best protect its fortunes if stabilization is scrapped." The result is that "since 1945, not a single major Latin American nation has been able to maintain a competitive political system and, at the same time, achieve sustained control of inflation once the latter exceeded 10% per year for three years or more."[15]

Carlos Diaz-Alejandro paints a similar stylized portrait of the disintegrative dynamics of Southern Cone populism:

During the last stages of populism there will be general agreement that "things cannot go on like this" and that something must be done. Within the populist coalition, some will argue for a bold move toward centrally planned socialism, thus further encouraging capital flight and a slump in private investment. Moderate populist technocrats may be able to attempt their own stabilization plans, which will come too late. The opposition will move for the kill, culminating in a military coup.[16]

Skidmore and Diaz-Alejandro bring to light the underside of Olson's argument. Distributional coalitions flourish in democracies; only strong states can tame them.

This conventional wisdom about the "elective affinity" between authoritarianism and IMF-planned adjustment is, I shall argue, open to challenge. The conventional wisdom is drawn from a few of the "strong" bureaucratic-authoritarian regimes in Latin America.[17] While it is true that the post-1964 military regime in Brazil or the post-1973 government in Chile could impose

14. Skidmore, "Politics of . . . Latin America," p. 149.

15. Cooper, *Currency Devaluation*, pp. 28–29; Sheahan, "Market-Oriented Economic Policies"; Skidmore, "Politics of . . . Latin America," p. 149.

16. Diaz-Alejandro, "Southern Cone," p. 122.

17. See David Collier, ed., *The New Authoritarianism in Latin America* (Princeton: Princeton University Press, 1979).

adjustment costs, these regimes are hardly typical of Third World authoritarianism. After all, the "authoritarian" category also includes highly personalistic or familial autocracies, for example Zaire and Haiti, in which the distinction between public and private finances is blurred. And even where such extreme personalism is not in evidence, state patronage is frequently a central pillar of political authority and legitimation in "authoritarian" regimes. Robert Jackson and Carl Rosberg describe the syndrome in the African context, using a patron-client framework:

> After independence [the need for political support] initially contributed to the demand for Africanization of the civil service and other agencies of the government (including the military).... When the Africanization resources were "spent," so to speak, African rulers who were short on loyalty had to search for additional resources by which the patronage polity upholding their rule could be fuelled. A major reservoir of fresh resources has been the alien-dominated private economy, which most African governments have sought to bring under the control of state or private African agencies.[18]

The maintenance of political authority through clientelism is most likely where governments are weakly institutionalized or where societies are ethnically divided. Political order in such "weak" authoritarian regimes rests on instrumental ties and the political leadership's discretionary access to state funds. The rationalization associated with adjustment and stabilization is thus, in an immediate sense, politically irrational.

Nor is the democratic record so dim, at least in the short run. Democratically elected governments may be more successful than authoritarian ones in eliciting support for adjustment measures; indeed, the desire to escape the problems of managing austerity may be one of the most powerful motives for the military's withdrawal from politics. Three conditions seem crucial to democratic adjustment. First, the policies of the previous government, whether authoritarian or elected, must be clear failures, giving the new government the political space to launch otherwise controversial policies. Second, the electoral opposition must remain weak or divided. Third, the antidemocratic right or the military, or both, must be either discredited or weak. Such a pattern is visible most clearly in Mexico and Sri Lanka.

In every one of the democratic cases, however, with the exception of India's peculiar program, IMF disbursements were interrupted or the program was canceled for noncompliance. The inital advantages of democracy were eroded by a process of "democratic stalemate." The reason may be traced in part to the political orientation of the governments in power, for the

18. Robert Jackson and Carl Rosberg, *Personal Rule in Black Africa* (Berkeley: University of California Press, 1982), pp. 43–44. The same point has been made from a Marxian or class perspective in discussions of the "state bourgeoisie"; see Rehman Sobhan, *The Crisis of External Dependence* (Dhaka: Dhaka University Press, 1982).

ideological projects of political elites naturally shape their approach to economic management and thus to IMF-style reforms. Attempts at democratic-socialist transformation face particularly severe constraints even in the best of economic times and are unlikely to receive the sympathy of the IMF during periods of austerity. But democratic stalemate appears common across governments of very different ideological orientations and follows a predictable sequence.

Elected officials start by manipulating macroeconomic policy for political ends, producing large fiscal deficits, rapid monetary growth, and an overvalued exchange rate. Governments then postpone or resist stabilization policies in anticipation of hostile reactions from key constituents that may also be organized along patron-client lines. "Losers" receive compensation that undermines adjustment. Forces opposed to stabilization use democratic channels or independent organizational resources to block or undermine reforms. Opposition parties gain ground with promises of deliverance from austerity (promises they are rarely in a position to fulfill). The very nature of the democratic system and the legal guarantees it affords limit the state's ability to act.

Democratic stalemate thus produces a zigzag or stop-go effort to adjust but need not lead to political destabilization, repression, or authoritarian installations. The economic conditions producing political change must be carefully specified. Is it the class conflict and polarization resulting from inflation or the political protest against attempted austerity that leads to repressive or authoritarian solutions? Critics of the Fund often rely on crude functional arguments—authoritarianism results from the "need" to stabilize— and generally refuse to pose the important historical counterfactual: what types of political changes would result from continued or accelerated inflation? In Latin America, conventional wisdom holds, those countries *failing* to stabilize early in the postwar period were more rather than less likely to get authoritarian regimes.

In none of the countries in my admittedly limited sample did economic conditions lead to the collapse of a democratic regime, though austerities produced changes in governments in Costa Rica and Jamaica and brought the new democracies of Peru and the Dominican Republic under severe stress. Reliable cross-national strike data are not available for the period, but strike activity appeared to increase in every case. Urban food riots followed subsidy cuts in several countries, though they could often be traced to poor timing and implementation on the part of the governments themselves.

Repression surfaced most clearly in the weakly institutionalized, low-income authoritarian countries in which *already* authoritarian regimes turned to increasingly coercive tactics to solve the problem of "political rationing." Coercion was most likely when economic protest was coupled, as it often was, with broader political challenges to the government's legitimacy. Many of these "weak" authoritarian regimes are sustained by extensive clientelism

Politics of adjustment

and state patronage, and coercion alone could not, in the end, address this most basic limitation on adjustment. Even well-institutionalized one-party regimes, such as Zambia and Mexico, face political limits when they try to impose the costs of adjustment on politically important constituents.

These points are illustrated in the case studies that follow. I begin with an analysis of the constraints on adjustment in low-income authoritarian regimes. The cases of Zaire and Haiti raise some important qualifications to the thesis that authoritarianism facilitates stabilization and adjustment. The left government of Michael Manley in Jamaica and the right government of J. R. Jayawardene in Sri Lanka both exhibit the dilemmas of democratic adjustment, albeit in differing degrees. An examination of Mexico shows that corporatism, while facilitating short-term pacts, is subject to a similar political entropy. I conclude by examining some alternative political hypotheses about the prerequisites for stabilization and adjustment and the problems that international organizations face in attempting to influence politically constrained national policy.

Weak authoritarian regimes

Personalism: Zaire and Haiti

Zaire and Haiti are examples of premodern, patrimonial, or familial forms of political authority that have proved remarkably resistant to the demands of external actors. Though very differently endowed, both countries are characterized by one-man rule, the repression of opposition, a mix of patrimonial and modern bureaucracies, and massively corrupt financial structures. State finances are used to maintain what Thomas Callaghy calls a "political aristocracy" located in the military, state-owned enterprises, central bureaucracy, territorial administration, and party.[19] Local understanding of the economic principles behind "adjustment" or "stabilization" as prerequisites for longer-term growth is weak. The small technocratic cadres that do exist have little autonomy from political demands on resources and little leverage on policy. Since political control of state resources is integral to political power, rationalization of the financial structure would entail a direct attack on the ruling elites themselves. Such states survive largely by seeking to manipulate their very poverty or their strategic significance to important donors.

Zaire presents this syndrome clearly, negotiating five stabilization plans with the IMF between March 1978 and December 1983, the fourth an EFF signed in July 1981. The Fund program pressed for greater emphasis on

19. The following is drawn from Thomas Callaghy, "The Political Economy of African Debt: The Case of Zaire," in John Ravenhill, ed., *Africa in Economic Crisis: Problems and Strategies* (London: Macmillan, forthcoming), and Callaghy, *The State-Society Struggle: Zaire in Comparative Perspective* (New York: Columbia University Press, 1984), pp. 194–204.

166   *Stephan Haggard*

agriculture and the improvement of supporting infrastructure but recognized that the main difficulty lay with economic mismanagement and corruption.[20] Previous efforts by the World Bank and the IMF to influence Zaire's economic policy had included the 19th-century solution of sending a team of experts, headed by retired German central banker Erwin Blumenthal, to take over key positions in the central bank, customs office, and planning and finance ministries. The team's efforts were not only circumvented but Blumenthal was physically threatened by government troops. Nor did the Fund have effective allies within Zaire's bureaucracy. *Institutional Investor* characterized the central bank's governor as "serious and relatively competent" but "ineffective in a chaotic system where corruption is rife" and exhibiting "little will or ability to prevail upon . . . Mobutu to accept economic reform."[21]

The program's overoptimistic projections of export earning and capital inflows contributed to the breakdown of the EFF of 1981, but the budget, outside Fund control, was the main sticking point. Expenditure in 1981 increased 58.6 percent over the previous year, much of the growth after the signing of the EFF. Expenditure overruns included the Office of the Presidency and Political Institutions and in education (where an estimated 15,000 mythical teachers were found on the rolls), and there were cost overruns on previous projects and a large subsidy to the state oil-importing company. In June 1982 the EFF was canceled and negotiations began on a fifth standby.

Haiti, the poorest country in the Western hemisphere, reflects a similar pattern of widespread corruption, familial rule, and administrative weakness. The year 1978 proved particularly disastrous, with drought and zero growth forcing Haiti to seek increased international assistance, including an EFF concluded in October. President Jimmy Carter's human rights policies placed new political constraints on the regime, forcing Jean-Claude Duvalier to reduce some of the more flagrant abuses in return for American support. Political protests and labor militance increased.[22] Donor governments were already exhibiting skepticism about Haiti's intentions by late 1980 but nonetheless offered a 20 percent increase at their December meeting. That same month saw the triumph of the hardliners ("les dinosaurs") within the government and a violent crackdown on political opposition.

In February 1981 IMF officials reported that the fiscal reforms on which the first tranche drawing of the EFF were predicated had not been made and the government's request for the second tranche would be denied. The IMF found that $16 million had "simply disappeared" from various state bodies over the last quarter of 1980, that Duvalier had obtained $20 million

20. See the World Bank's uncharacteristically blunt *Zaire: Current Economic Situation and Constraints* (Washington, D.C., 1979), sections 5 and 6.

21. *Institutional Investor* (international ed.), September 1983, p. 284.

22. Economist Intelligence Unit, *Quarterly Economic Review* (hereafter *QER*), 3d quarter, 1979; *Latin America Weekly Report* (hereafter *LAWR*), 14 March 1979; *New York Times*, 29 September 1984.

of state funds for his personal use in December, and that he had ordered the national bank to pay his wife a monthly salary of $100,000.[23] Despite pressure from the Fund and aid donors, the regime failed to jettison three costly projects on which Duvalier and his allies collected a reported $15 million in commissions. In addition, Duvalier had begun to hand over state monopolies in salt, sugar, and flour to his wife's family, aggravating shortages.[24]

In the course of 1981 donors sought to pressure Duvalier by curtailing aid commitments. Under U.S. prodding, Marc Bazin, a former World Bank official, was made finance minister in February 1982. Bazin sought to use his links to the international aid community to institute basic reforms, among them public accountability in tax collection, strict quotas on staples, and a crackdown on luxury imports, and to reopen negotiations with the Fund. But Bazin's import policies and his stated intention to investigate the disappearance of the EFF money proved his undoing. Bazin and two other "technocratic" ministers were forced out of office in July, and several members of the old regime's economic team brought back. The technocratic core of reformers was decimated. The Fund followed up the failed EFF with a standby agreement, but it was clear that the new economic team marked a return to the open corruption of the past.[25]

Both Duvalier and Mobutu have made constant appeals to Western governments for increased assistance. Both have argued that their domestic opponents are Communist or Communist-inspired and that their strategic significance, in the Caribbean and Central Africa respectively, warrant increased assistance. These appeals have not been ignored, and they have given both leaders a degree of maneuverability they would otherwise not have.

State patronage: Guyana and Sudan

In Zaire and Haiti the rationalization of state finances posed a direct threat to the discretionary power of extremely narrow ruling elites. Slightly different are those regimes in which political power has been maintained by the incorporation of broader social, ethnic, or professional groups into networks of "state patronage." In Guyana such patronage resulted both from ethnic cleavages and from the attempt to effect a socialist transformation of the economy. Austerity gave additional fuel to a coalition of forces challenging the basic legitimacy of the regime. With unions controlling sectors of the economy key to the earning of foreign exchange, repressive tactics not only added to the regime's political problems but proved economically counterproductive. The Sudan typifies a similar set of dilemmas in the African

23. *LAWR*, 20 February 1981.
24. *Latin American Regional Reports: Caribbean* (hereafter *LARR:C*), 27 March 1981.
25. *LARR:C*, 20 August 1982; 1 October 1982.

168   *Stephan Haggard*

context and also demonstrates the barriers to structural reform in the agricultural sector. The difficulty in lifting food subsidies, critical to the Fund's aims of both fiscal reform and "getting the prices right," proved a major constraint on Sudanese adjustment, as it did in nine EFF countries.

Playing coalition politics over the 1960s, Forbes Burnham's predominantly black People's National Congress (PNC) consolidated its hold on government against its main rival, Cheddi Jagan's People's Progressive party, which represented the numerically superior East Indian population.[26] In rigged elections in 1968 Burnham gained full control of both the legislature and the executive. Blacks already had overwhelming representation in the urban unions, civil service, and, what proved crucial, the army and police forces. The PNC used its newly gained political power to launch a socialist course, incorporating lower-class blacks into the regime through public employment. By 1977, 80 percent of the economy was in state hands and a black bureaucratic elite was being forged.[27]

The effort to consolidate the socialist experiment ran afoul of declining economic performance after 1977, particularly in the three sectors on which the economy rested: bauxite, rice, and sugar. Recognizing the political importance of external resources, Burnham appointed a powerful committee to oversee a 1978 standby agreement. An EFF was signed in June 1979.

Demonstrations and strikes against the regime increased in response to the economic downturn and Burnham's increasingly authoritarian political tactics. The response of the government was coercive. As austerity undercut the means of maintaining support through the state sector, so Burnham's reliance on the army and police increased. The opposition came under continual harassment. Strikes in the bauxite sector, once a PNC stronghold, were broken violently, and striking sugar workers were replaced by members of the armed forces and civil service. Elections held in December 1980 were found by international observers to be fraudulent in every regard,[28] and the U.S. State Department's 1980 report on human rights in Guyana noted "the blurring of the distinction between the ruling party and the government."[29]

In October 1980 the government admitted the failure of the first EFF, blaming setbacks on bad weather, strikes, and "political subversion."[30] A second EFF had already been signed, in July. One year later the Fund ap-

26. For background see Percy Hintzen and Ralph R. Premdas, "Guyana: Coercion and Control in Political Change," *Journal of Interamerican Studies* 24 (August 1982); Jay R. Mandle, "Continuity and Change in Guyana's Underdevelopment," *Monthly Review* 28 (September 1976); C. Enloe, "Civilian Control of the Military: Implications in the Plural Societies of Guyana and Malaysia," in C. Welsh, *Civilian Control of the Military* (Albany: SUNY Press, 1976); and Premdas, "Guyana: Socialist Reconstruction or Political Opportunism?" *Journal of Interamerican Studies* 20 (May 1978).

27. Kenneth P. Jameson, "Socialist Cuba and the Intermediate Regimes of Jamaica and Guyana," *World Development* 9 (September–October 1981).

28. *LARR:C*, 16 January 1981.

29. Cited in *LARR:C*, 22 March 1981.

30. *QER*, 1st quarter, 1980.

proved a request from Guyana to augment its drawing under the EFF by 50 percent. The new program was immediately followed by harsher measures: a long-avoided devaluation, cuts in government expenditures and subsidies, and a consumption tax on over a thousand items. Only top officials, already highly paid, received wage increases in full compensation for the effects of the devaluation. Work stoppages, malingering, and even sabotage increased in the crucial sugar, bauxite, and rice sectors, and production in all three sectors fell dramatically short of targets, contributing to shortfalls in foreign reserves. The government also proved unwilling to impose financial discipline on state-owned enterprises, an important target of Fund scrutiny.[31] Not until December 1982 did the government publicly admit that, after one drawing, the second EFF had also lapsed for failure to meet fiscal and foreign-exchange reserve requirements. Given Burnham's political goals and style, austerity bred coercive politics but coercion did not produce adjustment.

The Sudan exhibits, perhaps in exaggerated form, the political difficulties of stabilization and adjustment in countries with weak institutions, ethnic and religious factions, and low incomes.[32] In the absence of an integrative nationalist movement, political identification in the Sudan was initially mobilized around rival Islamic sects. Numeiri's 1969 coup sought to construct a progressive secular government: middle-ranking officers allied with the Communists against religious forces. The new government denied any political role to organized groups. It sought gradually to coopt key individual leaders into specific bargains, including a "reconciliation" with Mahdist religious leader Sadiq-al-Mahdi in 1977. Numeiri's selective cooptation probably contributed to his survival by fragmenting the opposition,[33] but it contributed to the country's economic woes.

The economic conditions triggering Sudan's difficulties included expansionary fiscal policies, subsidies for consumer essentials, and in the late 1970s large wage increases.[34] Cotton exports fell 21 percent between 1970 and 1979 due to an abortive effort to diversify production into other cash crops.[35] Some of these problems had political roots. Numeiri's settlement of the armed secessionist struggle in the south in March 1972 resulted in de facto recognition of the biracial and bicultural nature of the country. To cement the settlement, Numeiri launched an ambitious development program; gov-

31. *LARR:C*, 16 July, 20 August, and 30 September 1982.
32. See Jackson and Rosberg, *Personal Rule*, pp. 130ff.; Peter Bechtold, *Politics in Sudan: Parliamentary and Military Rule in an Emerging African Nation* (New York: Praeger, 1976); and Dunstan M. Wai, "Revolution, Rhetoric, and Reality," *Journal of Modern African Studies* 17, 1 (1979). For a review of the period under question with an emphasis on the agricultural sector see Robert L. Curry, Jr., "The Global Economy's Impact on Planning in Kenya and Sudan," *Journal of African Studies* 9, 2 (1982).
33. See *African Contemporary Record* (hereafter *ACR*), 1981–82, p. 392.
34. See Karim Nashashibi, "A Supply Framework for Exchange Reform in Developing Countries: The Experience of Sudan," *IMF Staff Papers* 27 (March 1980); *IMF Survey*, 7 May 1979, 1 September 1980.
35. *IMF Survey*, 7 May 1979.

ernment expenditures increased 70 percent in fiscal 1973–74 and more than doubled in 1974–75. Fiscal deficits were averaging 7 percent of gross domestic product (GDP) by the late 1970s. Government-owned enterprises, occupying a dominant position in the economy, were responsible for much of the government's borrowing.

In June 1978, after three years of resistance to devaluation by the Sudanese government, a program of economic reform was launched. It had three main components: the restructuring of agricultural incentives to promote exports; financial stabilization, including cuts in subsidies, a moratorium on new projects, and restriction of new credit; and the settlement of external debt and arrears. The EFF signed in May 1979 incorporated these goals.

The EFF did not run to its conclusion, however, despite a massive increase in the original resources in November 1980 from 200 to 427 million Special Drawing Rights (SDRs). As in many of the poorest countries, the failure of the program in the Sudan seems overdetermined, hamstrung by problems ranging from aid shortfalls to administrative weaknesses.

As in eight other EFF cases—the Dominican Republic, Egypt, Bangladesh, Guyana, Morocco, Pakistan, Senegal, and Sierra Leone—the issue of food subsidies proved a crucial sticking point. In four EFF countries, and arguably in Brazil as well, ill-timed and poorly implemented subsidy cuts provoked food riots, the most serious in Casablanca on 20 June 1981 when an estimated two hundred people were killed.[36] Additional political compromises played their part as well. The Sudanese government, like many of its counterparts, faced historically strong unions in state-owned enterprises. Labor responded quickly to the first round of austerities and the failure to deliver promised pay increases. The strikes were political, directed against the government rather than local management.[37] The government put the army on alert, but it also made critical concessions, rescinding increases in the price of petrol and promising pay raises and price controls on basic commodities.

The next year, 1981, brought much more serious strike action. The Sudan Railway Workers Union, the oldest and best organized union in the country, struck in support of wage increases and the reinstatement of workers purged for political reasons. The government declared the strike illegal and sought, unsuccessfully, to use the army to run the railway system. The railroad union was dissolved; illegal strikes were declared "high treason" punishable by death; strikers not returning to work would lose their jobs and benefits; and Numeiri even announced plans to denationalize and decentralize the railways—a move that would dramatically reduce union power. In breaking the strike Numeiri set the tone for a more repressive approach to workers in the public sector.[38]

36. See *Jeune Afrique*, 1 July and 8 July 1981.
37. *QER*, 3d quarter, 1979.
38. *QER*, 3d quarter, 1981.

It was the students and the urban poor, however, who responded most directly to the price increases and the cuts in subsidies. The "IMF riots" began as student affairs.[39] In August 1979, following a 66 percent increase in the retail price of petrol that led to higher taxi and bus fares, student riots broke out in Khartoum and other provincial capitals. Though the riots were broken up, the government was forced to decrease the price of petrol and to promise price controls on basic commodities.

Student action against the government was renewed in November 1981, following the effective cancelation of the EFF and the negotiation of a new standby that demanded additional austerities. Blaming the deterioration of the economy on the inefficiency and bad administration of his own government, Numeiri sacked his entire cabinet.[40] New measures included 30–40 percent increases in the price of petrol and a 62 percent rise in sugar prices. Massive demonstrations followed in Khartoum and spread to other towns. By mid-January 1982 the situation was so grave that there was talk of a military coup. In a surprise move Numeiri first dissolved his own party's leadership and then sacked his vice-president, defense minister, and twenty-two army officers. His action was in effect a palace coup, followed immediately by the formation of a People's Committee, which read like a "*Who's Who of Sudan tribal and family leaders,*"[40] to look into the reorganization of the political system and the question of economic reforms. Numeiri's balancing act of selective cooptation began again, but with little hope for a solution to the Sudan's economic problems.

The political irrationality of adjustment

Authoritarian or one-party rule does not necessarily facilitate adjustment, particularly where resource constraints are severe. Zaire and Haiti represent an extreme: with little or no inclination to stabilize, with the role of technocrats inside the government severely circumscribed, and with adjustment entailing an attack on the political elite's discretionary use of state finance, failure is hardly surprising.

Guyana raises a different set of problems. Austerity there did not so much pose a direct threat to the material interests of the ruling elite as it did to its ability to pursue a socialist course while maintaining ethnically based support through state patronage. Stabilization narrowed the regime's political base. The party, which had consolidated its grip on the state apparatus, was faced with a difficult choice. Should concessions be made and the political process broadened—at the risk of unleashing ethnic conflict and a loss of power—or should coercion be employed? By 1981 Burnham's regime had become severely repressive, but in doing so it had alienated labor in sectors that held the key to continued growth.

39. *Africa Research Bulletin*, Economic ser., 15 December–14 January 1982.
40. *ACR*, 1981–82.

172   *Stephan Haggard*

The Sudan presents the problem of a deeply factionalized and weakly institutionalized military regime with virtually no economic slack. Numeiri's skillful political juggling and cooptation, including the constant promise of broad political reform, kept the political opposition off balance, but it also involved economic compromises. Numeiri, unlike Burnham, may have felt unable to rely on a purely coercive solution, because of divisions within the Sudanese army. In both countries, however, political weaknesses of different sorts contributed to program failure.

Democratic stalemate

Stalemate left and right: Jamaica and Sri Lanka

In at least twelve of the twenty-four countries that negotiated EFFs, economic policy was made in the context of some political competition and electoral constraint.[41] Jamaica demonstrates most clearly and controversially the phenomenon of democratic stalemate and the broader difficulties of democratic socialism.[42] The ideological program and coalitional base of Michael Manley's People's National party (PNP) clashed repeatedly with IMF logic. While Edward Seaga's Jamaica Labour party (JLP) was able to capitalize on Manley's difficulties, Seaga was elected on the basis of promises he could not fulfill. Coupled with the economic failure of Fund advice, the system of patronage and popular organization that had blossomed under Manley saddled Seaga's regime with the same difficulties as his predecessor's.

The PNP was voted into office in 1972 on a populist platform appealing to the unemployed and large segments of workers and peasantry.[43] The government's economic program stressed the redistribution of income and

41. The democratic regimes are Costa Rica, the Dominican Republic, India, Jamaica, Kenya, Peru, and Sri Lanka. Mexico, Senegal, and Zambia are one-party dominant systems that operate under some electoral constraints, while Brazil and Honduras were undergoing transitions to democracy at the time of their EFFs.

42. The notoriety of the Jamaican case has generated its own literature. The IMF explains its position in *IMF Survey*, 15 December 1980. See Jennifer Sharpley, "Economic Management and IMF Conditionality in Jamaica," in Williamson, *IMF Conditionality*; Norman Girvan, Richard Bernal, and Wesley Hughes, "The IMF and the Third World: The Case of Jamaica, 1974–1980," *Development Dialogue*, 1980/2; Winston James, "The Decline and Fall of Michael Manley: Jamaica, 1972–1980," *Capital and Class* no. 19 (Spring 1983); Gladstone Bannick, "The Experience of Jamaica," in Dell Report, *The Balance of Payments Adjustment Process in Developing Countries*, UNCTAD/MFD/TA/5 (New York, 1980); Richard Burkholder, Jr., "The International Monetary Fund's Presence in Jamaica, 1976–1980: Its Effect on Factional Struggle within the People's National Party Government of Michael Manley" (ms., Harvard University, 1984); and for background on the Jamaican political system Carl Stone, *Democracy and Clientelism in Jamaica* (New Brunswick: Transaction, 1980). I am particularly indebted to the definitive study by Evelyne Huber Stephens and John D. Stephens, *Democratic Socialism in Jamaica: The Political Movement and Social Transformation in Dependent Capitalism* (Princeton: Princeton University Press, forthcoming), and to comments by the authors.

43. See Carl Stone, "Democratic Socialism in Jamaica, 1962–1979," *Journal of Commonwealth and Comparative Politics* 20, 2 (1982), p. 40, for electoral data.

the creation of short-term employment rather than investment and increased production. Private-sector investment slowed, particularly with the PNP's shift to a more radical and statist economic program after 1974. Efforts to adjust to the oil shock were delayed until after the elections of December 1976. During that election year government spending rose 20 percent, despite declining revenues. The PNP gained an unexpectedly sweeping mandate.[44]

Prior to the elections, treasury and central bank officials had negotiated a tentative two-year IMF standby on the basis of a wage freeze, a curbing of the deficit, and a 20–40 percent devaluation. Electoral victory served to strengthen the left wing of the PNP, however, which had been active in mobilizing electoral support. The left wing proved a critical constraint on Manley's freedom, forcing him to reject the tentative agreement and announce a structuralist alternative that included price increases, higher taxes, a wage freeze, and an extensive battery of trade and exchange controls. Despite this politicization, diplomatic support from Britain and Canada helped Manley to negotiate a surprisingly lenient agreement with the Fund, though still against the wishes of the party left. A large devaluation was avoided, wage guidelines allowed a maintenance of 1973 real wages and, though demand management was called for, specific policies were not spelled out in detail.

Nonetheless, Jamaica failed the first performance test in December 1977, in part because of retroactive pay increases for the police and military announced the same month. As Jennifer Sharpley concludes, "the 1977 breakdown illustrates both the lack of independence of the technocrats from their political context and the lack of flexibility of the Fund in view of changed external circumstances."[45]

Politics intruded in two ways when the EFF was negotiated in 1978. Fund officials resented Manley's ability to politicize the earlier standby and to extract concessions. However, Manley had gained politically on the basis of that very success, though hardly with the party left. The two political games clashed. The IMF's effort to extract more comprehensive terms under the EFF reactivated the PNP's left wing.

The terms of the EFF were a direct attack on Manley's entire ideological and political program. Not only did the program entail a major devaluation, the avoidance of which had become a point of honor in Jamaica's relations with the Fund, but the IMF demanded deep cuts in wages, a switch of resources from public to private sector, and a move away from administrative controls to reliance on market forces. Despite strict adherence to conditions, economic performance did not match Fund projections, eroding what little political slack Manley still had.[46] A "Social Contract" between the government, the private sector, and the unions traded a 10 percent increase in

44. Ibid.
45. Sharpley, "Economic Management," p. 246.
46. The Fund later admitted a political motivation in negotiating the EFF despite its harsh terms.

wages for similar restraints on prices. What Manley could not overcome was the tremendous uncertainty his government had created among domestic and foreign investors about the future of the private sector. Yet it was the private sector that held the economic resources required for the success of the market-oriented program.

The growth objectives of the renegotiated program were not met, either, and as real GDP fell in 1979, the left within the PNP was revivified. When Jamaica failed three performance criteria, negotiations were opened on a waiver. These negotiations stalled on the issues of further wage freezes and cutbacks in social programs. PNP union officials and the party's left demonstrated openly against government layoffs. In announcing the termination of negotiations with the Fund, Manley called elections, running them as a virtual referendum on the Fund.

His decision raised the question of the posture that the PNP was going to take toward further dealings with the IMF. The left argued that the IMF was bent on the political destruction of the PNP and that an alternative economic program was required—one that would rest on a radical expansion of the state sector.[47] The PNP blamed the economic crisis on external causes and the Fund's programs. Seaga's JLP argued that domestic policies were to blame and that foreign capital and good relations with the IMF were critical for Jamaica's future growth. In a campaign marked by widespread violence, the JLP won a dramatic victory, attracting voters from the working class, peasantry, and unemployed.[48] Seaga had apparently forged a coalition around a rejection of Manley's policies, yet the optimism over his election, both at home and abroad, was short-lived. Democratic stalemate emerged virtually at once, for Jamaicans had voted against hardship, not for more austerity. When "deliverance," the JLP's campaign slogan, did not materialize, public opinion turned against Seaga just as it had turned against Manley. The very system of state patronage and popular organization that had limited Manley's ability to act similarly plagued Seaga, and the targets associated with the 1981 EFF were repeatedly broken.[49]

If Jamaica typifies the stalemate of democratic socialism, Sri Lanka has been hailed as a model of the benefits of IMF-style reforms. There, the economic failures of the previous administration and the fragmentation of the opposition allowed sharp departures in policy within a democratic framework. Despite the sympathy of the new government for IMF-style policies, however, Sri Lanka also shows the difficulty of maintaining stable policies in a democratic setting.

Mrs. Bandaranaike returned to power in 1970 at the head of a united

47. See Burkholder, "IMF's Presence in Jamaica," for a discussion of the PNP's internal deliberations.
48. See Stone, "Democratic Socialism."
49. See *LARR:C*, 24 August 1984; Stephens and Stephens, *Democratic Socialism in Jamaica*, chap. 7.

front of her dominant Sri Lanka Freedom party and smaller leftist parties, and she pursued policies to the left of her main opposition, the United National party (UNP).[50] Government expropriations and macroeconomic mismanagement increased uncertainty and reduced profitability in the crucial tea, rubber, and coconut sectors. The steady deterioration of plantation production contributed to slower growth, which in turn placed a fiscal strain on the government's successful but ambitious and costly social welfare programs. These included free distribution of rice and heavy subsidies for food, public transport, utilities, and health care.[51] The government's political commitment to maintain these programs in the face of mounting economic difficulties led to an expansion of price controls, export and import controls, and shortages, and to the growth of a black market. Factional and ideological conflicts within the government produced erratic economic management. Moreover, Mrs. Bandaranaike's arbitrary responses to spreading strikes and protests raised questions about her willingness to govern within a democratic framework.

Exploiting economic and political grievances and moving his UNP to the center, J. R. Jayawardene was able to win a huge majority in the National Assembly elections of July 1977, for the first time completely excluding the left from national representation. Victory brought a cohesive new economic team into government, allowing for a shift in economic priorities and dramatic changes in the political structure that had the effect of giving the executive more power. Many of the economic reforms were consistent with the Fund's orientation toward structural adjustment, among them the liberalization of imports, a unification of the exchange rate, the end of state monopolies, the phasing out of subsidies, a raising of interest rates, and a general encouragement of the private sector. The new government's economic strategy also included three enormous "lead projects," however, projects that appealed to politically diverse constituents. The Accelerated Mahaweli River Development Project became a symbol of the regime's rural commitment, a series of urban and rural housing projects were launched, and a free-trade zone was to be constructed in Colombo. The IMF backed the new program with a standby and, in 1978, with an EFF.[52] The Fund saw the elimination of subsidies as centrally important, to free financing for the government's ambitious investment schemes. With a strong electoral showing in the local elections held in May 1979, the UNP felt able to move ahead on this sensitive issue and launched a phase-out plan.

After two years of accelerated growth, however, Sri Lanka's effort at struc-

50. *IMF Survey*, 3 June 1980. This also draws on Joan Nelson, "The Political Economy of Stabilization in Small, Low-Income Trade Dependent Nations" (ms., ODC, Washington, D.C., November 1983), and Joseph Stern, "Liberalization in Sri Lanka: A Preliminary Assessment" (ms., Harvard Institute for International Development, 1984). See also Ron Herring, *Land to the Tiller: The Political Economy of Agrarian Reform in South Asia* (New Haven: Yale University Press, 1983).
51. Paul Isenman, "Basic Needs: The Case of Sri Lanka," *World Development* 8 (1980).
52. *QER*, 2d quarter, 1978.

tural adjustment met unanticipated economic difficulties, suggesting limitations on the program's design. The private sector was hesitant in its response to new investment and export incentives. Administrative problems continued in the agricultural export sector, and balance-of-payments deficits grew. Politics also played a role.

The rapid growth of expenditure associated with the three major projects was the major contributor to budget deficits, leading to higher foreign borrowing, higher inflation, and diminished private-sector access to credit. Yet the "lead projects" were integral to the UNP's electoral pledges. Ministries were encouraged to become more active in formulating projects that would generate the "one million jobs in three years" that the UNP had promised in 1977. Appropriating too much on capital spending in the first place, the Finance Ministry acceded to parliamentary demands for supplementary additions.[53] The prime minister, Ranasinghe Premadasa, also the minister of local government, housing and construction, was particularly committed to the massive rural and urban housing program. His "village wakening movement" involved building one model village in each electoral constituency, arousing the interest of backbenchers in Parliament even though the program demanded the abrogation of Fund conditions.[54]

These incidents occurred after World Bank and IMF budget reviews showed that the Finance Ministry was losing control. EFF disbursements were interrupted and aid increases blocked by the donor consortium in an effort to scale down the 1980–1984 Public Investment Program.[55] In June 1981 the finance minister was able to negotiate a resumption of disbursements by agreeing to raise more revenues through a battery of new taxes, though allowing wage increases to the politically crucial workers in the public sector.

The debate within the government typified the political dilemma of democratically constrained adjustment. (Despite differences between the two governments, it bore a resemblance to debate within the PNP in Jamaica.) On the one hand were those around the Finance Ministry who saw inflation as the key economic as well as political problem. The finance minister sought to maintain the cooperation of the Fund, arguing that "more governments fall by inflation than by lack of development."[56] Other senior ministers argued, however, that employment remained the primary problem and public spending was the only palliative. They counseled disregard of the IMF and a search for alternative finance to sustain growth.

53. For example, in the 1981 budget announced in November 1980 the finance minister sought to cut spending on the Mahaweli project 25%, from Rs. 4 billion to Rs. 3 billion. The special minister in charge of the key project, however, asked for Rs. 4.5 billion, finally receiving Rs. 3.8 billion, over protests from both the World Bank and the IMF. See *Far Eastern Economic Review* (hereafter *FEER*), 16 October 1981, and Howard Wriggins, "Sri Lanka in 1981: Year of Austerity, Developmental Councils and Communal Disorders," *Asian Survey* 22 (February 1982).

54. *FEER*, 20 February 1981.

55. *QER*, 4th quarter, 1980.

56. *FEER*, 20 February 1981.

With the decision to hold elections in October 1982, the stop-go syndrome started to be driven by electoral politics more directly. Economic measures in the course of 1982 reversed the discipline of 1981, including large increases in wages and salaries. The opposition was factionalized, and the UNP won another five-year mandate. The new budget, postponed until after the elections, reflected once again the effort to cut spending.

Both Jamaica and Sri Lanka provide examples of democratic stalemate. In each country a strong electoral mandate provided the political basis for change in economic policy. In Jamaica, Manley's socialist project dictated a leftward shift in policy that could be sustained neither against adverse external shocks nor against the declining confidence of the private sector and the raised expectations of the left wing of the ruling PNP. Both groups held independent resources with which they could undermine the adjustment effort: the private sector by not investing, the PNP left wing by mobilizing opposition. Neither the Fund program nor the left's alternative could deliver Manley from his economic difficulties, and Seaga's conservative opposition had ample ammunition to carry him to electoral victory. In Sri Lanka, by contrast, an incoming government reacted against the "excesses" of its leftist predecessor. The new government gained IMF support, but over time the populist-expansionist faction in the party exerted greater influence and electoral politics dictated short-term economic compromises.

Stalemate under corporatism? Mexico

Corporatist political structures, which permit peak bargaining between labor, business, and government, appear ideally suited to forge social consensus on economic adjustment.[57] While not averse to selective coercion and manipulation, Mexico's ruling Partido Revolucionario Institucional (PRI) has a political dependence on corporatist labor and peasant organizations. Political reforms during the 1970s made Mexico's political system at least formally more democratic. Yet this very inclusiveness and the PRI's revolutionary claims to legitimacy have been in political terms both short-term assets and medium-term liabilities. Over the course of the López Portillo administration conflicting political imperatives from both inside and outside the bureaucracy led to the pursuit of an expansionary course, financed at first by oil revenues but increasingly by external debt. Despite optimism concerning the de la Madrid administration's performance through 1984, history suggests that the test of Mexico's corporatist adjustment may be yet to come.

In 1977 López Portillo inherited an economy suffering from a weak cur-

---

57. For a review and critique of the literature on European corporatism see Leo Panitch, "Recent Theorizations of Corporatism: Reflections on a Growth Industry," *British Journal of Sociology* 31 (June 1980).

178   *Stephan Haggard*

rency, a large trade deficit, and rising external indebtedness. Mexico approached the IMF with a sophisticated medium-term adjustment proposal that skillfully balanced traditional Fund criteria with an interest in accelerating growth and employment.[58] The IMF agreement included normal ceilings on monetary expansion and limits on net external borrowing. More ambitious were the expectations that budget deficits would be reduced from a projected 6 percent of gross national product (GNP) in 1977 to 4 percent in 1978 and 2.5 percent in 1979 and that fiscal reforms would be made.

The new government, needing to control labor, pressed for wage settlements limiting increases to 10 percent.[59] Despite strikes by independent unions, the PRI-controlled labor federation (the CTM) indicated a willingness to support the new administration by making visible sacrifices. While offering short-term support, however, the labor movement simultaneously signaled that it would not be willing to bear the full brunt of adjustment over the longer term.

The restoration of private-sector confidence demanded a series of political overtures, taking the form of a largely symbolic "Alliance for Production" negotiated between the private sector and the incoming administration. Leaders of the conservative Monterrey Group of industrialists lent public support to the alliance with a set of investment proposals in early 1977.[60] In return the government would increase the fiscal and financial supports to investors. New overtures were also made to foreign firms.

This openly probusiness strategy for stabilization faced important opposition within the government itself. The treasury secretary, Moctezuma Cid, defended the program, reflecting the continuity of a conservative orientation in that ministry. The secretary of the newly created Ministry of Planning and Budget (SPP), Carlos Tello, advocated an alternative, expansionist approach, however, using state investment to generate employment while increasing social and health expenditures. López Portillo also came to agree on the need for more rapid investments in the oil and gas sectors.[61] The

58. Mexico's memorandum to the IMF notes, for example, "Strong opposition must be overcome before it will be politically possible to stop the provision of consumer subsidies on basic consumption items and to dismantle the associated bureaucracy. Perhaps it will be even more difficult to get it recognized that the wage rises of recent years caused Mexico's loss of competitiveness and to obtain the necessary support for a policy of real wage cuts." Confidential text leaked to *El Heraldo*, 7 November 1977, quoted in Lawrence Whitehead, "Mexico from Bust to Boom: A Political Evaluation of the 1976–1979 Stabilization Program," *World Development* 8 (November 1980), p. 849.

59. Jose Luis Reyna, "El movemiento obrero en una situación de crisis: Mexico, 1976–1978," *Foro Internacional* 19 (January–March 1979). For a critique of labor's concessions see *Proceso*, 10 July and 13 November 1978.

60. *LAWR*, 8 April 1977.

61. In late June, López Portillo announced that "[These sectors] cannot be developed without modifying what we have called the IMF padlocks on deficit spending and external indebtedness . . . we are in a vicious cycle. We cannot get out of the trap because we do not have financial resources and we do not have them because we cannot get out of the trap." *Business Latin America*, 10 July 1977.

political tension inside and outside the government over stabilization and the Alliance for Production became clear in the course of 1977. Inflation rose above 20 percent, far outstripping the 10 percent wage gains given to labor, while private investment lagged. In August, López Portillo freed the unions to pursue wage settlements above 10 percent. When Tello's proposal for an expansionary budget was overruled by the cabinet, he resigned. López Portillo immediately relieved Moctezuma Cid as well, in order to avoid the appearance of siding with the right.

Oil appeared to promise deliverance from the continuing pressures on the president, but in fact it only sparked new debates over the industrial strategy that Mexico should pursue. The Ministry of Patrimony and Industrial Development favored increased state action to promote capital goods investment, expanded control over industry, banking, and foreign exchange, and increased outlays for social expenditures and rural reforms.[62] The Treasury and the Bank of Mexico, backed to varying degrees by the private sector, the World Bank, and the IMF, supported a continuation of the policies of the first two years, which relied on wage controls, tax exemptions, and credit to stimulate private-sector growth. Government would rationalize industry by pursuing phased liberalization, a positive posture toward foreign investment, and a realistic exchange rate.

Intrabureaucratic conflict produced an eclectic policy mix. By late 1978, however, a boom was under way that allowed early repayment to the IMF and made the conditions of the original agreement irrelevant. The boom did not, however, resolve the political divisions over the direction of economic policy. The interventionist National Industrial Development Plan revived the conflict over the respective roles of the private and the public sectors and "statization." Within the government the conservative Bank of Mexico cautioned that inflation and the external deficit were growing important as a constraint.

More strident, however, was the chorus of criticism from the left, which reached a high point during the Fourth Congress of Economists in May 1981.[63] The "national project" of the congress covered agriculture, industry, and energy, but also the underlying political commitments that would accompany different growth paths. The state, it argued, should take a lead role in industrialization and agricultural reform, imposing limits and conditions on private investment. Energy would be an instrument for achieving basic reforms, allowing attention to be given to housing, health, education, and the creation of jobs. This programmatic emphasis corresponded closely with

62. While this nationalist posture had clear historical and political roots and found support in the labor movement, it was given new intellectual justification by a group of economists in the Ministry of Patrimony and influenced by Cambridge School economics. See "Mexico's Cambridge Connection," *New York Times*, 24 October 1982 (sec. 3, p. 1), and the response by John Eatwell and Ajit Singh, *New York Times*, 29 November 1982.

63. See the essays in *El Economista Mexicano* 15 (July–August 1981).

the interests of most opposition parties on the left and the independent unions.

Politics explains government action and inaction in the course of 1981 and 1982. Left groups were beginning to argue that basic economic and social reforms were impossible given the corporatist nature of state structures, challenging the PRI's very legitimacy. More immediately, both the right-wing PAN and the left parties presented an electoral challenge. Neither came close to defeating the PRI, but the left, with access to the media, could plausibly seek to capture the symbols of the revolution for itself: democracy, anti-imperialism, development, justice, and equality. The right sought to capitalize on growing middle-class and regional discontent with economic mismanagement and inflation.

The pressures to preserve high levels of growth thus continued during 1981 despite growing inflation. Without the anticipated levels of oil revenue the government faced larger-than-expected deficits in the budget and the current account, and the capacity to borrow proved a great temptation. Over the course of 1981 external borrowing increased by more than 80 percent. In the summer of 1981 an "austerity plan" was instituted, seeking to cut government expenditures by 4 percent. In fact, actual spending for the year was 12 percent over the budget, with huge expenditures going to subsidize fuel and food. The federal deficit jumped from 7.6 percent of GNP in 1980 to 14.2 percent in 1981. Angel Gurria, the Finance Ministry's director of external borrowing, admitted in 1982 that "there was a political decision made not to stop the country's growth in the middle of the year."[64] By February 1982 it had become clear that the central bank would not be able to maintain a fixed rate of exchange, and the peso was floated. Successive austerity measures were announced, but all depended on a political settlement between business and labor. Labor now insisted on wage increases that would fully compensate workers for the effects of devaluation. The secretary of labor unilaterally announced a package of increases that by themselves would add 12 percent to the federal budget.[65]

Prices proved uncontrollable. Government subsidies, a major contributor to budget deficits, increased still further following the devaluation, particularly for basic foodstuffs (the lower-class subsidy) and fuel (the middle-class subsidy). In August the Ministry of Finance announced a second round of IMF-style reforms, marking a defeat for the expansionists within the cabinet. In a final political balancing act López Portillo reached out to the left by announcing the nationalization of the banking system in his last presidential address.

In 1977 López Portillo had attempted to reconstruct the pre-Echeverría growth coalition. The incoming government, as in Sri Lanka, sought to exploit

64. *Miami Herald*, 30 August 1982.
65. *LAWR*, 19 April 1982.

dissatisfaction with its predecessor in order to favor domestic and foreign investors, control wages, and stabilize the economy along lines acceptable to the IMF. Over time, however, political constraints made the temptation to escape from Fund strictures through oil-led growth irresistible. Continuing social problems gave visibility to leftist critics of the government, while on the right the PAN was able to make new appeals to the growing middle class. As in both Jamaica and Sri Lanka economic-ideological splits within the administration proved an additional source of policy incoherence. Above all, labor retained crucial political assets vis-à-vis the PRI. Willing to make short-run sacrifices, the CTM was unwilling and unable to accept stabilizing reforms over a longer time frame, particularly as inflation began to erode real wages and the traditional unions were challenged by independents on the left. The result was a democratic stalemate, "solved" only by overt economic crisis.

Over the last weeks of the López Portillo administration a new agreement with the IMF was negotiated. The incoming president, Miguel de la Madrid Hurtado, acted boldly and swiftly to contain wages, cut public spending, raise revenues, and attack corruption.[66] IMF targets were met or exceeded, making Mexico the success story for stabilization, though at the cost of deep recession, a decline in real income, and an erosion of support for the country's political institutions. De la Madrid's reformism proved wide-ranging, aiming at a significant reduction in the role of government, and he emphasized efficiency and selective liberalization of the economy in order to enhance international competitiveness. If the previous administration provides an insight into the future, however, the test of the new administration will come in the middle years of the *sexennio*. The 1984–85 budget was already marking a departure from previous austerity. Given the political and social pressures on the PRI, will this settlement be more durable than the last?

The political bases of "will"

The conventional wisdom that an "elective affinity" exists between authoritarianism and IMF stabilization programs is oversimplified. Authoritarian polities, both those dominated by narrow, clientelistic elites and those depending on broader systems of state patronage for their legitimacy, present daunting barriers to economic adjustment. These countries, among the poorest in the world and exhibiting consistently low levels of economic growth, pose a particular challenge to external actors, since reform seems to depend on the circumvention of the central government.

66. For an overview of the de la Madrid administration, see Wayne Cornelius, "The Political Economy of Mexico under De La Madrid: Austerity, Institutionalized Crisis and Nascent Recovery," *Mexican Studies* 1 (Winter 1985).

182   *Stephan Haggard*

Political leaders in developing democratic countries must work with narrow economic slack, and hence their problems of stabilization and adjustment should not be surprising, though Sri Lanka and Mexico indicate that short-run policy shifts are possible. Austerity led in both countries to higher levels of political mobilization and activism among labor and other groups, contributing to an erratic, stop-go policy, but it did not result in authoritarian or repressive solutions. The most repressive responses to austerity were to be found among those already authoritarian regimes in which opposition to austerity was coupled with broader political challenges to the regime.

The cases suggest that three other political factors are important in explaining a regime's capacity to make economic adjustments. They are the availability of nonconditional resources and, perhaps more importantly, the ideological orientation of bureaucratic elites and the strength of administrative structures.

Temptation

The case of Mexico suggests that the existence of alternative sources of finance—increased economic or military aid, remittances, export earnings, or commercial borrowing—leads to an abrogation of the Fund's adjustment programs. This is to be expected, as new resources make old conditions obsolete. Generally, however, such windfalls are short-lived and do not solve the structural imbalances that an EFF seeks to address; indeed, they may make them worse. The result is usually a return to the Fund. Six cases demonstrate this pattern: Gabon (declared by the IMF to be a success), Kenya, Egypt, Mexico, and possibly India and Pakistan.

This problem of temptation was found in one of the very first EFFs, signed with Kenya in 1975.[67] The only performance criteria imposed by the Fund were ceilings on the total expansion of credit and on government borrowing from the banking system. In the second half of 1975, however, coffee prices shot up, rising 69 percent over June levels by December. The government quickly expanded its borrowing in excess of the credit ceilings and, as Tony Killick summarizes, the program simply "fizzled out."[68] By late 1978, though, Kenya was drawing on its first credit tranche and borrowing commercially. These funds "gave the government an assurance that it would not be forced into devaluation during the politically sensitive period of a presidential election."[69] By the summer a deterioration in the current account had become apparent, and negotiations were under way for a two-year standby and a World Bank structural adjustment loan.

High politics play a crucial, if quiet, role in the IMF adjustment process.

67. Tony Killick, "Kenya: The IMF and the Unsuccessful Quest for Stabilization," in Williamson, *IMF Conditionality.*
68. Ibid., p. 400.
69. Ibid.

Otherwise weak governments can manipulate their strategic significance and ties with powerful patrons to secure additional resources. Egyptian commitment to a May 1978 EFF, for example, was probably undermined by the signing of the Camp David accord in March 1979 and the subsequent inflow of U.S. aid.[70] Egypt's EFF sought to support a broad program, rationalizing the exchange and domestic interest rates, curbing inflation, and reducing governments deficits. In January 1979 devaluation met the IMF guideline to eliminate the dual exchange-rate system and interest rates were raised. The main problem, however, was meeting the fiscal conditions due to politically sensitive food subsidies. The government's reluctance to act was wholly rational. In January 1977 the government had faced severe and widespread rioting after it had lifted food subsidies.

The IMF refused to release the second and third tranches of the credit in mid-1979. By then, however, Egypt had more money than it knew what to do with. Aid commitments in the first year following the Camp David accord totaled $1 billion in outright grants and another $1.8 billion in military contracts and "supplementary" aid. Government assessments showed that the average utilization rate for foreign finance in 1978 was 61 percent, and (as of December 1978) $4.3 billion in aid and credits had been committed but not spent. Record cotton harvests and increased revenues from petroleum and foreign remittances completely altered the balance-of-payments situation. IMF support—and economic advice—was not critical.

Nonetheless, the government sought to negotiate a new EFF, promising to increase its revenue through more vigorous tax collection and reduced subsidies. But the government's commitment to the negotiations is questionable. In May 1980 Sadat announced a 25 percent increase in the minimum wage and a 10 percent bonus for all private-sector workers. The mid-June budget saw increases in wages, subsidies, and social insurance coverage. Not surprisingly, negotiations with the Fund broke down. Only with the economic downturn of 1981 did the government reopen negotiations with the IMF.

Technocrats and adjustment

These cases suggest that the power, cohesion, and ideological orientation of technocrats is an important variable in explaining the fate of IMF programs. A "technocratic" style of economic decision making is generally viewed as one of the characteristic features of the "strong" bureaucratic-authoritarian regimes of Latin America and the newly industrializing countries of East Asia as well.[71] The ideologies of political elites in the developing world fre-

70. The following is drawn from *QER*, various issues. See also John Waterbury, *The Egypt of Nasser and Sadat* (Princeton: Princeton University Press, 1983).
71. See the essays in Collier, *New Authoritarianism*, and Stephan Haggard and Chung-in Moon, "The South Korean State in the International Economy: Liberal, Dependent or Mercantile?" in John Gerard Ruggie, ed., *The Antinomies of Interdependence* (New York: Columbia University Press, 1983).

quently dispose them against the market-oriented reforms associated with the IMF, however. In some cases the counterintuitive rationale for stabilization may simply not be understood. In the absence of a countervailing "stabilizing cadre" capable of articulating the long-term political, as well as economic, benefits of adjustment, programs are likely to fail. The core of this cadre is a cohesive group of sympathetic economic technocrats forming the domestic half of a transnational coalition with the Fund. Where these groups are absent or politically marginal, commitment falters.

The orientation of the economic bureaucracy is as important as its political presence. In more advanced developing countries, including Mexico and India, or in states attempting socialist transformations, such as Jamaica, structuralist alternatives to the Fund's adjustment strategies have been articulated within the economic bureaucracy and academic and intellectual communities. Substantive disagreements over the wisdom of Fund advice can divide the state into Fund supporters and detractors, undermining the cohesion of policy. These divisions reflect a complex mixture of bureaucratic and ideological interests. There is usually a key fault line running between central bankers and finance ministers, who take more orthodox, pro-Fund positions, and ministers of planning, commerce, industry, and trade. At the extreme, technocrats skeptical of Fund advice propose programs that would bypass or subvert an agreement with the IMF.

Administrative constraints

A final range of constraints is perhaps most important of all, particularly for microlevel reforms. Many limitations on the implementation of structural adjustment policies exist not at the level of the political and social system broadly conceived but within the bureaucracies themselves and where particular administrative structures and their environments meet.[72] The implementation of the central government's policies often rests on the compliance of administrative "subsystems." Those subsystems may resist central government incursion, or they may be politically captured or constrained by specific clients. The clearest example can be found in the difficulties that economic ministers routinely face in attempting to control the activities of state-owned enterprises. Moreover, the comprehensiveness of structural adjustment programs entails policies of such complexity that existing administrative structures and personnel may be simply unable to implement them. Not surprisingly, the World Bank has increasingly turned its attention to the problems of the "management" of economic development.[73]

72. John M. Cohen, Merilee S. Grindle, and S. Tjip Walker, "Policy Space and Systems Research in Donor Led Rural Development," Harvard Institute for International Development *Discussion Paper*, April 1984.

73. See the World Bank's *World Development Report 1983* (New York: Oxford University Press for the World Bank, 1983), pt. 2.

Should the IMF know what it's doing?

The power of the IMF rests not on the resources at its disposal but on the need of the target country for those resources and the stamp of approval they confer. One would thus expect the Fund to have most leverage when conditions are desperate and other options are foreclosed. This expectation assumes, however, that the program which the Fund offers is politically feasible; many IMF programs appear not to be. A more careful scrutiny of individual programs would no doubt reveal that plans went awry because of changed economic circumstance and poor design as well as politics. But the record of noncompliance raises an important policy question: how "understanding" should the Fund be of political constraints on program implementation? Is it better to retain the myth of political neutrality, or should political assessments become explict aspects of program design and the quest for alternative paths to stabilization?

Such understanding, one could argue, is critical. Programs designed without reference to political realities are likely to fail and even to generate undesirable political consequences. A more explicit and systematic consideration of political factors would help the Fund to design programs that enhance political commitment to adjustment. Joan Nelson has suggested several such stratagems, for example "political insurance" that would specify conditions under which additional resources might be made available in support of risky policies. She has also emphasized the critical importance of tactics, persuasion, and timing in reducing the political costs of reform measures.[74] Debate meanwhile continues over alternative means of stabilization and adjustment itself, and in particular over the search for an "adjustment with growth" that would relieve political pressures.[75]

The argument for understanding is not as obvious as it might appear, however, as from a slightly different angle the debate over the relative merits of shock treatment and gradual adjustment suggests. Supporters of shock treatment argue that expectations are best shifted by dramatic action; drawing out the adjustment process leaves too many opportunities for waywardness. Overly harsh conditionality may breed program failure, and shock treatment may demand coercive measures in the short run, but leniency *also* breeds failure and can lead to stop-go policies that may be even more costly for the economy over the longer term. Moral hazard thus haunts Fund conditionality just as it haunts any insurance scheme, though the degree of worry about the problem no doubt rests on one's faith in the IMF medicine: "failure" may be the easiest delivery from the costs of "success."

It is also forgotten that the Fund operates within its own set of constraints,

74. Nelson, "The Politics of Stabilization," pp. 114–18.
75. See Tony Killick, Graham Bird, Jennifer Sharpley, and Mary Sutton, "The IMF: Case for a Change in Focus," in Feinberg and Kallab, *Adjustment Crisis*.

including limited resources and a particular mandate. Larger programs and more lenient terms would demand a change of heart on the part of the advanced industrial states. It could also be argued that the entry of the Fund into the pseudoscience of political risk assessment would serve only to politicize even further the IMF's relations with Third World governments. The IMF's legitimacy is already in question; an explicit emphasis on the political would merely confirm suspicions about external meddling.

This consideration leads to a final point concerning the networks of transnational relations established through IMF and World Bank programs. These networks, perhaps more than resources per se, are the political bases for the power and influence of these organizations.[76] The existence of an IMF-sympathetic "stabilizing cadre" within the state appears to be a prerequisite for program success. The IMF and the World Bank have become more than simply the allies of already existing technocratic cadres, however. Indeed, where indigenously trained technocrats exist, as in the advanced developing countries, there is more likely to be an intellectually coherent alternative to Fund ideas. In lower-income countries, however, the Bank and the Fund are likely to play an increasing role in training bureaucrats and even in designing the institutional structures through which economic policy is carried out. Administrative "rationalization" is becoming the back door to deeper political reform.

There is no escaping the inevitable entanglement of the IMF and the World Bank in the bureaucratic and larger political milieus in which they operate. The IMF is an external lobbyist for policies that political leaders themselves view with skepticism. IMF staff can be critical allies of reform-minded technocrats, particularly if programs can be formulated that incorporate Fund guidelines but avoid the stigma of external imposition.[77] For political elites facing stabilization, the Fund might be equally useful as an enemy on which austerity can be blamed even as it is—albeit haltingly—pursued.

76. One study of these transnational relations in the context of an EFF is Robin Broad, "Behind Philippine Policy-Making: The Role of the World Bank and the International Monetary Fund" (Ph.D. diss., Princeton University, June 1983).

77. One example of this is India's EFF. See Catherine Gwin, "Financing India's Structural Adjustment: The Role of the Fund," in Williamson, *IMF Conditionality*.

Democratic and authoritarian responses to the debt issue: Argentina, Brazil, Mexico
Robert R. Kaufman

For Latin American governments, mediating between their national societies and the international economy, the contemporary debt issue poses some excruciating dilemmas. On the one side, these governments are under intense pressure to arrive at satisfactory formulas for settling their debts—satisfactory, that is, to the banks and creditor agencies that control access to international financial markets. Loss of such access would threaten vital capital and trade flows, and for this reason virtually every Latin American government has so far placed a high priority on meeting its external obligations. But governmental elites, if they are to remain in power, must also answer to (or repress) their own populations. And the price to be paid for external help with "liquidity problems" has typically involved politically dangerous stabilization measures (devaluations, wage and credit restrictions, and fiscal deficit reductions)—measures that often arouse the strong opposition of major social forces.

The disorienting uncertainties of current developments in international trade and finance, moreover, deepen this dilemma substantially. For regardless of the choices made by their governments, the basic "solvency" of Latin American societies also turns on unpredictable factors that neither they nor their creditors can control: interest rates, trade opportunities, oil and commodity prices, and so forth. Yet even in the midst of this uncertainty, Latin American governments must act—if only by deciding *not* to have a policy.

In this article I explore the way in which systems of electoral democracy and authoritarianism have shaped responses to this dilemma in Argentina, Brazil, and Mexico (the ABM countries)—the three largest debtor societies in the world. Governments in all three countries have, for reasons already

Written with the assistance of Laura F. Schoen. I also acknowledge the helpful suggestions of David Collier and Miles Kahler. Earlier versions were presented at the Lehrman Institute, New York City, as part of its series on Politics and International Debt, which was supported in part by a grant from the Ford Foundation, and at the 1984 Annual Meeting of the American Political Science Association, Washington, D.C., 30 August–2 September 1984.

suggested, attempted to project an image of responsibility in their dealings with creditors. But there have also been distinct national differences in willingness to pay the stabilization price.

The new democratic government of Argentina, established in December 1983 after seven years of antilabor military dictatorship, was by far the most defiant. Throughout most of 1984 the Alfonsín administration insisted repeatedly that it would not impose "recessionary" policies—a commitment that became the key issue in a protracted war of nerves over Argentina's international debt arrears and in a prolonged stalemate in negotiations with the IMF. Although an agreement finally signed with the IMF in October 1984 did clear the way for a restructuring agreement, it remains to be seen whether an austerity program can actually be sustained in the face of a strong, independent union movement seeking economic relief.

The Brazilian government, caught in a delicate moment of transition between military rule and civilian regime, has muddled. The official position of the outgoing Figuereido administration was based on a restructured loan agreement and on an austerity plan negotiated with the IMF. But the backsliding began well before the military government left office in March 1985. In an unprecedented display of independence, for example, the Brazilian Congress rejected the wage bill initially associated with the IMF settlement in 1983, forcing a much weaker compromise. By the end of 1984 failure to meet monetary and fiscal targets had led to a suspension of IMF disbursements and a new round of negotiations. And although economic moderates have important roles in the new civilian government, they will face strong pressures to modify even more of the orthodox policies adopted in 1983-84.

Mexico's party-based authoritarian regime has been most compliant. The tough austerity program imposed in December 1982 under the new presidential administration of Miguel de la Madrid has been widely praised in international financial circles as a "success story," holding out the hope of a significant recovery for Mexico as well as of the payment of its international debt.

To those familiar with the postwar histories of the ABM countries, these contrasting approaches to stabilization should come as no surprise. They are rooted in enduring features of the political systems of these societies.[1] In Mexico the sweeping land reform and nationalizations of the Cárdenas era helped lay the political foundations for a highly successful period of economic

---

1. As I argue in Robert R. Kaufman, "Mexico and Latin American Authoritarianism," in Jose Luis Reyna and Richard S. Weinert, eds., *Authoritarianism in Mexico* (Philadelphia: Institute for the Study of Human Issues, 1977). More broadly, I draw on the literature represented in Guillermo O'Donnell, *Modernization and Bureaucratic Authoritarianism* (Berkeley: Institute of International Studies, University of California, 1973); David Collier, ed., *The New Authoritarianism in Latin America* (Princeton: Princeton University Press, 1979); and Alfred Stepan, *The State and Society: Peru in Comparative Perspective* (Princeton: Princeton University Press, 1978).

expansion after 1945. The principal instruments of power, wielded most recently by de la Madrid, included a highly concentrated system of presidential authority based on a dominant single party (the PRI), which had coopted organized labor and peasant interests and substantially controlled populist electoral pressures. These resources have been used before to impose unpopular stabilization measures, in 1954 and 1976. Although the consequences of the 1976 measures were obscured by the subsequent oil boom, the 1954 policies have been widely credited with opening the way to two decades of comparative price stability.

Brazil and Argentina emerged from the 1930s and 1940s with far less institutionalized political regimes and substantially more pervasive problems with inflation and balance of payments. In Argentina alternating periods of military dictatorship and weak civilian governments, and sharp "stop-go" cycles of expansionist and austerity policies, have each been associated with deep sociopolitical cleavages centering around the strong, union-based Peronist movement. Brazil has been more stable, in part because the state-corporatist structures created during the Vargas era helped to weaken unions and to mute populist pressures. Unlike Mexico, however, Brazil has also experienced a major regime change in the postwar period; increased labor militancy, business fears, and economic crises contributed to the shift from an electoral-constitutional system to a "bureaucratic-authoritarian" regime in 1964.

Economic stabilization packages imposed under the Argentine and Brazilian military-authoritarian regimes of the mid-1960s did have some short-term success in relieving exchange and price pressures. But neither of these regimes nor the military government reestablished in Argentina between 1976 and 1983 was able to institutionalize political support for long-term models of development as in Mexico. By the 1980s an increasingly bankrupt regime was on the ropes in Brazil, and a thoroughly discredited military government had been displaced entirely in Argentina. In light of the democratizing trends now at work in these two countries, on the other hand, it is no less important to recall that no democratically elected government in Argentina and Brazil has ever managed successfully to initiate and sustain a stabilization program – a record of political immobilism closely connected with subsequent authoritarian takeovers.[2]

In the following pages we shall explore some of the factors that influence these patterns. Several assumptions should be spelled out explicitly. One is that in economies where annual rates of inflation now range from 100 to over 1,000 percent, some sort of economic retrenchment will be a necessary component of long-term recoveries. Although governmental elites might find

2. Thomas E. Skidmore, "The Politics of Economic Stabilization in Post War Latin America," in James M. Malloy, ed., *Authoritarianism and Corporatism in Latin America* (Pittsburgh: Pittsburgh University Press, 1977).

it appropriate to reject specific IMF formulas or to take a hard-line position on the debt negotiations, they will find it increasingly difficult to avoid the exchange-rate adjustments, credit and fiscal controls, and wage restraints conventionally linked to the politics of stabilization. Such policies, broadly understood, are one of the principal variables of the analysis.

A second assumption is that authoritarian and democratic regimes are only one set of factors shaping choice of policy. Other crucial determinants include not only international and domestic economic forces but also political factors that can conceivably cut across regimes: the economic ideologies of political elites, the organization of the public bureaucracy, the resources available to various groups operating within the political system.[3] Although all of these factors must necessarily be built into any general analysis of stabilization policies, the "regime issue" has a compelling practical and theoretical status in the ABM countries—theoretical, because in these highly politicized societies democratic or authoritarian changes in the "rules of public contestation" can be intimately linked to policy outcomes, and practical, because of the specific challenges that stabilization now poses for new and prospective democracies in Latin America.

How, then, do the "rules of public contestation" established under different sorts of political regimes affect the capacity to undertake stabilization initiatives? How do such initiatives in turn affect the stability of political regimes? I start to answer these questions by providing a general perspective on the coalitional spaces and lines of political conflict that have typically formed around stabilization initiatives in the ABM countries, emphasizing the kinds of challenges posed for political authorities by the labor-based populist heritage of earlier decades. I then review the stabilization records of the Mexican regime, which initially coopted this populism, and of the bureaucratic-authoritarian regimes of Brazil and Argentina, which attempted to purge it from the political system. The third section focuses on the options and opportunities open to democratic governments in the attempt to design and sustain stabilization initiatives.

Finally, I consider the political and economic consequences of different domestic responses to the stabilization-debt issue. In conditions of sustained international economic growth, I suggest, center-right coalitions may provide

3. On the general concept and analysis of "sustainability" I draw heavily on the work of Joan M. Nelson, "The Political Economy of Stabilization in Small, Low-Income, Trade-Dependent Nations" (ms., Overseas Development Council, January 1984), and Stephan Haggard, "The Politics of Adjustment: Lessons from the IMF's Extended Fund Facility," *International Organization* 39 (Summer 1985). For recent work on other aspects of the problems, see Benjamin J. Cohen, "International Debt and Linkage Strategies: Some Foreign-Policy Implications for the United States," *International Organization* 39 (Autumn 1985); Philip A. Wellons, "International Debt: The Behavior of Banks in a Politicized Environment," ibid. (Summer 1985); Charles Lipson, "International Debt and International Institutions," and Miles Kahler, "Conclusion: Dilemmas and Proposals for Reform" (The Lehrman Institute: Politics and International Debt Series, 21 March 1984 and 7 June 1984).

the most effective means of consolidating new democracies. In less favorable international circumstances, on the other hand, new democratic regimes might benefit most from the less orthodox approaches of center-left coalitions.

I shall not attempt to describe specific details of various stabilization episodes, nor shall I spend much time documenting assertions about the historical-political settings in which the episodes occurred. Instead, I offer an interpretative and speculative dissection of the limits and possibilities of democratic and authoritarian solutions to the problem. The discussion, finally, is limited to the ABM countries themselves unless otherwise specified. Although almost every developing country must confront the same issues, Argentina, Brazil, and Mexico share broad similarities that make it easier to assess the roles that different political institutions and strategies might play in the current situation. Because of the size of their debts and their economies, they are among the few societies with any real leverage in bargaining with international creditors. They have also traveled roughly comparable routes of industrial development. Finally, certain common themes of sociopolitical conflict, to be discussed in the next section, provide still another important ground for comparison.

Some general perspectives on stabilization conflicts

To understand the domestic conflicts associated with the politics of stabilization, we have to consider two broad issues. One can be mentioned here only in passing; it involves the factors influencing the "will and capacity" of governmental centers of initiative. As Stephan Haggard and Joan Nelson suggest, the ability of state elites to design and implement stabilization programs is often undermined "from within"—by the particularistic pressures of governmental agencies, by patron-client networks that erode the control of central authorities over the state apparatus, and by dissonant economic ideologies and political concerns within the state elite itself.[4] These forces have certainly been at work within the state bureaucracies of the ABM countries; on the whole, however, they threaten stabilization initiatives less there than they do in smaller, less developed societies with comparatively low degrees of "stateness." In the ABM societies comparatively articulated economic bureaucracies provide a technocratic counterweight to the politicization of the state apparatus. Staffed by large cadres of technocratic personnel and linked to international academic centers of professional training and research, such bureaucracies have acquired the degree of "relative autonomy" required to set stabilization plans in motion, even in the face of high political risks and uncertain economic results.[5]

4. Nelson, "Political Economy of Stabilization," and Haggard, "Politics of Adjustment."
5. Nicos Poulantzas, *Political Power and Social Classes* (London: NLB and Sheed & Ward, 1973).

system, not to destroy it—and it was military antagonism to the Peronist movement, rather than labor opposition to the IMF plan per se, that eventually dealt the fatal blow to the Frondizi regime. In the Brazilian case the fatal blow was dealt by the enigmatic Quadros himself; but, again, the principal pressures came not against the stabilization plan but from the right on foreign-policy issues. The point can be made more generally: however threatening and disruptive the street actions of labor and leftist groups may appear to governmental authorities, democratic regimes have typically faced far greater threats from antipopulist civil-military coalitions.

In this regard current elected leaders in Argentina and Brazil have greater leverage than their predecessors had to deal with labor-oriented political groups as a loyal opposition. The discrediting of military-authoritarian solutions reduces the chances that the armed forces will overreact to labor opposition as they did twenty years ago. In Argentina, in particular, the antagonism between the Peronists and the military poses far less of a threat to Alfonsín than it did to Frondizi. At the same time there may also be greater incentives for labor organizations to keep their opposition to stabilization within bounds. After several decades of military repression and political and economic turmoil, radical and reformist alternatives seem for the moment to have less appeal than they had in the 1960s and early 1970s, in the direct aftermath of the Cuban revolution. Thus, over the "medium term," labor might now be more willing to exchange economic concessions for political freedom—the opportunity to run candidates, organize unions, and bargain collectively within the framework of newly established political democracies. Unlike Alfonsín, Frondizi could deliver only belatedly and partially on this opportunity, in a context where expectations were high and where the Peronists had themselves only recently been deposed from the heights of power. Quadros, operating in a fifteen-year-old framework of electoral politics, had even less leverage in this respect. In contrast, a civilian president in the 1980s can capitalize on being the first to usher in a new democratic era.

The extent to which this leverage can be effectively employed depends in part, of course, on the political orientations of the democratic elites in power. In this connection we must draw a distinction between Alfonsín's center-left government, which formed after the Argentine military suddenly withdrew from power, and the more center-right orientations that could emerge in the new Brazilian regime as a result of a more gradual and controlled political transition. In the latter case the new civilian leadership, which now draws support from virtually every sector of Brazilian society, has an opportunity to forge a narrower, but conceivably more stable, electoral-legislative coalition by joining the large middle class in the southern states with the more conservative political bosses who control the northeastern regions. Even with such a coalition, of course, it would not be easy to initiate and sustain an IMF-backed stabilization program. But this type of government would find

The second issue, and my main focus here, concerns the foundations of the sociopolitical cleavages mobilized within civil society. It is fair to say, even after we take into account the heterogeneity of contending coalitions in Latin America, that conflicts over stabilization have typically divided along class lines. Major sectors of "big business"—not only the old agro-exporting elites but also large foreign and domestic industrial and financial groups—are usually at the center of the support coalitions that form around technocratic initiatives. Even when such groups quietly seek to evade austerity for themselves, they most often adopt positions of open support or benevolent neutrality toward stabilization programs in general. Conversely, although the other side often includes smaller businesses, military nationalists, and intellectuals, the principal opposition comes from the "popular sectors" incorporated into the political system initially during the 1930s and 1940s: blue-collar unions, allied white-collar organizations, and mass-based political parties. Even popularly oriented governments typically encounter resistance from such groups when they sponsor stabilization packages. And, in general, the ability to sustain stabilization initiatives in the ABM countries has varied inversely with the capacity of these forces and their leaders to escape the orbit of state supervision and control.

Such conflicts raise several questions, for democratic and authoritarian regimes alike. General experience since 1945 suggests, on the one hand, that there is a high price to be paid for "radical populist" policies, at least in their extreme form. The countries hit the hardest by inflationary and balance-of-payments crises during the 1960s and 1970s (Argentina and, to a lesser extent, Brazil) were those which in previous decades had experimented most drastically with state-administered, inward-oriented models of development; Mexico, which allowed somewhat greater scope to market forces, has experienced a smoother course.[6] At the same time the disastrous collapse of the "Chicago School" models adopted in Argentina and Chile during the 1970s indicates strongly that the radical laissez-faire policies often advocated by the leaders of antipopulist coalitions are cures worse than the disease.[7] In these circumstances the persistence (and at times the deepening) of such apparently destructive class-based cleavages poses an important puzzle. What has inhibited more moderate attempts to elicit cross-class cooperation? Why have populist groups clung so fiercely to distributive objectives? What accounts for their ongoing capacity to frustrate stabilization initiatives? Finally, what are the chances that "political learning" will induce a greater willingness to share short-term sacrifices in anticipation of sharing the longer-term benefits of an expanding economy?

6. John Sheahan, "Market-oriented Economic Policies and Political Repression in Latin America," *Economic Development and Cultural Change* 28 (January 1980); Robert R. Kaufman, "Industrial Change and Authoritarian Rule in Latin America: A Concrete Review of the Bureaucratic-Authoritarian Model," in Collier, *The New Authoritarianism.*

7. On the failure of neoconservative options see especially Alejandro Foxley, *Latin American Experiments in Neoconservative Economics* (Berkeley: University of California Press, 1983).

There is a long list of historically specific explanations, most of which are useful for understanding at least some aspects of the conflict, for the persistence of zero-sum tendencies. Such explanations include (although are not limited to) the failure of leadership and political persuasion, traditions of mistrust among Latin American parties and interest groups, and the inequalities and class antagonisms inherent in "dependent development" models based on alliances between big business and the state. On the other hand, class-based stalemates and polarization over stabilization issues are hardly unique to Latin America or the Third World, and the ubiquity of these tendencies suggests that more general explanations are needed to bring the dilemmas of the ABM governments into sharper focus. In this connection two quite different analytic traditions—one derived from rational choice theory, the other from sociological theories of class relations—are useful points of departure.

Mancur Olson's familiar argument about the logic of collective action provides one important perspective, for if we assume that many of the benefits to be derived from stabilization efforts are collective in nature (e.g., reduced inflation), appeals for cooperation based on the enlightened self-interest of competing groups can be expected to founder on the "free-rider" issue. It simply does not make sense for most labor unions or business firms to pay the costs of stabilization if they cannot be excluded from its benefits.[8] If all groups attempt to evade the costs, of course, the program fails—which is what typically happens in Latin America. But because most labor and business organizations are too small to have a direct influence on this outcome, they are still better off if they evade the "short-term" sacrifices asked by governmental elites. In any event, Olson argues, for all but very large peak associations the advantages of defending or enlarging distributive shares of wages will almost always outweigh the costs that the groups incur from consequent contractions of the national economy. It would benefit a firm or union that controls, say, 1 percent of the national output to strive for a larger share of a shrinking pie "unless the reduction in the value of the society's output is a hundred or more times larger than the amount won by the organization's clients in the redistributional struggle."[9] In a world composed of many interest-maximizing economic groups, in short, attempts to transfer the costs of stabilization onto others will be the norm rather than the exception.

At this point we can turn back to the class content of these redistributional struggles. I suggest that it derives in part from the power asymmetries inherent in the control of productive assets and investment decisions by business. This view is no longer associated exclusively with Marxist writers. Charles Lindblom, among others, has also emphasized the "privileged position" that

8. Mancur Olson, *The Logic of Collective Action* (Cambridge: Harvard University Press, 1965).
9. Mancur Olson, *The Rise and Decline of Nations* (New Haven: Yale University Press, 1983), p. 43.

business elites occupy as a result of their pivotal accumulation role in capitalist economies, a position further buttressed by their capacity to use informal channels of access, to finance political and public relations campaigns, and to occupy public office themselves.[10] The implication for our purposes is that capitalists are on balance in relatively good position to come out ahead in stabilization conflicts.

For labor organizations, of course, the opposite holds. In any distributional struggle with business they lack entirely the leverage that comes from direct control of productive assets. This asymmetry can be partially offset, as I shall suggest later, by the development of corporatist political structures, which provide large labor organizations with institutionalized access to the state apparatus—an arrangement approximated under some social democratic governments of Western Europe. For the most part, however, labor's structural disadvantage is compounded even in fully industrialized democratic societies by relative weakness in the conventional political resources it can deploy in the competition for political influence. These considerations, of course, apply with special force to labor movements in Latin America. There, in comparison with Western Europe and the United States, business control over assets has become especially pronounced in recent decades, while labor organizations are typically weakened by slack employment markets, political repression, and dependence on political authorities. But the structural foundations of these business-labor asymmetries are characteristic not of some particular form of "dependent development" but of capitalist systems generally. Given these disadvantages—*even in the case of equitably designed stabilization initiatives*—labor bears a greater portion of short-term risks and must attach a significantly greater discount for long-term benefits. It follows that labor organizations, if they have the political freedom to do so, will typically resist more strongly than will business.

Against this conceptual backdrop we can bring some specific features of the political-economic polarities of the ABM countries into clearer relief. One important point, already noted, is the especially sharp concentration of capitalist economic power, characterized in recent decades by increasingly close cooperation between state enterprises, international banks, and large transnational and domestic industrial companies. The second feature, rooted for almost half a century in the political frameworks established during the heyday of populism, is a politicolegal space and organizational infrastructure that politicians and union leaders can employ to defend the distributive interests of their constituents. This combination, though varying in its precise configuration from one ABM society to the next, creates the potential for unusually combustible, politicized, and persistent conflicts over stabilization.

In several instances, it should be noted, stabilization coalitions of big

---

10. Charles Lindblom, *Politics and Markets: The World's Political Economic Systems* (New York: Harper & Row, 1977).

business and technocrats have been strengthened considerably by the antiunion and antileftist fears engendered in these conflicts. In both Argentina and Brazil, for example, these fears made it possible for bureaucratic-authoritarian regimes to attract, for a time, the support of military nationalists and segments of the middle class that otherwise opposed policies aimed at restricting demand and liberalizing controls on prices and trade.[11] But the openly antilabor character of these coalitions has also done much to undermine (or "demystify") technocratic claims to political neutrality, and this in turn has facilitated the activation of very broad, antistabilization coalitions organized around vaguely anti-oligarchical and nationalist themes. Labor oppositions gain strength from the fact that even moderate austerity measures threaten the political foundations of states that have historically linked their legitimacy closely to the material rewards and administrative protections derived from import-substituting growth models.

As I implied in the introduction, the role of the labor organizations at the center of these coalitions varies with the institutional legacy of the populist era, with economic conditions, and with the regime choices of political elites.[12] In each of the ABM countries, however, unions and popular movements have acquired a political presence that is quite extensive when compared to other, less developed Third World countries or to the "new industrial countries" of Asia, which did not pass through comparable populist phases. Labor's distributive militancy, viewed broadly, derives from efforts to use its considerable organizational leverage to offset economic and political weaknesses. High levels of urban and rural unemployment limit opportunities for the kind of "nonpolitical" collective bargaining adopted in the United States, although workers in strategic export, port, or transport areas do have some leverage in this regard. On the other hand, as we shall see in more detail below, the very heterogeneity of the populist movements that have mobilized working-class organizations inhibits the formation of autonomous programatically oriented "labor parties" that might actually take control of government. The alternative has been to draw upon the loyalties, expectations, and resources generated in the 1930s and 1940s to politicize distributive issues and defend existing footholds within the system. Such capabilities are almost exclusively defensive and are highly vulnerable to manipulation or coercion from above. Nevertheless, labor opposition is a force to be reckoned with, even by harshly antilabor authoritarian regimes.

Authoritarian regimes and economic stabilization

In the face of these political conflicts authoritarian regimes have some apparent advantages over competitively elected governments. They can repress op-

11. See O'Donnell, *Modernization and Bureaucratic Authoritarianism.*
12. See especially the work by Ruth and David Collier, "Inducements versus Constraints: Disaggregating Corporatism," *American Political Science Review* 73 (December 1979), and their "Unions, Parties, and Regimes in Latin America: An Introduction" (Rutgers University Political Science/Political Economy Workshop, March 1984).

position from unions and popularly based party organizations; their executive authorities, operating outside a framework of institutionalized accountability, can overrule particularistic business opposition to stabilization schemes; and at the same time government technocrats are in a good position to promote policies aimed at winning the general "confidence" of local and international capital. Authoritarian regimes in the ABM countries are, in fact, so far the only ones in which stabilization programs have actually restored some degree of price and exchange equilibrium and a resumption of economic expansion. The main "success stories" are Brazil between 1964 and 1968, Argentina between 1966 and 1970, and Mexico in the mid-1950s and, arguably, in 1976.[13]

But authoritarian regimes have also produced some colossal failures, even in the "short term" (e.g., under Argentine economy minister Martinez de Hoz in the late 1970s). The decade of the 1980s, moreover, has revealed some major problems in the capacity of such systems to deal effectively with longer-term development questions as well. With the Argentine military government in defeat and the Brazilians in retreat, the weaknesses of the Southern Cone's bureaucratic-authoritarian regimes have been especially apparent, but the Mexican system is also showing signs of serious strain. In this section we look first at some of the issues confronting Mexico and then at the cruder, less institutionalized forms of military authoritarianism in Argentina and Brazil.

Mexican authoritarianism

Stabilization policies in Mexico have been framed within a political system characterized by a unique blend of revolutionary legitimation and robber-baron capitalism. It is a paradoxical and very uneven balance. On the one side, the state apparatus is wrapped in symbols derived from the civil wars of the 1910s and from the convulsive period of popular mobilization, land reform, and oil nationalization of the 1930s. The radical legacy of this era is such that domestic business organizations are not even entitled to formal representation within the PRI. Since the 1940s, on the other hand, no other ABM government has so extensively and consistently attempted to promote development by providing incentives to local and foreign private capital. By the mid-1970s, before the unsettling effects of the oil boom, the track record put other, ostensibly more probusiness, systems to shame. The direct governmental role in the economy was relatively limited (government share of gross fixed investment was only 40% in Mexico, 60% in Brazil), and tax rates were also extremely low (10% of gross domestic product [GDP] in

13. Skidmore, "Politics of Economic Stabilization"; on the 1976 Mexico case see Laurence Whitehead, "Mexico from Bust to Boom: A Political Evaluation of the 1976–1979 Stabilization Programme," *World Development* 8 (November 1980); Rosemary Thorp and Laurence Whitehead, eds., *Inflation and Stabilization in Latin America* (New York: Holmes & Meier, 1979).

Mexico as compared with 25% in Brazil). A very high premium was placed from the mid-1950s until the mid-1970s on the promotion of private savings—through low rates of inflation, stable exchange rates and a fully convertible currency, and high interest rates relative to U.S. levels. The result was a long period of high profits, massive inflows of direct foreign investment, and high, relatively steady rates of economic growth.[14]

Organized labor, in contrast to authoritarian experiences in Brazil and Argentina, has not been entirely excluded from this "alliance for profits."[15] Successive Mexican presidents (e.g., López Mateos in the 1960s and Echeverría and López Portillo in the 1970s) attempted to bolster the legitimacy of the Mexican system with distributive reforms, and comparative income distribution data indicate that they had some effect. In Brazil, for example, only the upper 10 percent gained during the "miracle years" of 1967–74, whereas in Mexico, during a comparable period, the top four deciles of the population (a sector that includes much of organized labor) were able to maintain constant or increasing shares of the GDP.[16] Even so, income disparities were increasing in the society as a whole—the bottom 60 percent of the population lost ground in relative terms, and a substantial portion may have experienced a deterioration in their absolute standard of living as well. For these reasons, few people would deny that the Mexican system has been tilted toward a profound concentration of income and assets, a trend that has probably been accelerated by the recent oil boom. Even before the debt-stabilization crisis of 1982–83, therefore, there were major questions about the amount of strain that the system could absorb.

One should not underestimate the very considerable sources of durability. The key, as indicated, is the official party, which serves as the base of legitimation and control for a cohesive political elite with strong vested interests in the stability of the system. The party is, first and foremost, a vast electoral machine, which draws upon revolutionary loyalties and habit, as well as on fraud and intimidation, to dominate the electoral arena. This in turn virtually guarantees presidential control of the governmental machinery—the congress, state and municipal offices, and the presidential succession—without at the same time requiring the systematic suppression of press freedom or intellectual dissent. The organization of the PRI into labor and peasant sectors, finally, is the principal mechanism through which state authorities coopt and manipulate organized urban and rural interests. For the leaders of officially connected unions, and sometimes for the rank and file as well, an expanding

14. On the Mexican model see Roger D. Hansen, *The Politics of Mexican Development* (Baltimore: Johns Hopkins University Press, 1971); Leopoldo Solis, *Economic Policy Reform in Mexico: A Case Study for Developing Countries* (Elmsford, N.Y.: Pergamon, 1981); David Felix, "On Financial Blowups and Authoritarian Regimes in Latin America," Department of Economics, Washington University, *Working Paper* no. 60 (1 October 1983). Data are from Felix, pp. 32–33.
15. Hansen, *Politics of Mexican Development*.
16. Felix, "On Financial Blowups," p. 32.

economic pie has until recently made possible a reward structure of mobility and economic benefits. For groups that resist cooptation the treatment can be much harsher: grudging toleration at best, imprisonment, dissolution, or reorganization at worst.

It was this political apparatus which apparently made the difference between Mexico's relative success with stabilization in the mid-1950s and the difficulties encountered by more populist governments in Argentina and Brazil, which attempted to impose similar measures at about the same time.[17] In the 1980s, once again, the Mexican government seems able and willing to pull levers that the other countries lack. Budget cuts deemed "impossible" in Brazil (from 16.5 to 8.5% of GDP in 1982–83) have actually been approximated in Mexico.[18] Wage increases have been held well below the rate of inflation, in a society where indexing does not cushion the shocks of price rises, and imports and industrial output have each contracted drastically during 1982–84. And, as in earlier periods, the government has been able to enlist the cooperation of some union bosses and to face down threatened union protests. Efforts by labor and political dissidents to organize general strikes have fizzled.

These patterns repeat themselves, however, within a context less favorable than that of thirty years ago. With the future course of the world economy itself uncertain, it is far from clear that sustained recovery will follow stabilization this time. The decades since the 1950s, moreover, have produced major changes in Mexico itself. The generations whose loyalties were formed during the Cárdenas era have now mostly disappeared from the scene. A population explosion has overloaded the system with demands for food, employment, and government services.[19] And the oil boom of the late 1970s, while ushering in a brief new period of expansion, also introduced new disequilibria: increased inflationary pressures, more corruption, and a middle class hooked on a standard of living that is now out of reach. In this general context of fading revolutionary legitimacy and frustrated expectations, it is particularly important to highlight two specific aspects of deterioration in the PRI's apparatus of control.

On the one side is an apparent decline in the capacity of the PRI to channel populist pressures. The rate of voter abstention has risen sharply while membership in official unions and peasant organizations has not kept pace with the growth of the urban and rural work force. The late 1960s saw bloody confrontations between students and police; the mid-1970s, episodes of land

17. Kaufman, "Mexico and Latin American Authoritarianism," and "Industrial Change and Authoritarian Rule."
18. Ariel Buira, "The Exchange Crisis and Adjustment Program in Mexico," in John Williamson, ed., *Prospects for Adjustment in Argentina, Brazil, and Mexico: Responding to the Debt Crisis* (Washington, D.C.: Institute for International Economics, June 1983).
19. Susan Kaufman Purcell, "The Future of the Mexican System," in Reyna and Weinert, *Authoritarianism in Mexico.*

seizures and rural terrorism. Recently legalized left opposition parties, intended to drain off some of this political pressure, add a further note of uncertainty to the political situation, even though they pose no serious threat to the electoral dominance of the PRI. Finally, it is doubtful that the "preemptive" reforms launched under Echeverría and López Portillo have had much success in replenishing the system's declining stock of legitimacy. In one major survey of industrial workers' attitudes, conducted at the height of the oil boom in 1979–80, about three-quarters of the sample (including those affiliated with the PRI) gave negative ratings to the government's performance in stimulating employment and promoting economic equality—the two issues of vital concern in the current politics of stabilization.[20]

On the other side, and even more threatening to the system, are signs that an increasingly assertive business sector will not tolerate even these very limited reformist orientations. Echeverría's distributive programs of the early 1970s were greeted by organized business interests in Monterrey and Mexico City with fierce opposition, including massive publicity campaigns, producers' strikes, and even rumors of military intervention. Business interests also had enough strength to block the tax reforms sought in the early 1970s to contain inflation and strengthen public-sector developmental capabilities, and they did not deliver on the promises of increased investment that López Portillo had extracted as part of his stabilization program during the mid-1970s.[21] The conservative National Action party (PAN), financed extensively by the private sector, has emerged on the right of the political spectrum as the PRI's major electoral challenger, actually winning several mayoral contests in the early 1980s. Finally, the recourse of sending capital across the long border with the United States has been used periodically throughout the last decade—not only a symptom but also a cause of the deterioration in the old alliance between business and government.

The social and economic difficulties that have beset the Mexican system over the past decade, in a word, both reflect and exacerbate the weakening of the once very strong political-institutional balances on which the system has rested. This change, in turn, makes it difficult to project far beyond the current situation. The dramatic and decisive response to the debt crisis since 1982 indicates the considerable resources still available to political elites, and the possibility of a sustained economic recovery would certainly alleviate some of the pressures. But the record of the past decade also indicates that even with a recovery, the old equilibrium between business, labor, and the state will not be restored completely. At best, we are likely to see new instances of the crises and retrenchments that have accompanied the last two presidential successions. At worst, should the crises accompanying these cycles

20. Kenneth M. Coleman and Charles L. Davis, "Preemptive Reform and the Mexican Working Class," *Latin American Research Review* 18, 1 (1983).
21. On tax reforms see Solis, *Economic Policy Reform in Mexico*.

become more intense, we may see a more militarized articulation of the state-business alliance and a turn toward more coercive responses to perceived threats from the unions, peasants, and salaried middle class.

Military-authoritarian regimes: Argentina and Brazil

During the mid-1960s strict stabilization plans were closely associated with the formation of military governments in Brazil (1964) and Argentina (1966). When the retrenchments imposed by these governments seemed to relieve the pressure of inflation and external deficits and to lay the ground-work for a new round of expansion, the interest in "military solutions" grew throughout the region. But the political price of these efforts has been much higher than in the Mexican case. In hindsight, in fact, experience in both Argentina and Brazil illustrates weaknesses that may be associated generically with attempts by the military to organize its own governing coalition and to impose stabilization plans by force. Whereas the Mexican regime derived legitimacy from the popular mobilization of its revolutionary past, the Argentine and Brazilian regimes were saddled at their inception by delegitimating "birth defects" associated with military exclusion of previously activated parties and unions. Neither was able fully to replace the coercive apparatus used for the initial stabilization programs with the more flexible forms of participation and cooptation required to manage development over the longer term. The weakness in the mechanisms of feedback and intermediation, moreover, also undermined relations between the government and its own support coalition—contributing at various points to sclerotic stalemates, the prolongation of costly policy errors, and even self-destructive adventurism.[22]

These problems have been more apparent in Argentina, where the military has twice (in 1973 and in 1983) had to beat a hasty and unplanned retreat back to the barracks. The first political failure, ironically, occurred after the implementation of the most balanced program executed in any of the ABM countries, designed under the supervision of Finance Minister Adalbert Krieger Vasena in 1966–67.[23] Imposed in the context of comparatively mild inflationary pressures, the program succeeded both in preventing a major decline in wages and in generating a rapid and brisk recovery by 1968–69. But the sharp concentration of executive authority associated with this program also cut the government off from key industrial and export groups and alienated important nationalist factions in the military that objected to the

---

22. See Guillermo O'Donnell, "Tensions in the Bureaucratic-Authoritarian State and the Question of Democracy," in Collier, *The New Authoritarianism*; Stepan, *State and Society*; Juan J. Linz, "The Future of an Authoritarian Situation or the Institutionalization of an Authoritarian Regime: The Case of Brazil," in Alfred Stepan, ed., *Authoritarian Brazil* (New Haven: Yale University Press, 1973).

23. See Gary Wynia, *Argentina in the Postwar Era: Politics and Economic Policy Making in a Divided Society* (Albuquerque: University of New Mexico Press, 1978).

liberalization of the economy. The government's method for dealing with the powerful Peronist movement, moreover, was to proscribe parties and elections entirely, to decree a wage freeze and a ban on strikes, and to use intimidation, selective intervention, and bribery to neutralize union organizations. By 1969, even with a rather vigorous economic expansion already under way, official efforts at military exclusion had generated strong counterpressures from below in the form of worker riots organized by union leaders and students and centered in the city of Córdoba. Police and military force eventually succeeded in putting down these upheavals, but riots demonstrated clearly the political costs of attempting to destroy independent unions and thus served as a catalyst in the unraveling of the regime. By the end of 1969 Krieger Vasena had been forced out as finance minister, followed after another year by the military president himself, Juan Carlos Onganía. By 1973, after several more years of deteriorating military control, a transitional government transferred authority to an elected Peronist regime.

A second round of military authoritarianism followed this Peronist "interlude" in 1976. It shared all of the defects of the first but was far bloodier and in economic terms far less successful. Again the principal technique was to use military force and intimidation to impose "order"—this time through the much more widespread and systematic use of a military intelligence network, mass arrests and "disappearances," and extensive censorship. The ostensible targets of this campaign were the left-wing guerrillas who had begun to organize in the early 1970s. In fact, however, virtually all forms of organized working-class, middle-class, and left-wing opposition came under official siege. The stabilization package imposed under these circumstances (in the context of infinitely worse economic conditions) was also much less successful. The hallmark of the plan was a deliberately overvalued peso, designed to bring down inflation, along with high interest rates and a liberalized tariff structure aimed at mobilizing domestic savings and stimulating efficiency. By 1980 the plan had clearly backfired, with widespread capital flight, public deficits, and bankruptcies.[24] At this point other political and institutional weaknesses associated with this form of military rule compounded the initial miscalculations: without any basis of legitimacy to cushion the shocks of its failures and with no systematic input from civil society, the military high command careened completely out of control. In an effort to deflect attention from failures at home the generals launched the desperate Malvinas/Falkland adventure and then attempted to disguise the tragic blunders of the campaign with false reports of victory in the government-controlled press. By the time the bubble burst, the wild excesses of the Argentine high command had performed at least one important service for Argentine society: for the time being they had shattered faith, even among most officers, in the viability of the "military option."

24. José Maria Dagnino Pastore, "Progress and Prospects for the Adjustment Program in Argentina," in Williamson, *Prospects for Adjustment*; Felix, "On Financial Blowups."

The post-1964 Brazilian regime—despite having imposed a perhaps unnecessarily harsh cut in lower-class incomes[25]—was founded on somewhat more secure institutional foundations. As long as it was backed up by military force, the state-corporatist framework of labor control served as a cornerstone of the regime. With labor organizations thus tied to the state, military authorities in their turn felt freer than in Argentina to govern through controlled party competition and elected legislative assemblies. But the armed forces, at least until political liberalization began to gather a full head of steam in the late 1970s, were the overwhelming force on the political scene. As such they suffered, in much more subtle fashion than in Argentina to be sure, the contradictions inherent in this form of unmediated political authority.

First, notwithstanding the "economic miracle" of 1967–74 (and perhaps because of it), the exclusionary "birth defects" of the regime systematically prevented it from employing elections as a legitimating mechanism. Even with electoral rules stacked heavily in its favor, the "government party" lost virtually every major electoral contest. By the mid-1970s the liberal-democratic apparatus, originally established as a constitutional fig leaf for military authority, had become an important arena within which opponents of the system could push for political liberalization. By the end of the decade authorities were using this apparatus to negotiate an "orderly" return to civilian government.

A decade ago, moreover, it became clear that the revolutionary élan and rhetoric of the late 1960s masked growing tensions among the groups that supported the system. As in Argentina, crosscutting lines of cleavage divided economic nationalists from liberal free-traders, state enterprises from private businesses, civilian political liberals from military hard-liners. Although these divisions did not contribute to collapse, as they had in Argentina, they did sap the autonomy of the government, especially as growth rates began to slow after 1974. On the eve of the debt crisis an aging regime thus seemed increasingly hedged in by entrenched and contradictory business, technocratic, and military interests, unable either to construct a base of popular support or to move decisively toward a new economic project.

The zigzagging course of Brazilian economic policy throughout the late 1970s and early 1980s reflects this decline in steering capacity: in 1979–80, in a rather desperate attempt to maintain the high growth rates that had held the authoritarian coalition together, the regime chose *not* to put brakes on the economy, despite the oil shocks and the growing external debt. Then, in the face of rising inflation during 1981, the government reversed course sharply, imposing the "tightest monetary policy ... since the turn of the century."[26] Finally, after having attempted to save its prestige by declining

---

25. Albert Fishlow, "Some Reflections on Post-1964 Brazilian Economic Policy," in Stepan, *Authoritarian Brazil*.

26. Edmar L. Bacha, "The IMF and the Prospects for Adjustment in Brazil," in Williamson, *Prospects for Adustment*.

to request IMF assistance in 1980–81, the government agreed in 1982–83 to conditions so harsh that they prompted the resignation of the director of the central bank. "Desperate ad hocism," in the words of one economist, "had replaced policy coherence."[27]

By 1984 Brazil under military rule had in certain respects been brought full circle to its position twenty years earlier. As civilian government grew nearer, an important part of the legacy bequeathed by the 1964 revolution was political immobilism, profound recession, crippling external deficits, and rates of inflation almost twice as high as in the earlier crisis. It is in the context of this kind of legacy that we now turn to the record and prospects of democratic regimes.

Stabilization policies in democratic regimes

The democratic record for sustaining stabilization programs provides very little ground for optimism. Since 1945 democratic regimes in Argentina and Brazil have initiated at least six stabilization programs.[28] Three were abandoned almost immediately by the presidents who sponsored them. The others helped to undermine the political authority of the regime, while at the same time failing to restore economic equilibrium. But although in every instance there was failure, the programs failed in different ways and for different reasons. In this section I consider several cases of democratic stabilization and the strategic assumptions behind them. My purpose is twofold: to bring out more fully some of the past weaknesses of democratic systems, and to assess future political options. The experiences to be discussed illustrate three such options: social pacts; containment of labor opposition; and the search for alternatives to stabilization.

Social pacts

The program launched in mid-1973 under Juan and Isabel Perón is the only clear example (within a competitive electoral framework) of an attempt to ground stabilization policies in state-sponsored agreements between organized labor and business. The "contract" (actually nineteen separate pieces of legislation) involved a carefully balanced system of shared sacrifice: a one-time wage increase to be followed by a two-year freeze, a price freeze aimed at reducing inflationary expectations and credit and tax incentives to increase agricultural exports. These provisions were formally endorsed by virtually every major Argentine interest group, including the Peronist Labor Confed-

27. Felix, "On Financial Blowups," p. 52.
28. My primary source is Skidmore, "Politics of Economic Stabilization." The relevant programs are: *Argentina*: Frondizi (1959–60), Perón (1973–75); *Brazil*: Vargas (1953), Kubitschek (1957–58), Quadros (1961), and Goulart (1963).

eration and the conservative Union of Argentine Industrialists. The package had the tacit support of the military establishment, which (as in the current situation) had recently emerged from a divisive period of authoritarian rule. And it was ratified by both Radical and Peronist parties in the national legislature.[29]

As social experiments go, this one was quite unprecedented in the normally divided society of Argentina. The implicit logic was that a Peronist government, by building labor organizations into the decisional process, might be able to offset the inherent socioeconomic disadvantages, mentioned above, that provide such strong incentives for labor to oppose stabilization programs. The societal corporatist mechanisms sponsored by social democratic movements in Western Europe suggest that such cooptive arrangements can sometimes work extremely well. Indeed, in Europe wage restraints, government tax revenues, and lower rates of inflation are all positively associated with the degree of social democratic political influence and peak-association bargaining.[30] The Argentine experience raised the question whether governments originating in more populist labor movements might be able to find a comparable formula. The social pact experiment, coming in the aftermath of Onganía's effort to exclude the labor movement, seemed at the time to hold out some hope of breaking the bitter political stalemates of the past.

In the Argentine setting, however, the results were catastrophic, particularly after the death of Juan Perón in July 1974 removed the major impediment to centrifugal forces within Peronism itself. By October 1974 ultrarightist and anti-unionist forces close to Isabel Perón succeed in ousting the architect of the pact, Jose Gelbard, as minister of economics. By May 1975, as one writer put it, the "union leaders were fighting for their political life" against highly restrictive government wage offers, responding with a strength and militancy that could "only be understood as a means of bringing about the downfall of the right-wing of the party."[31] In the context of this open political warfare between the unions and the government, Mrs. Perón first retreated, then advanced—acceding to the ouster of her ultraconservative advisers but then in 1976 attempting to impose a harsh new IMF-backed stabilization plan. Meanwhile, annual inflation was approaching 500 percent; the authority of the regime had been shattered; and the army, with the assent of the Peronist government, had begun to engage Peronist terrorists in the "dirty war" that would become the hallmark of the next military regime.

29. Wynia, *Argentina in the Postwar Era.*
30. See David R. Cameron, "The Politics and Economics of the Business Cycle," in Thomas Ferguson and Joel Rogers, eds., *The Political Economy: Readings in the Politics and Economics of American Public Policy* (Armonk, N.Y.: Sharpe, 1984); Philippe C. Schmitter, "Interest Intermediation and Regime Governability in Contemporary Western Europe and North America," in Suzanne Berger, ed., *Organizing Interests in Western Europe: Pluralism, Corporatism, and the Transformation of Politics* (Cambridge: Cambridge University Press, 1981).
31. Guido Di Tella, "The Economic Policies of Argentina's Labour-based Government (1973–76)," in Thorp and Whitehead, *Inflation and Stabilization in Latin America*, p. 199.

What went wrong? What are the implications for future efforts to find a social pact solution to stabilization problems? Even if we went beyond the superficial historical sketch presented here, it would obviously be unclear how much of the blame ought to be pinned on such "accidental" factors as Perón's death, the oil shocks of 1974, or the design of the stabilization plan itself. But bad luck, bad judgment, and exogenous problems are constant features of *any* stabilization situation; and even after making appropriate allowances for these factors, the failure of this particular experiment does seem to illustrate more pervasive problems characteristic of the diffuse, multiclass, and personalist forms of populism through which labor organizations were mobilized into politics and tied to the state. Far more than in the more institutionalized party-union connections in Europe, the personalist shadow cast by Perón—the principal focal point of cohesion for a highly heterogeneous movement—left a host of unresolved questions about the role that labor organizations should play within the Peronist government itself. By 1973, after almost twenty years in opposition, the incoming coalition included business groups as well as unions, along with ultrarightists, white-collar workers, social democrats, and left-wing terrorists. As in the Onganía period, therefore, the stakes in the union-government confrontations involved questions of political power, not wages. Perón himself helped for a time to link the unions to his coalition, but his personalistic and autocratic style was in the longer term as much a part of the problem of the social pact as of its solution. For, both before and after his death in 1974, it precluded the development of any clear institutions through which labor organizations could participate in the making of economic policy.[32]

The immediate prospects for a favorable social pact seem hardly better under Argentina's present democracy. On the one hand, Alfonsín's initial approach to the union question, typical of earlier Radical presidents, was an attempt to undercut Peronist syndical leaders by sponsoring internal union elections aimed at weaning the blue-collar rank and file away from Peronist identifications. In mid-1984 Alfonsín began to adopt a more conciliatory posture, but only after his reorganization initiatives had been defeated by the Peronist delegation in the national legislature. On the other hand, even if the Alfonsín government had moved earlier and more decisively toward a social pact strategy, it is doubtful that the Peronists could have cooperated effectively. Notwithstanding the Peronists' encouraging general commitment to the role of a loyal opposition, their historic rivalry with the Radical movement inhibits broad and systematic collaboration on policy. And even more important, after seven years of military dictatorship and the first electoral defeat in their history, they are more divided than ever. With profound intraparty struggles for dominance unfolding between Isabel Perón and rival union officials and electoral politicians, it is difficult to imagine how any one

32. Wynia, *Argentina in the Postwar Era*, p. 220.

faction of the movement could systematically identify itself with government-sponsored stabilization measures without being fatally undercut by the others.

Notwithstanding a populist legacy very different in some respects, leaders of a prospective Brazilian democracy would face similar obstacles. In Brazil, as in Argentina, the central issue would be who would speak for workers and how. In the current transition period union activists have adopted no clear stance toward the system of governmental financing and jurisdictional regulations that have served as the foundation of Brazil's state corporatist structure. Thus there is considerable uncertainty about the role that "official" unions will play within a newly established democratic order. Although Brazilian unions do not generate the degree of hostility that has surrounded the Peronists, moreover, they are even more divided in their political allegiances. Effective labor collaboration in a social pact is virtually inconceivable without fundamental and potentially very conflictual organizational change and consolidation. In this respect, as the contrast with the more cohesive European social democrats has already implied, the principal problem that populist movements have posed for democracy in both of these South American societies is not that their party and union organizations are too strong but that they are too weak.[33]

Containment of loyal opposition

If democratic governments cannot draw labor interests into direct collaboration, their other major choice (assuming they go ahead with stabilization) is to deal with labor organizations as a loyal opposition. This approach, of course, like the social pact strategy, depends on a degree of collaboration between a stabilizing government and its labor-based critics, including both tacit and explicit efforts to narrow policy differences over the issue of stabilization. By definition, however, the approach also assumes labor criticism rather than labor's formal and sustained cosponsorship of the stabilization process. Most important, it presupposes that both government and opposition sectors share an interest in drawing a line between system-threatening violence and turbulent but acceptable forms of political contestation such as political campaigns, strikes, mass demonstrations and rallies, media criticism, and even various forms of nonviolent civil disobedience.

Something along these lines was tried in Argentina by Arturo Frondizi (1959–60) and by Brazil's last directly elected president, Janio Quadros, in 1961. It is also, of course, what usually happens in advanced industrial

---

33. It remains to be seen in this connection whether Venezuela might be an exception that proves the rule. The close articulation between urban and rural unions and the governing AD party might provide a more solid basis for gaining the cooperation of working-class organizations through social pact arrangements. For similar reasons, social pacts might conceivably be viable in a future Chilean democratic system, although the profound ideological divisions in the traditional Chilean party system would probably make this more problematic than in Venezuela.

democracies (e.g., Britain or the United States), which are governed by centrist or rightist coalitions. Although at present it would be very difficult for any elected government in either Argentina or Brazil to sustain a stabilization program under these conditions, strong external pressures and internal inflation are pushing in that direction. And ironically the containment option, despite the high odds against it, might prove to be more sustainable than a social pact strategy, especially in Brazil.[34]

Let us first glance at the unsuccessful Frondizi and Quadros prototypes. The Frondizi experience contained very little hope from the start. The new president, elected with the support of the recently deposed and outlawed Peronists, was kept on a very short leash by the then violently anti-Peronist military establishment. The stabilization plan, imposed at the insistence of the military high command, further undercut Frondizi's credibility and authority.[35] There was, to be sure, a remote possibility that a speedy recovery, together with a promise to legalize the Peronist political party, would eventually attract blue-collar support for Frondizi. But these hopes were dashed entirely when the Peronists won the congressional elections of 1962 and the military ousted the increasingly isolated president.

Quadros's circumstances were less confining. His IMF-backed stabilization program had been directly foreshadowed in a highly successful presidential election campaign aimed explicitly at mobilizing middle-class opposition to the "corruption and inefficiency" associated with Vargas-style populism. At the same time Quadros linked his conservative "clean-up" campaign at home with a "nationalist," mildly pro-Cuban foreign policy, in an attempt to appeal to some working-class sectors of the population. It is at least conceivable that, in the context of still rather modest economic problems, such an approach might have kept the working-class opposition to stabilization to manageable proportions. We shall never know, however, for when his foreign policy came under attack by the civilian right, Quadros suddenly resigned in August 1961, ushering in the turbulent Goulart period and the 1964 military revolution.[36]

What are the chances that new versions of these stabilization strategies would fare better? As just suggested, they are perhaps somewhat better than might be expected.

In each earlier failure, it must be emphasized, the fatal opposition pressures came from the military or the civilian right, not from labor organizations as such. The Peronists in the late 1950s were seeking to *reenter* the electoral

34. For a general discussion of the containment option, see Nelson, "Political Economy of Stabilization," pp. 25–26.
35. Wynia, *Argentina in the Postwar Era*. Alvaro Alsogaray, the cabinet chief charged with implementing the program, was appointed only after a military ultimatum that threatened to depose Frondizi (p. 94).
36. See Thomas E. Skidmore, *Politics in Brazil, 1930–1964* (New York: Oxford University Press, 1967).

it easier to absorb the political threats posed by union-backed opposition than would one that depended on a capacity to attract working-class support.

Alfonsín's center-left government, by contrast, may incur very high political costs if it is forced to shift gears and opt for a stabilization program. Alfonsín's strategy, like Frondizi's, has been built on the possibility of undercutting the Peronists and adding blue-collar workers to his own middle-class base of support. *If* he can find a way to keep his promise not to impose a recession, and *if* he can arrive at an appropriate developmental formula (i.e., one that involves less inequality than in the past), and *if* he can continue to reorganize the military establishment—then he has a chance to capitalize on the current crisis and to consolidate a working-class base of support. It is, however, a high-risk strategy. If events force Alfonsín to adopt a stabilization program, he will have the worst of all worlds. In seeking to undercut the Peronist union leadership he has burned (or badly damaged) the bridges that lead toward a social pact. By raising expectations about an immediate economic recovery, he has left himself vulnerable to a substantial erosion of support if he cannot deliver.

The search for alternatives

For the time being democratic governments in the 1980s are likely to try hard to avoid policies that have the "short-term" effect of conspicuously undermining wages and employment. This decision in turn means that they must also seek ways to shift the costs of price and exchange stabilization onto upper-income sectors, particular groups of white-collar employees (i.e., in the public sector), banks, and creditor governments. For short-term domestic economic policy this tactic implies higher and more progressive tax rates, reductions in military budgets, the elimination or restructuring of state enterprises, and tighter control of foreign-exchange earnings. Regarding the debt itself, the corollary is not necessarily repudiation but rather the use of the *threat* of repudiation to extract the maximum advantage from restructuring negotiations. Also implied, finally, is a shifting of longer-term development priorities toward more carefully planned import substitution, an expansion of the state's extractive capacity, and possibly also a renewed emphasis on direct foreign investment. As might be expected, there is considerable support for some version of this strategy among many politicians and intellectuals in both Argentina and Brazil.

Although there are no parallels to this approach in the post-1945 era, the "developmentalist" model pursued by Brazil's Kubitschek administration (1956–61) offers some instructive, if sobering, perspectives. The essential feature of the Kubitschek model was that domestic market demand would drive the economy while foreign direct investment, public enterprise, and long-term finance capital would supply the investment resources. This approach did yield very high growth rates for a time, despite declining coffee prices and domestic inflationary pressures. By the late 1950s, however, increasing external deficits had begun to raise serious questions among creditors about the security of new long-term loans, and it became clear that some sort of adjustment was necessary. One possibility might have been a version of the "hard-line" strategy sketched above, although it was never, at the time, really on the agenda. A second approach would have been the conventional retrenchment measures then being urged by the IMF. But Kubitschek also rejected this option in 1958–59, even though his decision reduced the availability of the long-term financing previously used to fund developmental projects. Instead, the presidential choice was to temporize, financing the inflow of vital growth-sustaining imports through the accumulation of short-term debts scheduled to come due in the early 1960s. "It was a successful strategy," remarks one critic, "of reaping the benefits and deferring the costs until someone else would be president. For Kubitschek's political popularity the strategy may have been optimal, but for his successors [Quadros and Goulart] caught between the IMF and national bankruptcy, it was disastrous."[37]

Contemporary governments in the ABM countries do not, of course, have the "Kubitschek option." They may, it is true, seek debt relief in the form of short-term emergency loan packages that defer, for a time, hard choices with respect to retrenchment and long-term access to international credit markets. But such stopgaps, in contrast to Brazil in the late 1950s, would be aimed not at postponing the slowdown of expanding economies but at preventing utter economic collapse. With such limited slack, there appears to be little room for maneuver in the space between a conventional retrenchment and a harder-line strategy.

The risks of a hard line have already been alluded to. Even if its "real" objective is to renegotiate its debt, a hard-line government (if only to be effective in the negotiations) must be prepared to assume the costs of economic isolation should negotiations fail. On the other hand, restructuring negotiations, even if they succeed under these conditions, are not likely to produce significant increases in the level of "voluntary" lending. One way or another, then, governments adopting a tough line toward creditors will probably have to find ways to wean their economies away from their current dependence on external private financing—which almost certainly implies major dislocations and contractions. It could be the case, as Michael Wallerstein has suggested, that "austerity for the sake of nationalism [might be] easier to sell to the working class than austerity for the sake of foreign capital."[38] But it is not easy to imagine how to accomplish this goal within a competitive electoral democracy.

37. Michael Wallerstein, "The Collapse of Democracy in Brazil: Its Economic Determinants," *Latin American Research Review* 15, 3 (1980), p. 34.
38. Ibid.

Yet the preceding analysis implies that, in the context of the mid-1980s, conventional stabilization alternatives may carry even greater economic and political risks for democratic governments. By the end of 1982 private voluntary lending had come to a halt, while debt service ratios had already far exceeded levels that were considered "impossible" only a decade earlier: 87 percent for Brazil and 103 percent for Argentina, up from 21 and 25 percent in 1973. The figures for Mexico were almost as bad: 58 and 36 percent.[39] Moreover, the economies that must bear these burdens are already reeling. In 1983 the once buoyant Brazilian economy suffered its third consecutive year of economic contraction. The Argentine economy did show positive growth rates in 1983 (2.0%), but it still remained mired at pre-1970 levels of per capita income.[40] Finally, for reasons already discussed, the working-class groups that are now most threatened by conventional stabilization programs also bore most of the costs of previous models of economic development.

In strictly economic terms it can be argued that debt repudiation begins to make sense once the costs of interest payments due on existing debts exceed the anticipated gains from new loans. If we consider only annual net financial flows (omitting future access to credit and the possibility of wider trade disruptions), the ABM countries exceeded that point by 1982 and were expected to continue to do so at least through the mid-1980s.[41] This observation does not mean that their governments will or should decide to suspend payments. In any event, the choices now are between a tough and a cooperative line on the issues of restructuring and stabilization rather than for or against outright repudiation. And such decisions must be made on the basis of prudential judgment or the struggles among interests, or both, rather than on the basis of mathematical calculation. But the point may be approaching at which even rather conservative governments may be prepared to assume the risks of a tough line. A fortiori this proposition may be true of new *democratic* regimes that are attempting to establish a new basis of order and legitimacy within a framework of electoral accountability.

On the consequences of stabilization: international conditions and domestic coalitional choices

We thus move from a discussion of the political causes of sustained stabilization policies to some speculation about their consequences. This concluding section begins with the assumption that although experiences of the recent

39. William R. Cline, *International Debt and the Stability of the World Economy* (Washington, D.C.: Institute for International Economics, September 1983), p. 131.
40. Comisión Económica para America Latina (CEPAL), *Sentesis preliminar de la economia latinoamericana durante 1983*, E/CEPAL/G. 1279, 20 December 1983 (n.p.), p. 32.
41. Cline, *International Debt*, p. 89.

past must be taken into account in such speculations, the uncertainty of world developments makes simple linear projections even more hazardous than usual. The failure of governments to adjust their national economies to "objective" international forces can, to be sure, produce major destabilizing consequences for their societies. But so can "adjustment" policies based on assumptions that no longer reflect international realities.

In this connection several aspects of the current debt crisis, already mentioned in passing, distinguish the post-1982 stabilization dilemmas from earlier ones. The first is the depth of the economic crisis within the ABM countries. From 1981 through 1983 per capita GNP declined by over 13 percent in Argentina, by almost 12 percent in Brazil, and by about 5 percent in Mexico.[42] This period of sustained contraction is, by most accounts, the worst since the 1930s. The second is the exposure of the banks. The banks may still have the greater leverage in bilateral restructuring negotiations, and they can probably absorb the losses that would be involved in any single case of default or repudiation. Still, the possibilities of provoking a chain reaction provide debtor governments with far greater leverage over creditors than they have had since 1945. Also distinctive is the discrediting of conservative "military solutions" in Argentina and Brazil. As we have seen, the debt crisis has highlighted political and economic contradictions that were already accumulating under military governments and that contributed to a particularly severe *coup de grace* in Argentina. Because in politics the ghosts of the past have a disturbing way of haunting the future, we should by no means rule out the possibility that either "orthodox" or more economically nationalist military options might surface again sometime in the next three to five years. But civilian elites, now more than at any other time in the past several decades, may have some breathing space in Argentina and Brazil to find solutions of their own.

The final point of distinction is the indeterminacy of the international trade system. For the first time since 1945 there is the serious possibility that debtor countries as a group may be confronting problems of "solvency," as a result of a prospective decline in trade opportunities and rising interest rates. If this is so, the "case-by-case" framework of the restructuring negotiations is based on incorrect, even economically fatal, assumptions about the variables that will determine capacity to pay. "Liquidity" issues are in principle resolvable through prudent economic management and financial cooperation between the governments and banks dealing with each debtor country. But this assumption could be undermined, or even counterproductive, if the real issue is a general contraction of the world economy.

The close connection between the size of Latin America's external deficits and developments in the advanced industrial countries is strikingly demonstrated in a recent series of simulations by William R. Cline. Capacity to

---

42. CEPAL, *Sentesis preliminar*, p. 33.

pay (as measured by debt service ratios and current accounts deficits) improves very considerably by 1987 under the following conditions: annual growth rates in advanced countries of 3 percent between 1984 and 1987; interest rates (LIBOR) declining to 8 percent by 1986; and stable oil prices ($29 per barrel through 1985 rising to $34 in 1986). Under these conditions—which, Cline argues, are based on hopeful, but not unrealistic, assumptions—the model projects a sharp decline in the debt burden, especially for Argentina and Brazil. The more general implication is that the problem these countries face is one of medium-term "illiquidity," which can be resolved through prudent economic management. The obvious corollary, on the other hand, is that the problem is likely to become far less manageable if world economic developments fall short of these assumptions. The projections on interest rates, for example, appear quite problematic; and Cline suggests as well that the 3 percent growth rate is a critical threshold below which ABM exports are unlikely to reduce the very large external deficits that exist at present.[43]

We do not really have to chose between "optimistic" and "pessimistic" world economic scenarios for the purposes of this article. The more useful approach is to ask how each might affect the consequences of the stabilization decisions now being made in the region.

Under conditions of world economic recovery (a "liquidity scenario") the political elites most able to contain (or coopt) the opposition to conventional stabilization strategies would presumably receive the highest payoff—in terms of a general economic recovery and increased room for political maneuver. Such developments would not, to be sure, obviate the likelihood of increased turmoil, political uncertainty, or surprising turns of fortune within specific countries. Moreover, in view of the unusual leverage that each ABM government has in debt negotiations, such twists can have a significant impact on the global recovery itself. Nevertheless, under "conventional" post-1945 world conditions the "conventional wisdom" is likely to prevail.

The result for Argentina, Brazil, and Mexico would be something along the following, "medium-term" lines. First, and rather surprisingly, the Cline model suggests that Mexico, as an oil exporter, might not benefit as much as Argentina and Brazil from a sustained world economic recovery, since one of the conditions of such a recovery would be stable international petroleum prices.[44] Under favorable international conditions, however, the strict stabilization plan now in place in Mexico would compensate for this disadvantage.[45] The result would be accelerated economic expansion by the late 1980s based on a renewed capacity to attract external loan and direct investment capital. Although this expansion would not solve the very serious political problems outlined above, it would probably slow for a time the

43. Cline, *International Debt*, pp. 44–73.
44. Ibid., p. 56.
45. Buira, "Exchange Crisis and Adjustment Program in Mexico."

erosion in the power position of the Mexican political elite by providing new resources for electoral patronage and selective rewards for organized interests.

In Argentina, conversely, the characteristic inability of democratic governments to sustain stabilization in the face of working-class and white-collar opposition might in a few years produce yet one more round—probably sharper and more violent—of the political cycle so familiar since the overthrow of the first Perón regime in 1955: democratic stalemate, political polarization, and the reemergence of the now apparently dead authoritarian "solution." Moreover, although initial versions of the new militarism might reflect "inward-looking," statist orientations, in the context of opportunities provided by an expanding world economy the heirs of Onganía and Videla are more likely to prevail in the end. I leave the reader to speculate on what would happen next.

The typically "muddling" Brazilian response presents an unclear picture, with the change from a military to a civilian president in March 1985 adding to the general uncertainty about policy. One strong possibility, unfortunately, is that Tancredo Neves's successor, José Sarney, will be unable to sustain a stabilization plan. Under these circumstances, Brazilian military elites (which unlike their Argentine counterparts are not likely to be far from the centers of power) would undoubtedly attempt to pull again on the reins (perhaps next time allowing a civilian president to remain in office). On the other hand, as I have suggested above, there are opportunities for a civilian center-right government to sustain a stabilization program. If so, with a renewed Brazilian expansion dulling the lines of political conflict, the next president could play the role of a Suárez to some future Felipe González.

What would happen if the international economy does not expand with the necessary rapidity? The answer depends, of course, very much on the responses of the banks, creditor governments, and international lending institutions—as well as on labor unions, taxpayers, consumer groups, and business organizations in the advanced countries. Ad hoc bailouts and rescue packages would, in contrast to the 1930s, provide some cushioning, and ABM governments would continue to find it in their interests to avoid outright repudiation. Still, in a context of basic insolvency produced by the contraction and regionalization of trade opportunities, the political and economic lessons drawn from the Depression might prove at least as instructive as those drawn from the years since World War II.

This picture is, to say the least, not encouraging. Although in some parts of the region the Depression did produce "progressive" governments and speeded up industrialization, no government—either of the left or of the right—made a major dent in the problems of deepening poverty. Throughout the region the 1930s was a period of unrelieved material hardship that did not really begin to ease until after 1945. On the other hand, profound crises of this sort, though they offer no good economic choices, can at times open the political space for the forging of new domestic coalitions and institutional loyalties. Elites, in other words, may have the opportunity to break old patterns and to restructure the basic constitution of the state—perhaps in ways that position them better to take advantage of future developmental opportunities.

Something of this sort did happen, it appears, in the ABM countries during the Depression era. What is striking, however, is that success in seizing these opportunities varied directly with the extent to which governmental elites were willing to *defy* conventional wisdom and to test the prevailing limits of international capitalist orthodoxy. The incorporation of workers and peasants at the base of the Mexican political system was integrally linked to Cárdenas's radical land reform and to his decision to challenge U.S. dominance by nationalizing the American oil companies. Vargas's Estado Novo, though more elitist and less institutionalized than the Mexican system, also sought to broaden the social base of the central state through nationalist appeals and social reforms engineered from above. Although such measures had only limited economic impact during the Depression, they established the politico-institutional pivot for the high-growth policies of the post-1945 era.

The conservative oligarchies that seized power in Argentina during the Depression marched in an entirely different direction, with much more divisive long-term consequences. The "political project" of 1930s governments was to restore the cattle-ranching elites to the unchallenged dominance that they enjoyed before middle-class parliamentarism was inaugurated in 1916. While Cárdenas and Vargas were mobilizing new groups into the political structure, therefore, the Argentine elites were attempting to roll back the political clock. A close identification with the prevailing economic wisdom of the day was also very much a part of the total package. Argentina was the only ABM government to honor its external debt obligations during this period; and notwithstanding some experimentation with import substitution, it relied extensively on meat and wheat exports to lead the hoped for recovery.[46] But in a rapidly contracting world economy this decision meant major, delegitimating trade concessions to the British and a "savage deflation" to avoid suspension of debt payments.[47] In these ways, then, the 1930s set the stage for the strident political stalemates and missed economic opportunities that have characterized Argentina ever since.

In the 1980s the roles of the countries are reversed: Argentina, with expanding political participation, is so far most inclined to test the rules of the international game, whereas Mexico has acted most consistently as a prudent and responsible participant in the international financial structure. What are the implications of such contrasts? How far can we expect the parallels of

46. Carlos F. Diaz-Alejandro, *Essays on the Economic History of the Argentine Republic* (New Haven: Yale University Press, 1970).
47. The characterization is from Marcello de Cecco, "The International Debt Problem in the Interwar Period" (The Lehrman Institute: Politics and International Debt Series, 13 April 1984).

the 1930s to extend into the present? Although the following scenarios are written as declarative sentences, they should obviously be read as questions and hypotheses.

Unlike the Argentine elite of the Depression era, the contemporary Mexican government has major leverage derived from its geopolitical centrality to U.S. security interests. It can thus reasonably anticipate special aid and attention from the U.S. government, even if its current austerity measures do not produce an economic recovery.[48] With the most stable and "responsible" of the ABM governments, moreover, Mexico would be in a better position than Brazil or Argentina either to seek bilateral rewards for good behavior or to carve a profitable role for itself as the leader of a debtor block.

Nevertheless, in a contracting world economy it is doubtful that either the U.S. government or the private banks could do more than prevent the collapse of the local economy. Since the system has depended heavily on the distributive resources derived from growth, this outcome would put it at serious risk. An induced recession that did not lead to a strong recovery would almost certainly exacerbate some of the profoundly destabilizing trends already discussed: increased conflicts within the political elite itself over the future course and direction of economic policy; accelerated loss of leverage over organized business and labor groups; increases in the level of "turmoil"— land seizures, guerrilla movements, terrorism, and so forth; increased reliance on military force to contain popular and revolutionary pressures; and increasingly visible links of dependence on U.S. governmental and private-sector support.

New or prospective elected regimes in Argentina and Brazil, on the other hand, might (like Mexico in the 1930s) reasonably hope to capitalize on the legitimacy derived from international assertiveness and popular mobilization. Short-term refusal to impose stabilization would not matter as much and could even be a symbolic "plus." In a failing world economy democratic governments could blame both their predecessors and exogenous forces for continuing economic problems while at the same time taking credit for incremental improvements in the material situation. Most important, these governments could offer expanded political participation to populations that have been forcibly excluded from the political system for the better part of several decades.

As in the 1930s, Brazilian-style caution—appropriate in an expanding world economy—might not be as effective in this connection as a bolder and more assertive approach. In an expanding economy, where the debt reflects a "liquidity" problem, a compromising center-right government may have a greater chance of finding an "appropriate" stabilization formula. More broadly, it would be comparatively well positioned to accommodate the domestic and foreign business interests that would drive an economic re-

48. Cohen, "International Debt and Linkage Strategies."

covery. In a contracting world economy, on the other hand, where the debt issue reflects a solvency problem, extended continuities with the old order become liabilities rather than assets. A new regime in this situation would hence be deprived of important symbolic resources that might allow it to consolidate a broad base of electoral support, without at the same time being able to compensate for this loss with access to export or credit markets. In contrast to the first scenario, a much more statist form of military authoritarianism would be the likely alternative to a failed democracy.

Finally, it is probable, under these circumstances, that the center-left orientation of an Alfonsín would have the best chance of success. With both the Peronists and the military badly weakened by the experiences of the last decade, the moment may be at hand for an attempt to reorganize and tame these historical veto groups. International insolvency would make less relevant the problems that this political restructuring might pose for conventional stabilization policies, since such policies might well be counterproductive in any case. Meanwhile, taking on the banks could, in a manner analogous to the Mexican oil nationalizations, become the kind of nationalist rallying point needed for the consolidation of a new popular constituency.

Accommodation as well as confrontation would, to be sure, have to be a component of this process if it is to issue in a stable democratic outcome. Moreover, a nationalist democratic government would have to face the very considerable challenge of finding a politically suitable "developmental model." The odds against this happening are very high—just as they were in Mexico fifty years ago.

International debt and international institutions Charles Lipson

The arrangements for handling international debt problems are informal but well articulated. They are based on extensive cooperation among major banks, the ability of these banks to secure cooperation from numerous smaller creditors, and the capacity of the International Monetary Fund to supervise economic adjustment in debtor states that are overextended.[1]

Private actors are clearly central to these arrangements. Any account of debt rescheduling must begin with the banks' discussions with one another, and simultaneously with debtors, over lending terms, fees, new credits, and amounts of principal to be covered. The numbers of creditors involved and the complexity of such refinancing make the extent of private cooperation striking.

Even so, public institutions have become much more involved in the last few years, as debt problems have deepened and spread. The IMF, which has long supervised economic adjustment, has begun to indicate an appropriate level of private credits that commercial banks should provide to troubled debtors. In a few significant cases the U.S. Federal Reserve and the Bank of England have specifically urged "involuntary" lending to troubled debtors, even arranging short-term loans themselves. At the same time they have expanded their supervision of bank assets and liabilities, which they, like monetary authorities in several other developed countries, now audit on a consolidated, worldwide basis. Aware that national banking systems are now intertwined, they have also coordinated their supervisory responsibilities for international banking and have at least discussed the problems of lenders of last resort.[2] Taken together, these various new forms of public involvement

I thank Miles Kahler, Cynthia Lichtenstein, Michael Mandelbaum, Kenneth Oye, and members of the Lehrman Institute's seminar on Politics and International Debt for their comments. This research was supported by a grant from the German Marshall Fund of the United States.
    1. See Charles Lipson, "The International Organization of Third World Debt," *International Organization* 35 (Autumn 1981), pp. 603–31.
    2. This coordination is publicly acknowledged in the so-called Basle Concordats, negotiated under the auspices of the Bank for International Settlements.

have reinforced and modified private arrangements for handling problem debts. They have not, however, fundamentally transformed them.

A complex but stable set of private rescheduling arrangements developed in the 1970s, I shall argue. These arrangements came under severe strain during the debt crisis of 1982 and 1983; they were modified not by grand design but by a series of small, yet cumulatively significant, steps. These steps have moved in a clear direction. They are aimed directly at overcoming deficiencies in cooperation among creditors. *Greater public involvement in international debt issues can best be understood as a series of incremental reforms designed to overcome inherent gaps in private cooperation,* gaps such as a fatal slowness that might produce defaults and turbulence in financial markets.

Rescheduling before the debt crisis

The basic features of commercial debt rescheduling were in place by the late 1970s. Rescheduling depended heavily on interbank cooperation, managed largely by the banks themselves, and the role of public institutions was carefully circumscribed. Of course, the IMF played an essential role in supervising debtors' economic programs, but neither the Fund nor major central banks intervened to establish rescheduling terms or to ensure their ratification by private creditors.

Restructurings were relatively infrequent in the 1970s. Although debts grew rapidly after the oil crisis of 1973–74, most principal did not come due until the early 1980s. In any case, borrowers had accumulated little prior debt and were paying low (or even negative) real interest rates. Between the mid-1970s and 1982 only nine countries restructured their debts to commercial lenders.[3]

The track record on foreign-aid loans was equally strong. Donors had made such loans throughout the postwar period, and inevitably some had required rescheduling. Such renegotiations were rare, however, and their terms stiff. Since the mid-1950s donors had seldom negotiated with more than one or two problem countries annually. Between 1956 and 1980 only twelve less developed countries had renegotiated their official loans.[4] (When these countries also faced problems with commercial creditors, such

3. M. S. Mendelsohn, *Commercial Banks and the Restructuring of Cross-Border Debt* (New York: Group of Thirty, 1983), p. 3.
4. John S. Odell, "The Politics of Debt Relief: Official Creditors and Brazil, Ghana, and Chile," in Jonathan David Aronson, ed., *Debt and the Less Developed Countries* (Boulder: Westview, 1979), p. 253. Some countries had to renegotiate their debts repeatedly, in part because of the creditors' conservative, short-term approach. According to Odell, the twelve countries that did reschedule their official debts in the 1950s, 1960s, and 1970s engaged in some 38 separate negotiations.

debts were handled in separate negotiations.)[5] The basic terms—for both official and private reschedulings—provided little relief from debt obligations, postponing only immediate amortization of principal.

Rescheduling was thus approached as an isolated event, not as a problem that broadly affected LDCs. The causes of repayment problems, it was assumed, lay at the national level, usually in economic mismanagement, and their solution lay at the national level as well. The standard remedies were to cut government budgets, restrain monetary growth, and realign overvalued currencies.[6] These measures, and corresponding performance targets, were embodied in agreements drawn up by IMF staff and signed by borrowers as a condition of IMF loans from higher credit tranches. As part of these agreements, the Fund staff monitored changes in national economic policies and assessed the overall economic performance of borrowers.

Supervisory duties gave the IMF an essential role to play in resolving debt problems, but its role also had important limitations. The Fund had little impact on the structure of national reserve assets. It certainly did not provide systemic management of global payments imbalances. Nor did it provide long-term assistance for structural adjustment. In short, the IMF was neither an embryonic central bank nor a development planning agency. Instead, it focused on short-term funding and oversight for balance-of-payments adjustment.

Rescheduling requires written agreements with both the IMF and the creditors, but the negotiations themselves have been kept deliberately informal. Foreign-aid donors meet on a case-by-case basis at the French Treasury, relying on a small secretariat for staff work. Negotiations remain informal despite occasional protests by debtors who would prefer to see reschedulings supervised by a multilateral organization of debtors and creditors. Donors have resisted such demands on the plausible grounds that more elaborate institutionalization would encourage more applications for debt relief, might be controlled by debtors, and could shift the terms of bargaining.[7]

These informal "Paris Club" arrangements do not provide concessionary funds or long-term relief. They postpone only payments of *principal*; interest payments must be kept current. In addition, they require debtors to

5. Many debtors now borrow from both official and private sources. When repayment problems arise, the two groups meet separately and negotiate their own arrangements. Official creditors are particularly concerned that they not offer more favorable terms than private lenders do, which might be viewed as an illegitimate "bailout" of the banks. The agreement with the debtor typically provides that no other creditors receive more favorable treatment, but the provision is practically unenforceable.
6. Cf. John Williamson, "The Economics of IMF Conditionality," in Gerald K. Helleiner, ed., *For Good or Evil: Economic Theory and North-South Negotiations* (Oslo and Toronto: Universitetsforlaget and University of Toronto Press, 1982), pp. 121–31.
7. This is the "moral hazard" problem that appears so frequently in discussions of financial institutions. The classic cases are those of property insurance and the lender of last resort.

promise corrective action. Donor states, in practice, will reschedule only after debtors have reached agreement with the IMF, pledging austerity and establishing targets for economic performance.[8] It is the IMF, not the donors or the private creditors, which oversees the subsequent economic retrenchment. Finally, creditor states have preferred to reschedule only near-term payments, deferring consideration of broader development issues. Payments of principal falling due over the next two or three years may be stretched out for eight or ten years, including a grace period when no principal is due. On the other hand, interest obligations, as noted above, must be paid promptly even during the grace period and may even be increased to a penalty rate. Countries that face severe and prolonged economic problems can seek additional reschedulings, but donors prefer to see some evidence that new adjustment policies are working before they will postpone more distant obligations.

These arrangements were established during the late 1950s and early 1960s, when aid recipients first experienced repayment problems. They have remained remarkably constant through several waves of large-scale rescheduling in the first half of the 1980s.[9] The most significant change recently has been to reschedule several years of principal instead of one or two years. The reasons for this change are clear. Creditors, faced with the need to restructure loans to dozens of countries, wanted to minimize their transaction costs. Equally important, they recognized that high debt burdens (high, that is, relative to gross domestic product and export earnings) required longer-term adjustments in debtor states. Multiyear reschedulings, in conjunction with IMF programs, set the stage for such adjustments.[10] Even so, creditors have adopted these multiyear restructurings with reluctance and, so far at least, have extended them selectively.

Commercial debt reschedulings have followed a similar pattern. Like the Paris Club agreements, they require a debtor's commitment to economic adjustment, embodied for IMF member states in Fund agreements, as a quid pro quo for rescheduling. They also share basic procedural norms: rescheduling is carried out only on a case-by-case basis and requires mutual agreement between debtor and creditor.

When sovereign debtors confront serious problems with commercial loans, as some started to do in the late 1970s, they must approach their major lenders and ask them to convene a creditor committee. These committees are organized on a case-by-case basis and include the largest creditors from all major financial markets. The banks have resisted formal institutionaliza-

8. This assumes that the debtor is an IMF member. All LDC debtors are, but several important East European debtors are not.
9. See M. S. Mendelsohn, "International Debt Crisis: The Practical Lessons of Restructuring," *Banker*, July 1983, pp. 34–36, and Mendelsohn, *Commercial Banks* pp. 31–33.
10. World Bank, *World Development Report, 1985* (New York: Oxford University Press, 1985), p. 29.

Debt and international institutions 223

tion. Like aid donors, they have focused on near-term problems, demanded that interest payments be kept current, and extracted new fees and penalty interest rates on renegotiated loans. Their position regarding the IMF also resembles that of official creditors: Fund involvement is an essential complement to rescheduling.[11] Lenders have been unwilling to negotiate any reduction in the present value of their assets, and neither official nor private creditors have been willing to link debt-service payments to any measure of debt-service capacity.[12]

Private creditors obviously aim to maximize the present value of their assets under difficult conditions. Donor states have more institutional flexibility, but they too are remarkably attentive to the value of their loans, even charging penalty interest rates on occasion. In many ways, then, the two types of creditors hold similar views of their interests in managing troubled debts and have produced similar organizational arrangements.

Private cooperation in rescheduling

Commercial banks and official creditors *do* differ in one crucial way beyond the banks' obvious attention to their operating profits. Coordination among private creditors is much more difficult and complicated because the number of institutions involved is much larger.[13] Only a few states hold outstanding aid loans and trade credits, so they can restructure obligations quickly, usually in a two-day Paris meeting. By contrast, hundreds of banks have assets outstanding in even the smallest debtor.[14] To coordinate they must overcome all the problems of large numbers—difficulties in communicating and forging joint positions, in monitoring creditor behavior that could undermine group efforts, and in responding effectively to individual threats to defect from joint arrangements.

To cope with these problems, commercial lenders draw upon their experience with troubled domestic loans. If a domestic borrower is potentially viable, then unsecured creditors may be best served by a "workout" agreement

---

11. Whether a conditional loan from the IMF is a *sufficient* condition for involuntary bank lending is a point very much at issue—and a central question of institutional reform. The Fund, as I shall show, is now attempting to make its approval of stabilization packages a sufficient condition for bank rescheduling, at least in major cases.

12. Linking debt-service payments to current economic capacity is precisely the point of a proposal by Peruvian president Alan García Pérez. In his inaugural address, in July 1985, he said that he would limit debt payments to 10% of the country's export earnings and would not accept an IMF program.

13. For a more complete treatment of strategic interaction among creditors, see Charles Lipson, "Bankers' Dilemmas: Private Cooperation in Rescheduling Sovereign Debts," *World Politics* 38 (October 1985), pp. 200–225.

14. A 1983 rescheduling in Ecuador, for instance, involved only $1.2 billion in overdue foreign debts but required agreement from more than 400 commercial banks. *Wall Street Journal*, 8 September 1983, p. 31.

that keeps the company operating (under specified conditions) and out of bankruptcy court.[15] In workouts the largest creditors form a committee, reach agreement among themselves and with the debtor, and negotiate with smaller creditors and secured lenders to ensure that they do not disrupt the agreement.

In many ways, that is exactly what international creditors do. Yet the analogy between domestic and international reschedulings is far from exact. Domestic U.S. law provides small creditors with legal protections that are not available internationally. Domestic loans, for instance, may be protected by secured assets, such as liens on specific property, while virtually all sovereign loans are unsecured. Domestic creditors, no matter how small, have legal rights to demand prompt repayment and to petition the courts to declare involuntary bankruptcy. The mere presence of these rights, even if they are not exercised, affects bargaining in loan workouts, for it increases the bargaining leverage of small creditors relative both to large creditors and to debtors.

No such protections are available in syndicated lending to sovereign entities such as central governments, state agencies, and state-owned corporations. There is no sovereign bankruptcy, of course. Even the calling of a major default requires a vote by lending syndicates. That is, lenders must formally recognize a violation of their loan agreement and then vote to accelerate repayment. Votes are weighted according to each lender's share of any particular credit, so big banks can prevent smaller banks from accelerating repayments. Many larger syndicate leaders also decided to change their loan documentation after widespread debt problems emerged. Their new loans require a two-thirds vote (rather than a simple majority) before calling a default—an additional control on small banks.[16] Major lenders thus can control the treatment of syndicated Euromarket loans and, in a rescheduling, impose solutions on smaller creditors.[17]

Large lenders are not, of course, a monolithic bloc. They have different levels of exposure, different relationships with borrowers, and different regulatory settings. As a result, they have somewhat different interests in particular reschedulings. But they also have an overriding interest in reaching agreement with each other, and powerful constraints prevent them from obstructing such agreements. Their extensive reciprocal ties range from shared

---

15. For the transcript of a simulated domestic debt renegotiation, with experienced professionals representing all sides, see "The Business in Trouble—A Workout without Bankruptcy," *Business Lawyer* 39 (May 1984), pp. 1041–87.

16. These special majorities also protect European banks in case their preferences should diverge from American money-center banks.

17. The state may also provide domestic rules that facilitate collective action—rules that are not available internationally. Under U.S. law, for example, any debts repaid during the ninety days prior to bankruptcy must be returned by the individual creditor and redivided among all creditors. The aim is to minimize bankruptcies caused by nervous creditors rushing in to claim assets. Obviously, no political institution can forge such rules internationally or facilitate collective action so effectively.

Debt and international institutions 225

syndicate lending to cross-depositing, and these ties, it should be underscored, are the very essence of large-scale international banking.[18] A major Euromarket bank, with a continuing stake in international finance, cannot afford to rupture vital, ongoing relationships for short-term gains.[19] The crucial issue in interbank bargaining, therefore, is not *whether* to reach agreement but *on whose terms*.

Major international banks, in sum, have powerful incentives to reach cooperative solutions among themselves and few incentives to defect. Defections for narrow, self-interested reasons would be irrational, because large international banks expect to interact repeatedly and must preserve their reputation as reliable partners; because noncooperators can be identified readily; and because noncooperators can be punished individually for defection (for instance, others can refuse to cooperate with them in the future). Noncooperators that did not expect to deal extensively with other banks in the future would be indifferent to reputation and less readily punished, for the immediate costs of providing involuntary credits would not be balanced by concerns about future relationships. Iteration thus produces what may be called a "coordination game," in which all players unconditionally prefer cooperation and need only choose a common point of agreement.

Small creditors have little direct choice about which point of agreement is chosen. They are much less involved than major creditors in shaping rescheduling agreements. Their consent, however, is needed to restructure existing legal obligations, and, equally important, their participation is needed to provide new involuntary funds to beleaguered debtors. Major creditors, fearing that they would have to cover any shortfall, are particularly concerned that everyone provide new credits on a prorated basis. Thus any proposed level of new funding must take into account the problem of extracting involuntary credits from smaller institutions.

Smaller lenders may have incentives to refuse, especially if substantial new credits are required. Smaller lenders are not regular participants in international finance and usually have weaker ties to the debtor. Furthermore, they know that larger lenders, who have so much more at risk, will be reluctant to see negotiations fail because of their nonparticipation. "If we are obstinate," the small fry may think, "major lenders may simply buy out our portion of the loan." Big banks understand this bargaining strategy all too well, however, and usually respond by threatening negative sanctions. The basic strategy of the large creditors is to isolate any mavericks who refuse to ratify the basic agreement. A maverick bank, standing alone, faces possible exclusion from other, more profitable syndicate loans and possibly even

18. In addition, creditor banks often have direct and important ties to the sovereign debtor and to major enterprises operating in that country. Obstructing a debt rescheduling or failing to participate equally in new "involuntary" lending could jeopardize these relationships.
19. Such banks will, however, bargain hard to defend their particular interests and achieve coordination on their most-preferred terms.

from correspondent services. It is threatened, in other words, with ostracism in a world where financial institutions are highly interdependent and depend for their continued profitability on their links with one another. Such threats, which rarely need enforcement, are typically made by money-center banks with extensive ties to the maverick bank.

The threat of isolation is a powerful one, and so far it has produced broad support for rescheduling agreements. Nevertheless, the process of reaching agreement is marked by uncertainty, compromise over the level of new credits, and slowness in sorting out complex financial details. Moreover, the problems of creditor coordination have worsened as the debt crisis has stretched out. When the debtor has good prospects for growth and is expected to return soon to voluntary borrowing, small creditors have far fewer incentives to refuse to provide their portion of new loans. When the debtor faces a long period of economic retrenchment and will need repeated infusions of involuntary capital, however, the incentives to defect are much greater. For small creditors, they may be overwhelming.

Institutional reforms in the 1980s: How much is really new?

In the late 1970s and early 1980s, arrangements among commercial lenders to reschedule debts were stable and effective, despite their informality and reliance on private institutions. Few countries needed to reschedule, and vast, involuntary credits were not required to meet current-account needs. These arrangements were seriously strained, however, in the early 1980s, when the world economy plunged into deep recession and dozens of sovereign debtors found themselves seriously overextended. A sharp rise in U.S. interest rates compounded the problems. Unable to refinance their existing debts, many LDCs found themselves unexpectedly forced to repay these obligations as they fell due. They could not do so.

Looking back, it is easy to identify the sources of this global debt crisis. At the macroeconomic level one can cite unusually high real interest rates, the worst recession since the 1930s, the prolonged strength of the dollar (in which most debts are denominated), excessively rapid borrowing by many LDCs, and, as credit conditions began to tighten, capital flight from developing countries and a dangerous reliance on short-term loans for balance-of-payments financing.[20] Contingent factors also played a role. The fall of the shah of Iran heightened awareness of the political risks in international lend-

20. Capital flight is best measured in the "recorded errors and omissions" category of balance-of-payments statistics. LDCs that borrowed on the commercial capital markets reported these errors and omissions at an annual average of about $4 billion in the late 1970s. In 1980 the amount increased fivefold and rose still further in 1981 and 1982. A major source of LDC improvement in external accounts in the mid-1980s has been the rapid decline of this extraordinary capital flight. IMF, *World Economic Outlook, April 1985* (Washington, D.C., 1985), Table 38, p. 250.

ing, and the confusion and uncertainties associated with the Falklands War halted virtually all new lending to Latin America in early 1982.

Adversity and imprudence together produced serious repayment problems and widespread debt reschedulings. A first round of crisis negotiations in 1982-83 was followed by another, even tougher set of negotiations when it became clear that short-term adjustment measures, however painful, would not be enough to restore creditworthiness. Although the crisis was global, the reschedulings were always handled on an ad hoc, nation-by-nation basis. They still are. Attention focused on immediate payment problems and not the longer-term issues of structural adjustment and resumption of growth.

Despite these continuities, some procedures and institutional roles have been modified in the early eighties. National monetary authorities have assumed more explicit responsibility for safeguarding international banking against major systemic shocks. They have provided short-term, emergency loans to major debtors and have extended their banking supervision to offshore facilities. These changes are clearly designed to enhance stability in closely linked financial markets, but their scope should not be exaggerated. As long as international lender-of-last-resort responsibilities remain unclear, the "safety net" for international banking must be considered uncertain. On the other hand, central banks have conferred regularly about such issues, and their private understandings may well exceed their public disclosures.

Institutional changes at the International Monetary Fund have been very public indeed and have taken the IMF beyond its traditional role of supervising economic adjustment. The Fund now plays a role in constructing overall financial packages for debtors, even specifying the amount of new credits to be provided from private sources in major cases. Other international financial institutions, notably the World Bank and the Bank for International Settlements, have also helped arrange financing for troubled debtors, although their roles have been more circumscribed.

The 1982 Mexican debt crisis as a catalyst for reform

We can date this greater public involvement with painful precision. On Thursday evening, 12 August 1982, Secretary of the Treasury Donald Regan received a telephone call from his Mexican counterpart, Jesus Silva-Herzog. What Silva-Herzog told him transformed the slowly building problem of international debt into a full-blown crisis. Mexico, he said, had no reserves left and could not continue to service its debts.

Mexico's finances had been eroding badly for several months—the result of slipping oil prices, heavy debt service, and economic mismanagement—but the depth and immediacy of the problem came as a profound shock to the Americans and, indeed, to Mexico's other creditors. After all, Mexico's $80 billion external debt ranked with Brazil's as the world's largest. Even worse, every major American bank had committed a substantial portion of its capital to Mexico. The potential for catastrophe was enormous.[21]

In the hurried weekend meetings that followed—and before the financial markets opened on Monday morning—the U.S. Treasury and Federal Reserve managed to assemble a $3 billion emergency rescue package.[22] On 18 August the world's major central banks met in emergency session at the Bank for International Settlements in Basle and put together an additional loan of $1.85 billion. The BIS and American credits would serve as a "bridge" until an IMF stabilization program was worked out.[23] Over the next several months the Mexicans accepted painful austerity, slashing imports and halting economic growth.[24] At the same time negotiators agreed on a comprehensive rescheduling of Mexican obligations, covering some fourteen hundred commercial banks worldwide.

The Mexican rescheduling marks a turning point in the treatment of sovereign debt. Not only did it put international debt squarely on the public agenda, it produced a new mixture of institutional arrangements and procedures to cope with the obvious and immediate problems caused by excessive debt burdens among less developed countries.

The changes at the IMF are particularly significant. Before 1982 public and private creditors had negotiated separate arrangements with the debtor, each arrangement contingent upon a national stabilization program supervised by the IMF. Lenders considered the Fund's role essential, but they determined for themselves the appropriate terms for debt restructuring, including the provision of new funds. The IMF had no say in the matter.

In 1982, however, confronted both with a need for massive rescheduling and with uncertain cooperation from some private lenders, the Fund moved to establish comprehensive terms for stabilization programs—*including* the element of private financing. For the first time the Fund indicated as part of an overall economic package the level of new commercial lending it required. It refused to sign a stabilization agreement until that level was met. The Fund's aim was to ensure that enough credits were available to pay for essential imports as well as to service debts. The terms themselves were hardly onerous for the banks, nor were they very different from the propos-

21. See Stanley Wilson, "America's LDC Troubleshooter," *Institutional Investor (International Edition)*. May 1983, pp. 80–85, and Alan Robinson, "Finance Minister of the Year [Jesus Silva-Herzog]," *Euromoney*, October 1983, pp. 264–65. Speed was obviously crucial, and the initial emergency package drew on any sources available, including $1 billion in credits from the U.S. Agriculture Department. *Business Week*, 20 December 1982, p. 37.
22. Wilson, "America's LDC Troubleshooter," pp. 80–85.
23. The United States and Britain took leading roles in arranging the BIS loan, and the United States contributed half the total. Joseph Kraft, *The Mexican Rescue* (New York: Group of Thirty, 1984), pp. 18–19.
24. See "The Debt Bomb," *Economist*, 7 May 1983, pp. 25–26; Lawrence Rout, "Mexico Proposes to Restructure Some of Its Debt," *Wall Street Journal*, 13 December 1982, p. 26; and Federal Reserve Bank of Chicago, *International Letter* no. 489 (17 December 1982), pp. 1–3.

als made by major lenders. But the IMF's involvement in such a way was itself new. Never before had the Fund intervened so directly in the affairs of commercial lenders.

The role of national monetary authorities changed as well. Aware of the risks of large-scale default, the major central banks, and especially the U.S. Federal Reserve, acted quickly to provide emergency foreign lending (on a short-term basis) and to ensure the stability of their own banking systems. Because national banking systems are closely linked, through cross depositing and syndicate lending, the major central banks also cooperated to draw up more complete guidelines for the supervision of foreign banking. Using the BIS as their forum, they once again discussed their responsibilities as lenders of last resort, reinforcing and extending agreements reached in the mid-1970s.

The Mexican crisis also galvanized the U.S. executive branch and led to another significant policy change: American support for a stronger IMF. The U.S. Treasury not only helped arrange the emergency loan to Mexico, and a later one to Brazil, it pushed for a new attitude toward the IMF. Before the Mexican crisis the Reagan administration had been resisting calls for a substantial, immediate increase in Fund resources, despite nearly universal support for the proposal among other IMF member states. As the full implications of the Mexican crisis sank in, however, the administration shifted its position on both the timing and the amount of the IMF quota increase. It joined with congressional Democrats to support immediate funding of the quota increase.[25]

Finally, the Mexican rescheduling dramatically changed the climate for new commercial lending. "I think that the Mexican experience has been shattering for a large number of regional banks," a leading New York banker told *Euromoney* in 1983. "In the past they were always eager to participate in international syndications. Now, it is very hard to interest them in anything."[26]

In fact, it had become hard to interest any bank, large or small, in sovereign lending. Voluntary credits had been slackening for some time, but after the Mexican rescue they virtually ceased.[27] Between 1977 and 1981 LDC external debt had doubled, reaching $660 billion. In 1983–84, by contrast,

---

25. Despite support for these changes, the Reagan administration remained steadfast on one important point: it wanted the IMF to concentrate on short-term, balance-of-payments problems. The administration wanted to reverse what it saw as the Fund's drift in the late 1970s toward longer-term adjustment programs that were linked to broader issues of economic development.

26. Anonymously quoted in Erik Ipsen, "After Mexico, the Regionals Are in Retreat," *Euromoney*, January 1983, p. 58. This view of Mexico's impact on regional bank lending is widely shared. Ipsen's article, for example, also quotes a similar statement by Frederick E. Schwartz, a senior vice president for international credit at Bankers Trust.

27. The only significant LDC market borrowers in the mid-1980s were fast-growing Asian exporters.

the net increase in private lending to LDCs was $30 billion, and only $7 billion of that was loaned outside restructuring agreements.[28]

The first to feel the impact of this credit crunch was Brazil, which needed a continuing flow of funds to service its huge debt. In 1983, after the flow had stopped, it replaced Mexico at the negotiating table. Its case proved to be even more difficult. Brazil decided to act patiently and deliberately in order to retain banker confidence, but the strategy proved far less effective than Mexico's decisive action. Instead of the usual steering committee, Brazil insisted on four separate committees, each in charge of a different facet of the rescheduling. This unusual procedure introduced considerable confusion and repetition into an already complex and difficult situation. Equally important, Brazil's strategy required that interbank credit lines be maintained at high levels. The task proved troublesome indeed, demanding continuous monitoring and suasion. Eventually, commercial banks did manage to roll over $5 billion in principal payments and to provide $6.5 billion in "new" money, much of it to meet arrears of interest. But the negotiations were difficult and protracted.[29]

Mexico and Brazil posed the largest and most immediate problems in 1982 and 1983, but they were hardly alone. Ultimately the combination of heavy debts and no new lending forced every Latin American borrower except Colombia to reschedule—some of them repeatedly. In fact, four major regional borrowers—Argentina, Brazil, Mexico, and Venezuela—now account for three-quarters of all bank debts from countries with debt-servicing difficulties.[30]

These large Latin American loans have created acute dilemmas for North American banks, but debt-servicing problems are truly global in scope. The only developing countries to escape have been the richest and least populous oil producers and the most successful East Asian exporters. The result is a debt problem of extraordinary proportions. In 1983–84 some forty-seven countries completed renegotiations with either commercial banks or official creditors (see Table 1).[31]

These are grim figures, but the consequences for financial markets could

---

28. IMF, *World Economic Outlook, April 1985* (Washington, D.C., 1985), pp. 3, 261 (table).

29. Subsequent negotiations to renew these interbank lines and short-term trade credits have been plagued by Brazil's repeated failure to meet performance targets agreed upon in talks with the IMF. Economist Intelligence Unit, *Quarterly Economic Review of Brazil, Annual Supplement, 1985*, pp. 48–52. For a good summary of the negotiations, see Nigel Adam, "How They Tried to Rescue Brazil," *Euromoney*, October 1983, pp. 76–87. See also Geraldo de F. Forbes, "How Not to Do It, or the Brazilian Renegotiation Affair," *Journal of International Affairs* 38 (Summer 1984), pp. 81–89.

30. C. Fred Bergsten, William R. Cline, and John Williamson, *Bank Lending to Developing Countries: The Policy Alternatives*, Policy Analysis no. 10 (Washington, D.C.: Institute for International Economics, 1985), p. 6.

31. Calculated from World Bank data in *World Development Report, 1985*, Figure 2.4A, p. 28.

TABLE 1. *Multilateral debt renegotiations, 1975–84 (in $ millions)*

Type of Negotiation	1975–80	1981	1982	1983	1984
Paris Club	8,166	1,284	641	10,559	3,341
Commercial Bank	5,638	4,473	1,741	41,005	112,853

Sources. World Development Report, 1985 (New York: Oxford University Press for the World Bank, 1985), p. 28, and World Bank data in David Folkerts-Landau, "The Changing Role of International Bank Lending in Development Finance," *International Monetary Fund Staff Papers* 32 (June 1985), pp. 328–29. Data for 1984 include agreements in principle.

have been much worse. Renegotiations and crisis financing have succeeded in preventing any major default. There has been occasional talk, mainly from the Cubans and Peruvians, of a Latin American debtors' cartel, but the idea has never gained crucial support from major market borrowers, who hope eventually to return to international capital markets. In spite of the shocks, furthermore, and in spite of the losses to banks and the austerity required of debtors, the international financial system has not been seriously disrupted.[32]

A larger role for the IMF

The difficulties of rescheduling such massive debts from so many financial institutions, together with the need for swift action to preserve the integrity of Western finance, have facilitated the entry of public institutions into the rescheduling process. Collective action has been at a premium. In case after case the creditors need to reach a common position on rescheduling terms and to determine the amount of new credits (if any) they will supply, and often they need to do so quickly. Institutions that help creditors to achieve such coordination have generally increased the scope of their authority.

The IMF, in particular, has moved decisively. No more did it simply inform commercial banks of its proposed terms for stabilization agreements

32. The fear of disruption in financial markets has been most acute after major bank failures. There have been several since the mid-1970s, but, significantly, none has spread across national borders. Equally significant, none of the failures has been due to bad sovereign loans. Most have been due to unauthorized currency speculation or domestic loan problems. There have been no "falling dominoes" in which one bank failure produces severe illiquidity in other major institutions. By contrast, the failure of Austria's Credit Anstalt in 1931 led to runs on banks in Hungary, Czechoslovakia, Romania, and Poland; to a financial crisis in Germany; and ultimately to President Hoover's decision to place a moratorium on all intergovernmental debts. Charles P. Kindleberger, *The World in Depression, 1929–1939* (Berkeley: University of California Press, 1973), pp. 148–57; Paul Bareau, "The Lessons of an Earlier International Debt Crisis," *Banker*, December 1983, pp. 35–39. For financial relations during the whole interwar period, see Benjamin M. Rowland, ed., *Balance of Power or Hegemony: The Interwar Monetary System* (New York: New York University Press for the Lehrman Institute, 1976).

and then allow them to choose their own courses of action. Rather, it demanded a specific level of commercial credits as a precondition for its own participation.[33] The effect was to isolate reluctant regional banks, pitting them not only against a solid phalanx of larger international banks but also against an international financial institution known for its conservative policies. True, there was some grumbling over the banks' loss of autonomy,[34] but large banks generally appreciated the IMF's stance because it facilitated collective action among lenders. On the other hand, they are reluctant to see this approach become an integral feature of IMF stabilization programs, extended routinely to smaller debts in calmer times.

The IMF's unique capacity to oversee domestic stabilization programs is the key to its involvement in debt negotiations. Fund loans, at least those in the higher credit tranches, are conditioned upon approved programs. Borrowers submit to such programs only reluctantly, and they do so less to get IMF funds than to get additional funds from private banks and official creditors. These other lenders consider IMF programs a necessary precondition for their own participation. The basic bargain, then, is that debtors submit to IMF-supervised austerity in order to qualify for a funding package from the IMF, private banks, and official creditors.

The Fund is well aware that its bargaining leverage with debtors is greatly enhanced because other creditors rely on it. But it is also aware that its leverage is potentially fragile because these other creditors do not consider IMF programs a *sufficient* condition for additional lending. This uncertainty about other creditors' participation poses problems for the Fund. If banks, aid donors, and export credit agencies fail to make vital new loans, they would not only obstruct the individual debtor's stabilization program but also undermine the IMF's bargaining with *all* troubled debtors. If the IMF is to coordinate economic stabilization at a time of widespread debt problems, then it must be certain that its programs will include adequate credit from all sources. That is why it has moved to shape involuntary private loan packages. The Fund is simply ensuring that it can deliver on its own implicit bargain with debtors and thereby negotiate effectively with them. The Fund's initiatives increase the likelihood that debtors will sign stabilization agreements promptly and reinforce its capacity to provide international coordination in cases of troubled debt.

The IMF's recent prominence in the debt crisis has reversed a decade of

33. See Art Pine, "IMF Chief Turning Table on Banks," *Wall Street Journal*, 25 January 1983, p. 35, and "Jacques de Larosière: Hero of the IMF," *Euromoney*, October 1983, pp. 196–97.

34. Americans were especially sensitive about the question of autonomy because their major enterprises, in contrast to those in continental Europe, developed without much centralized state support. Given the political economy of American industrialization, the problem of corporate autonomy is a recurrent one in U.S. economic policy debates. See Charles Lipson, *Standing Guard: Protecting Foreign Capital in the Nineteenth and Twentieth Centuries* (Berkeley: University of California Press, 1985), chap. 7.

declining importance. The modest resources of the Fund were eclipsed during the 1970s by the ready availability of commercial credit, which came with no strings attached. Moreover, the IMF's conditional lending program, which began in the 1950s, was ill-equipped to deal with the structural adjustment problems posed by the oil crisis. The sharp and unanticipated shift in energy prices required fundamental changes in patterns of production and consumption in all importing states. Yet most IMF funds are available only for temporary needs. They are most useful for rapid retrenchment and for the alteration of monetary and fiscal policy. They are not designed to effect the more basic economic reorientation needed to cope with permanently higher fuel costs. In the 1970s, as a result, IMF quota funds were not much used (although members did borrow readily from several special IMF facilities that carried no conditions). Alternative funding was available in the Euromarkets, at least for creditworthy applicants, such as the newly industrializing countries. The major Latin American economies, in particular, turned to these financial markets to support their continued growth (which was considerably more rapid than that of the OECD in the 1970s) and to cover their resulting payments needs.[35]

The IMF thus played a small role immediately after the first oil crisis. In a longer perspective, however, the IMF was becoming a more central actor as debt burdens grew steadily and adjustment problems became more pervasive. Such problems became even less tractable after oil prices doubled again in 1979, interest rates soared, and the West fell back into recession. When oil prices finally receded in the early 1980s, many producing countries (including Mexico, Venezuela, Nigeria, and Indonesia) found that they had borrowed far too much on unrealistic assumptions about future energy prices. Yet the price relief was hardly enough to rescue LDC oil *importers*, who still had to cope with stagnant export markets and unprecedented interest payments. With current accounts still deep in deficit, debt burdens were beginning to reach dangerous levels and lenders becoming unwilling to commit themselves to new, long-term credits. Desperate borrowers grabbed whatever short-term credits they could find. The stage was set for a debt crisis.

That crisis arrived in August 1982, when Mexico announced that it could not pay. The Euromarkets slammed shut on sovereign borrowers, and new voluntary lending to these states, which had already slowed as perceived risks had risen, now stopped abruptly. Many LDC borrowers, no longer able to roll over their loans, could not meet their upcoming obligations. To minimize the consequences for their own banking systems, the major Western central banks, led by the United States, stepped in with bridging loans for debtors and liquidity support for financial markets. At the same time the

---

35. Benjamin J. Cohen, *Banks and the Balance of Payments: Private Lending in the International Adjustment Process* (Montclair, N.J.: Allenheld, Osmun, 1981).

IMF departed from its traditional role and helped organize private debt restructuring.

The World Bank

The IMF's sister institution, the World Bank, has played a much less important role in dealing with troubled debt. Its mandate, after all, is to lend for economic development rather than for balance-of-payments shortfalls. This distinction is blurred, however, when deep-seated problems in external finance lead to serious economic contractions and lower per capita income, as they have in major debtors in the 1980s.[36] Against this background, Bank officials have pushed for greater capitalization, broader lending programs, and swifter loan disbursals. So far, their proposals have met with only limited success.

The traditional strength of the Bank lies in lending for specific development projects, ranging from new productive assets to economic infrastructure. Noted for their careful preparation, these loans take years of study and consultation before gaining approval. Even then the Bank's funds are released slowly, as the projects proceed.[37] The success of these projects has in turn assured prompt loan repayment, contributing to the Bank's own high credit rating while minimizing the costs to developed members. Lending for such carefully planned investments is the Bank's basic mission; developed countries, which provide the Bank's capitalization, have opposed any significant alteration.

The Bank's impact on debt and adjustment issues derives mainly from its smaller programs. Its sectoral adjustment program, for instance, is designed "to support comprehensive policy changes and institutional reforms in a specific sector."[38] In fiscal year 1985 the Bank lent slightly over $1 billion (or 7.4% of its total commitments) for such sectoral reforms. The Bank has maintained this level for the past several years.[39] These one- to four-year

36. Among major debtors, gross domestic product has not kept pace with population in the 1980s. For the ten largest debtors, per capita GDP has declined almost 10% since 1980–81. See Morgan Guaranty Trust, *World Financial Markets*, September–October 1985, Table 1, p. 2.

37. According to the World Bank, the disbursement period for specific investment loans is usually four to nine years. World Bank, *Annual Report, 1985* (Washington, D.C., 1985), p. 50. For a standard account of the bank's focus on project lending, see Edward S. Mason and Robert E. Asher, *The World Bank since Bretton Woods* (Washington, D.C.: Brookings, 1973), chap. 8. The definition of a suitable development project was broadened under former Bank president Robert McNamara, but the project focus remained. See Robert L. Ayres, *Banking on the Poor* (Cambridge: MIT Press, 1983), pp. 41–46. The task of evaluating projects at the World Bank is discussed in William Diamond and V. S. Raghavan, eds., *Aspects of Development Bank Management* (Baltimore: Johns Hopkins University Press for the Economic Development Institute of the World Bank, 1982).

38. World Bank, *Annual Report, 1985*, p. 50.

39. Ibid. See also Morgan Guaranty Trust, *World Financial Markets*, September–October 1985, Table 17, p. 10.

loans often serve as a follow-up to IMF stabilization programs and require continuing Bank surveillance.

Potentially more important are the Bank's efforts to encourage medium-term adjustment, including institutional reforms and changes in macroeconomic policy. Its Structural Adjustment Loans (SALs), begun in 1980 after the second oil price shock, mark an important departure for the Bank. As one program consultant observed, "For the first time in its history the Bank introduced, in a systematic manner, a form of lending which was entirely policy-focused."[40]

The Bank's structural adjustment lending has a longer time horizon than the IMF's standby arrangements do, but the two are closely linked. Indeed, the Fund and the Bank have carefully harmonized their roles to prevent borrowers from shopping around for better conditions. Like the Fund, the Bank requires pledges of policy reforms as a precondition for structural loans.[41] But the IMF focuses on immediate reductions in domestic absorption and changes in exchange rates to improve the current account balance while the World Bank encourages more fundamental institutional changes. The Bank reviewed the SAL program in 1982 and concluded that its "structural-adjustment lending operations and the IMF programs were, in practice, both complementary and mutually reinforcing."[42]

Even so, the SAL program has proved to be far less important than planned.[43] In the first five years of the program the Bank made only thirty-one such loans, to seventeen countries, totaling $4.5 billion.[44] (The IMF, by contrast, concluded 140 stand-by arrangements during the same period.)[45] The lending ceiling for SALs was initially set at 10 percent of the Bank's annual commitments, a limitation that reflected the program's novelty and uncertainty about its connection to the Bank's traditional activities and expertise. The program failed to reach even that modest ceiling at a time when developing countries were desperately short of external financing. In the SAL program's peak, in 1983–84, the Bank was lending slightly over $1 billion annually, or about 8 percent of its total commitments. In fiscal 1985 new SAL loans were scaled back to $200 million, or 1.4 percent of Bank commitments.[46] As a result the World Bank has been at best a periph-

---

40. Stanley Please, *The Hobbled Giant: Essays on the World Bank* (Boulder: Westview, 1984), p. 18.
41. See Don Babai, "The World Bank, Structural Adjustment and Commercial Co-Financing" (paper delivered at the 1983 Annual Meeting of the American Political Science Association, Chicago, Illinois), and Babai, "Between Hegemony and Poverty: The World Bank in the World Economy" (manuscript, University of Maryland, 1983).
42. World Bank, *Annual Report, 1982* (Washington, D.C., 1982), p. 40. See also World Bank, *Annual Report, 1985*, p. 53.
43. See the World Bank's discussion of the program's origins and aims in its *Annual Report, 1980* (Washington, D.C., 1980), pp. 67–68.
44. World Bank, *Annual Report, 1985*, p. 53.
45. IMF, *Annual Report, 1985* (Washington, D.C., 1985), Table I.4, p. 97.
46. Morgan Guaranty Trust, *World Financial Markets*, September–October 1985, Table 17, p. 10.

eral actor in the debates over LDC adjustment to debt problems. Equally important, the modest scale of the Structural Adjustment Loan program means that no international institution is offering significant support for medium- and long-term adjustment.[47]

The Bank has tried in other ways to spur long-term capital flows, however, and has embarked on some lending in tandem with private investors. The Bank's goal is to stretch its limited resources, multiplying the funds it can provide for suitable projects. Private investors hope, of course, to reduce the risks of lending to LDCs and to avail themselves of the Bank's extensive project evaluation. Because no borrower has ever defaulted on a World Bank loan (to do so would jeopardize a major source of concessional finance), private lenders are eager to couple their loans with those of the World Bank. For the Bank, however, linking the two kinds of lending is a difficult and delicate matter.

The Bank's original cofinancing program involved parallel loans: one from the World Bank, one from private investors. The contracts did not require the World Bank to declare default unless its *own* loan was in arrears, although it could choose to do so if the accompanying private loan was in default. With these arrangements private investors still faced significant risks. A borrower, aware that the confinanced loans were separate, might not be deterred from defaulting on the private portion. What lenders wanted, then, was a contract that required the Bank to declare default if the private loan was in default.[48]

The World Bank has carefully guarded its autonomy in so sensitive and important an area, but it has also been willing to consider new forms of cofinancing that involve more direct relationships with private capital. In 1984 it replaced its traditional cofinanced loans, with their optional cross-default clauses, with a pilot program of "B-Loans." Several basic types of B-Loans have been made, each entailing closer connections between the World Bank and commercial lenders than the older program did. The Bank can choose, for example, between guaranteeing the late maturities of cofinanced loans or participating directly in those late maturities. Or it may accept a contingent obligation to finance some of deferred principal payments as part of a private, floating-rate loan.[49] The effect, in each case, is to encourage longer maturities in LDC lending. In 1984 and 1985 the pilot pro-

47. Longer-term adjustment would include the expansion of export capacity and changes in state policy instruments, such as tariff reductions. See Fahrettin Yagci, Steven Kamin, and Vicki Rosenbaum, *Structural Adjustment Lending: An Evaluation of Program Design*, World Bank Staff Working Papers no. 735 (Washington, D.C., 1985), pp. 4–19, 97–133.

48. Cf. Jacques Cook, "Maintaining the Flow of Loans: The Cofinancing Alternative," *Banker*, May 1983, pp. 55–63; *Banker*, February 1983, p. 22; *Banker*, July 1983, p. 77; and Roger S. Leeds, *Co-Financing for Development: Why Not More?* Development Paper 29 (Washington, D.C.: Overseas Development Council, 1980).

49. The operations of this pilot program were reviewed by the Bank's executive directors in December 1984, who expressed satisfaction and renewed the program. World Bank, *Annual Report, 1985*, p. 55.

gram produced almost $1.5 billion in loans, and the Bank is now considering ways to cofinance projects with major export credit agencies.[50]

The Bank's cofinancing efforts are clearly fueled by its own shortage of resources. Proposed large increases in the Bank's capitalization were rejected in the early 1980s, and actual disbursements remained constant during this turbulent period.[51] The Bank's role may increase, however, now that major players have shifted their policy focus to longer-term issues of economic recovery. Cofinancing is likely to be an important instrument in this new setting because it promises what has been so very difficult to achieve: increased flows of voluntary private capital.

The U.S. Treasury, in particular, resisted consideration of these broader issues during the early 1980s. Its approach changed, however, after James Baker succeeded Donald Regan as secretary. At the 1985 IMF–World Bank annual meeting, Baker proposed a significant increase in the World Bank's lending capacity, along with other measures to increase capital flows to developing countries. He openly linked World Bank lending to the resolution of debt problems and stressed the Bank's cofinancing program as a key to mobilizing private capital.[52]

Although these changes are not fundamental reforms, they are significant steps in restoring medium-term lending to major LDCs. They signal a more important role for public institutions, including the World Bank, in the next round of debt talks.[53]

The BIS and the central banks

The World Bank and IMF have been involved in global debt problems because of the financial resources and organizational capabilities they possess. The Bank for International Settlements (BIS) is, by contrast, a much more modest institution, with limited resources. Yet its exclusive membership of major central banks gives it unique advantages as a forum for joint action. The members meet regularly in complete privacy and can act swiftly without public discussion if emergency measures are called for.[54]

The BIS can be used, therefore, to provide critical short-term financing on a multilateral basis; indeed, it has been so used. Despite the central bankers'

50. Ibid.; *IMF Survey*, 12 August 1985, pp. 244–46.
51. World Bank, *Annual Report, 1985*, p. 8, table.
52. Reported in, for example, *Economist*, 12 October 1985, p. 75.
53. One recent study that calls for a greater role for the World Bank is Donald R. Lessard and John Williamson, *Financial Intermediation beyond the Debt Crisis*, Policy Analyses in International Economics no. 12 (Washington, D.C.: Institute for International Economics, 1985).
54. See Gidon Gottlieb, "Global Bargaining: The Legal and Diplomatic Framework," in Nicholas Greenwood Onuf, ed., *Law-Making in the Global Community* (Durham, N.C.: Carolina Academic Press, 1982), pp. 109–30, and Dominique Carreau, *Le système monétaire international* (Paris: Colin, 1972), pp. 31–32, as quoted by Gottlieb, p. 118.

reservations about providing such finance through the BIS, and despite their desire to end the practice, the BIS has been used regularly in emergencies when a failure to get substantial new credits quickly might lead to serious arrears or even default. Thus the BIS, which had made a few bridging loans in the mid-1970s, was called on for many more in the early 1980s. The central banks used it to provide emergency money first to Mexico and then to Argentina, Brazil, Hungary, and Yugoslavia.

The BIS, unlike the IMF or the World Bank, is less an institution in its own right than a reflection of the major central banks' need to communicate continuously and to coordinate episodically. These needs stem from the interdependence of national financial markets. Central banks now acknowledge, as the Basle Concordats on bank supervision show, that they must pay close attention to the global distribution of private bank assets. Their own tasks as supervisors, regulators, and lenders of last resort all require continuous surveillance of offshore banks, whatever their legal form. Likewise the presence of foreign banks in every financial center requires central banks to cooperate if they are to oversee the liquidity and solvency of branches, subsidiaries, and consortiums.

This process of extensive and regular consultation began with the exchange-rate crises of the 1960s, when monetary authorities worked together to repel speculative runs against par values and sustain the Bretton Woods system.[55] Ties were renewed and strengthened in the mid-1970s, when integrated financial markets were threatened by the failures of the Bankhaus Herstatt and the Franklin National Bank.[56] It was these failures which led to the first Basle Concordat, in which central bankers assigned responsibility for supervising the liquidity and solvency of foreign branches and subsidiaries. The status of such branches had previously been uncertain—a potentially dangerous gap in regulatory responsibility in an era of extensive offshore banking.

These discussions continued under BIS auspices in the Basle Committee on Banking Regulations and Supervisory Practices, chaired originally by George Blunden and later by Peter Cooke, both of the Bank of England.[57] After the failure of Banco Ambrosiano's Luxembourg affiliate in 1982, supervisory responsibility was reasserted and refined in a second Basle Con-

---

55. I am indebted to Richard Erb for calling my attention to this point. See also Charles A. Coombs, *The Arena of International Finance* (New York: Wiley, 1976).

56. For details, see Joan Edelman Spero, *The Failure of the Franklin National Bank* (New York: Columbia University Press for the Council on Foreign Relations, 1980), p. 153; Robert Solomon, *The International Monetary System, 1945–1981*, rev. ed. (New York: Harper & Row, 1982); and John Williamson, *The Failure of World Monetary Reform, 1971–1974* (New York: New York University Press, 1977).

57. Cf. George Blunden, "International Co-operation in Banking Supervision," *Bank of England Quarterly Bulletin* 17 (September 1977), pp. 325–29; W. P. Cooke, "Developments in Co-operation among Banking Supervisory Authorities," ibid. 21 (June 1981), pp. 238–44; and G. G. Johnson with Richard K. Abrams, *Aspects of the International Banking Safety Net*, IMF Occasional Paper 17 (Washington, D.C., 1983).

cordat.[58] The second concordat requires that bank assets and liabilities be supervised on a consolidated, worldwide basis and that parent authorities take responsibility for the solvency of banking affiliates abroad.[59] But like the first concordat, it avoids any discussion of lender-of-last-resort responsibility (perhaps because of the problem of moral hazard it would raise).[60] The omission is a critical one. Although supervisory responsibilities are divided between authorities in the host and the parent countries, neither authority is assigned responsibility for remedying any setbacks that might occur.[61]

Conclusions

Concern with the stability of Western financial markets is fundamental to public involvement in debt issues. It underlies the U.S. Federal Reserve's swift intervention in the Mexican and Brazilian cases, and the Bank of England's active encouragement to private lenders in the Mexican rescheduling. This basic concern with the liquidity of interdependent capital markets and the integrity of national banking systems provides the deep, and often unspoken, fear behind any serious discussion in advanced countries of global debt problems. It is why the Group of Ten and Switzerland have committed themselves to provide "temporary liquidity to the Euromarkets . . . if and when necessary."[62]

---

58. See Richard Dale, "Basle Concordat: Lessons from Ambrosiano," *Banker*, September 1983, pp. 55–60; Spero, *Failure of the Franklin National*, p. 153; H. J. Muller, "The Concordat," *De Nederlandsche Bank, N.V., Quarterly Statistics*, September 1979, pp. 84–91; and the text of the 1983 Basle Agreement in "Basle Concordat Mark II," *International Currency Review* 15 (July 1983), pp. 5–9.

59. Johnson with Abrams, *Aspects of Banking Safety Net*.

60. This theme recurs in the work of Charles P. Kindleberger, especially his *Manias, Panics, and Crashes* (New York: Basic, 1978) and Kindleberger and Jean-Pierre Laffargue, eds., *Financial Crises* (Cambridge: Cambridge University Press, 1982). Also see Thomas M. Humphrey's analysis of Walter Bagehot and Henry Thornton in "The Classical Concept of the Lender of Last Resort," Federal Reserve Bank of Richmond *Economic Review*, February 1975, pp. 2–9. At one point, Kindleberger calls the IMF the "lender of last resort for developing countries." He then adds that the IMF cannot play the same role independently for financial centers (its resources are too limited), but that it may be "part of a larger package." Kindleberger is only partly correct. The IMF's resources are too small and its procedures generally a bit slow for it to act alone as a lender of last resort, even to LDCs. That is why the debt crisis has evoked a two-tiered approach. Central banks, which can act rapidly, have put together the emergency rescues. The IMF has then coordinated the follow-on loan package and adjustment program. To the extent that it acts as a lender of last resort, it does so in its role as catalyst and leader, directing the resources of others. To act as a lender of last resort when one was needed during the debt crisis, the IMF had to enlarge the scope of its own authority regarding private lenders. See Kindleberger and Jean-Pierre Laffargue, "Introduction," to their *Financial Crisis*, p. 10.

61. See the critical editorial, "The Interbank Fire-Chamber," in *Banker*, October 1985, p. 3.

62. Ibid.

If financial chaos is the ultimate issue, the day-to-day problems of debt negotiation are about much more concrete and immediate issues: preserving the value of bank assets, coordinating lenders with differing interests, and negotiating politically acceptable economic programs between the debtor and the IMF.

So far, financial markets have muddled through these day-to-day problems, as serious as they are. What has occurred is incremental adaptation by all actors, including greater involvement by central banks and the IMF. The roles of these public institutions have evolved directly to address gaps in creditor cooperation. Private cooperation remains critical to the handling of troubled debts, to be sure. It is both extensive and effective. But it also has inherent limits. Private creditors can mobilize substantial funds in rescheduling but they cannot act quickly, so others (the parent central banks) must supply emergency loans—as they did to Mexico, Brazil, and Yugoslavia. Nor can private lenders prevent liquidity crises from spreading or adequately monitor economic stabilization programs.[63] Finally, and perhaps most important, private lenders cannot assure a continuing net inflow of capital to debtor countries. It is uncertain how long debtors can sustain the combination of negative credit flows and prolonged austerity. Such problems will only worsen if interest rates rise or the export markets of developed countries weaken.

It is these limitations on private coordination which have set the agenda for institutional reform in international debt issues. I am not advancing the strictly functionalist argument that gaps in private coordination somehow *must* be overcome, nor that they require specific institutional changes. There is surely scope for policy initiative, strategic interaction, error, and choice. But I am claiming that *the growing role of public institutions in managing international debt is a response to coordination failures among private creditors and is limited by the extent of those failures.*

Consider, for example, the coordination problems posed by the large numbers of international lenders and by the variety of their outstanding claims. The 1982 Mexican case involved some fourteen hundred banks, as I have already noted, and some twenty-five different kinds of loans.[64] With such complexity the renegotiation of sovereign debts inevitably takes months. In a crisis, however, faster action may be required to avert a major default and financial disruption. National monetary authorities, which are constituted for precisely such purposes, have acted quickly and decisively to avert chaos in financial markets, most notably in the Mexican case. Similarly with Brazil, a loan was arranged multilaterally, with central banks working through the Bank for International Settlements. In both cases, pri-

---

63. Private creditors did try such surveillance in Peru in the mid-1970s, and it proved unworkable. G. A. Costanzo, then vice-chairman of Citicorp, later remarked, "I want *no* part of deals with that kind of discipline in the future." Quoted in Nancy Belliveau, "What the Peru Experiment Means," *Institutional Investor (International Edition)*, October 1976, p. 34.

64. Kraft, *Mexican Rescue*, p. 44.

cordat.⁵⁸ The second concordat requires that bank assets and liabilities be supervised on a consolidated, worldwide basis and that parent authorities take responsibility for the solvency of banking affiliates abroad.⁵⁹ But like the first concordat, it avoids any discussion of lender-of-last-resort responsibility (perhaps because of the problem of moral hazard it would raise).⁶⁰ The omission is a critical one. Although supervisory responsibilities are divided between authorities in the host and the parent countries, neither authority is assigned responsibility for remedying any setbacks that might occur.⁶¹

Conclusions

Concern with the stability of Western financial markets is fundamental to public involvement in debt issues. It underlies the U.S. Federal Reserve's swift intervention in the Mexican and Brazilian cases, and the Bank of England's active encouragement to private lenders in the Mexican rescheduling. This basic concern with the liquidity of interdependent capital markets and the integrity of national banking systems provides the deep, and often unspoken, fear behind any serious discussion in advanced countries of global debt problems. It is why the Group of Ten and Switzerland have committed themselves to provide "temporary liquidity to the Euromarkets . . . if and when necessary."⁶²

---

58. See Richard Dale, "Basle Concordat: Lessons from Ambrosiano," *Banker*, September 1983, pp. 55–60; Spero, *Failure of the Franklin National*, p. 153; H. J. Muller, "The Concordat," *De Nederlandsche Bank, N.V., Quarterly Statistics*, September 1979, pp. 84–91; and the text of the 1983 Basle Agreement in "Basle Concordat Mark II," *International Currency Review* 15 (July 1983), pp 5–9.

59. Johnson with Abrams, *Aspects of Banking Safety Net*.

60. This theme recurs in the work of Charles P. Kindleberger, especially his *Manias, Panics, and Crashes* (New York: Basic, 1978) and Kindleberger and Jean-Pierre Laffargue, eds., *Financial Crises* (Cambridge: Cambridge University Press, 1982). Also see Thomas M. Humphrey's analysis of Walter Bagehot and Henry Thornton in "The Classical Concept of the Lender of Last Resort," Federal Reserve Bank of Richmond *Economic Review*, February 1975, pp. 2–9. At one point, Kindleberger calls the IMF the "lender of last resort for developing countries." He then adds that the IMF cannot play the same role independently for financial centers (its resources are too limited), but that it may be "part of a larger package." Kindleberger is only partly correct. The IMF's resources are too small and its procedures generally a bit slow for it to act alone as a lender of last resort, even to LDCs. That is why the debt crisis has evoked a two-tiered approach. Central banks, which can act rapidly, have put together the emergency rescues. The IMF has then coordinated the follow-on loan package and adjustment program. To the extent that it acts as a lender of last resort, it does so in its role as catalyst and leader, directing the resources of others. To act as a lender of last resort when one was needed during the debt crisis, the IMF had to enlarge the scope of its own authority regarding private lenders. See Kindleberger and Jean-Pierre Laffargue, "Introduction," to their *Financial Crisis*, p. 10.

61. See the critical editorial, "The Interbank Fire-Chamber," in *Banker*, October 1985, p. 3.

62. Ibid.

If financial chaos is the ultimate issue, the day-to-day problems of debt negotiation are about much more concrete and immediate issues: preserving the value of bank assets, coordinating lenders with differing interests, and negotiating politically acceptable economic programs between the debtor and the IMF.

So far, financial markets have muddled through these day-to-day problems, as serious as they are. What has occurred is incremental adaptation by all actors, including greater involvement by central banks and the IMF. The roles of these public institutions have evolved directly to address gaps in creditor cooperation. Private cooperation remains critical to the handling of troubled debts, to be sure. It is both extensive and effective. But it also has inherent limits. Private creditors can mobilize substantial funds in rescheduling but they cannot act quickly, so others (the parent central banks) must supply emergency loans—as they did to Mexico, Brazil, and Yugoslavia. Nor can private lenders prevent liquidity crises from spreading or adequately monitor economic stabilization programs.[63] Finally, and perhaps most important, private lenders cannot assure a continuing net inflow of capital to debtor countries. It is uncertain how long debtors can sustain the combination of negative credit flows and prolonged austerity. Such problems will only worsen if interest rates rise or the export markets of developed countries weaken.

It is these limitations on private coordination which have set the agenda for institutional reform in international debt issues. I am not advancing the strictly functionalist argument that gaps in private coordination somehow *must* be overcome, nor that they require specific institutional changes. There is surely scope for policy initiative, strategic interaction, error, and choice. But I am claiming that *the growing role of public institutions in managing international debt is a response to coordination failures among private creditors and is limited by the extent of those failures.*

Consider, for example, the coordination problems posed by the large numbers of international lenders and by the variety of their outstanding claims. The 1982 Mexican case involved some fourteen hundred banks, as I have already noted, and some twenty-five different kinds of loans.[64] With such complexity the renegotiation of sovereign debts inevitably takes months. In a crisis, however, faster action may be required to avert a major default and financial disruption. National monetary authorities, which are constituted for precisely such purposes, have acted quickly and decisively to avert chaos in financial markets, most notably in the Mexican case. Similarly with Brazil, a loan was arranged multilaterally, with central banks working through the Bank for International Settlements. In both cases, pri-

---

63. Private creditors did try such surveillance in Peru in the mid-1970s, and it proved unworkable. G. A. Costanzo, then vice-chairman of Citicorp, later remarked, "I want *no* part of deals with that kind of discipline in the future." Quoted in Nancy Belliveau, "What the Peru Experiment Means," *Institutional Investor (International Edition)*, October 1976, p. 34.
64. Kraft, *Mexican Rescue*, p. 44.

vate lenders and the IMF eventually provided longer-term credits, but they could never have arranged the necessary emergency financing. The sums were too large and the time too short. State authorities, however, could act—and did. By the same token, they have largely confined themselves to solving these acute problems.

Banks and financial markets are now so well integrated internationally that a severe crisis in one national market could spread quickly.[65] As a result, monetary authoritics have worked closely and systematically with each other to clarify their supervisory responsibilities and to ensure adequate surveillance of multinational lending institutions. In general, national monetary authorities have intervened directly when market disruption was a genuine threat or when one bank's illiquidity carried costs well beyond the institution immediately involved.

Likewise, the IMF has played a more directive role as the rescheduling exercises have become larger and more expensive for individual creditors. Some smaller creditors, especially those in weak financial positions, have been reluctant to accept costly solutions devised by major money-center banks. Smaller banks, with fewer long-term ties to the whole process of international lending and less compelling stakes in the resolution of any particular debt problem, can plausibly threaten to defect, to walk away from any responsibility to supply new loans to impoverished debtors. The IMF has no direct leverage over these smaller creditors. But it has openly supported the agreements negotiated by major banks and has refused to ratify the debtors' austerity programs until creditors unite behind the agreement and share in the provision of new funds.

The IMF, which once limited itself to negotiations with debtor states, has thus insinuated itself into creditor relationships. Even so, its role is indirect. The ratification of rescheduling agreements depends principally upon the creditors' ability to achieve consensus and to compel recalcitrant banks to contribute. The Fund, in effect, seeks to reinforce these existing relationships among creditors and relies upon them to produce involuntary credits for stabilization packages.

These institutional reforms have staved off disaster in Western financial markets, at least through the initial phases of crisis rescheduling. Despite hard bargaining over terms, debtors have accepted their obligations and adjusted their economies rapidly to constraints in external financing. In fact, LDCs slashed current-account deficits from over $100 billion annually in 1981 and 1982 to under $40 billion in 1984.[66] These deficits are currently about 6 percent of exports, the lowest ratio in two decades.[67]

65. Cf. Robert Z. Aliber, "The Integration of the Offshore and Domestic Banking System," *Journal of Monetary Economics* 6 (1980), pp. 509–26.
66. IMF, *Annual Report, 1985*, Table 8, p. 22. The figures exclude eight major oil exporters in the Middle East.
67. According to J. de Larosière, quoted in *IMF Survey*, 28 October 1985, p. 318. In 1982, by contrast, current-account deficits were over 14% of LDC exports. IMF, *World Economic Outlook, April 1985*, Table 33, p. 240.

But there is a dark side to this adaptation. Per capita income losses have not been recouped, and voluntary lending has not resumed. The problems have been especially severe among market borrowers in Latin America and among aid recipients in sub-Saharan Africa. Furthermore, outstanding debt ratios have not declined despite austerity measures. External LDC debt has remained at about 150 percent of exports since 1982, and it has actually increased as a fraction of gross domestic product.[68] Nor have debt service payments abated. Approximately $124 billion in 1982 and $134 billion in 1985, they are projected to continue their slow rise. These payments are equal to about one-quarter of LDC exports, a fraction that has not declined in the 1980s.[69] What is worse, perhaps, is that these debt ratios remain high in spite of moderation in interest rates and strong export markets. Global debt problems, in other words, are far from solved.

As these problems persist, old solutions become more difficult to sustain. Slow or negative growth is politically painful, and adjustment programs will be increasingly difficult to sustain without the prospect of significant external financing. Likewise, small creditors will be increasingly reluctant to contribute involuntary loans unless they believe borrowers are on the road to recovery. And bank regulators, charged with overseeing the solvency of lending institutions, must be very careful about encouraging such lending to weak borrowers. The prospect of another economic downturn in developed countries' markets and rising protectionism (which hits LDC manufactured exports especially hard) only sharpens these difficulties.

This is the new and somber background for reform proposals, such as the one advanced in 1985 by Secretary of the Treasury Baker. Private institutions, with help from the IMF and central banks, were able to cope with crisis refinancing in the early 1980s. But since then they have been unwilling to extend new loans or to underwrite economic adjustment with long-term loans. Hence the American proposals seek new private commitments to major debtors coupled with additional lending from the World Bank and regional development banks. These proposals signal an important departure in several ways. They suggest a longer-term, more comprehensive approach to debt problems and a more active role for public institutions, including the U.S. government.

These are critically important steps but hardly fundamental reforms. The scale of proposed new lending is not large, and even that depends heavily on private cooperation. The U.S. proposals are best understood as an incremental approach to the latest gap in private international finance: the absence of voluntary lending to major debtors, who need additional external finance to proceed with economic adjustment and debt service.

The stakes are high. Debtors cannot sustain their austerity programs

---

68. External debt in developing countries was equal to 32.9% of GDP in 1982. It rose to 36.7% of GDP in 1985. IMF, *World Economic Outlook, April 1985*, Table 48, p. 266.

69. Ibid., Table 49, p. 268.

indefinitely. Modest reforms of international institutions may not hold out the hope of renewed economic development or provide sufficient funds for needed structural adjustments. There is real uncertainty, then, about whether these incremental changes are adequate. So the query with which I began these concluding remarks still stands: Are we really muddling through—or just muddling?

Conclusion: politics and proposals for reform Miles Kahler

Following the Mexican rescue, cooperation without reform went virtually unchallenged as a solution to the debt crisis for nearly two years. That outcome, described in my introductory chapter, was supported by a widespread consensus within the political leadership of the industrial countries (with the possible exception of France) that the improvised solutions of the post-1982 period were the best solutions—temporary operations until the commercial banks resumed spontaneous lending. That "official optimist" view was reinforced by economic analyses, both official and unofficial, suggesting that the debt crisis was manageable, though the narrow assumptions built into those projections were often overlooked.[1] The policy prescriptions of official optimism became a familiar refrain after 1982: the debt crisis threatens international financial stability; the parameter for managing that crisis is fixed by the supply of finance from official sources and from the commercial banks; the burden of adjustment to the changed parameter falls almost entirely on the developing countries.[2] A final and crucial assumption of official optimists was that with industrial country growth, such adjustment—both conventional stabilization and more fundamental changes in development strategy—would produce recovery in the countries in question. In this sense the prescriptions briefly noted here echo the idea of "self-levitation" that has become familiar with the Thatcher experiment and "new classical" arguments in the industrial countries. Get prices right, get inflation down, reduce the role of the public sector, and the private sector will do the rest.

1. Two influential examples are the models of William Cline and the International Monetary Fund. Both emphasize the importance of maintaining a level of growth in the industrial countries high by the standards of 1980–83; both also suggest the importance of stable oil prices and stable (or declining) real interest rates (though Cline awards interest rates a less central role than the IMF does). See William R. Cline, *International Debt and the Stability of the World Economy* (Washington, D.C.: Institute for International Economics, 1983), pp. 44–73; IMF, *World Economic Outlook*, Occasional Paper 27 (April 1984), pp. 20–25, 59–77.

2. It is essential to underline this assumption, which pervades the arguments of Cline, the IMF, and Richard S. Dale and Richard P. Mattione, *Managing Global Debt* (Washington, D.C.: Brookings, 1983): the limits to financing are fixed (though how they are fixed is left obscure), but there are no limits to adjustment on the part of the developing countries.

The political presuppositions of the official optimist view, though less often noted, were perhaps more important than the economic ones. It is best to review them in terms of the three political processes outlined in the introduction and considered by the authors in this volume: the politics of ensuring the stability of the international financial system, regulatory politics, and the politics of adjustment. Political intervention had certainly increased, in the interests of crisis management, but only within narrow limits. The relatively high level of cooperation among a large number of actors, public and private, which had been essential to the ad hoc renegotiation strategy pursued after 1982, was assumed to persist. The corollaries of that assumption were continued participation by the money-center and regional banks, willingness of industrial country governments to reschedule official debt and supply new finance, a central role for the International Monetary Fund, and little collaboration among debtor countries. All were put to the test at various times after the Mexican rescue.

Because policy makers were absorbed during rescheduling exercises by a need for new finance, they tended to regard regulatory change to avert future overlending as a less pressing matter. Nevertheless, demands in the United States for increased regulation (during debate on the IMF quota increase) should have alerted officials to change in the political process of regulation in the United States and, potentially, change in the delicate balance between closer regulation and the need for bank cooperation in providing new finance. Finally, the official optimist view seemed oblivious to the question of whether the major debtor countries could, in political terms, sustain adjustment: William Cline, for example, reviewed the incentives and disincentives for default and concluded that repudiation or even radical restructuring was unlikely, principally because he hypothesized that the dominant concern of developing country elites would be for future access to international credit markets. The *political* calculations that developing country elites might make were ignored in this and most other optimistic scenarios.

Perhaps the most important support for the official optimist view came from the apparent success of crisis management—success, that is, by Northern criteria. No debtor country defaulted or repudiated its debt; no major bank failed as a result of its involvement in international lending. Some of the major debtors, such as Brazil, Mexico, and Yugoslavia, achieved dramatic shifts in their current accounts. And despite dire predictions, there had been no political or social upheaval during the difficult initial period of adjustment. The apparent success of the "case-by-case, on a short leash" approach led to a general presumption that the debt crisis would remain manageable in coming years, that the pattern set could continue until the adjustment of the debtors provoked a willingness on the part of the bankers to resume spontaneous lending. Exactly when that would happen, in this view, would vary from country to country, but there should be no need in the interim for additional and more drastic solutions to the debt crisis.

Official optimism at bay: stirrings of reform

Since the consolidation of debt crisis management in late 1982, the official optimist view and the outcome of cooperation without reform have not gone unchallenged. On two occasions, changes in the economic environment heightened debtor resistance and strengthened debtor bargaining power. On each occasion, changes called into question the political assumptions of the official consensus in the North. And on each occasion, reform proposals previously dismissed were considered seriously, though not adopted.

A change in economic parameters—an increase in the U.S. prime interest rate—touched off the first round of discussion of shortcomings in the case-by-case, short-leash approach in mid-1984. That movement in a key economic indicator produced cracks in the solid front of Northern complacency and shifted bargaining advantages somewhat toward the debtor countries. West European governments seemed to become more skeptical of the existing course and more inclined to see the problem of Latin American debt as a U.S. problem. Within Northern governments, bureaucratic consensus frayed. It was central bankers, curiously enough, who took the lead in stimulating discussion of the next stage in the resolution of the debt crisis. Renewed discussion among central bankers—one was modest enough to comment that the debt crisis was so vast as to be beyond the scope of central bankers alone—derived from two concerns. A pressing dilemma of the U.S. Federal Reserve, in the absence of action on the American budget deficit, was the need to control inflation in the United States without increasing the debt burdens of the developing countries. Some suggested reforms, such as a cap on interest rates, provided a partial delinking of American monetary policy from the fortunes of the major debtors. A second concern of central bankers was stirred by the whiff of a banking panic that surrounded the rescue of Continental Illinois. The massive infusion of capital by the Federal Deposit Insurance Corporation and the extraordinary guarantee to depositors made by that agency and the Federal Reserve aroused fears for the stability of the international banking system which had been stilled since 1982. Moreover, the bailout of Continental not only concentrated the minds of central bankers on the stability of the banking system, it also called into question the trend toward deregulation of banking, with unpredictable consequences for the flow of finance to developing countries. Worried central bankers were joined in their questioning of the official consensus by some of the banks themselves. Rimmer de Vries of Morgan Guaranty, for example, endorsed some form of interest-rate relief, not excluding the capitalization of interest. Morgan, long the "pessimist" among the major banks, was opposed by Citibank, which continued to take a tough line.[3]

3. Morgan Guaranty Trust, *World Financial Markets*, February 1984, p. 11; Art Pine, "Debate Likely to Continue over Proposal to Cap Interest Rates for Debtor Nations," *Wall Street Journal*, 18 May 1984, p. 28.

Although changes in economic prospects and threats to the banking system stimulated rethinking and public debate among former supporters of the orthodox, short-term view, the principal challenge came from the South, from long-ignored political constraints on adjustment. From the point of view of creditors, the political horizon in the major debtor countries was not bright. It seemed increasingly unlikely that debtors would be able politically to sustain a combination of low (or no) growth and the exportation of capital to service their debt. The weak link in the chain continued to be Argentina, which had bargained to the brink in March 1984 and continued to delay final agreement on an IMF standby arrangement. Although the Brazilian government managed to stagger through the vote on direct election of the country's next president, widespread public opposition suggested the likelihood of a less pliable government in 1985. In Chile and Peru, ministers who had endorsed IMF programs were sacked. The Dominican Republic suspended its negotiations with the Fund after riots over price increases that were publicly blamed on the IMF. The Marcos government emerged from Filipino elections with a weaker political base from which to negotiate an acceptable adjustment program with the Fund.

In mid-1984, then, the IMF and the banks confronted the strong probability that political changes in prospect would produce successor governments even less likely to participate in the cooperative arrangements assembled since 1982. In May 1984 Bolivia announced a "temporary" suspension of payments on debt owed to commercial banks; a few weeks later Ecuador followed suit. Economic hardship was most severe among some of the smaller debtors, but domestic political pressures were pushing all debtors toward a tougher bargaining stance. The new circumstances also produced the first signs of genuine collaboration among the larger debtors, in a joint statement by the presidents of Argentina, Brazil, Colombia, and Mexico calling for substantially more lenient terms on renegotiated debt. The statement was later supported by Peru, Venezuela, Bolivia, Ecuador, Chile, and the Dominican Republic.[4] The pronouncement was aimed at the London summit of leaders of the industrialized countries in early June; a further meeting of the debtors at Cartagena after the summit threatened more militant action.

The case-by-case, short-leash strategy had hardly collapsed, although the only true believers seemed to reside in the U.S. Treasury and certain large commercial banks. The new context required revision, however, and the revised strategy produced by the creditor countries and the International Monetary Fund was only a modest change in the existing pattern.[5] While the

4. See Edward Schumacher, "4 Latin Chiefs Ask Easing on Debts," *New York Times*, 21 May 1984, p. D1; Richard J. Meislin, "Latin Plan on Debts Reported," ibid., 25 May 1984, p. D1.

5. The revised strategy was put forward by Managing Director de Larosière at the International Monetary Conference in Philadelphia, 4 June 1984, when he singled out Mexico for a multiyear rescheduling because of its record of adjustment. Multiyear reschedulings were endorsed at the London summit: G-7 leaders accepted such a pattern for public debt in Paris Club reschedulings. See *IMF Survey* 13 (18 June 1984), pp. 180, 189.

original case-by-case approach had offered additional bank credits through involuntary lending (as well as a promise of industrial country markets and an eventual return to the financial markets), the new approach concerned itself with the *terms* of rescheduling. Those debtors which had completed successful adjustment programs should be rewarded with eased terms. Multiyear agreements would relieve some of the instability and strain inherent in the annual renegotiations. The principal candidate for such treatment was Mexico—central as well to any effort at debtor collaboration.

The new emphasis by officials in the North on multiyear reschedulings with eased terms quickly crowded out the other candidate in a modest reform package, an interest-rate cap, which in any of its variants would have breached the long-standing refusal of banks to capitalize interest. Such an initiative, quite apart from regulatory obstacles and resistance from the banks, seemed unnecessary as the modification ("rewards for adjustment") in existing practice seemed to take hold.

Mexico appeared to receive its reward in the negotiations that produced a provisional agreement in September 1984: not only multiyear rescheduling with repayment stretched out over ten to fourteen years but also waiver of a commission by the banks and a reduction of the spread on the package, which was pegged to the London Inter-Bank Offered Rate (preferable to the U.S. prime rate). Brazil and Venezuela looked forward to a similar easing of terms in their own restructurings. Argentina, continuing to pursue its own course, declined an adjustment program satisfactory to the IMF and again seemed isolated. Although the debtor countries that met at Cartagena issued another call for a "direct political dialogue" at Mar del Plata in September, debtor collaboration that might fundamentally challenge the existing pattern of crisis management seemed distant once more.

Although Northern preferences about managing the debt crisis had reasserted themselves, the challenge to case-by-case, short-leash in mid-1984 suggested underlying political weaknesses. The structure of collaboration among commercial banks, industrial country governments, and debtor governments, overseen by the International Monetary Fund, could be gradually undermined.

First, a fraying of cooperation was likely in the postcrisis period, whatever the economic indicators. The bargaining process until 1984 had resembled a game of chicken, with the penalties for noncooperation large and largely unknown. Fear of the abyss kept the process going, whether the abyss concerned was a collapse of confidence in the financial system or a cutoff of debtor countries from international exchange. The wear and tear on participants, as in any process of crisis management, grew with a declining belief that the only alternative was collapse or economic disaster. The iterative process that originally produced the high level of cooperation then undermined it, by breeding a certain confidence that led to growing brinksmanship by the participants—a tendency amply demonstrated in the March 1984 Argentinian accord.

A second weakness was the continued absence of the market: politics, though disguised, remained in command. The Bank for International Settlements reported some revival of spontaneous lending to developing countries, but all of that lending had been outside Latin America, where involuntary lending prevailed.[6] The persistence of involuntary lending to the major Latin American borrowers, the development of what the BIS labeled a split market, affected management of the debt crisis. It reinforced the view of Europeans that the crisis was a concern of American banks and American clients. It reduced the bargaining power of creditors, based in large measure on future creditworthiness, for the value of future creditworthiness declined as the resumption of voluntary lending continued to be postponed. It eliminated an appeal to the market as a means of dispute resolution. (As noted above, the official consensus was based on the notion of fixed limits to financing and no limits to adjustment—in a world of involuntary lending, one might ask why these limits and not another set?) Finally, the persistent redlining of Latin America, creating difficulties for a country like Colombia which had managed its external debt prudently, created another basis for debtor collaboration, though it also weakened likely support for a wider resolution of the debt crisis from other, non–Latin American countries.

A weakening of collaborative pressures among the industrial countries was accompanied by a domestic push toward tougher bargaining and a greater collaboration on the part of some of the debtor countries. Although revision of the existing approach to rescheduling fragmented that challenge, it was clear that the politics of adjustment could tug cooperative elites away from the ad hoc and short-term approach.

Finally, the international organization that had seen its role expanded during the debt crisis was at considerable risk as the foundation of its role—the cooperative structure among the major actors—was threatened with erosion. Previously the IMF had been able to trade adjustment programs for additional bank and official lending. In 1984 it faced a number of dangers—particularly an inability to deliver results on its adjustment programs satisfactory to both the creditors and the debtor countries. As the period of adjustment lengthens and recovery in Latin America lags, the willingness to accept IMF programs declines and the likelihood of negotiation followed by rapid abrogation grows. As shifts occur among the participants in its fragile coalition and as relative bargaining advantages change, so the Fund faces a difficult task: how to modify its own stance so as to maintain its successful image without alienating any of the coalition members. The organization also faces the simple problem of overload, too many tasks undertaken too quickly, a danger that is present in many of the reform proposals considered below.

Changes in the economic and political environment in 1984 created enough questions about the established consensus on the debt crisis to pro-

6. BIS, *International Banking Developments*, April 1984, pp. 9–12; Morgan Guaranty Trust, *World Financial Markets*, January 1984, pp. 2–3.

vide the space for a renewal of debate on medium-term solutions. What quickly became apparent was the limited nature of the changes that Northern officialdom would countenance, even those Northern officials who expressed their dissatisfaction with the present structure.

For those who had been skeptical about the ad hoc crisis management approach from the start, however, such measures merely extend the effort to shore up a structure that, they believe, must be overhauled before it crumbles under the pressures outlined above. Expressions of discontent in Latin America provided valuable ammunition to those who advocated more radical reforms as a solution to the crisis. Their proposals can be classified in terms of their aims and their diagnosis of the crisis: radical restructuring (usually coupled with some debt relief), provision of new finance, and prevention of future crises. Most of those proposals accept the existing system of intermediation and the large role played by the commercial banks, but a final set of proposals looks more carefully at the desirability of the system that ballooned during the 1970s and reached its limits in the 1980s. It asks whether the financing needs of the developing countries are best served by that system, even in altered form.

In these proposals for reform, however, the political underpinnings remain crucial. Some erosion of the political bases for the existing system may have taken place. It is not, however, clear that the bases for a new and radically altered system are in place or even that they can easily be created.

Global reform: restructuring, financing, and prevention

A simple solution: laissez-faire

One set of proposals, a "reform" of sorts, was important because of its political power in the United States and its prominence in the debate over the IMF quota increase: nonintervention by governments in the debt crisis (except in the lender-of-last-resort role that national central banks play for their banking systems). In this view the day of reckoning should not be postponed: banks should accept their losses and the economy should accept the likely failure of a number of banks; developing countries should adjust to the reduced financing that will result if they are unable to service their debts. Any restructuring or renegotiation should be a matter for the banks and the developing countries, without intervention by governments or the International Monetary Fund. The latter organization, according to this view, is simply seeking a new role after the demise of the Bretton Woods system. Even if there is some value to an IMF "seal of approval" on country policies, that value is not a justification for the IMF itself to lend.[7]

7. For example, Roland Vaubel, "The Moral Hazard of IMF Lending," and Larry A. Sjaastad, "International Debt Quagmire—To Whom Do We Owe It?" both in *World Economy* 6 (September 1983), pp. 291–304 and pp. 305–24 respectively; Deepak Lal, "The 'Debt Crisis': No Need for IMF Bailout," *Wall Street Journal*, 27 April 1983, p. 33.

These arguments did not carry the day within the Reagan administration, as its endorsement of the IMF quota increase and its support for the new role of the Fund demonstrate. The risks of doing nothing, for the financial system and for the interests of the United States in the Third World, finally seemed too great. Quite apart from these pragmatic arguments in favor of managing a system that grew with government encouragement, Jeffrey Sachs and others have demonstrated that the present structure of international lending displays market imperfections that justify public intervention and a role for the IMF.[8] Nevertheless, such arguments do emphasize the moral hazard that any management of the debt crisis entails. In that sense they support those who are principally concerned with preventing a recurrence of crisis through encouraging an unregulated environment for lending and preventing the transfer of the mistakes of past lending to the public.

Radical restructuring: reducing the burden of debt

A very different set of proposals came from the center and left of the political spectrum. Rather than less government (or IMF) intervention, most of these proposals argue for more. Their criticisms of the crisis management structure devised since 1982 have already been enumerated: that the margin for error in economic prognoses is too narrow and the threats to the stability of the financial system too great to permit the present ad hocery to persist; that even with a fairly robust recovery the burden of debt servicing would be politically unsustainable in the developing countries; that the short-term devices are wasting and finally unstable solutions.

Although these schemes differ in their institutional and burden-sharing dimensions, they share for the most part a common analogy—that of the troubled or bankrupt domestic firm. It is no accident that in the private sector the most vigorous proponents of such schemes have been investment bankers, comfortable with extending the analogy to the international sphere. In some cases the present mechanisms are regarded as adequate or likely to be upset by efforts at more drastic reform; therefore the restructuring plan is proposed as a contingency plan in the event that crisis management procedures collapse.[9]

8. Jeffrey Sachs, "Theoretical Issues in International Borrowing," mimeo. (August 1983).
9. The following reform proposals have been reviewed: Norman A. Bailey, "A Safety Net for Foreign Lending," *Business Week*, 10 January 1983, p. 17; C. Bogdanowicz-Bindert, "Debt: Beyond the Quick Fix," *Third World Quarterly* 5 (October 1983), pp. 828–38; Felix G. Rohatyn, "A Plan for Stretching out Global Debt," *Business Week*, 28 February 1983, pp. 15, 18; Peter A. Kenen, "A Bailout Plan for the Banks," *New York Times*, 6 March 1983, p. F3; Richard S. Weinert, "International Finance: Banks & Bankruptcy," *Foreign Policy* 50 (Spring 1983), pp. 138–49; and Jack Guttentag and Richard Herring, "The Current Crisis in International Banking," mimeo. (University of Pennsylvania, Wharton School, October 1983). *Towards a New Bretton Woods: Challenges for the World Financial and Trading System* (London: Commonwealth Secretariat, 1983) endorses such restructuring schemes as contingency measures only.

The devices proposed are all designed to stretch out debt repayments in a more orderly and sustainable fashion than the present ad hoc procedures, correcting the mismatching of maturities that emerged, particularly after 1980, and permitting adjustment by the developing countries in a way that has lower economic and social costs. Most plans suggest an agency, either an existing international organization or a newly created one, to purchase the loans of troubled debtor countries from the banks and to issue in return a longer-term instrument (usually at fixed interest). The benefits that proponents argue would flow from such a restructuring are an improvement in the quality of bank portfolios through the acquisition of the new assets in place of doubtful loans, a reduction in risk to the international financial system, and some measure of debt relief for the developing countries involved. The proposals vary on how much of the cost of debt relief is to be borne by the banks and by public entities (and ultimately taxpayers in the industrial countries) and how much of the risk is to be transferred from the banks to other entities. The central question of burden sharing cannot be sidestepped, and Felix Rohatyn, at least, confronts the question by admitting that "The allocation of such costs among bank stockholders, taxpayers, and countries would be the subject of difficult negotiations."[10] None of the various proposals indicates the *political* mechanism through which such a difficult division of burdens and risks would take place.

Critics of these proposals, who most often defend the "manageability" of the debt crisis under present procedures, also claim that perverse and even destabilizing effects would result from such government-sponsored efforts at a radical restructuring of the debt burden.[11] It is clear that one critical difference between the proponents of such reforms and their critics is an assessment of the determinants of bank behavior (just as a key element in the case-by-case procedures was a rigid view of how much new financing the banks would be expected to provide). The allegedly adverse impacts of the reforms are twofold. First, by reducing bank exposure in the debtor countries the plans undercut any incentive for banks to provide new financing to protect their old loans. Second, by ensuring even modest losses on the old loans, which could be replicated in new lending under some of the schemes, the plans provide another disincentive to new lending. Supporters of these plans would argue that such adverse impacts could be avoided by additional measures such as guarantees for new loans (see below), by refusing the swap of all of a bank's exposure in a given country, and by altering the regu-

10. Rohatyn, "A Plan," p. 15. Guttentag and Herring, "Current Crisis," avoid the issue of debt relief through their issuance of consols at a penalty interest rate, but the banks would be penalized in their scheme by the "marked to market" rule.
11. Criticisms of the proposals are given by Cline, *International Debt*, pp. 117–18; Dale and Mattione, *Managing Global Debt*, pp. 42–48; Pedro-Pablo Kuczynski, "Latin American Debt: Act Two," *Foreign Affairs* 62 (Autumn 1983), p. 33; and C. Fred Bergsten, William R. Cline, and John Williamson, *Bank Lending to Developing Countries: The Policy Alternatives* (Washington, D.C.: Institute for International Economics, 1985), pp. 181–99.

latory environment. They assume that the banks will resume spontaneous lending if there is money to be made in the developing countries and that new, spontaneous lending there will look more promising if some of the debt burden is removed and recovery begins.

A second criticism of the plans concerns their impact on bank capital: such losses, even with modest debt relief, would serve to undermine the financial stability that the reformers hope to preserve. Here the response, from some of the reformers at least, is that the bank regulators could cushion the impact of such losses on the banks. Although Robert Roosa does not endorse the creation of any new entity, he does accept the need for radical restructuring under existing institutional arrangements. He deals with its impact on bank behavior by raising once again the domestic analogy:

> . . . such an array of credit arrangements may seem to imply that the commercial banks would be expected to carry a disproportionate share of the effort to bring the LDCs to viability and growth. Perhaps it would be too much to expect that the banks would go along with all of this simply to help preserve the value of the loans to LDCs already carried on their books. But there are other analogies with the "bailouts" of domestic concerns in the United States, for the banks could surely expect to receive warrants and other potential claims related to the revival of the private borrowers. Moreover, there should be terminal dates on any interest-rate concession.[12]

The debate between reformers and managers, then, hinges in large part on divergent views of bank behavior, a subject whose political dimensions have been explored in this volume by Philip Wellons.

To the degree that reformers distribute the burden of debt restructuring to the public, critics note a poor record of support for established international lending organizations in recent years, let alone the creation of any new ones. Some reformers, such as Richard Weinert, sidestep the issue by means of the device of unpaid subscriptions, but clearly all of the reform proposals are alert to the political difficulties inherent in any proposal to bail out banks or debtor countries with public resources.

Removal of a substantial measure of debt burden from the debtor countries raises once again the problem of moral hazard. Could the international organization that assumed the debt maintain control over the policies of the debtor when the short leash had been lengthened? How would the exercise affect the borrowing behavior of developing countries in the future? Efforts by reformers to circumvent this issue include the requirement of a mandatory program with the IMF before a country may receive debt restructuring, though that seems to be imposing an enormous burden of surveillance on the Fund while removing one of its most important levers. Other reformers insist that use of the facility must be a one-shot affair and cannot be repeated.

12. Robert Roosa, "The International Financial System in Crisis?" mimeo. (Washington, D.C.: Johns Hopkins University, 1984), pp. 14–15.

Finally, to the degree that debt relief is granted, a question of equity arises: Why should countries receive what is in effect foreign assistance as a reward for what was (in part at least) imprudent borrowing behavior? The question is particularly pressing when most of the largest debtors are middle-income developing countries. The "well-managed poor," such as India or China, face the prospect of a replenishment from the International Development Association lower than expected while the not-so-well-managed middle-income would be rewarded. It is clear, to the degree that a debt crisis is perceived in the North and that relief will be granted, that only those countries with the potential for system destabilization are likely to receive relief, and they will get relief in proportion to their "destabilization capabilities" rather than to their need.

Ensuring new financing: the role of guarantees

If one set of reformers has been concerned with relieving the burden of existing debt, their critics (and other reformers) are much more concerned with the dramatic falling off in commercial bank lending that produced the debt crisis. Two means have been suggested for increasing the flow of finance and thus easing the burden of adjustment in the short-to-medium term.

An acceleration or increase in lending by the multilateral development banks is favored by almost all observers of the debt crisis: the institutions are in place, they have a proven lending capability, and the maturities of their loans are more in keeping with the needs of the developing countries. One means to bring about more and quicker lending would be simply to institute more rapid and flexible lending policies, and that course has already been adopted in part. A significant increase in lending from this source, however, would require either an increase in the World Bank's gearing ratio or an increase in its callable capital. An alternative would be to create a subsidiary of the Bank that would be more highly leveraged.[13] World Bank lending could be more directly linked to commercial bank loans through varieties of cofinancing, serving to reduce the risk to the banks and increase the total lending to the developing countries beyond the Bank's own resources.[14]

Cofinancing points to a second means of offsetting the withdrawal of commercial bank lending: guarantees or insurance of new lending. Such guarantees could be part of a sponsored or a spontaneous restructuring of existing debt; they would in any case serve to offset the adverse effects on new bank lending of such a restructuring and could be varied to take into account

---

13. For differing views on the wisdom of changes in World Bank financing, see Kuczynski, "Latin American Debt," p. 32; and William H. Bolin and Jorge Del Canto, "LDC Debt: Beyond Crisis Management," *Foreign Affairs* 61 (Summer 1983).

14. World Bank cofinancing alternatives are evaluated in Bergsten, Cline, and Williamson, *Bank Lending*, pp. 118–22.

the existing incentives for lending. The entity undertaking the guarantee has been variously proposed as a G-10 facility administered by the IMF (Zombanakis), the IMF itself (Witteveen, Dale and Mattione), or an agency established by national export credit agencies (Lever). Apart from their effect on new lending, such guarantees are attractive for their low direct costs to national budgets.[15]

Prevention: the dilemmas of regulation

If restructuring threatens the flow of new finance to the developing countries, so do recommendations for greater regulatory scrutiny of bank lending in an effort to avert a new round of overlending. The proponents of such regulatory shifts accept that the old system of commercial bank financing will be resumed, and that despite the present aversion to lending to developing countries, the volatile lending cycle is likely to repeat itself.

The drawback to additional regulations on international bank lending in the crisis management phase is that virtually all of the proposed changes would serve to reduce new lending to the largest debtor countries at a time when the IMF and national authorities are urging *increases* in such lending, through programs that include involuntary lending. In addition, some proposals would serve to punish the banks after the fact rather than prevent overlending before the debt crisis emerged. Nevertheless, the politics of regulation in the United States became entwined in the autumn of 1983 with legislation to increase IMF quotas, and congressional pressure served to tighten somewhat the regulatory environment of the banks. Several principal changes have been urged or adopted.

New capital requirements (new standards of capital adequacy) have been issued by the Federal Reserve Board for major multinational banks in the United States. The importance of such requirements in dealing with overexposure in particular countries has been questioned, however. Even if country exposures were included in the measure of capital adequacy, they would serve to deter higher exposures only if the marginal cost of capital were very steep.[16] In such a case, capital requirements come to resemble merely another prudential measure.

Country lending limits have been rejected to date by American regulators, who argue that uniform limits will not take account of the differing needs of

15. See Minos Zombanakis, "A Way to Avoid a Crash," *Economist*, 30 April 1983, pp. 11–14; Lord Lever, "A Concerted Way Out," ibid., 9 July 1983, pp. 14–16; H. Johannes Witteveen, "Developing a New International Monetary System: A Long-term View," The Per Jacobsson Lecture (Washington, D.C.: IMF, 1983); Dale and Mattione, *Managing Global Debt*, pp. 46–47; and Bergsten, Cline, and Williamson, *Bank Lending*, pp. 69–72, 110–18.

16. Guttentag and Herring, "Current Crisis," pp. 38–40; Dale and Mattione, *Managing Global Debt*, p. 36. An approach directed more toward Europe is taken by Witteveen, "Developing a New International Monetary System," pp. 9–10.

Politics and proposals for reform 257

countries. Differentiated limits impose a large burden of information gathering and analysis on the regulators as well as being politically sensitive. Jack Guttentag and Richard Herring note that a "rigid" limit has long applied on loans to individuals; few would argue that the rule should be removed. In the present setting, in which most banks are already well above prudent country limits, the impact of limits on current lending seems decisive.[17]

In response to new legislation enacted at the time of the IMF quota increase, U.S. federal regulators introduced a new *system of classifying loans* and new requirements for *reserves against losses*. The new procedures establish three categories of classification for loans, two of which (loss and value impaired) would require a partial write-off or the establishment of loan-loss reserves. The new procedures did not immediately affect the major debtors, however: banks were required to set aside reserves for Poland, Sudan, Zaire, Bolivia, and Nicaragua. Not until late 1985 was Peru, with large interest arrears, added to the list. The delay in the Peruvian decision suggested that the "trigger" was set at a level to avoid curtailing desired lending to major debtors.[18]

Other accounting changes have included *the amortization of fees*, already adopted by regulatory authorities, which serves to end a bias toward international lending, and the more radical proposal of Guttentag and Herring that loans should be "marked to market." Not only would that change serve to reduce international lending—particularly to the debtors—but it would also require a secondary market to serve as a standard for the value of loans.[19]

Increased information is a final step to have received widespread support, though even here political difficulties loom. Under congressional pressure, American regulatory authorities have conceded a measure of required disclosure of country exposure on the part of banks, so that outsiders can more effectively evaluate the condition of loan portfolios.[20] Other observers have suggested increased information about the borrowing countries through expanded cooperation between the banks and the International Monetary Fund. Member countries would resist such a breach of confidentiality, however, and so the banks have themselves established an Institute for International Finance to encourage such collaboration.

International coordination among regulators in the industrial countries has been instituted to make certain that there are no gaps in regulatory cover-

17. Guttentag and Herring, "Current Crisis," pp. 37–38; Dale and Mattione, *Managing Global Debt*, pp. 34–35.
18. Guttentag and Herring, "Current Crisis," pp. 27–35; Dale and Mattione, *Managing Global Debt*, pp. 36–38; "Interagency Statement on Examination Treatment of International Loans" (Washington, D.C., 15 December 1983).
19. Guttentag and Herring, "Current Crisis," pp. 13–19; Jack Guttentag and Richard Herring, "What Happens When Countries Cannot Pay Their Bank Loans? The Renegotiation Process," *Journal of Comparative Business and Capital Market Law* 5 (1983), pp. 224–25.
20. Guttentag and Herring, "Current Crisis," p. 37; Dale and Mattione, *Managing Global Debt*, p. 38.

age, at least for major banks, and that banks do not seek out locations known for regulatory laxity. The 1975 Basle Concordat, described in Chapter 1, was a first step in this direction: it was subsequently revised after the Banco Ambrosiano failure in 1982. Shortcomings remain: tighter international standards of regulation meet opposition from those states which benefit from international financial markets; the coordination that has taken place has not (at least in public statements) been extended to lender-of-last-resort responsibility; and finally, efforts to include the less regulated offshore banking centers have only just begun.[21]

The view from the South: reform, adjustment, default

The benefits that debt restructuring might confer on two groups of developing countries suggest one reason for the weak response of the Third World to the debt crisis. The crisis affects two regions most severely: Latin America, which has been dependent on private financial markets, and low-income African countries whose debt is largely, though not exclusively, public. The latter group has not presented enough of a threat to the financial system to challenge it; the former has been too deeply involved in the system to want to.

Within Latin America the differential political effects of stabilization, described by Robert Kaufman, and the differentiated strategy of the creditors—favoring large over small debtors and rewarding adjustment efforts—have undermined attempts to construct a debtor coalition. The benefits that financing through the Eurodollar markets conferred on the middle-income Latin American countries, and their own hopes (parallel to those of the banks) that the system might be restored, are another principal reason for their cooperation in the crisis management procedures developed in 1983 and 1984. Official assessment in Latin America has been that of Carlos Diaz-Alejandro and Edmar Bacha:

> . . . on balance, semi-industrialized countries were helped during the 1970s by the emergence and expansion of private international financial markets. True enough, private credits were more costly and shorter-term than official bilateral or multilateral finance. However, volumes were larger, procedures were more expeditious, and looser strings were attached, both at the political and the economic-policy levels.[22]

Lingering hopes for a relatively rapid restoration of creditworthiness led the larger Latin American debtors to distance themselves until very recently

21. G. G. Johnson with Richard K. Abrams, *Aspects of the International Banking Safety Net*, IMF Occasional Paper 17 (March 1983), pp. 16–17; Richard Williams et al., *International Capital Markets*, IMF Occasional Paper 23 (July 1983), pp. 18–19, and for the Basle Concordat revision, pp. 49–53.
22. Edmar Lisboa Bacha and Carlos Diaz-Alejandro, *International Financial Intermediation: A Long and Tropical View*, Princeton Essays in International Finance 147 (Princeton, May 1982), p. 28.

from any collective bargaining effort and to undertake formidable programs of adjustment. They also inhibited the development of any far-ranging program of reform; although their bargaining stance might change with fluctuations in international economic and domestic political circumstances, Latin American elites were restorationists not reformers.

Of course, the diagnosis of the debt crisis and the definition of an "appropriate" balance between financing and adjustment was very different in the South. The relative weights assigned to bad domestic policies and adverse external conditions reversed those in the orthodox Northern view. Appropriate paths of adjustment remained a bone of contention with the International Monetary Fund, and the debtors argued, as the developing countries had for some time, in favor of a longer period of adjustment, more supply-oriented measures, and a greater attention to political sustainability.

Still, one can only be impressed by the meekness with which officials in the South accepted the need to sustain the existing system of international finance. At the Caracas conference of the Organization of American States in September 1983, in the Quito Declaration, and again in the presidents' statement and Cartagena proposals in 1984 there were no clarion calls for joint action nor even any insistence on reforms resembling those described above. A recent study of the debt problem by the Economic Commission for Latin America and the Caribbean favored "bilateral agreements compatible with positive adjustment": essentially a renegotiation of debt on more favorable terms coupled with a modest degree of debtor collaboration to share information. The study views a public and multilateral solution as a medium-term ideal that could not be negotiated in time to meet the pressing needs of the region. More radical alternatives, such as a moratorium or a unilateral conversion of bank debt into bonds, it dismisses as prejudicing future access to bank credit—the promise that has kept Latin American elites inside the existing structure since the onset of the debt crisis.[23]

Tough bargaining by Argentina and Venezuela in 1984 and more recently by Peru, however, suggests that brinksmanship and even disguised default may eventually become an acceptable option. The balance of incentives outlined by Cline and others may have overstated the case for cooperation.[24] A reassessment by Anatole Kaletsky argues that while intensified debtor collaboration and outright repudiation are unlikely, because they would dramatically raise the probability of sanctions, a "conciliatory" default by some debtors is not unlikely.[25] The debtor country might offer what Kaletsky terms "a unilateral rescheduling formula": something labeled a

23. ECLAC, *External Debt in Latin America* (Boulder, Col.: Rienner, 1985), pp. 88–97. See also Carlos Geraldo Langoni, "The Way Out of the Country Debt Crisis," *Euromoney*, October 1983, pp. 20–26, and the Brazilian views given in Lenny Glynn, "Is Time Running Out for Brazil?" *Institutional Investor*, April 1984, pp. 73–84.
24. Cline, *International Debt*, pp. 87–93; Guttentag and Herring, "Current Crisis," pp. 214–16.
25. Anatole Kaletsky, *The Costs of Default* (New York: Priority, 1983), p. 64.

renegotiation would continue, further fragmenting the creditors and (depending on the country) possibly separating governments from their banks. The final weapon of the banks against default or repudiation is generally held to be the harassment that the banks could institute against the international economic transactions, particularly the trade, of the debtor. The effectiveness of the weapon might be reduced by the forced reliance of many debtors on countertrade and barter, an experience that could substantially lessen dependence on trade finance, especially if the debtors have accumulated reserves. In a deregulated and competitive financial environment, it is also an open question whether the banks could maintain a solid front against the wayward debtor; the difficulties in imposing any form of economic sanctions are numerous and well-documented.

The principal impetus toward such a course would come if the political sustainability of adjustment programs, as examined by Robert Kaufman and Stephan Haggard, seemed doubtful. One major restraint is lingering attachment to the old order, if it could be restored on more favorable terms, and the absence of any clear economic alternative that would legitimate a "delinking" risk. Unlike in the 1930s, populist programs are not being proposed by the elites of Latin America. Despite their aversion to "recession," those elites seem, in fact, to agree with some of the prescriptive emphases of orthodox adjustment, such as export orientation.

If hopes for a restoration of bank lending serve as a barrier to radical options, they are equally significant in distancing elites in the debtor countries from many of the reform proposals circulating in the North. As Diaz-Alejandro and Bacha noted before the onset of the debt crisis, debtor interests would not be served by any increase in collaboration among banks that might lead toward a cartelization of credit flows, nor would they be helped by any increase in regulation that might dampen the resumption of bank lending or endanger what involuntary lending survives. Debtors would certainly reject the greater IMF role over their domestic policies that many of the radical restructuring proposals include as the price for debt relief. They would also be skeptical of any new role undertaken by the IMF as a de facto allocator of credit—the traffic cop giving a green or red light to commercial bank lending.

Any turn by the Latin American elites toward a more militant stance would hold a substantial irony. These technocratic revolutionaries, like so many revolutionaries in the past, would be seeking a restoration of a golden, if somewhat tarnished, past and endorsing domestic policies that even their Northern critics might applaud.

Alternatives in the longer term: the antirestorationists

The discourse of both reformers and those who favor the status quo ante, North and South, holds a common theme, the notion that the system of commercial bank lending to the middle-income developing countries can be and should be restored. The purpose of short-term crisis management or debt restructuring, both groups agree, is the eventual resumption of "spontaneous" lending.

Even in official circles, however, some have voiced doubts about the adequacy of the old regime. The Federal Reserve Bank of New York stated flatly in its annual report that "short-term variable rate bank loans are not the means for transferring savings from rich nations to poor nations." Rimmer de Vries has declared that "the industrial countries can no longer neglect the need for adequate long-term capital flows to developing countries, which commercial banks are ill-equipped to provide."[26] Several shortcomings of the system that brought us the debt crisis are commonly cited: the mismatching of maturities (developing countries borrow short or medium term for long-term projects), volatility in levels of lending and in interest rates, and the risks posed for the banking systems of the industrial countries—riots in Brazil produce tremors on Wall Street. The alternatives presented are usually much vaguer than the reform proposals outlined above, but they divide neatly between politics and markets, favoring expansion of public international organizations or of private financial markets.

Redressing the balance between public and private: international organizations

For some observers skeptical of the virtues of markets in international finance (or their existence), the present crisis results from an overdependence on private financial markets. H. Johannes Witteveen portrays "a monetary system where official liquidity—and thus official influence—has gradually been overwhelmed by gigantic masses of quickly movable private international liquidity."[27] The solution is to move back to a system in which national regulators and international organizations play a larger role.

An expanded role for the IMF, as Charles Lipson has detailed, was a major feature of the present crisis management strategy, but reformers and antirestorationists seem to wish an endless proliferation of new tasks for the Fund: guaranteeing loans, making country credit ratings (providing a green light for private loans), circulating information, constructing new facilities (such as an interest-rate compensatory financing facility), and so on. The developing countries have been conspicuously silent because they face the prospect of confronting an IMF with expanded powers of surveillance and tougher conditionality.

The great advantage of the IMF in the eyes of those who wish to expand its role is precisely its ability, through surveillance and conditionality, to af-

---

26. In Morgan Guaranty Trust, *World Financial Markets*, February 1984, p. 13.
27. Witteveen, "Developing a New International Monetary System," p. 3.

fect the economic policies of members. But its boosters neglect several weaknesses, which in brief involve resources, policies, and role.

Although the United States finally consented to an enlargement of IMF quotas (while simultaneously seeking to rein back the policy of enlarged access instituted in 1981), the resources provided by the quota increase and the expansion of the General Arrangements to Borrow are hardly adequate for a major shift in the balance between the Fund and the private banks, even in providing balance-of-payments financing. And beyond the present crisis, the leverage that the Fund can exert depends in large measure on the scale of financing that it can provide in exchange for the policy changes demanded. As the United States in particular is unlikely to consent to a further quota increase any time soon, many have urged that the Fund supplement its existing borrowing from official sources with borrowing in the private financial markets.[28]

Those policy changes already alluded to are summarized in the concept of conditionality, which has long been a point at issue between the Fund and the developing countries. The debate over Fund programs may be moving to a different plane, less polemical though not uncritical.[29] The Overseas Development Institute proposal for a cost-minimization goal in Fund programs, while accepting the primary role of the Fund as the provision of temporary balance-of-payments financing, may stimulate a new reformist debate. To the degree that the Fund becomes more deeply involved in the policies of member countries, however, and particularly in structural deficits, its political skills will be taxed. Stephan Haggard remains a skeptic on the need for greater political analysis by the Fund; the ODI team, on the other hand, argues for more expertise in this area.

Pressure for the Fund to become involved in correcting structural deficits, a familiar demand of the developing countries, involves changes in Fund policies and, some fear, a change in the traditional role of the Fund. The Reagan administration and other industrial country representatives have resisted what they see as an effort to transform the IMF into another multilateral development bank. Certainly the overlap between the Fund's role and that of the World Bank and other multilateral banks has grown in recent years, with the institution of the Extended Fund Facility and multiyear standbys at the IMF and an increase in program lending by the World Bank.

Since the onset of the debt crisis, however, striking innovations in crisis management at the Fund have sharply contrasted with the absence of such new roles at the World Bank. The Bank figures in many reform proposals, particularly those that attempt to fill the medium-term finance gap.[30] Al-

28. Cf. Group of Thirty, *The IMF and the Private Markets* (New York, 1983).
29. As suggested by the appearance of two large, collaborative studies in 1982 and 1984; see John Williamson, *The Lending Policies of the International Monetary Fund* (Washington, D.C.: IIE, 1982), and Tony Killick, ed., *The Quest for Economic Stabilisation: The IMF and the Third World* (London: Heinemann, 1984).
30. Bolin and Del Canto, "LDC Debt," pp. 1110–12.

though the Bank has accelerated its project lending, expanded structural adjustment loans, experimented with more cofinancing, and most recently instituted a version of the interest-rate cap, it has failed to fill the gap in program financing that many regard as the most pressing need of the developing countries, whether touched by the debt crisis or not. Why the Bank did not step in, when so many believe that it is underused, is a matter of debate. Some see a failure in leadership at the Bank itself. Others point to the strict limits that the Reagan administration imposes on all of the multilaterals, exemplified in its rejection of a higher U.S. contribution to the IDA and then its delay of the IDA increase as part of its bargaining with Japan on unrelated trade questions. But there is no bar to the Bank's involvement in longer-term loans for stabilization purposes, nor would it be impossible to craft country programs that included involvement by Bank and Fund; their cooperation has been growing in recent years.[31]

The magic of the market place: bonds and foreign direct investment

For those who reject an expansion in public finance (or even public guarantees) yet admit the shortcomings of the existing structure, private financial alternatives provide the key to changing the pattern of developing country finance. Favored options include greater reliance on the bond market and foreign direct investment; most advocates of these alternatives to commercial bank lending suppose that they will emerge spontaneously, however, thereby overlooking the crucial role of the political environment in stimulating or thwarting financial innovation.

The bond market is seen by some as a virtual panacea, providing fixed-interest, long-term lending more suited to the needs of developing country borrowers. This positive view is shaped by a nostalgia for earlier periods when borrowers and lenders confronted one another with less governmental interference, a rosy view of the pre-1914 and interwar financial markets undercut by Albert Fishlow in this volume. Before 1914 political interference in the London financial market was limited, but capital flows were directed primarily to relatively rich countries (and those similar in political regime to the lender). Political intervention and regulation figured more prominently in interwar financial flows. In neither period did bond markets entirely escape the volatility that characterizes commercial bank lending in the 1980s; the relatively smooth reschedulings described by Fishlow resulted from a particular *private* organization of the market.

In any event, hopes for filling gaps in developing country finance through the bond markets as presently organized seem slight. In part as a legacy of the collapse of developing country debt in the 1930s, the regulators of na-

---

31. Sidney Dell has recently pointed out a long-standing authorization for the Bank to engage in long-term stabilization loans: "A Note on Stabilization and the World Bank," *World Development* 12, 2 (1984), pp. 165–67.

tional bond markets demand credit ratings that most developing countries (particularly the indebted ones) could not meet. Although participation of developing countries in the Eurobond and national bond markets grew in the 1970s, conditions there were volatile both in the supply of funds and in interest rates. Some of the innovations introduced in the bond markets during this period of turmoil—such as floating-rate notes—offset the putative advantages of bonds as a source of finance.[32]

The case for foreign direct investment as a long-term solution also seems overblown. While it is true that some of the large Latin American countries have discouraged foreign direct investment and preferred commercial bank finance, it is difficult to make such an argument regarding Brazil or the Philippines. (Often overlooked is the attraction that policies of import substitution—and heavy trade protection—may have for foreign investors.) In circumstances of deep economic depression and high political risk, it is difficult to imagine that private investors, already less enthusiastic about Third World prospects after Iran and the second oil shock, would substantially increase their involvement.

The orthodox consensus in the North assumes that simple changes in developing country policies will produce new sources of private finance. The authors in this volume, whether describing the past or the present, demonstrate conclusively that such an assumption is unmerited. The pattern of financial intermediation has always been shaped—often unwittingly—by political and regulatory action. What is required is careful thinking about new forms of financial intermediation that will better serve the interests of lenders and borrowers. Like most new technologies, such new forms may need initial public support if they are to develop. The report of the Commonwealth experts' group suggests, too briefly, the range of alternatives— guarantees or partial guarantees for bond issues, inventive ways of unbundling the investment package, investment insurance, and new equity-type forms of finance such as the "conditional loan."

Renewed challenge and American response: politics and reform

After official debate within the North and between North and South intensified in early 1984, consideration of even such modest reforms as the

---

32. The Bank for International Settlements recently seconded concerns expressed by central banks on the possible risks involved in a shift from syndicated bank lending to other international financial instruments; see Peter Norman, "International Bond Issues Pose New Risks, BIS Says," *Asian Wall Street Journal*, 29 October 1985, p. 4. A recent study of private financial innovations that could increase capital flows to developing countries is Donald Lessard and John Williamson, *Financial Intermediation beyond the Debt Crisis* (Washington, D.C.: Institute for International Economics, 1985), which appeared after this article was completed. The experience of the developing countries in the international bond markets is summarized in the *IMF Survey*.

interest-rate cap or an interest-rate facility at the IMF was set aside as the revised case-by-case approach, rewarding adjustment with a longer leash and easier rescheduling terms, reduced debtor resistance and dissolved the threat of debtor collaboration. Although some warned that the Mexican model was not widely applicable or even desirable, by early 1985 official optimism reigned once again; Brazil and Venezuela began negotiating their own rescheduling agreements with the banks.[33] Even Argentina, long the brinksman among Latin American countries, signed an agreement with the IMF in December 1984 and came near to success in its negotiations for a new $4.2 billion credit with the commercial banks. Confidence in the existing strategy was indicated by the industrial countries' continued resistance to developing country demands for an allocation of special drawing rights, an interest-rate subsidy account at the IMF, and more resources for the Bretton Woods organizations.

Within weeks, however, the new pattern of cooperation was shaken by a stalling of the new round of rescheduling negotiations, by worsening economic conditions in the debtor countries, and most important, by political changes in the debtor countries. These shifts, taken together, represented yet another challenge to the case-by-case approach, deeper than that of 1984 because they followed years of painful adjustment on the part of major debtors.

Rescheduling negotiations with Argentina and Brazil were delayed in early 1985 when the International Monetary Fund declared their adjustment programs off track and suspended disbursements. The sensitivity of the Fund surprised some analysts; its actions seemed designed to reestablish its credibility during a time of political transition. The dilemmas inherent in the Fund's role as manager of the cooperative structure were rapidly becoming clear: as conditionality blurred into "enhanced surveillance," first appearing in the Mexican rescheduling, the Fund's leverage declined, because its own resources were not involved. Some criticized its new role as too much the policeman for the banks; others argued that the policeman was still needed but was now disarmed.[34]

A second challenge to the credibility of the IMF came from an unexpected quarter: sub-Saharan Africa. Its debt crisis had not threatened the international financial system through the commercial banks and had always had a priority lower than the crisis in Latin America. Now, however, African countries that had undertaken programs with the IMF in the early 1980s were finding it difficult to repay their drawings on the Fund. With the IMF

33. Cautions about the Mexican model were voiced by Jeffrey E. Garten, "Don't Use Mexico's Solution as a Model," *New York Times*, 23 September 1984.
34. Edmar Bacha discusses the dilemmas of the new enhanced surveillance role in "The Future Role of the International Monetary Fund in Latin America: Issues and Proposals," mimeo. (Department of Economics, PUC/RJ, June 1985), pp. 17–19; see also Garten, "Don't Use Mexico's Solution."

the linchpin of the collaborative structure erected since 1982, the threat of default on those payments—which would also bar those countries from further Fund programs—threatened the structure itself. Failure to repay either of the Bretton Woods institutions, even for reasons of economic distress, called into question the credibility of the sanctions and rewards that underlay the system of debt management.[35]

The economic decline of sub-Saharan Africa was shared by many of the smaller debtor countries in Latin America and the Caribbean. Their economic performance had lagged behind the larger debtors in 1984; in 1985 it worsened as export revenues declined further. Weakening export performance soon began to affect larger debtors as well, with the same result in 1985 that rising interest rates had had in early 1984: it called into question the soothing reports that the debt crisis was over, that modified rescheduling coupled with continued adjustment would restore economic growth and hasten the return of debtors to the private financial markets. The weak response of commodity prices to the economic recovery that began in 1983 had been clear for some time. Now, as American growth declined in 1985, developing country exports declined significantly.[36] Brazil seemed to reach the limits of import compression and confronted the threat of increased protectionism in the United States; Mexico and Venezuela had to contend with declining petroleum prices, which led to new measures of austerity early in the year.

Maintaining the original structure of cooperation in the absence of more extensive reforms was further complicated by political changes in the principal Latin American debtors and their effects on elite commitment to adjustment. Mexico's ruling political party, the PRI, had appeared the most secure of governing coalitions among the major debtors, but only blatant rigging in July prevented electoral losses to the opposition in the northern states of Sonora and Nuevo Leon. In Brazil the death of President-elect Tancredo Neves produced a less secure administration under José Sarney. The new president, like Raul Alfonsín of Argentina, pledged that he would not accept a recession as the price of an agreement with the IMF. His government equivocated between the expansionist programs urged by the Planning Ministry and the more orthodox line of the Finance Ministry and the Central Bank; the orthodox line seemed to concede defeat with the resignation of both finance minister and central bank president in late August.

35. By mid-1985, two countries had been declared ineligible for use of Fund resources in 1985—Vietnam and Guyana. In Africa, meanwhile, Sudan, Zambia, Liberia, Chad, Equatorial Guinea, and Gambia were reported to be in arrears on their payments to the IMF. On the debt crisis in Africa see Thomas M. Callaghy, "Africa's Debt Crisis," *Journal of International Affairs* 38 (Summer 1984), pp. 61–79; Melvyn Westlake, "The IMF's African Nightmare," *South*, July 1985, pp. 31–35; and Clyde Farnsworth, "U.S. Plans Proposal on Aid to Africa," *New York Times*, 21 September 1985, p. 41.

36. See "Dollar Value of Developing Country Exports Drops Sharply in First Quarter of the Year," *IMF Survey*, 12 August 1985, p. 246.

More significant for the future was the pattern established in Argentina and Peru by governments more populist in their rhetoric. After sixteen months of strenuous bargaining with commercial banks and the IMF, and repeated last-minute financial rescues, the Alfonsín government produced in June 1985 a drastic program of currency reform, devaluation, price and wage controls, and fiscal austerity that went beyond IMF demands. Initially the recessionary consequences of the program were less evident than its success in curbing the country's accelerating inflation; Alfonsín was able to confront resistance from Peronist unions and won an electoral victory in November 1985. But the Alfonsín government gave no indication of changing its demands for a more equitable solution to the debt crisis: its legitimacy and its ability to carry out a drastic adjustment program were being used to extract additional support from its creditors and the industrial countries.

The same pattern of adjustment and demands for a new bargain on debt management characterized the new government of Peru, headed by a charismatic populist, Alan Garcia Pérez. Garcia came closest to "conciliatory default" by announcing in his inaugural address that Peru would limit its debt payments to 10 percent of its export earnings—the first such explicit linkage by any debtor country. (Some saw the announcement as conciliatory, since Peru was one year in arrears on its debt payments.) While pledging to repay the debt, he also ruled out a program with the IMF and pledged to seek debtor collaboration in order to strike a better bargain with creditors. At the same time—and here Garcia diverged from the early Alfonsín—he instituted a program of adjustment matching that of Argentina in its severity. Latin American elites were taking the revised bargain for debt management—rewards for adjustment—and declaring that the rewards were inadequate and that adjustment without further concessions by creditors could not be politically sustained.

The new civilian governments of Latin America thus took a tougher line toward their creditors as well as accepting some orthodox adjustment prescriptions. The Alfonsín government had pursued a policy of brinksmanship in its first eighteen months, externalizing hard economic choices and pursuing a political agenda. The new Argentinian and Peruvian line, and possibly that of Brazil, traded *legitimacy* in the pursuit of desired adjustment policies in favor of greater concessions from creditors. New governments could also place a political goal on the bargaining table—the new regime itself. As President Garcia bluntly stated in his address to the UN General Assembly in September 1985, "We are faced with a dramatic choice: it is either debt or democracy."[37]

Flagging economic prospects and changes of political regime had placed the revised case-by-case strategy in question by late 1985. Efforts at debtor collaboration had not intensified, but increasingly each debtor country

37. James Brooke, "Peruvian President, at the U.N., Warns I.M.F. That Debt Repayment Must Be Eased," *New York Times*, 24 September 1985, p. A15.

voiced the same bargaining position. Perhaps the most damaging blow to the existing strategy came from Mexico, the model for successful adjustment duly rewarded. Even before its catastrophic earthquake Mexico had announced the need for at least $2.5 billion in new credits from the commercial banks. Within a few weeks the IMF suspended further drawings by Mexico in the last months of its program, because of failure to meet performance criteria.[38] Finally Mexico's bankers had to accept a postponement for six months of $950 million in loan repayments intended as a "downpayment" to reassure the financial markets. Case-by-case, even on a lengthened leash, seemed to have reached the end of its tether.

Of the various political dimensions to the debt crisis discussed in this volume, the political capability to sustain adjustment programs was clearly the weak element in the debt management strategy pursued after 1982 and revised in 1984. A worsening of economic parameters—in this case, a decline in export earnings—as well as an unwillingness to continue policies that seemed likely to produce no or low growth in a democratic political setting finally eroded the strategy.

At this point, however, a second political parameter changed: the attitudes of the U.S. government and in particular its willingness to exercise greater leadership at somewhat higher cost. At each point in the development of the debt crisis, American preferences had been key. Benjamin Cohen has documented the key conversion of the United States to an expanded role for the IMF in 1982; "jawboning" by Paul Volcker was part of the revised "rewards for adjustment" strategy in 1984. As that strategy in turn began to unravel in 1985, the U.S. Treasury and the Federal Reserve indicated that cooperation without reform would henceforth have to include a larger measure of reform if the fragile structure of cooperation were to survive.

The turn toward greater activism on the part of the United States was reflected in international monetary cooperation (the Group of Five agreement of 22 September 1985 to encourage "some further orderly appreciation of the main nondollar currencies against the dollar") and a push to begin a new round of trade negotiations. The new initiative in the debt crisis reflected changes in the obstacles to U.S. leadership examined in the first chapter: the primacy of domestic politics (and domestic economic goals), and ideological resistance to government intervention. By 1985 foreign economic policy was having a clear domestic impact. Throughout the debt crisis, concern for the stability of the American financial system had propelled official actions. Even if not directly connected to foreign lending—as in the failure of Continental Illinois, for example—strains in the banking system affected management of the debt crisis. Those strains had not disappeared: the farm

38. Considerable outcry greeted the IMF announcement, which coincided with the Mexican earthquake. The Fund soon indicated willingness to extend emergency assistance to Mexico.

credit system in the United States followed the savings and loan institutions in showing alarming signs of weakness. The possibility of a loss of confidence in the system forced policy makers to pay more attention to potential external shocks and to take more of an activist position toward managing the debt crisis.

Trade was even more significant for the debt crisis. Import penetration induced by the strong dollar had stimulated a wave of protectionist legislation in Congress, some of it directed against major debtor countries such as South Korea and Brazil. Protectionist pressure pointed toward American activism. One crucial element in the original bargain on debt management had been open markets in the industrial countries; it now appeared that the United States might not be able to keep its side of the bargain. Further, the American trade deficit itself had widened because of the deep recession in Latin America: U.S. exports to the region declined by $17.2 billion (in 1980 dollars) from 1980 to 1983, and one study estimated that almost 440,000 jobs were lost because of the drop in exports.[39] Finally, developing country cooperation would be required to make the new trade round a success: a conciliatory debt management strategy was more likely to win such cooperation.

Foreign-policy goals also figured in the new turn of American policy. Fidel Castro's intervention in the debt crisis, while hardly greeted with uniform enthusiasm in the region, did raise the specter of radicalization and debtor collaboration. As one Latin American diplomat commented: "Castro is pushing for all of us. He is saying things we don't dare say. He may help us find some middle ground, and we appreciate this." And the new civilian governments offered the United States Garcia's choice of "debt or democracy" as well as cooperation on other issues of concern, among them Peru's efforts to stamp out the drug trade.

Ideological resistance to American activism weakened with the appearance of a new team at the Treasury. The treasury secretary, James Baker, and his deputy, Richard Darman, were known for a more pragmatic style than the Regan-Sprinkel team. The new line of monetary cooperation, trade liberalization, and expansionary adjustment in the debtor countries found favor in the supply-side wing of the Republican party, long critical of IMF prescriptions and floating exchange rates.

Politics and prospects for reform: the Baker initiative

The "Program for Sustained Growth" introduced by Treasury Secretary Baker at the annual meeting of the IMF and World Bank in October 1985 re-

39. Overseas Development Council, "U.S. 'Costs' of Third World Recession: They Lose, We Lose," *Policy Focus* no. 2 (Washington, D.C., 1985), pp. 5–6.

sponded to the changed economic and political context of the debt crisis. It also reflected the political limits to any efforts at reform, however modest. Although the Baker plan only outlined a new bargain, it clearly reflected some of the suggestions for reform described above.

For the debtor countries it held out the promise of growth rather than stagnation, meeting some of their objections to existing adjustment policies. The revision in the time horizon for adjustment to the medium and long term did not mean that the United States had foresworn efforts to change Third World economic policies, of course. Rather, the American emphasis would shift to structural adjustment—trade liberalization, efforts to encourage private enterprise and foreign direct investment, a reduction in the public sector.

Any growth-oriented adjustment policy required additional financing, which, apart from the IMF quota increase, the Reagan administration had long resisted. Baker supported the formation of a special low-conditionality fund at the IMF to assist those poorest developing countries which face "protracted balance-of-payments problems."[40] This special fund would be particularly directed to the sub-Saharan African countries whose difficulties in repaying the Fund and the Bank appeared to threaten the system. For the middle-income debtors, whose system-threatening potential was even greater, Baker proposed an increase in bank lending of $20 billion over the next three years coupled with an enhanced role for the World Bank—a major element in reform proposals—and other multilateral institutions, which would increase their lending by $9 billion.

The Baker plan was yet another effort, and by far the most ambitious by the United States, to meet the weaknesses in the existing management of the debt crisis on a multilateral and cooperative basis. It was the first to have global outlines. Nevertheless the Baker package and the various reform proposals described in this chapter depend on political assumptions that must be tested against the findings of the authors in this volume.

The United States, as Benjamin Cohen shows, has played an equivocal role throughout the debt crisis. Intent on restoring American military leadership, the Reagan administration was initially unwilling to exercise leadership in the world economy, preferring reliance on market solutions and expressing skepticism toward the organizations representative of postwar managed capitalism (the IMF and the World Bank). The onset of the debt crisis did produce a shift toward more activism and a more positive attitude toward the IMF; the Baker initiative demonstrates even greater willingness to exercise leadership in the international political economy. Nevertheless, the record of U.S. behavior and the cooperative patterns that have emerged suggest three fairly narrow limitations on possible longer-term solutions to the debt crisis.

40. Financing for the special fund would initially come from Trust Fund repayments received by the IMF, although additional funding could be added from other sources.

The first is the *international structure of power*. Whatever one's estimate of the theory of hegemonic stability, the last decade of economic change and devolution in economic power does strongly suggest that the construction of new international regimes (or rules of the game) is very difficult in a pluralistic structure of power. The relative decline of American weight in the world economy did not prevent a high level of cooperation among many participants during the debt crisis—the arguments of Charles Kindleberger that there must be "one stabilizer" do not seem to hold. But the failure to move beyond crisis management must be due in part to the obstacles posed by a more pluralistic system. Even the modest proposals of the United States in 1985 foundered initially on the resistance of other countries and international organizations: the U.S. preference for an expanded program of World Bank cofinancing was thwarted by resistance by other industrial countries to increased World Bank funding, and plans to make the special fund for low-income countries a joint operation of the IMF and the World Bank could not surmount the bureaucratic resistance from those organizations. American influence could no longer overcome such obstacles to intensified cooperation, at least in the short term.

As important as these structural considerations, however, are two domestic ones that affect the dominant economic power. The United States seemed to have overcome some of its *ideological* opposition to the postwar model of managed or regulated markets. Nevertheless, the "new conditionality" offered by Baker was still committed to the magic of the market place and intent on changing the economic policies of developing countries in directions consistent with American ideological preferences. Second, the United States has become increasingly unwilling to bear the *costs* associated with economic activism. Baker's plan might have received a warmer welcome had it included the commitment of new American resources. It did not. It only offered vague indications that a capital increase for the World Bank might be sought if necessary. Every reform proposal entails costs, and the apportionment of those costs becomes more difficult as the United States becomes more unwilling to bear the economic burdens of leadership.

These three elements affecting the role of the dominant economic power suggest severe constraints on any global solution. Two other central political variables have also been considered in this volume. *The behavior of the banks*, discussed by Philip Wellons, is difficult to predict and yet of key importance to any scenario or solution. As described above, both optimists and reformers make certain assumptions about the banks, assumptions that are seldom tested. The Baker plan itself left unclear the incentives for its projected increases in bank lending. In part it was hoped that a "pull" would result from increased growth in debtor countries, yet bankers seemed unconvinced by arguments for less orthodox adjustment rather than more.[41] An

---

41. See Eric N. Berg, "Banking Opposition to Debt Plan Seen," *New York Times*, 1 October 1985, p. D6.

expansion of cofinancing by the World Bank could also provide a lowered level of risk that would stimulate the projected growth in lending.[42] It was unclear how the plan would deal with the pressures on bank syndicates as regional banks grew enthusiastic about participation in debt reschedulings. The idea of a "superbank," a new organization to replace the mechanism of syndication, was floated and then apparently dropped by American policy makers. Perhaps the most important incentive to bank participation, however, could come in the sphere of regulation, and many saw the need for a trade, similar to the relaxation that had occurred in the early stages of the debt crisis. Statements by Federal Reserve chairman Paul Volcker seemed to rule out regulatory concessions as part of the Baker plan bargain, however.[43]

Finally, the *politics of adjustment* will profoundly influence the attitude of the debtor countries toward the Baker plan and any other proposals for resolving the debt crisis. The original case-by-case approach depended on the cooperative attitude of its technocratic interlocutors in the South, and it finally foundered as the political bases for sustained and drastic adjustment programs dissipated. Although the newest U.S. initiative appears more generous to the debtors, it could still be seen as substituting one form of conditionality for another, structural adjustment—which could be politically *more* sensitive—for old-style stabilization. And as the recent debate in Brazil demonstrates, elites in Latin America are themselves divided on the appropriate economic strategy to follow.

The political parameters of the debt crisis are set by governmental tasks: ensuring the stability of the financial system, the regulation of financial intermediaries, and adjustment. Those parameters have shifted in a way that may permit the emergence of a new pattern of cooperation with limited reform in managing the debt crisis. That reform exercise, however—induced by political change—itself has political limits, domestic and international, that may force it in directions too modest to ensure the persistence of the cooperative bargain.

42. The model often employed is Chile, which completed its latest financing package only with the help of a World Bank cofinancing.
43. "Is the Superbank a Flier?" *Economist*, 19 October 1985, p. 90; Monica Langley and Phillip L. Zweig, "Volcker Rejects Appeals to Relax Conditions on U.S. Foreign Loans," *Asian Wall Street Journal*, 23 October 1985, p. 3.